# A
# GUIDE TO
# CONTEMPORARY
# ITALIAN LITERATURE

## From Futurism to
## Neorealism

**SERGIO PACIFICI**

SOUTHERN ILLINOIS UNIVERSITY PRESS

*Carbondale and Edwardsville*

FEFFER & SIMONS, INC.

*London and Amsterdam*

Library of Congress Cataloging in Publication Data

Pacifici, Sergio.
    A guide to contemporary Italian literature, from
futurism to neorealism.

    (Arcturus books edition, AB 99)
    Bibliography: p.
    1.   Italian literature—20th century—History and
criticism.  I. Title.
[PQ4087.P23    1972]          850'.9'0091          72-5472
ISBN 0-8093-0613-1
ISBN 0 8093-0593-3 (pbk.)

ARCT
URUS
BOOKS ®

Copyright © 1962 by Sergio Pacifici
Reprinted by special arrangement with Sergio Pacifici
All rights reserved
Arcturus Books Edition  September 1972
This edition printed by offset lithography in the
United States of America

FOR JEANNE

*"amica mia e non della ventura"*

# ACKNOWLEDGMENTS

It is a particular pleasure for me to acknowledge here at least a few of the numerous debts of gratitude I owe to individuals, libraries, and foundations, whose friendly interest helped make the present volume possible.

I wish to express my thanks to Yale University for awarding me a Morse Fellowship in 1958-9 for research and writing in Italy, where this book was begun, and for a supplementary grant from the Fluid Research Fund in 1960 to defray certain expenses connected with the final preparation of the manuscript; and to the American Philosophical Society of Philadelphia for a travel grant in 1958-9.

From both the professional and personal points of view I was fortunate to have the constant encouragement of my friends and colleagues: Rigo Mignani, Joseph G. Fucilla, Charles Speroni, Thomas G. Bergin, Dean William De Vane, and Henri M. Peyre. My sojourn in Italy, during my tenure of the Morse Fellowship, was made extremely rewarding and fruitful thanks to the assistance of the staff of the Angelica and the Alessandrina libraries. I am indebted to Giacomo Debenedetti for many hours of stimulating conversation about literature and the arts, and for the graciousness with which he lent me books and periodicals not readily available elsewhere. In New Haven, I was always able to count on the efficient cooperation and unfailing good will of the staff of the Sterling Memorial Library, of Miss Elizabeth Butler of the Acquisitions Department, and of Miss Lorene Taylor of the Linonia and Brothers Library.

I am grateful to the numerous writers and critics, among whom are Alberto Moravia, Elio Vittorini, Vasco Pratolini, Guglielmo Petroni, Natalia Ginzburg, Italo Calvino, Enrico Falqui, and Salvatore Quasimodo, for the courtesy and patience with which they answered, candidly and at length, my detailed questions about their work. While in Rome, I was privileged to meet Signor Goffredo Bellonci and his exquisite wife, Maria, whose warm hospitality I shall not soon forget.

The United States Information Agency, through the kind offices of Mr. John Brown, Cultural Attaché in Rome, and Miss Frances Coughlin, Assistant Cultural Affairs Officer, extended several invitations to me to speak before Italian audiences on Italo-American literary relations. The trips I undertook under the auspices of the U.S.I.A., especially those to the *Mezzogiorno*, helped me acquire a firmer understanding of certain problems discussed in the pages that follow.

Finally, I am deeply grateful to Norman Cousins and Rochelle Girson, of *Saturday Review*, for giving me the frequent opportunity to write about current Italian fiction in their magazine; to my daughters, Tina and Sabrina, for their willingness to give up a good share of the time their daddy would otherwise have spent with them; and to my wife, Jeanne, without whose affection and companionship this book would probably never have been written.

Certain sections of this book were originally published in: *The Modern Language Quarterly, Symposium, Yale French Studies, Books Abroad, Cesare Barbieri Courier,* and *Saturday Review*. They appear here, considerably revised, with the kind permission of the editors of the respective journals.

My analyses are based upon a reading of the works in the original. In order to make the text easier to read, I have used, whenever possible, the standard English translations listed in the Selected Bibliography. In all other cases the translations are my own.

S. P.

*Rome, September 1961*

# CONTENTS

# ERRATA

| Page, Line | Errata | Correction [Read] |
|---|---|---|
| 64, 14 | *Cronache* | *Cronaca* |
| 117, 10 | Vittorio [Brancati] | Vitaliano [Brancati] |
| 117, 11 | Quarantotto | Quarantotti |
| 153, 31 | blank verse (*verso libero*) | *verso sciolto* blank verse |
| 155, 1 | Rea | Pea |
| 168, 1 | Ungaretti (1888-     ) | Ungaretti (1888-1971) |
| 179, 28 | accart occiarsi | accartocciarsi |
| 187, 3 | blank (date of death) | 1968 |
| 200, 20 | Children of Life | *Ragazzi* |
| 256, 14 | between 1868 and 1871 | 1869 and 1871 |
| 265, 11 | Contini (b. 1900) | Contini (b. 1912) |
| 266, 24 | Flora (1891-     ) | Flora (1891-1962) |
| 314, 8 | Buzzati (1906-     ) | Buzzati (1906-1972) |
| 314, 34 | Comisso (1895-     ) | Comisso (1895-1969) |
| 315, 26 | Pascara | Pescara |
| 317, 26 | Marotta (1902-     ) | Marotta (1902-1963) |
| 319, 38 | Piacenza | Vicenza |
| 320, 39 | Tecchi (1896-     ) | Tecchi (1896-1968) |
| 333, 13 | figura | figure |
| 333, 20 | ano | anno |
| 342, 12 | rivisti | riviste |
| 347, 3, col. 2 | 166-7 | 266-7 |
| 347, 16, col. 2 | Quarantotto | Quarantotti |

# PREFACE TO THIS EDITION

Next to writing a book, the hardest assignment for a literary historian or a critic frequently turns out to be the preparation of a new introduction for a subsequent edition of his work. Presenting one's own intellectual labors in finished form for the first time is like celebrating the birth of a special child. But what can an author legitimately say when his book, like a child, has been around for some time, living its own special life? After all, once published a book becomes public property and there is little its maker can rightfully add to something which, if still valid, should speak for itself. The mere fact that this *Guide* is being reprinted seems to signify that the passing of time has not diminished its usefulness—and that calls for at least a modest celebration. It may be argued that perhaps this *Guide* should have been enlarged and brought up to date. I have resisted this temptation on three grounds: first, additions tend to alter the design and the balance of a book; second, the final volume of my *History of the Modern Italian Novel*, now in progress, will examine the fiction of a number of writers—including Gadda, Pizzuto, Lampedusa, Pavese and Bassani—who, for one reason or another, are not covered in this *Guide;* third, fortuitous circumstances do not make the case for a reassessment of the chief figures and trends discussed in this work very compelling. The novels Vasco Pratolini has brought out since 1962 add little, if anything, to his stature as a writer; Elio Vittorini's last published novel before his untimely death in 1966 was a revised version of *Le donne di Messina;* two of Italy's most distinguished poets, Salvatore Quasimodo and Giuseppe Ungaretti died (in 1968 and 1971 respectively) without producing anything that would alter my evaluations; and the same is true of Petroni, Ginzburg, Silone and others discussed in this book.

Turning to the cinema, it is fair to say that if recent Italian films have frequently been of good quality, they have not been particularly daring or innovative. Finally, the level of literary criticism has shown much sophistication, even though its best practitioners (Edoardo Sanguineti, Umberto Eco, Guido Guglielmi) who are working within the theoretical orbit of the international avant-garde, have yet to make a genuinely original contribution to the field.

It is good to note that since 1962 interest in Italy, particularly her poetry and fiction, has dramatically increased in this country. Among the serious critical studies that have appeared lately, the following should prove to be helpful and illuminating to both the general and the specialized reader: Donald Heiney's *America in Modern Italian Literature* (New Brunswick, N.J.: Rutgers University Press, 1966) and *Three Italian Novelists: Moravia, Pavese and Vittorini* (Ann Arbor: University of Michigan Press, 1968); Glauco Cambon's *Giuseppe Ungaretti* and Luciano Rebay's *Alberto Moravia* (both published in the series "Columbia Essays on Modern Writers," N.Y., 1967 and 1970 respectively), Joseph Gary's *Three Modern Italian Poets: Saba, Ungaretti, Montale* (N.Y.: New York University Press, 1969), and Joan Ross's and Donald Freed's *The Existentialism of Alberto Moravia* (Carbondale: Southern Illinois University Press, 1971).

In the "Preface" to the first edition of this book, Professor Thomas G. Bergin wrote: "In truth the book before us is well called a 'guide'; it should serve explorers—and even tourists—in the field of twentieth-century Italian culture for many years to come." I will be pleased if this *Guide* will continue to fill the need which impelled its preparation. But it would be for me an even greater source of satisfaction if, aside from offering some perspective on Italian culture, this volume will encourage further studies of an absorbing and perplexing era.

Sergio Pacifici

*Larchmont, New York*
*January 23, 1972*

*A GUIDE TO*

## Contemporary Italian
## Literature

*Ond'io per lo tuo me' penso e discerno
che tu mi segui, ed io sarò tua guida.*
DANTE, *Inferno*, I, 112-13

## A NOTE ON TITLES

For convenience and clarity, the following system
of listing titles is used in this volume:
English titles of works mentioned
are given in parentheses immediately after the original Italian,
in *italic* type if the work has been published in translation,
and in roman type
if the work has not appeared in English.

# Prolegomena

One of the outstanding events on the cultural scene since the end of the last war has been the extraordinary success enjoyed by Italian culture in its broadest manifestations. The American appearance of a film and a book, Roberto Rossellini's *Open City* (1946) and Carlo Levi's *Christ Stopped at Eboli* (1947), paved the way for what a few years ago was called "the rediscovery of Italy." Shortly after the publication of H. Stuart Hughes's book *The United States and Italy*, Renato Poggioli offered the first brilliant comment on "the Italian success story," and compared the fate of Italian letters to Cinderella's, both of which repeat the ever-popular saga "from rags to riches."

Several years have passed since the first analyses of the phenomenon were made and at present American interest in things Italian is still gaining momentum. What at first seemed to be only a temporary fashion has instead turned out to be a permanent and fruitful trend. Indeed, as Leslie Fiedler recently pointed out, there is something unique about current American fascination with Italy, since "it touches more kinds of people at more points and has had a more direct influence on the shape of life at home."

One of the truly intriguing qualities of contemporary Italy is its capacity to evoke different things for different people and exert a totally diverse impact upon those who are exposed to it on the cultural or human level. Thus Italy may call to mind the unforgettable movies of the so-called neorealistic school, the plastic face of Giulietta Masina, the sophisticated fashion of Roman and Florentine couturiers, the daring architecture of Pier Luigi Nervi, the sculpture

15

of Manzù, the canvases of Di Chirico and Morandi. For those who have experienced a "physical" exposure to Italy, the country inevitably conjures up visions of lamentable social conditions, bureaucratic inefficiency, and cold *pensioni* made bearable only by the warmth and generosity of the people.

For the large group whose interest is primarily literary, Italy today is symbolized by the fiction and poetry of Alberto Moravia, Elio Vittorini, Mario Soldati, Vasco Pratolini, Italo Calvino, the recent Nobel Prize winner Salvatore Quasimodo, or any of the many writers whose work has been translated into English over the past decade and a half. The total sum of our exposure to Italian culture has made possible a concept of that country thoroughly different from the one inherited from the past. If it is possible to generalize about such matters, one might say that the "new" Italy is at once more human and compassionate, less rhetorical and provincial, than the "old" Italy of Mussolini. It is a country less committed to perpetuating the myth of its having the greatest cultural heritage in the Western world than to working toward the gradual formation of a truly modern culture. Modern art must, of course, be highly conscious of the past; but its roots must be in the present and its eyes turned toward the future. Recent Italian writing has revealed a nation conscious of its flaws as well as it virtues, aware of its vast and as yet unresolved problems that demand action, not rhetoric. Above all, contemporary Italian literature, probably the most humane written in the world of today, has proved its immense capacity to speak of the joys and sorrows of man in a language accessible to people everywhere.

It is a promising sign that our interest has by no means confined itself to contemporary Italian art. What the critic P. M. Pasinetti once called "the Italian vogue" has extended to the classics. Dante (whose *Divine Comedy* is destined never to be adequately translated), Boccaccio, Petrarch, Machiavelli, Ariosto, Michelangelo, Leopardi, Manzoni, Verga, Svevo, and Pirandello have been studied anew and freshly retranslated: their magnificent work has at last been presented to an audience only vaguely aware of their "presence."

Speculations and inquiries seeking to explain the popularity of Italian literature have not been lacking. Mr. Poggioli, bringing to his interpretation an immense knowledge of Italian culture and an unusual perceptiveness of its quality, has synthesized the theme of his analysis in the opening statement of his essay "The Italian Success Story":

> Italy has gained the sympathy and admiration of an alien world after she has started acting and feeling like Cinderella. . . . Before doing so, she had failed to tear off the veil of foreign indifference, having chosen to play the part of Cinderella's stepmother or of her sisters. It is my contention that foreign literary opinion had been turning its back to the cultural values of modern Italy not through any lack of intellectual generosity on its part, but rather because of Italy's inability to win or to woo non-Italian hearts.

Mr. Fiedler, on the other hand, analyzing the situation from his special perspective as a student of American life and literature, has underscored the fact that "if America welcomes the flood of Italian fiction (and the closely related pseudo-documentary films) it is welcoming itself, a deliberate reflection of its own stylistic devices." There is a good deal of truth in the observations just quoted. Certainly no one would want to minimize the part played by American publishing houses, which have demonstrated astuteness and good judgment in their selection and presentation of Italian novelists. Nevertheless, the reader may feel considerable dissatisfaction with views that, intelligent as they are, do only partial justice to their subject. The success of a literature in the context of the international cultural community is determined by a multitude of factors—literary, psychological, human, and even political. But above all passing fashions and the sort of appeal achieved through devious means, literature receives its share of recognition when it proves that it has something to say and a capacity for speaking to the body, heart, and soul of mankind without respect to national barriers. Only creative writing that addresses itself to fundamental questions of life in our time, and hence of all time, deserves to endure. Italian literature, after a miraculous self-rejuvenation of language and themes, has once again regained the privilege of speaking to the world.

American interest in contemporary Italy has not yet produced a body of sustained literary criticism. It is not difficult to wonder, with René Wellek, why "Italian literature, with the exception of Dante, has, strangely enough, almost ceased to excite critical interest." There is, however, substantial promise in the criticism of some penetrating observers, such as Leslie Fiedler, Irving Howe, Francis Fergusson, Eric Bentley, and R. W. B. Lewis.

Where the situation of criticism of fiction leaves much to be desired is in Italy itself. Although Italian fiction is at last experiencing its first international "moment," it is still slighted on its native soil, where American, French, and English novels, frequently inferior to the local product, are avidly read. The novel, popular everywhere in the Western world (despite the regular dramatic announcements of its impending death) has not yet achieved in Italy a status comparable to that accorded it in other European countries. The entire cultural system is perhaps to blame for this situation. From the moment when the youngster begins his serious studies he is nurtured almost exclusively in the classics. Contemporary writers are seldom studied in Italian schools; even more seldom are they recognized and analyzed as significant forces in the culture of the country. Extensive courses on contemporary novelists are seldom offered except in the few cosmopolitan universities. The student who wishes to acquaint himself with the literature of his own time is denied the guidance of the seasoned reader and left to his own resources. It is not unusual for him to confront the fiction and poetry of his own generation wholly untrained and unprepared to understand it.

Books *on* fiction, rare as they are anywhere, are even scarcer in Italy. Over the past two or three decades only a handful of volumes dealing with the novel have appeared, most of them academic collections of essays (or even reviews) without a central focus. None of these studies has dealt with the problem of the novel in Italy in a unified manner, and much less with such a speculative topic as "the theory of the novel." Paradoxical as it must seem, foreign critics have frequently taken the lead and have been the first to receive and enthusiastically analyze Italian fiction, and to applaud the vitality and courage of postwar Italian letters.

The predilection traditionally shown by Italians for poetry is understandable in the context of the native tradition, as is the disparagement critics have always shown toward fiction, a genre far less "pure" and "aristocratic" than poetry. Poetry has been widely and successfully practiced from the beginning of Italian literature. It is indeed to its poets—Dante, Petrarch, Ariosto, Tasso, Leopardi, and D'Annunzio (to mention a few important names)— that Italy owes most of its international literary reputation.

The fact that the novel emerged in Italy almost a century and a half later than in France does not mean that there was no narrative tradition. Quite the contrary: from the earliest times, Italy has produced an imposing array of amazingly interesting and influential short-story writers. The anonymous *Novellino*, Boccaccio, Franco Sacchetti, Agnolo Firenzuola, and in modern times (with a pause in the eighteenth century), Verga, D'Annunzio, Buzzati, and Moravia are internationally known raconteurs. The concentration on the short story, or *novella*, I find significant in that it is revealing of the Italian creative temperament. Traditionally, the *novella* tells a striking, extraordinary incident. In P. M. Pasinetti's definition, "the classic Italian short story is episodic, anecdotal. Historical or not, its overt assumption is that the author comes up with a worthy piece of news about an actual or memorable event." The nature of the short story, its length and subject matter, are at once its strength and weakness. Although it lends itself to be read or recited quite rapidly, only at the hands of an unusual writer can it become the kind of serious, sustained comment upon society a good novel generally is. However colorful a tableau of manners and people, the short story is seldom transformed into a critical judgment of society or into an effective dramatization of a "vision" of the world.

Numerous factors were not only instrumental in delaying the emergence of the novel in Italy but also rendered difficult its acceptance until the latter part of the nineteenth century. England and France, the countries where the novel was "invented," and where the new art form achieved almost immediate recognition and popularity, enjoyed a considerable amount of political and intellectual freedom and autonomy. Freedom itself, it is true, can hardly guarantee the worthiness of the artist's product. Yet it seems to be an indispensable prerequisite for the formation of a climate conducive to the creation and strengthening of a genre that deals with and is frequently critical of the *living* world. Such a condition could not exist in Italy which, until the year 1860, was divided and ruled by more or less benevolent despots. Living without freedom, in a state of perpetual fear of recrimination, persecution, or exile, few dared to criticize the established social, political, and moral order. It is significant that the publication of the first modern Italian novel, Manzoni's *I promessi sposi* (*The Betrothed*) in 1827, and in its final version in 1842, coincided with the beginning of the *Risorgimento,* which was to culminate in the unification of Italy some twenty years later.

Recent scholars of English literature have amply documented their thesis that the rise of the novel in the Western world was made possible by changing social conditions, and particularly by the arrival on the scene of the middle class. The bourgeoisie, of whose life the novel became the best literary expression, was composed of merchants and tradesmen; it was an adventurous, practical, liberal lot. It was, as has been stressed by Arnold Kettle, "a revolutionary class. . . . The commercial bourgeoisie were revolutionaries against the feudal order because the feudal order denied them freedom. It denied them freedom, physically, legally, spiritually, to what they wanted to do, to develop the way they must develop." The arrival of the middle class marks the beginning of the decadence and the rapid collapse of a feudal society and with it a medieval view of life clearly incompatible, or out of tune, with the new times. By the seventeenth century, England particularly had reached unorthodox philosophical and religious positions from which society was no longer interpreted as being a product of God but of men, and as such, subject to considerable changes in its structure.

The popularity soon achieved by prose fiction (as contrasted with verse fiction, the romances of chivalry, for example, which were sung or recited before groups of people) is also traceable to the growth of a large, widely distributed reading audience, interested in taking stock of the new world and vitally willing to be amused. The increased literacy of certain nations was naturally accompanied by an intensive demand for reading matter. The improved economic situation made possible a more regular purchase of books, while the increase in the number of free loan libraries encouraged reading habits that were to prove quite beneficial to prose fiction and to intensify its popularity.

By the end of the seventeenth century, society in France and England had reached a highly developed stage. In almost every European nation, the Reformation itself played a positive part. But as Salvatore Rosati pointedly remarked:

> The whiff of freedom of the conscience and the orientation toward human conceptions which the Reformation brought about, in Italy determined nothing more than a tightening of brakes and a stiffening of theocratic positions. . . . Even later on, the conditions of our country (political absolutism, *spagnolismo*, etc.) did not favor the formation of an organic, highly enlightened social life. Nor did such conditions favor the consciousness and the dignity of the individual, the spirit of independent thought, and, by extension, the growth of observation and criticism.

A rapid glance at the fiction produced in Italy during the first half of the nineteenth century supports these negative observations. Aside from Manzoni's great novel, *I promessi sposi*, no other work of imaginative prose was written in that period. The record is bound to appear all the more meager if we remember that by 1850, Stendhal's *Le rouge et le noir* had appeared, while Balzac's gigantic project, *La comédie humaine* (which was to consist of almost one hundred volumes) was well under way, after having been launched in 1829. In England, Defoe, Richardson, and Fielding, the great early masters of the new genre, were followed by a new group of novelists, Austen, Scott, Dickens, and Thackeray. The novel was moving from its original autobiographical and "fantastic" stage into a new area where it became a perceptive and vigorous instrument of social and philosophical criticism.

Only with political unification did Italy finally produce its first novelists, and the novel commence to express the modern experience. In such circumstances it was inevitable that the Italian writer should be inspired by and be concerned with describing a reality with which literature had lost touch: the reality of his immediate milieu—his native town or region. The first important novelists wrote about life in the provinces and, out of a genuine feeling for the backward social conditions of the people, wrote tales "documenting" and dramatizing the ills that for centuries had plagued the country.

The second half of the nineteenth century produced fiction that, from a qualitative and quantitative point of view, was far superior to that published during the first fifty years. There was Matilde Serao's devastating critique of Neapolitan life, *Il paese di Cuccagna* (*The Land of Cockayne*); Verga's *I Malavoglia* (*The House by the Medlar Tree*) and *Mastro-don Gesualdo*, the first two volumes of a projected series of five novels entitled *I Vinti* (*The Vanquished*), whose single theme was that of man's innate desire to improve his lot, and the ultimate failure of his attempts; Ippolito Nievo's *Le memorie di un ottogenario* (*The Castle of Fratta*), retitled *Confessioni di un Italiano;* Federigo de Roberto's *I Vicerè* (The Viceroys), a long novel about the transition experienced by the South when it ceased being a Bourbon state and instead became a province of Italy; and Italo Svevo's masterful novels *Una vita* (A Life) and *Senilità* (*As a Man Grows Older*), dealing with the psychological life of the Triestine bourgeoisie.

The freedom won at so dear a price after centuries of political enslavement lessened another problem, which throughout Italian history had involved practically every important scholar and creative writer. The problem is not peculiarly Italian although in Italy it assumed a seriousness unknown elsewhere. It is a language problem known as *"la questione della lingua."*

Dante Alighieri was not the first writer to use the Italian language, or the vulgate, the new language that had emerged after the year A.D. 1000 and which had previously been used almost exclusively as an instrument of oral communication. But it was Dante who, after the early and still rough poetry of the Sicilian school of the court of Emperor Frederick II, produced the first sustained literary expression in Italian prose, *La vita nuova* (*The New Life*), and poetry, *La Divina Commedia* (*The Divine Comedy*). The poets who came after him—Petrarch, Boccaccio, and Poliziano—continued the tradition begun by the Florentine. They composed their work in either Italian or Latin, remaining convinced to the end of their lives that it would be their Latin work that would make their names endure in the history of letters.

After the disappearance of the masters of the *Trecento* and beginning with the sixteenth century, the community of intellectuals took up rigid positions with respect to the Italian language. They held either that the work of Dante, Petrarch, and Boccaccio should serve as a model to be scrupulously followed (in which case they engaged in long, frequently fruitless debates about questions of morphology, pronunciation, or linguistic "purity"); or they rejected completely the use of Italian, deeming the language incapable of the loftiness, precision, range, and scholarship of Latin. The outcome was a disconcerting lack of agreement that resulted in antagonistic positions impossible to reconcile. The spread of Italian as a standard language, nationally spoken, understood, and written with a modicum of conformity was thus further delayed.

It was only with Alessandro Manzoni that the problem, aggravated meanwhile by a deep split between the oral and written tradition that had developed in the intervening centuries, approached a satisfactory solution. After publishing the first version of his novel in 1827, with the provisional title *Fermo e Lucia*, the author visited Florence and set himself the task of "rinsing [his] clothes in the Arno River," by which he meant polishing his style to conform with the living language as spoken in its birthplace, Florence. The result of his long labor was an entirely new novel retitled *I promessi sposi*. It was rewritten from beginning to end and cleansed of most traces of expressions, words, and mannerisms of his native Milanese dialect. The work has long been considered the major novel produced in the nineteenth century in Italy, as well as a model of prose style that gave the country a linguistic unity only dimly envisioned before.

The political division of Italy had its negative effect in the involved "*questione della lingua*" to which these rapid remarks can hardly hope to do justice. In other countries the language problem was resolved by the ruling sovereign, who played either a direct or indirect role as arbiter of linguistic issues. The political situation in Italy only fostered continued reliance upon the various dialects, colorful and expressive to be sure, but hardly appropriate as vehicles of communication on a national level. The situation has persisted to this very day. The majority of Italians still learn their native dialects well before they master the national language taught in the schools; even then, most continue using the dialect at home or in the intimacy of friendly communion. This, as Dr. Barbara Reynolds justly observed, puts the novice writer in a strange situation, for he is "using a language he has hardly ever spoken . . . [and] is therefore bereft of that secure communion between himself and his readers and the confidence of using an instrument equally intelligible to them both."

The continuous, almost exasperating confrontation with the language problem made the writer excessively sensitive to the problem of "style," to the point where he placed an unusually heavy premium on the *formal* quality of his work at the expense of its content. For centuries, the "*bello scrivere*" remained the most coveted goal a writer could achieve, and many poets conveniently forgot that literature is communication of experience, and that prose fiction in particular must have a large relevance to life. In a little-read essay on the Italian novel, Salvatore Rosati once reminded his readers that "while the contemporary novel makes an effort to reconcile two things shown by experience to be irreconcilable, namely, the narration and writing at a high artistic level . . . [in our tradition] the second tendency, which is congenital [to our letters] gets the better at the expense of the first." No one in Italy dared to proclaim,

in the manner of Frank Norris, "Who cares for fine style!
. . . We don't want literature, we want life."

An outline of the difficulties traditionally encountered
by the novel in Italy is incomplete without mentioning the
gulf that has always separated life and literature. Ever
since its beginning, and with rare exceptions, Italian culture has been created in, by, and for the academies, the
closed circles, the aristocratic elites. As a social system,
literary patronage undoubtedly produced an impressive
culture. As the poet Quasimodo remarked in his Nobel
Prize acceptance speech, it could only be justified by those
who considered "creative intelligence . . . a moral conta-
gion." It was instrumental, from the sixteenth century
(when Italy lost her independence) to the last century,
in giving rise to an art of superior intellects who addressed
themselves to the "happy few" countrymen. For the next
two centuries literature in Italy ceased being a vigorous
element that at once made the meaning of life and of man's
condition clearer to people. It became a game skillfully
played by the literati, who were often blessed with a superb sense of craftsmanship but were spiritually empty. In
the last analysis such a literature could not help lulling the
human sensibility to a placid, undisturbed sleep so that
man might not see nor hear nor feel the tragic character
of existence. Poetic virtuosity was carried to its final,
extreme perfection by the Arcadia in the seventeenth
century. Indeed, Arcadia, as Leo Olschki brilliantly commented, "as a cultural phenomenon . . . reveals both the
generalization and passion of the Italians and the suprem-
acy of literary technique over a human and spiritual substance of inspiration."

Recent events tend to confirm the possibility, first envisioned in the months immediately after the last war, that
the separation of literature from life is narrowing steadily.
Already in the thirties, Antonio Gramsci (the co-founder
of the Communist Party in Italy), writing from the jail
where he had been put by the Fascists and where he was
to die a few years later, noted what he termed "the non-
national popular character of Italian literature." Many of
his notes and articles, published posthumously by Einaudi
of Turin, relate to the general subject of literature and ex-

amine individual works, authors, and the background of traditions and conflicts peculiar to Italian culture. The terms "national" and "popular" need qualification, and Gramsci went a long way in his effort to sharpen such concepts and arrive at a satisfactory definition. While he affirmed that literature need not divest itself of its poetic and artistic form in order to be popular, Gramsci pointed out that before the ideal of a "popular national literature" could be realized there would have to be a reconciliation between the artist's vision and that of his audience. "A work of art," he wrote, "is so much more 'artistically' popular when its moral, cultural, and sentimental content is closer to the morality and sentiment of the nations, understood not as something static, but as an activity of continuous development."

Postwar trends in Italian creative writing confirm the validity of Gramsci's insights and forecast its possible realization in the future. The following pages will show that the factor that has clearly set apart postwar fiction and poetry from prewar Italian letters is an intentional, sustained, and vigorous concern with *real* issues, *real* people, *real* facts.

In this respect there is less difference between Italian and French or English writing of the same period than one would ordinarily be justified in assuming. The starting point in most cases has been provided by a situation rarely experienced by contemporary writers. Intellectually, religiously, socially, and politically, the bulk of postwar European fiction has been of the "engaged" variety. The important themes and practitioners of the novel will be discussed in the chapter devoted to the "young writers."

To say that the war is largely responsible for the situation just described is, of course, a truism. Yet it may not be useless to remind the reader that the effect of the last war is quite similar to the plague, an event admirably depicted in Manzoni's *The Betrothed*. It has been the broom that has swept away much of the rhetoric and bombast that infested prewar Italian writing. The war, too, has succeeded in frightening away (for how long it is hard to predict, for *"il lupo perde il pelo, ma non il vizio"*) the ghost of past glories. Contrary to all the pessimistic forecasts of Italian critics, present circumstances may indeed see Italian fiction entering its most productive and stimulating phase.

I trust that I am not running ahead of my story if I conclude these introductory comments with one or two observations on the character of the contemporary literary scene in Italy. Particularly striking is the emergence of a new literary generation, an able and intelligent nucleus of novelists partially rooted in the tradition of that great master Giovanni Verga and moderately influenced by the linguistic and formalistic experiments of writers like Vittorini, Gadda, and Pasolini. Most of today's novelists would not find it difficult to accept the definition of the novel recently given by Italo Calvino: "A narrative work which is enjoyable and significant on many levels that intersect one another." The fact that contemporary Italian novelists invariably have continued to set their tales against a regional background—the Rome of Moravia and Pasolini, the Naples of Rea and Marotta, the Florence of Pratolini, the Sicily of Sciascia, and the South of the "Southern group"—is no longer as significant as it was at one time. The writers of postwar Italy, young and old alike, are showing an uncanny ability to confront in their art complex human situations. As the editors of the unorthodox magazine *Il Menabò* recently stated, "the new facts (French, English, American, . . . Russian, or Italian as they may be) need perhaps to be seen from a different perspective." It will be evident in the pages that follow that the novelists of the "new" Italy are less interested in dealing with provincial situations than in trying to bring out, by dealing with what are only on the surface "regional" problems, their universal applicability. Hunger and destitution, destruction and poverty—of the flesh and of the spirit—are not Sicily's and Naple's alone. Today as yesterday, Vittorini's words ring true: "The word [Sicily] sounds, to me, more harmonious than Persia and Venezuela. Moreover, I expect that all manuscripts come out of a single bottle."

It is ultimately both unfair and impossible to define and describe closely, in a few pages, the kind of fiction recently produced in Italy. It is not, on the other hand, unreasonable to state that it has demonstrated its capacity to deal, with an increasingly greater perception and range, with the dominating problems of our age. Whether such problems are social or political or human depends largely on the individual sensibility of the artist. But all of them would readily subscribe to the statement that man's great concern is to find himself in a chaotic universe and that the writer's supreme goal is to achieve an understanding of, and write with compassion for, human events and human frailty. If we can agree with F. R. Leavis that serious literature dramatizes life in such a way as to promote our awareness of its possibilities, then beyond any doubt Italian letters at last deserves our attention, and calls for a sympathetic and discerning analysis.

# CHAPTER ONE

# Alberto Moravia

About three decades ago a young writer published at his own expense a novel that had been turned down by several publishers. The appearance of the book caused a wave of protests and outcries—a reaction not unlike the one following the first showing of Federico Fellini's film *La dolce vita*. Critical reaction was similarly discordant: thus, while some of the more cautious and traditional readers expressed their shock at the amorality of the author, others expressed their regret that the talent of such a fervid imagination should be wasted on a decadent theme. The book was alternatively praised to the skies or condemned, on thematic, stylistic, or even moral counts. Yet, within a few weeks after the first notices had appeared, the inevitable had happened: talk of the book was on everyone's lips and the novel had achieved the rare distinction of being both a critical success and a *succès de scandale*. In due time, the publication of the work was to be hailed as one of the most exciting events to have taken place in Italy since D'Annunzio's day.

The year was 1929. The work responsible for skyrocketing its author into a prominent position in the literary firmament was *Gli indifferenti* (*The Time of Indifference*); and the protagonist of this singular literary phenomenon was a twenty-two-year-old youth named Alberto Pincherle whose *nom de plume* was Alberto Moravia.

More than three decades have passed and a prolific production has amply justified the early favorable verdict of Giuseppe A. Borgese, who first discovered the young author and reviewed *Gli indifferenti* in the authoritative pages of *Il corriere della sera*. Considerable luster has since been added to Moravia's name. His work has been translated into practically every European and Oriental language; he has been the recipient of numerous literary prizes, including the Viareggio Prize in 1961; three of his novels and a score of his short stories have been adapted for the screen (one, *Two Women*, was a resounding success in 1960-1), and two for the theater. He has become one of the most widely known and esteemed of contemporary Italian novelists. Although his work should by no means be considered representative of avant-garde writing, it is nevertheless indicative of the intelligence and maturity of postwar Italian fiction.

In his native country Moravia's name has already been immortalized (a bit hastily, perhaps) by the publication of his *opera omnia* in a de-luxe edition, an honor generally reserved for the classics. The demand for his critical and creative contributions continues to mount. Moravia is the motion-picture critic of the weekly *L'espresso*; a frequent contributor to *Il corriere della sera*; the co-editor (with Alberto Carocci) of the bimonthly magazine *Nuovi Argomenti*; a scenario writer; and the occasional spokesman of the liberal intellectual wing on cultural and political matters. His extraordinary activity has led some suspicious critics to urge him to write less but better—advice he has not heeded.

Little is known about Moravia's life, for he is unusually retiring, as Latins go. He has occasionally made known some of the more important events of his life, but he has never encouraged the publication of a biographical study or a sustained critical work on his fiction. By most, he is considered unco-operative when he is asked to discuss his own work or the general situation of literature in Italy. Aside from the scant information generally available, the reader wishing to penetrate his closed personality must do so by reading him. His attitude is as unusual as it is highly commendable.

He was born in Rome in 1907, the only son of a moderately well-to-do Venetian architect. At an early age he showed an inclination toward humanistic studies: with the help of his governess he soon mastered French and achieved a reasonable fluency in English and German, lan-

guages that were to be useful to him in later years. He must
have had a lonely childhood for, as he once wrote, it was
not at all unusual for him to spend the entire afternoon
recounting stories to himself, which he would only inter-
rupt at suppertime and continue, without the slightest difficulty, the next day.

When he was nine years old he was taken ill, and the
doctors recommended that he be sent to a sanatorium to
cure what was diagnosed as a severe case of osteomyelitis.

He educated himself by reading a good deal and more
seriously and intensely than the average youth of his age.
In the wards of the sanatorium, where he spent the next
few years, he discovered the classical writers normally
despised by schoolchildren and developed a considerable
interest in literature. His favorite authors were Ariosto,
Goldoni, and Boccaccio. Certainly he must have found
them amusing and humorous. Ideally they afforded him
the best escape from his own real world. As he grew older,
his interests expanded and he read the plays of Molière
and Shakespeare, both of whom were to have considerable
impact upon his sensibility. By the time he had reached
the end of his adolescence he was well read in French,
English, Russian, and Italian literature. American letters
were not to attract his interest until much later, at which
time he translated some of the naturalists for the Vittorini-
Cecchi anthology, *Americana.*

His early years, as can be seen from the brief sketch,
were anything but "normal" in the current sense of the
word. The experience of living far away from his family,
in the isolated sanatorium, without any real friend of his
own age, hastened his maturity. A sensitive record of this
period may be found, in fictional form, in the perceptive
short story "*Inverno di malato*" ("*A Sick Boy's Winter*"),
in which the loneliness and timidity of a hospitalized adolescent (Girolamo) and the crisis brought about by the
awakening of his senses are aggravated by the teasing
and scorn heaped upon him by his roommate, Brambilla,
a traveling salesman.

By the time he was eighteen, Moravia had written three
novels—none of which was published. But they served
as preparatory exercises for an ambitious "work in progress"
entitled *Gli indifferenti.* After the publication of his first

work, Moravia began enjoying the reputation of a precocious writer whom the Fascist regime regarded with considerable suspicion. His tales did not please the government, which was anxious to create an image of Italy far
rosier than Moravia's. An effort was made to discourage the
writer by asking him to sign his articles with a pseudonym.
His life since then has been generally calm and devoted to
writing and working. Aside from some interesting long
trips to the United States and Mexico, in the mid-thirties,
and one to the Far East shortly afterward, the most exciting experience of what is otherwise an uneventful life
(biographically speaking) took place during the last
months of World War II. Shortly after the capitulation of
fascism, the Germans took over the city of Rome. Moravia,
who had written an anti-Fascist polemical article in the
Roman newspaper *Popolo di Roma,* edited by Corrado
Alvaro, headed south with his wife, Elsa Morante, in order
to reach the Allied lines. Circumstances forced the two
to hide in the hills of the Ciociara region, on the outskirts
of Rome, and there wait for the liberating troops. Out of
the experience of living for nine months in a miserable
pigsty where the couple had taken refuge has come the
successful novel *La Ciociara (Two Women),* one of the
few works to be directly inspired by autobiographical
events.

Since 1929, Moravia's position in the world of letters
has grown increasingly important; yet there is general
agreement among his critics that his first novel remains,
in many respects, the most representative and best work
he has produced to this day. It is upon his first novel and
some of his excellent *novellas* that his reputation may be
said to rest. The prevailing feeling is that, barring unfore-
seen surprises, Moravia's position in literature will be determined by his shorter fiction. It is in the less sustained
genres of the short story and the *novella* that he has found
a felicitous vehicle to dramatize, effectively and succinctly,
the few themes close to his sensibility.

Although Moravia's first novels began reaching the international audience in the thirties, our own acquaintance
with him is barely ten years old. Along with a score of
other contemporary Italian novelists, Moravia also had to
wait for the postwar vogue for things Italian to find a re-

ceptive audience in the English-speaking world. Privately, he has been known to blame the fact that his early novels were too mature, too ahead of their time, so to speak, to be assessed and understood in all their implications. There is some truth in his contention, but it is more likely that the intolerably bad English translations of his early works were largely responsible for the lukewarm reception they received, and for delaying an otherwise well-deserved recognition.

His real presence on the international scene begins with the publication in English of *The Woman of Rome* (*La Romana*), in 1949, a novel that also marks the beginning of Moravia's real productive period. Soon afterward, his short stories began appearing in avant-garde magazines, furthering the suspicion professed by some readers inadequately informed about Italian literary trends, that Moravia was a representative of avant-garde writing in his own country. Time has corrected such a misconception, and recently an increasingly greater stress has been placed on his "themes" and his skillful handling of them. Without renovating the novel form in any way, Moravia has succeeded in saying something "new" about existence—and this may well be the basis for his popularity abroad. He belongs, as someone remarked some years ago, "to that rather select international group of writers who have something to say that other men, regardless of national barriers, want to know." By the same token, however, it is important to bear in mind that by extracting from his native tradition that which is essential to his sense of form and to his vision, and by blending it with interests and themes outside of his tradition, Moravia has achieved an unusual reconciliation of national and cosmopolitan attitudes, avoiding at the same time the provincialism or the regionalism of some of his colleagues.

A first reading of his work may recall to mind a distinction, once made by Virginia Woolf, between types of novelists. In her lecture "Mr. Bennett and Mrs. Brown" the noted writer divided writers of fiction into two distinct categories, the Georgians and the Edwardians. It is to the latter group that Alberto Moravia obviously belongs, since "he does not give us a house in the hope that we may be able to deduce the human beings who live there." It is Moravia's firm belief that not only are novels "first of all about people," but that it is the writer's business to give us as complete a picture as he can of people and of what they are about. He does not subscribe to the theory that the reader is in a sense duty-bound to co-operate with the writer to the extent of supplementing, with his own fantasy, whatever has been left out due to the novelist's negligence or incompetence or lack of intuition. Moravia's greatest gift consists precisely in his ability to leave his reader with the distinct feeling that he has said all that could possibly be said about his characters, and that he has reached as deep an understanding of them as it is possible to obtain in their special circumstances.

Structurally, his work is deeply rooted in the tradition of nineteenth-century narrative. His books are marked neither by confusing techniques nor by daring stylistic experiments. In the majority of cases, the tale begins with a situation that has already reached a critical juncture. We are told something of the background of the characters, just enough to understand them and become sufficiently curious about them to want to know the nature of their situation and how it is resolved in the context of the story. Here Moravia departs from the traditional manner of handling a tale. While the nineteenth-century writer was sure of finding in objective reality the cause and the eventual solution of his characters' "problem," Moravia gives us the instinctive feeling that such causes must be found in man's inner self. Like many of his contemporaries, Moravia believes far more firmly in the reality of man's inner feelings than in that of the external world. Because the anguish felt by his heroes is essentially metaphysical or psychological, but never physical, the situation therefore demands that it be met and resolved in new ways.

Ever since his first book, Moravia has consistently demonstrated a keen appreciation of (coupled with an unusual deftness in using them in fiction) certain philosophical ideas whose "popularity" is quite recent. The idea of nausea, the notions of the absurdity of life and the nothingness of existence, the chaotic quality of the modern world, could well be mistaken for gratuitous borrowing from the existentialists (whose work Moravia admires), were it not for the fact that the novelist had found his "themes" and was stating them in the late twenties. He thus became, unconsciously, the first existentialist writer in his own country, well before Camus and Sartre in France. Unlike the French novelists, Moravia arrived at his own conception of life not by way of philosophical speculation and study but through intuition. Similarly, without any attempt on his part to turn his novels into economic-psychological tracts, he fictionalized life around two big aspects that really matter, sex and economics, life "just as it happens in times of great change and uncertainty such as ours." But for him Freud's insights into our psyche and Marx's revolutionary theories can hardly be used by a novelist, unless they are filtered through his sensibility: they must first be understood, but they must also be lived.

As for his style, Moravia is far from being a polished writer, and charges that he "writes badly" or even "ungrammatically" are often leveled at him. His plain, realistic prose has at times a tendency to border on a pseudo-scientific language. His manner of telling a story is not, therefore, one that could be properly defined as "poetic"; but it is factual, often cold, generally precise, and occasionally prosaic. If the reader should find it difficult to be fond of Moravia because of "how" he writes, but finds himself attracted by "what" he says, then he must be reminded at this point that, as with any significant writer, *what* Moravia says can only (for better or worse) be said in his particular style.

Some years ago Moravia confessed that, after several attempts at composing poetry, he began his first novel, *Gli indifferenti,* writing it in the hotels and *pensioni* in Northern Italy where he was recuperating from his illness. The book was written with certain literary models fresh in his imagination. "At that time," he stated, "I was reading plays more than anything else—especially Molière, Goldoni and Shakespeare—and I gradually formed an ambition to write a novel combining the technique of drama and narrative. In 1926, I read James Joyce's *Ulysses.* Joyce seemed to me to have resolved the problem of the duration of time in the same way as the dramatists, that is to say, by bringing out its flexibility and conventionalism. So I conceived the idea of writing a novel describing minute by minute the life of a bourgeois family in Rome. *Ulysses* describes only one day. My ambition, if I remember correctly, was to apply to the novel Aristotle's principle of unity of time, place, and action."

Such recollection, valuable as it undoubtedly is, must be accepted with some reservation. Moravia read *Ulysses*, probably with the help of the French translation of Valéry Larbaud. One wonders, however, how much he could really make of the book, in view of its enormous linguistic and structural difficulties. Granted that he had seized the significance of the book, there is hardly any evidence in *Gli indifferenti* that Moravia had been affected by the problematic nature of Joyce's work. Indeed, the structure and style of *Gli indifferenti* betray, in a certain sense, the conventionality of the book. Its importance rests not only in the treatment of a traditional theme (the famous love triangle) but in the fact that it formulates with astonishing precision and maturity the problems Moravia was to treat at length in his future books. It also contains *in nuce* the seeds of the themes developed in the more recent novels and short stories. The thesis, once advanced by this writer, that Moravia's constant efforts have been directed toward restating, more concisely and clearly, the world first sketched in *Gli indifferenti,* finds confirmation in a comment recently made by Moravia: "Good writers are monotonous, like good composers. Their truth is self-repeating. *They keep rewriting the same book.* That is to say, they keep trying to perfect their expression of the one problem they were born to understand." (Italics mine.)

*Gli indifferenti* is built around a single problem, the question most deeply felt by all Moravia characters to be fundamental in contemporary life: "How are we to act in the face of reality?" The question is being asked *here* and *now* and poses consequences and dilemmas that can hardly escape the sensitive reader. How are we to behave in a universe where man finds it difficult, and at times impossible, to accept complacently the vast baggage of social, religious, and moral beliefs inherited from the past? It is this singular question that gives Moravia's work a homogeneity not easily found among many other writers. From the very beginning of his creative activity, Moravia found himself confronting the problem of "how man was to

deal with reality," man "who found himself incapable of
establishing a relationship with his own world, a world
that had become dark and unplumbable—worse still, it
had disappeared." Moravia's numerous novels and short
stories are dedicated to a search, a quest for the clue to
a harmonious relation between Man and Nature that exists
no more. When considered as part of such an attempt the
figures and symbols of a "limited" writer appear clearly
as integral and necessary elaborations in the unceasing
struggle to reach a unified vision of life.

The story of *Gli indifferenti* revolves around the doings
of a middle-class Roman family. There is Mariagrazia
Ardengo, an aging widow who for several years has been
the unloved mistress of a cynical businessman (Leo
Merumeci); Carla, her pretty daughter; her son, Michele, a
law student with a definite flair for self-analysis. The
*dramatis personae* are rounded out by Lisa, also an aging
woman, who is presently hoping to become Michele's mistress.

The family's predicament is, first of all, of a practical
sort. Its small fortune has dwindled away; its only remaining possession, the villa in which they live, is heavily mort-
gaged and is soon to be sold if the numerous debts incurred by the Ardengos are to be paid. On other counts
the situation is hardly more encouraging. The empty life
led by the trio has brought them dangerously close to the
point where each of them will lose completely man's most
prized possession: his moral conscience. Fewer and fewer
are the acts that succeed in shaking them: people and
events slowly drown in the vast sea of their "indifference."

Their state of mind becomes total blindness in the face
of their impending ruin. The first climax of the story, developed within a forty-hour span, is reached when Carla
allows herself to be seduced by her mother's lover. She
consents to this in the faint hope that her life might take
a different direction and become, if not happier, at least
more meaningful. In her desperate search for some solid
ground onto which she may anchor her vanishing hope,
Carla brushes aside any question concerned with the moral
or indeed even the practical propriety of her act. The
yielding of her virginity proves to have been totally useless. Soon enough, Carla finds herself in an even worse

predicament when her lover, having satisfied his purely libidinous passion, gives unmistakable signs of being bored with her naïve thirst for affection, adventure, and security.

Michele, aside from being the antihero of this singular story, provides the reader with a suitable vantage point from which the unfolding (and the implications) of the drama may be observed. Conscious of the degrading life led by his family, he regrets the decay and the senselessness of their doings; yet he cannot persuade himself that he can change the situation in any positive manner. Through his articulate, monotonous comments we sense both the irony and the tragedy implicit in his life. However, tragedy itself is something denied to the Moravian hero—indeed as it is denied to the hero of the contemporary imagination. "I perceived," wrote Moravia apropos of *Gli indifferenti,* "the impossibility of tragedy in a world where nonmaterial values no longer had any justification, and where the moral conscience had become callous to such an extent that men, moving through sheer appetites, tend more and more to resemble automatons."

One element of tension in the novel is provided by Michele's apparent inability to gain enough courage or indignation about his family's behavior to do something about the situation and eventually restore a minimum of dignity to their lives. Being himself indifferent, his impulses materialize in a series of increasingly more violent but ultimately meaningless demonstrations of urgent manly conduct. As the novel moves toward the end, Michele is told by Lisa that Carla has become Leo's mistress and that the two may be caught, *in flagrante delicto,* in Merumeci's apartment. The young man realizes that this may be his last chance to test his sincerity and courage. He formulates a plan to murder Leo and proceeds to purchase a revolver. For a while he even surrenders to his facile fantasy and he imagines the consequences of his criminal act. He lives through the scene of the trial, the lawyer's pleas and the judge's final pardon, the tears, the indignation, the shame of it all. Upon reaching Leo's apartment he aims his pistol and fires it. But the weapon misfires. In his haste, Michele had curiously forgotten to load the gun. A tragic finale is turned into a farce, a cheap and shabby melodrama.

The other element of tension is provided by the constant awareness Michele preserves of his own indifference, and of the stakes involved in the struggle to grow up to his place in life, and to his responsibilities as an adult. Another novelist might have seen in the contrast between what is *to be* done and what in actuality *is* done, in the contrast between good and evil, the subject for a potentially stirring tale whose resolution is to be found in an active posture. Moravia, on the other hand, chose the reverse path. Unlike the heroes of Sartre and Camus, similarly involved in existential situations, his characters achieve their fullest realization through *nonaction*. Michele becomes what he is by refusing to participate in correcting an intolerable situation. Similarly, Michele, the intellectual hero of *Two Women*, when queried as to what the peasants should do about the German proclamation to evacuate the entire zone, states: "Do you want to know what you ought to do? You ought to do nothing at all." Michele, as the author remarks, having refused to conform to Fascist requirements had remained an individual, which could only mean that he had become an anti-Fascist. Through his lack of participation he established his own autonomy. He becomes truly free, in a society without freedom, by refusing to commit himself to notions readily accepted by the masses.

Italian critics, when they first analyzed *Gli indifferenti*, could not possibly grasp or predict the large meaning the author's unusual posture would eventually have in the larger body of his narrative. They concentrated instead upon the novel's overt criticism of the decay and sterility of the bourgeoisie. True enough, the book severely condemned, in the particular manner of fiction, the mores of the middle class. Yet, as Moravia himself has repeated again and again, such condemnation was accidental rather than intentional. The development of Moravia's subsequent fiction could only vaguely be guessed at the time of *Gli indifferenti*. His postwar fiction has demonstrated that Moravia is less interested in painting an objective canvas of a corrupt world (although such a preoccupation is by no means to be excluded) than with portraying a universe robbed of the possibility of being tragic because it can no longer *feel*. In modern times, man has neither the ability, nor the will, and much less the desire, to fight the gods of fate in order to mold the world in his own image. Indifference itself, rendered in his first novel in terms of attitudes and feelings, transcends the easy formula, apathy + indolence = futility. Although it started out as a condition shared by the limited cast of one novel, it has been gradually turned, in the neurotic world of Moravia, into one of the dominating symbols of man's inability to "find" himself in a world without beliefs.

What is the world Moravia writes about? Ever since his first novel, and with one or two brief interludes (the most notable being *I racconti romani*), Moravia has fictionalized the world of the middle class. His orientation is a matter of some interest since traditionally Italian novelists, the majority of whom come from the middle class, have dealt with the problems and mores of the working class. Svevo and Pirandello had little or no influence with respect to changing this pattern, although the ties Moravia has with both would indicate more than a mere coincidence of interests. From Svevo, who was in the process of being "discovered" at the time of *Gli indifferenti*, Moravia inherited the disinterested, clinical method of character analysis, while Pirandello transmitted something of his metaphysical curiosity about life, which is a pervasive feature of Moravia's fiction. Literary influences, especially in his early works, are numerous indeed (Manzoni and Verga, Boccaccio and Shakespeare, and, of course, Goldoni, are among them); certainly enough of them to justify amply the suggestion of R. W. B. Lewis that Moravia is "one of the most incorrigibly *literary* novelists of his generation." The passages and situations willfully lifted from the classics he has been reading since his adolescence are too obvious to be enumerated here. But Moravia expects his reader to understand that his overt borrowings have a definite place within the broader strategy of his fiction. What were in the classics occasions for lyricism and tragedy are cunningly turned into occasions for irony and ridicule—and hence unmistakable and necessary instruments to dramatize a world stripped of its meaning. In the nightmare of our modern world, about which Moravia writes with forcefulness in his better creative moments, "the air is too foul to breathe." Michele, in *The Time of Indifference,* longs for the world of real tears and indignation—a world of sincerity and real feelings that has apparently vanished. We are all well acquainted with the new, efficient world of our century; and Moravia is right in reminding us that modern literature (Kafka, Camus, and Sartre are its typical, but not its only worthy representatives) gives us "the same sense of suffocation and claustrophobia. We seem to lack air; we want to free ourselves from whatever surrounds us; it is as if the sky itself were too low. All modern poetry, in different ways, expresses this feeling of suffocation. Poetry, the eternal Cassandra, warns man that his world has grown absurd." Michele himself "felt he was suffocating . . . everything around him was without weight and without value, fleeting as a play of light and shade."

It is fitting, too, that the special habitat of Moravia's characters should be Rome, seldom specifically mentioned by name, to be sure, but recognizable in the kind of activity and life that takes place. It is in the big cities, Boston or Bologna, Milan or San Francisco, Rome or New York, that modern man understands most intensely, amidst so many other men, how it feels and what it means to be alone. Today as yesterday Borgese's remark apropos of *Gli indifferenti* has retained its relevance and validity: "there is little of Rome here . . . the scene is made up of lights and draperies, as in certain *mise en scène*." But geography and history matter little in Moravia's fiction: and the locale of his tales, even when minutely described (as in *Two Women,* for example) is always raised to the symbolic value of a place somewhere, or anywhere in the Western world. There is enough in his fiction to make us "feel" Rome without our ever being certain we are there. In some instances (as in *The Conformist* and *Two Women*) Moravia sets his story in a definite historical milieu, that of fascism and World War II. Unlike his contemporary novelists who have been effectively inspired by the war, Moravia rarely deals with history with an eye to exploring its phenomena and its chain of cause-effect. The historical dimension holds no interest for Moravia, who is too sophisticated and too intelligent to forget that history repeats itself with unending regularity. He prefers rather to deal with human vices, desires, frustrations, and the existential problems of individuals. He is therefore equally at home depicting characters living in Fascist Italy (as in *The Woman of Rome, The Conformist,* and *Two Women*) or in sixteenth-century Florence, as in the intriguing play *Beatrice Cenci.*

Generally speaking, Moravia's characters, much like Svevo's, are comfortably settled in society and seldom plagued by the harsh necessity of earning a living. In the majority of cases, their occupation is readily given: they are architects, students, lawyers, teachers, businessmen, government employees, writers who, even when unemployed, never worry about their future. Invariably, however, their professional life matters little because Moravia seldom focuses on the problems brought about by their jobs. There is also a large, colorful group of workers—those who, because of their occupation and standing in society, must be classified as "the lower class," the *plebe.* The point of distinction between the middle and working classes is not an idle one since each group, well distinguished by its conventions and its socioeconomic structure, plays a particular role in Moravia's fiction. The critic Fernandez has been the first to suggest, to the best of my knowledge, that each social group incarnates certain problems. Thus, for instance, the relationship between mother and daughter is dramatized by characters belonging to the working class; the relationship between mother and son is always seen in a middle-class family; and, finally, the relationship between husband and wife is explored in situations involving only intellectuals. That the sympathy of the author goes unmistakably to the working class is something that may surprise us only momentarily. For the author, simple and unsophisticated as the workers generally are, they constitute the only group blessed with a special sort of ignorance and philosophical endurance, a wisdom and serenity invariably denied to the comparatively well-off, well-bred, literate bourgeoisie. Once again, no one better than Michele (in *Two Women*) articulates a view that has in time betrayed its polemical content vis-à-vis the intellectual. It is Rosetta who speaks first:

> "Peasants don't know anything except the land, they are ignorant and live like beasts." He started laughing, and answered: "Some time ago it wouldn't have been a com-

pliment, but today it is. Today it's the people who read and write and live in towns and are gentlefolk who are really ignorant, the really uncultivated, the really uncivilized ones. With them there's nothing to be done, but with you peasants one can begin from the very beginning."

The absence of pressing financial problems does not prevent Moravia's heroes from being concerned with money. On the contrary, some of the early works (particularly *Le ambizioni sbagliate*) center around the struggle for money and for the kind of station in life only money can buy. Of course, the working people are also concerned with money; but for them the problem is of an entirely different nature, determining only whether or not they will be able to buy sufficient food the next day. Cesira, one of the *Two Women*, speaking of the peasants' attitude toward money, refers to it as "a kind of god . . . for them it is money that is the most important thing, partly because they haven't any, and partly because it is from money —from their point of view, anyhow—that all good things come." But beyond this first, realistic meaning, there lurks a greater one; for money is only seldom seen as a means to achieve power and security. Its meaning is frequently more Freudian; money symbolizes not so much what it *can* do (its purchasing power, so to speak) but what we are truly like. This is reflected in the varying attitudes we assume toward it. A greedy person or a miser, for example, is for Moravia both incapable of and unfit for love, since love is a feeling that flows from within and does not ordinarily expect anything tangible in return. Money also becomes an instrument for establishing or for arresting a rapport with the world. The best illustration of this is provided by the youngster Luca, in the *novella La disubbidienza* (*Two Adolescents*), who accidentally sees his parents putting away some bonds and cash in a safe concealed behind a reproduction of Raphael's Madonna, the painting before which he customarily kneels down at night when he says his prayers. Luca is undergoing a critical period of his life, the time when an adolescent tries to find his place in his family's life amidst the confusion and difficulties presented by his other problems of adjustment. When he becomes aware that the money he himself had painfully saved from his allowances "bound him to the world and forced him to accept it, he felt a raging hatred for these objects and for his savings. . . . Those objects and that money were not merely objects and money, but living, tenacious strands in the woof of which his existence was woven." Since the youngster wishes to cut off his ties with a world he feels he can no longer love, his first impulsive act is to bury the small treasure of money he has saved, and thus "in burying the money he would also in a certain way be burying himself—or at any rate that part of himself that was attached to the money."

> He discovered that he felt a profound hatred for the money, the sort of hatred one might feel for a tyrant against whom one has rebelled. The idea, too, that money was held in such esteem by his parents and that he himself without knowing it had for so many years said his prayers in front of a safe full of money contributed to his resentment. . . . Luca . . . wanted to destroy [its value] not merely by his own desire to do so but in actual fact. Detested idol as he felt it to be, nothing less than this blasphemous tearing to pieces could serve utterly to desecrate it.

Although projected against a background of material comfort, Moravia's heroes lack the feeling of security they badly need. An ironic twist is added here: money itself, so necessary to enable people to lead an easy existence, proves ultimately to be a useless commodity since it is incapable of purchasing what Moravia's protagonists most desperately need—love. There are times, indeed, as in the short story "L'avaro" ("The Miser"), when the protagonist at last finds the woman whose affection and companionship will make his life far happier than it has been. Upon serious reconsideration of the whole situation he decides not to become deeply involved with her. To him it is the preservation of his fortune that matters, and therefore he must not run the risk, however remote, of its being squandered by the woman.

There are, to be sure, other ways for humans to become involved with one another, and Moravia has always explored, with unusual perception, the "sentimental" relations between two people. If his recent fiction is indicative of the conclusions he seems to have reached, I would say that he believes that a meaningful human rapport, based on understanding, respect, and what he has defined in a long and little-read essay, "the reasonable use of reason" is possible. In the case of two persons of different sex such a rapport must be preceded by a successful satisfaction of their physical craving for affection. Several of his critics have constantly complained that love as a traditional unselfish kinship has ceased to exist for him. Though this may be true up to a point, the "deficiency" is due less to the artist's alleged inability to portray such a feeling than to his relative lack of interest in it. For Moravia is primarily concerned with depicting that breakdown of rapports that we all acknowledge to exist in our twentieth-century life. His position is that of a mere observer who disclaims any intention to play the role of a moralist. "Let society change," he is reputed to have said, "and I'll describe it, as it is." For reasons that he should hardly be called upon to explain, he analyzes what happens when the so-called normal equilibrium between two people is (for a variety of circumstances) disturbed and how and why it is eventually re-established. In his fiction, therefore, mothers are estranged from their children while the children are alienated first from their parents and then from each other—to the point where what used to be accepted as a normal (or conventional) and usually controllable rapport is expressed in terms of hate and indifference. Adriana, the lowly prostitute in *The Woman of Rome*, is distressed by the hatred her lover, Mino Diodati, shows for his family; Stefano, the sickly and penniless degenerate of *Mistaken Ambitions*, agrees that the death of his sister "might be a good thing"; Luca Mansi, of *Two Adolescents*, realizes that once his love for his family and friends, and for his studies and possessions, has disappeared, his strong *raison de vivre* is no more.

Love, robbed of its affective connotations, is then distilled into an activity that is hardly anything more than purely sexual. Moravia's gamut, when it comes to describing the passions of the senses, is among the most engrossing in modern literature. There is enough in his fiction to satisfy every reader: the bombastic sensuality of Brambilla ("*A Sick Boy's Winter*") is a mild affair when compared to the masochism of Lorenzo ("*End of a Relationship*"), who in a moment of anger and ennui throws his mistress's clothes under the bed and all over the room for the sheer pleasure of watching her assume "awkward attitudes like those of a disabled animal." There is also the sadistic sensuality of the members of the Tennis Club (*"Crime at the Tennis Club"*), who, after undressing an older woman notorious for her past love affairs, finish what began as a farcical jest by accidentally killing her and hiding her body in a trunk. These may be taken as examples of Moravia's range. It is often on the purely physical aspect of man's relation with woman that Moravia dwells at length. In his fiction the cult of sexual love is seldom allowed to be transformed into a cult of true love.

A generation brought up under the influence of Freudian psychology and well read in the sexual behavior of men and women of all ages can hardly be shocked or annoyed by Moravia's supreme concern with sex. It is important to stress here, as Mr. Lewis has aptly done, that there is, *in fondo*, far less "sex" in Moravia than in most other contemporary writers. For him sex matters only as an important force in modern life; as a force that may afford freedom from the futility and boredom of our existence or one that may grant us a momentary consciousness of the "being" we otherwise lack in our spiritual world. It is refreshing that, granted the world being described, we should occasionally find a character like Adriana. Her love for the numerous men who come to her (perhaps to unburden the least lovable part of their personality) is transformed into a kind of pseudo-religion whose particular strength is in its Christian concept of Love as *Caritas*. The uniqueness of Adriana consists precisely in her being able to find in promiscuous love, generally deemed humiliating, the very strength to accept with cheerfulness an otherwise sordid existence.

More often Moravia's characters see in sexual love the one way to seek a release or find an escape from a wretched world. For them, such love is the only avenue left open to humans who have never experienced or have never possessed the capacity *to* love. When in the short story *"End of a Relationship"* Lorenzo declares to his mistress that his difficulty is that he does *not* love her, he is formulating in simple terms the kind of predicament shared by a good many Moravian heroes. Their situation is all the more painful in view of their material comfort: "A home, a car, travel, clothes, amusements, sport, holidays in the country, society, a mistress—sometimes it happened that he counted up, with a kind of vain, boastful weariness, all the things he had in life, only to conclude, in the end, that the source of his trouble should be looked for in some physical disorder." Tullio, in the short story "The Miser," confesses his inability to love and the wretchedness involved in the miserable awareness that he is not to experience the tenderness of *being* loved: "My life is empty. . . . It is true that I eat and sleep well, but who doesn't do the same? It is love that I really care about, love which itself *can* give a purpose to life. When it doesn't exist, it cannot be replaced by anything: such love is denied to me." By the same token, the failures to come to terms "sexually" with life can only lead to further and more hopeless alienation from the rest of the world.

Sex does not always play a negative role in the tales of the novelist. A thorough reading of his work would prove that the sexual encounter yields the possibility of redemption, the beginning of a new, more meaningful relation. The two youngsters Agostino and Luca (portrayed in the two *novellas* entitled *Two Adolescents*) find in the promised or realized sexual experience the reason that impels them to go on living and accept what had previously filled them with nausea. In *The Woman of Rome*, or in such a story as *"The English Officer,"* the sexual act is described as something through which an otherwise meaningless world may achieve some sense. When the sexual encounter fails to occur, the possibility of establishing a harmonious relation with the world is wiped out and the individual's own well-being is severely threatened. Moravia's fiction, as has frequently been remarked, reads much like a catalogue of failures, many of which begin at the sexual level. Beginning with Carla and her lover Leo, in the early work, *The Time of Indifference*, to Riccardo Moltesi, in the more recent *A Ghost at Noon*, such failures are symptomatic of still larger failures as human beings. Moreover, as the critic Fernandez has written:

> The contrary of indifference will never be, for the Moravian hero, a straight forward and coherent moral conscience; only an acknowledgement—without reservations—

of the sexual fact will permit them to rid themselves of their indifference and adhere once again in a strong manner to reality; and the novelist, making of the body the last truth, will at once have found the means to reduce the universe to a comprehensible universe and offer to the investigative capacity of his style an entirely explorable subject.

Through sexual integrity and through the spontaneous and unselfish giving of oneself it is possible to lessen the isolation to which man is condemned and to achieve a deeper, more satisfying understanding of our condition. The novel *Il disprezzo* (*A Ghost at Noon*) centers on a writer, Riccardo Moltesi, who becomes a hack in order to earn more money. The drama itself pivots on the uncertain relationship between him and his wife, and climaxes in the disastrous end of what had been a relatively happy marriage. This pathetic situation is reached when Riccardo surrenders his artistic integrity and, from a subconscious desire to please his employer, allows him to make advances to his wife.

> During the first year of our married life my relations with my wife were, I can now assert, perfect. By which I mean to say that, in those years, a complete, profound harmony of the senses were accompanied by a kind of numbness—or should I say silence?—of the mind which, in such circumstances, causes an entire suspension of judgement and looks only to love for an estimate of the person. Emilia, in fact, seemed to me wholly without defects, and so also, I believe, I appeared to her. Or perhaps I saw her defects and she saw mine, but, through some mysterious transformation produced by the feeling of love, such defects appeared to us both not merely forgivable but even lovable, as though instead of defects they had been positive qualities, if of a rather special kind. Anyhow we did not judge: we loved each other. This story sets out to relate how, while I continued to love her and not judge her, Emilia, on the other hand, discovered, or thought she had discovered, certain defects in me, and judged me and in consequence ceased to love me.

Not much different in the case of Silvio Baldeschi, the would-be writer, self-defined dilettante, hero of *Conjugal Love*, who at the outset of the story confesses readily that "there were only two things that could save me [from despair]: the love of a woman and artistic creation." The book eventually shows how Silvio, having temporarily suspended making love to his wife (when he decides that only marital abstinence will prevent a disruption of his creative activity), is eventually betrayed by her and becomes conscious of his failure both as an artist and as a husband.

When the world cannot be comprehended through the love of the senses Moravia's characters experience a range of emotions that move from violence to hate. Their world is desolate enough without love. The women and men are forced to enact their drama on a bare stage and although neither fear nor dread haunts their hearts they must accept what they are, without questions.

The parable of a sick humanity is repeated time and again. Michele accepts indifference as a *modus vivendi;* Pietro (*Mistaken Ambitions*), having failed in his attempts to "redeem" Andreina, reverts to the role of the ambitious journalist that he really is; Marcello Clerici (*The Conformist*) persists in his foolish conformity to the very end, and the lesson of history is of no avail. To accept what we are and to make peace with our reality, so that we may find through it the strength to go on living, that appears to be Moravia's implicit message. A moment of spiritual tranquillity can only seldom be found by his characters. Religion rarely offers any comfort to his struggling souls, and when it does it is clearly expressed in terms of a form of superstition. Adriana in *The Woman of Rome* says:

> I liked the Madonna because she was so different from mother, so serene and tranquil, richly clothed, with her eyes that looked on me so lovingly, it was as if she were my real mother and not the mother who spent time scolding me, and was always worn-out and badly dressed.

Such reflections are unusual, however, and more frequently it is anger that reigns. Life, completely emptied of any ideal or purpose, however foolishly idealistic, is turned into something hard to bear: "I am sad. . . . I am angry and restless. . . . Why should I laugh? . . . what necessity do I have to laugh? . . ." asks Luca Sebastiani, the architect in the short story "The Storm." Gemma Foresi (*"The Wayward Wife"*) listens to her fiancé's plans for their forthcoming wedding and, as the author admits,

"It very often happened that she felt inwardly boiling with rage and boredom and restlessness." After her husband, Professor Vagnuzzi, is refused an appointment to a Rome school, this disappointment added to many others that had preceded it, "plunged Gemma back into the old raging, desperate boredom. . . . Thoughts charged with rage and impatience came more and more to dominate her." Hate and anger are two feelings experienced by Moravia's characters with an almost exasperating regularity: hate for the mother, for society, for the whole wide world, whose history, as Mino Diodati sternly proclaims in *The Woman of Rome,* is nothing but "a long yawning of boredom."

Their hate is basically reflective of their inability to reconcile themselves with the reality of life. Incapable of shaking off their moral indifference, unwilling to participate more fully in life around them, they view life as a carrier of tedium and wretchedness to be met with a philosophy of negatives: suicide, murder, anger, spite, rage, rebellion. Luca Mansi, having perceived that things and people show an undue insubordination to his will, experiences a "violent rage." He feels first that he should kill himself (as does indeed Silvio Baldeschi in *Conjugal Love*). Having discarded the idea of suicide, the youngster decides to "disobey."

> The word "disobey" pleased him because it was familiar. Throughout his childhood and a great part of his boyhood he had heard his mother say that he must be obedient, that he was disobedient, that if he didn't obey she would punish him, and other similar phrases. Perhaps by starting to be disobedient again on a more logical, higher plane, he was merely rediscovering an attitude of mind which was native to him but which he had lost. So far he had been disobedient only in the sphere of his school life, which was the fullest and most absurd part of his existence. But since the incident of the football game, he was discovering that this disobedience could be extended to other spheres as well: it could embrace other things which, because they were normal and obvious, had hitherto escaped him—the affections, for instance; and—an extreme case which immediately fascinated him—the actual fact of living.

Life is to be denied then, because it offers a pre-established order which Moravia's characters are often unfit, or unable, or unwilling to change—even in the smallest way. Hence the disorder, the streak of meanness and deep-running spite in their temperament.

When viewed from this perspective, other elements in the fiction of Moravia appear to be perfectly consonant with what we have come to recognize as the essential characteristics of his world. The weather, for example. The attentive reader must certainly have noticed how frequently Moravia describes turbulent weather. Heavy and steady rain falls forever upon his landscape—a landscape of such desolation and despair that it can never offer mankind a source of consolation. No discord is ever registered between the mood of the characters and the weather. It rains steadily throughout the action of *Gli indifferenti*, most of *Le ambizioni sbagliate*, and much of *La Ciociara*; a rain which when accompanied by a furious wind makes the atmosphere appropriately violent. The rain, insistent and monotonous, seems to deny the possibility of either salvation or survival. Perhaps rain stands for more than an atmospheric phenomenon: it becomes profound melancholy, the objectified longing and pain experienced by Moravia's heroes. The symbolic value of rain as anguish and loneliness is nowhere better exemplified than in *Gli indifferenti*. Michele, walking in the crowded yet "empty" streets of Rome, thinks about the sorry mess in which he finds himself and the predicament that will ultimately lead him to his final ruin. Suddenly he finds a striking analogy between his own life and the rainy boulevards: "Whatever he was, he was the same—idle, indifferent; this rain-soaked street was his own life, which he traversed without faith and without enthusiasms, his eyes dazzled by a deceptive splendor of the advertising signs. . . . His distress oppressed him." Whether it is the rain or the wind, or the unbearable, torrid heat beating inexorably upon Moravia's wasteland, it is certain that the elements of nature are as hard to withstand as is the rain of fire falling upon Dante's sinners in hell. In the tormented world of Moravia, the heroes are seldom left in peace by the continuous fever of their senses.

The reader may legitimately assume from the observations made in the previous pages that Moravia's world is one particularly distinguished by an excessive spiritual aridity, and that he is, by accepted standards, an uninspiring, depressing novelist. Several Italian critics have been quite articulate in pointing out the apparent inability of the novelist to depict honesty and courage, goodness and true love. Gaetano Trombatore, in a devastatingly polemical essay entitled "The Point About Moravia," concludes that:

> His is a world of purely conventional rapport, not held together by anything, without true affections and real interests; a world that lives only of appetites easily satisfied and that takes nothing seriously, not even sex which plays such a large part in it; a world where even the most innocent things, rain and *pasta*, become impure, and where, next to artificial perfumes, one breathes the stench of coitus and vomit. The vital motives of this "small" humanity do not go beyond the small intrigues and gratuitous perfidy, the shabby tricks of vanity, of calculation.

Justified as it may seem, the charge is largely unfounded. A careful reading of Moravia's fiction is bound to yield the image of an intelligent humanist writing of the condition of our time, without necessarily sympathizing (for all his emphasis) with the situation man has been instrumental in imposing upon other men. The evidence supporting such a view is scattered through the large body of fiction authored by Alberto Moravia. The signs are there, sure enough, if we but take the trouble to recognize them, the signs pointing to a distinct longing for what Michele of *Gli indifferenti* had, in 1929, defined as "the paradise of reality and truth." In the postwar *novella* *Agostino* (*Two Adolescents*), for example, the protagonist, confronted with a reality that is largely shaped by violence and cruelty,

> walked about for a little, naked on the soft, mirroring sand, and enjoyed stamping on it with his feet and seeing the water suddenly rise to its surface and flood his footprints. There arose in him a vague and desperate desire to ford the river and walk on and on down the coast, leaving far behind him the boys, Saro, his mother and all the old life. Who knows, whether, he was to go straight ahead and never turn back, walking, walking on that soft sand, might

he not at last come to a country where none of these horrible things existed; a country where he would be welcomed
as he longed to be, and where it would be possible for him
to forget all he had learned, and then learn it again without all that shame and horror, gently and naturally as he
felt that it might be possible.

The desire is always there: the desire to awaken from
a terrible nightmare and live, for to live is what matters.
"I am not alive . . . I am dreaming, this nightmare cannot possibly go on long enough to convince me that it is
not a nightmare but reality; one day I shall wake up and
recognize the world again, with the sun and the stars, the
trees and the sky and all the other lovely things. Therefore I must have patience: the awakening is bound to
come." A touch of tenderness, a bit of sympathy, is what
would seem to be lacking in Moravia, if we are to listen
to his commentators. It is my contention, however, that
during his thirty-odd years as a writer Moravia has been
working to sum up the dilemma of modern man, or better
still, how man has used—and abused—other men. "To
use man as a means and not as an end is the root of all
evil," Moravia wrote in an essay entitled "Man as an End
in Himself." He continued: "The use of man as a means
indicates a lack of respect for a man; and this presupposes
that one does not sufficiently know what man actually is,
or have a clear and adequate idea of what it signifies to
be a man."

What it signifies to be a man. The order is a big one, to
be sure, and in his own way Moravia has striven to achieve
his own definition, however inadequate it may be. Behind
the petty intrigues, the shabby conventions, the grotesque
behavior, the sloth and indolence, the futility and indifference, that are the qualities of his fiction, there looms
*that* purpose to which only a poet may aspire. It is a
wicked, difficult life, the novelist implies, and it is impossible (and inconsequential, in the last analysis) to retrace
our steps, so as to discover the reason at the root of our
mistakes. Many of his characters are no longer concerned
with finding out who or what is responsible for their
faults: "The fault was everyone's; impossible to discover
its source, the original cause of it," says Michele. The prostitute Adriana comes to much the same conclusion. "No

one was guilty; and . . . everything was as it had to be; although everything was unbearable . . . everyone was innocent and guilty at the same time."

Through the years, the vision of Alberto Moravia has expanded. In *The Time of Indifference* you may see the indictment of a whole way of life in a given generation; in *The Conformist* (no matter how unsuccessful the work may be as a finished novel), you will perceive the attempt to "explain" the evil of conformity and the worst plague it carries with it—the loss of identity. *Two Women* is, of Moravia's long novels, not only the most successful but the most human. It is also the finest tale about the war and the deepest statement about life made to this date by the novelist. The story consists of the trials and adventures of Cesira, a widow of a shopkeeper, and of her beautiful daughter Rose—two women of Rome's lower class. When the war begins to make itself felt in Rome, the two decide to leave for the country and finally take refuge in nearby Fondi. But aside from the few episodes at the beginning of the story much of the novel is essentially without a plot. There are some extraordinary effective descriptions of the months spent in a small hut atop a hill; of the women's friendship with Michele, an anti-Fascist intellectual, who is only distantly related to the host of intellectuals ever-present on the Moravia stage; there is the episode of Michele's final sacrifice, when he is slaughtered by the Germans; and finally, the shocking, deeply moving episode of Rosetta's loss of virginity when she is raped by the Moroccan troops, and her subsequent calm, dignified acceptance of her new condition. All that the two women go through—and it is quite a lot in terms of fear and trepidations by the end of the story—is not in vain. Cesira, the narrator of the story, confesses toward the end of the tale that she has discovered an important truth about life. She thinks about the episode of her innocent daughter:

> I said to myself that purity is not a thing that you can receive at birth as a gift of nature, so to speak; it is a thing that we acquire through the trials of life, and lose all the more disastrously for having been confident of possessing it; and, in short, it is almost better to be born imperfect and gradually become, if not perfect, at any rate better, than to

be born perfect and to be then forced to abandon that first transient perfection for the imperfection that life and experience bring with them.

Of all the women adroitly depicted by Moravia, Cesira is the one who seems to have successfully synthesized the author's view of the human condition. Indeed, it seems almost paradoxical that the novelist, after having created a wasteland of corruption and confusion, of cruelty and violence, is a profound believer in life, in the miracle of life. With Henry James and the poet Giacomo Leopardi, Moravia has discovered that a poet cannot be concerned with dying. There is a passage (it happens to be the last page of *Two Women*) in which Cesira gives a poignant analysis of her experience:

> Sorrow. I thought of Michele, who was not with us in this eagerly longed-for moment of return and would never be with us again. I remembered the evening in the hut at Sant' Eufemia when he had read aloud to us the passage from the Gospel about Lazarus, and had been so angry with the peasants who had failed to understand anything, and had cried that we were all dead and waiting for resurrection, like Lazarus. At the time Michele's words had left me in doubt, but now I saw that Michele had been right, and that for some time now Rosetta and I had indeed been dead, dead to the pity that we owe to others and to ourselves. But sorrow had saved us at the last moment, and so in a way the passage about Lazarus held good for us too, since at last, thanks to sorrow, we had emerged from the war which had enclosed us in its tomb of indifference and wickedness, and had started to walk again along the path of our own life, which was, maybe, a poor thing full of obscurities and errors but nevertheless the only life that we ought to live, as no doubt Michele would have told us if he had been with us.

As the characteristics of the world of Moravia have been briefly touched upon in these pages, we have discerned the element that has already given its first fruits. To enlarge the vision, to broaden the perspective, moving constantly on to higher perspectives would seem inevitable indications of maturity—and these, no one would deny, the novelist possesses. But to see and to touch, to paint and to tell, is clearly not enough. Lately Moravia's fiction has shown how much richer it has become in human knowledge and sympathy, demonstrating a capacity for depicting as well as understanding not merely vice but sorrow as well.

If he ranks with the genuine artists of our century, it is not, I suggest, due to his sheer ability to handle the medium, although that is an important aspect of it. It is because, after years of writing, and despite the fact that time itself has not changed in any substantial way the *manner* of his writing, he has come closer to saying something vital about the condition of modern man. We are isolated and lost, faithless and cruel, and yet we are committed to the perennial search for that measure of truth that finite man can achieve. In his most recent books, and particularly in *Two Women*, Moravia has come still closer to dramatizing his answer to that eternal riddle of existence. "Our entire world," he has recently written, "is built with . . . human pain. . . . The vicious circle which paralyzes our world is similar to that which governs the act of a sadist. He wants to be loved, but, in order to love, he must inflict suffering. The more he wishes to be loved, the less he is loved. He does not realize that, in order to be loved, he must be capable of love." For thirty-odd years Moravia has been trying, in his own humble and imperfect way, to say just that.

# CHAPTER TWO

# Vasco Pratolini

Italy is more than a single country.
She is a continent in miniature, each
of her regions a world in itself.
ELIZABETH MANN BORGESE

It is highly doubtful whether at any other moment in
the history of Italian letters the critics were more betrayed
by their political views than when Vasco Pratolini's novel
*Metello* was published in 1955. The first work of a projected trilogy, entitled *Una storia italiana* (An Italian
History), *Metello* fictionalizes Italian life of a certain social
stratum from 1875 to 1902, in terms of class struggle and
class consciousness. Its publication gave rise to an intense,
enlightening literary debate—probably the most thought-
provoking to have taken place in postwar Italy. It is fair
to add at once that the criticism, frequently polemical and
even bitter, was directed solely at the author's method and
technique. Pratolini has come out of the debate as popular
as ever, his reputation hardly damaged. His sentitive
autobiographical volumes and his readable fiction have
already earned him a permanent place in Italian literature, as "the poet of his quarter," as Luigi Russo called
him. Beyond his immediate merit as a creative writer, it
seems certain that he will be remembered for many decades as the novelist who succeeded, unintentionally perhaps, to raise through *Metello* some fundamental questions
about neorealism, realism, and the fate of the Italian novel.

Vasco Pratolini's first book dates back only two decades.
*Il tappeto verde* was published in 1941 in an edition limited to a few hundred copies. Its author remained unknown,
except to a small literary elite. By contrast, *Cronache di*

*poveri amanti* (*A Tale of Poor Lovers*), published in 1947, became an immediate best seller. Winner of the Lugano Prize, it was *Cronache* that made Pratolini's name familiar to an international audience and that stimulated a wider interest in the fiction of postwar Italy.

Unlike many Italian novelists whose entrance into the world of letters has been sudden and noisy, Pratolini chose a cautious pace. He has made the best of the opportunity— denied to those to whom success has come unexpectedly and even undeservedly—to dedicate himself seriously to the business of writing. At all times he strives to make his books finished literary expressions, not mere personal documents.

The beginning of his literary career could hardly have been more modest. He was published only sparsely in the Florentine reviews during the thirties, undergoing several literary experiences that were to leave an indelible mark upon his writing. Although his early work was largely autobiographical, he has gradually become more inventive. Similarly, his early lyricism was attenuated by his exposure to hermeticism and to the *prosa d'arte;* since the war he has moved toward an engaged, social kind of realism. With the passing of time, too, his vision has acquired depth, expanding from the restricted "frame" of family life into a vast interpretation of Italian life, from the end of the *Risorgimento* to the Second World War. In contrast with Moravia, Pratolini's trajectory is definitely an ascending one. Moravia's *Gli indifferenti* is already a complete expression of the world of its precocious author; Pratolini's *Il tappeto verde* indicates, at best, merely a mood, the general tone of the novelist. It is but a tenuous prologue to the complex and richer discourse of Pratolini's recent novels.

Pratolini belongs to the generation of writers born at the beginning of this century, raised under fascism, and involved in the drama of the last war. Like many of his fellow writers, he is self-taught and comes from the working class. His father was a laborer and a cook, his mother a maid. Such biographical details may help us understand his interests and his vision. Similarly, the superb ease with which he handles the language is normal for a writer born in Florence, the birthplace of the Italian language and of some of the finest Italian poets and novelists. It is considerably easier for a writer to begin his creative work if he grows up in a region where the spoken and written language are nearly the same. Although he once attempted to set one of his novels in postwar Naples (a book that for linguistic reasons he was never able to finish), his milieu is Florence. The only exception is *Un eroe del nostro tempo*, which takes place in a northern Italian city. The major concern of the novelist has always been the individual and his socioemotional life; never his anxiety or his metaphysical dilemmas. His heroes confront life at the most fundamental, and even practical, levels. Whatever drama there is in his tales arises out of the necessity (and frequently the difficulty) of solving pressing, elementary problems. Emotionally, man's loneliness finds a resolution through companionship and affection. Actually the work of Pratolini yields much more than what may appear from my cursory definition thus far. There is the movement of the great city of Florence and its streets, its well-known quarters, and its friendly atmosphere. His fiction succeeds admirably in recapturing the dimension of "real" people who, as true Florentines, are "defined" frequently through amusing and lively descriptions of their everyday life. The people we see, almost invariably in groups, are always gesticulating, shouting, laughing, working, confiding in each other. His characters—and here is certainly one side of their uniqueness—are eager to speak about themselves not because of immodesty or egocentricity, but because they profoundly feel the need, the supreme need, to communicate with each other. Their basic drive is to make articulate their condition and give of themselves as much as they can. In the manner they do this we easily detect their hunger for understanding and solace. Because they have suffered and have learned the meaning of suffering, they are anxious to share, and are willing to let others share with them, the troubled or happy part of their daily life, their disappointments and failures as well as their happiest moments. Pratolini's fiction is quite effective when it succeeds in focusing upon the instant of human communion when the personal experience of poverty and solitude is understood, accepted, and conquered through the act of love.

I have mentioned that Pratolini is an autodidact. Early in life, his eagerness to read, his insatiable curiosity to know people and places, a distinct feeling for the written word, led him to such disparate authors as Jack London, Dickens, and Manzoni. Guided by his intuitive good taste and by the advice of his cultured friends (among them Ottone Rosai) he acquainted himself with the work of his contemporaries, Saba, Palazzeschi, Campana, Ungaretti, and later on, Eugenio Montale and the difficult hermetic poets.

For some years he led an irregular life, working in a variety of jobs (from soft-drink vendor in the streets of Florence to typographer) while trying to educate himself. As he privately remarked, any job that would give him ample free time to pursue his real interests—to read and engage in creative writing—was perfectly acceptable to him. The difficult life he led caused a deterioration of his health. His subsequent illness, erroneously diagnosed as tuberculosis, forced him to spend several months in the sanatoriums of northern Italy. His experiences there led him to write a few pages that are memorable for their lyrical tone and natural expansiveness. In the secluded life of the sanatorium, conducive to the meditation necessary to serious study, he thought of the possibility of death and of his personal destiny. He began reliving those days of his life that had brought him, as he perceived, sorrow but also happiness. He then undertook to transform his autobiographical events into poetic matter, discovering that only by writing about himself would he eventually come to grips with his destiny, as he saw it.

During those very years he met the young novelist Elio Vittorini, who soon became his intimate and helpful friend. Vittorini, though only in his twenties, was unusually mature. He had already published a collection of short stories as well as several chapters of his first novel, *Il garofano rosso*. It was Vittorini who introduced to his friend a host of new writers, including some of the English and American novelists he himself was discovering and translating; and he encouraged Pratolini to pursue his vocation.

In 1936, finally discharged from the sanatorium, Pratolini began a new phase of his life. He decided that he could devote his time to writing and eventually become a productive artist only if he gave up the jobs he had held in the past. He began earning his living by translating from the French and by contributing to the literary page of *Il Bargello*, the paper of the Florentine Fascist unit "Fasci di Combattimento." After he had struck up a friendship with Vittorini and Romano Bilenchi, his political views underwent notable changes. He realized at that time the failure of a regime which, after having labeled itself "revolutionary," had turned into a static, unimaginative government aiming to please the conservative big business and the middle class. During those years, too, Pratolini began contributing to the excellent literary review *Letteratura*, where the best avant-garde creative and critical elements were being published.

Eventually, with the poet Alfonso Gatto, he founded and co-edited his own "little magazine," called *Campo di Marte*, whose bold and positive interpretations of foreign literature soon incurred the wrath of the irate censor, who ordered the permanent suspension of its activities. The magazine thus came to an end barely nine months after its inception.

Pratolini's first important piece, a short story entitled *"Prima vita di Sapienza"* ("Sapienza's First Life"), appeared in 1938. Not until the early forties, however, did his books commence to be published, in rapid succession: *Il tappeto verde*, written between 1935 and 1936, was published in 1941; *Via de' Magazzini* was completed in 1940 and published in 1941; *Le amiche* (The Girl-Friends) was published in 1943, but had previously appeared in the literary page of *La Stampa* of Turin and other periodicals. The first period of literary creativity, which includes *Cronaca familiare* (Chronicles of the Family), published in 1941, was an important one. Recently, the author himself has stressed the meaning of his early work in the broader context of his writing by reprinting the best pieces from it in a single volume, aptly titled *Diario sentimentale* (Sentimental Diary).

The second edition of *Via de' Magazzini* carries a statement that clarifies the nature of Pratolini's immediate problem when he began writing: "I was incapable of speaking in the name of mankind and of revealing to men their own sorrow. I avoided the obstacle and began to tell of my own private anguish." It was inevitable that the literary production of his "first" period should dramatize the author's confrontation with the world of his own city.

The central portion of *Il tappeto verde* is made up of a short story entitled *"Una giornata memorabile"* ("A Memorable Day"), in which we see the hero-author as a child, playing and joining a gang of children in their mischievous games. It is with them that Pratolini identifies for the first time in his life—just as it is with young people in general, their aspirations and problems, that he has continued to sympathize. His world is reminiscent of the minuscule universe of the poets of the Twilight school, a world of pathos and of longing for the small, seemingly unimportant things in life, tinged with considerable melancholy. The death of the author's mother, the entrance of his stepmother into the household, the first months spent living with his grandparents, the hate he felt for the woman who had come to replace his mother—these are the events Pratolini writes about.

The volume published the following year, *Via de' Magazzini*, defines even more closely the author's world. The Florentine streets (first Via de' Magazzini, later on Via del Corno, the San Frediano Quarter, Via dei Leoni) become familiar geographical references of Pratolini's universe and the natural habitat of his all-too-human characters. The story begins where the previous book had left off, or at least from that sentence in the book that rather coherently synthesizes Pratolini's initial problem: "Nothing satiates us, nothing helps us; the vice is in us; the vice is to renew our daily fear of living. I know that we must free ourselves of such a fear, *find ourselves:* we shall have bunches of roses, baskets full of bread on the day of our salvation." Feeling that belief in life could be achieved through communion with others, Pratolini turned his deep-seated desire to share his experiences with other humans so as to reenforce the ties binding him to his friends into the very themes of his work. As the awareness of the need—to find through friendship not so much a style of life as a reason to live—increased, so did his love for, and understanding of, his environment, of the people in it and the fact that they are living the only possible life they can actually have. Such a vision of the world can be traced to Pratolini's youth. His life was never calm or secure, but was one of continuous hardships until he became an adult. He was barely five years old (he was born in 1913), when his mother died, shortly after having given birth to her second child. Entrusted to the care of his grandparents, after his father's death, he became a passionate walker, developing much interest in his city and its mysteries. An avid and curious observer, he learned much of the geographic and human map of Florence. Raised without the usual parental love, he realized the importance of affection and comradeship in human rapports, to the point of making them the fundamental factor of a happy existence.

*Via de' Magazzini* has a greater consistency and feeling for order than *Il tappeto verde*. While it has lost none of the lyrical quality of the previous book, it is arranged more episodically and develops its theme more systematically.

One of the stylistic problems posed in earlier writings is more visible and critical in *Via de' Magazzini*. Unable to fuse entirely his lyricism with the individual parts of the book (the descriptive and the reflective sections), Pratolini is the victim of a fracture that runs from the beginning to the end of the tale and that damages the structure of the total work. The story is divided into sections in which the author either describes the factual events or reminisces and meditates about them. The two are invariably kept separate by the use of parentheses or by a special typographical arrangement. It is not inappropriate to speak of two "styles" of the book, employed alternatively to recapture the mood and feelings of Florence during and after the First World War and to describe the boy's first confrontation with life.

*Le amiche* (1943) is another work that belongs to Pratolini's first period. It is a collection of sketches whose main importance—from the point of view of the author's growth—is in their focusing, with a tenderness bordering on romantic sweetness, upon the "type" that becomes a recurrent one in his fiction. *Le amiche,* as the title implies, is a series of pieces about various girls who, through their sentimental function in the life of a man, exercise a positive role in his destiny. Exposed to them, man realizes that his loneliness and sorrow are equally experienced by the opposite sex. He arrives at the conclusion that he needs a woman as a life companion: through a mutual love they will survive the tough struggle of everyday life and find in each other the reason to continue to live in hope. One critic has compared the women delicately and perceptively depicted by Pratolini to priestesses who disclose (so to speak) the mystery of life to their men. "It matters little," Alberto Asor Rosa continues, "whether they be honest or lost souls or prostitutes, since in all of them, without distinction, he, who is able to understand them, can find the freshness, the purity, the uncontaminated capacity to love that are parts of their character."

With the exception of another brief excursion into autobiography, represented by the slim *Cronache familiari*, written in 1945 in memory of his deceased brother, Pratolini's entrance into the world of the novel begins with *Il quartiere* (*The Naked Streets*). The book is an obvious prologue to the longer, engrossing *Cronache di poveri amanti*. It is *Il quartiere* that reveals Pratolini's gifts as a fiction writer, his ability to spin his story out of a reality both lived and imagined. A whole world, the familiar cosmos of Florence and its Santa Croce district, is vigorously brought alive. The milieu and the characters of *Il quartiere* are familiar to the faithful reader of the novelist. Unlike the previous books, there is no attempt to hide the historical or political implications of the story. The action is, in fact, set in the thirties, several months before the outbreak of the war against Ethiopia. The central problem of the world described here is clearer and more resolutely indicated. Although the rapports of friendship and affection common to Pratolini heroes still matter a great deal, they have been enriched by an awareness of the future roles they will have to play in the life of the nation. The burdensome problems have been hopelessly bungled, their solution postponed. Some day the youngsters who for the moment are trying to grow up and understand themselves a little better will have to confront them: but it is in the present, in the most critical period of their development, that they sense the existence of something vitally "wrong" in the conduct of national affairs and in the individual participation in these affairs. In the novel, there is also a concerted effort to establish a firmer relationship between the socioeconomic background of Pratolini's characters and their political beliefs. Through the first years of the post-war period, indeed including *Metello,* the poor and exploited working class is identified with the socialist or Marxist cause, just as the middle class and wealthy industrialists are implicitly identified with conservative thinking.

The hero of *The Naked Streets* is a youngster named Valerio. He is, in many respects, the same Valerio encountered in the frankly autobiographical volumes of the novelist. But what in his earlier works were emotional problems and attitudes toward the world shaped almost entirely by "sentimental" feelings, here become impregnated with other preoccupations, clearly of a political nature. Through the story of the young Valerio, Pratolini dramatizes not only the necessity to pull together, but the significance of his characters' reaction vis-à-vis the issues of their times Therefore, the perspective has become more historical, imbued with thinking at the social and political level. The characters themselves are transported from the autobiographical and personal into the historical and realistic context.

*Il quartiere* revolves around the doubts, the fears, the first loves, and the restlessness of the younger generation, a subject that has always been found to be quite attractive by novelists everywhere. As a story, it has a definite beginning, a middle, and an end reached through a logical, believable development of events. For the first time, Pratolini describes his city Florence less emotionally and more objectively. His pages are replete with a polemical spirit that does not in any way lessen either the author's or our understanding of the ills and qualities of its people.

> We liked our Quarter. It stretched from the fringe of the center of town all the way to the first houses of the suburbs, right to the beginning of Via Aretina, with its street-car tracks and market gardens, its middle-class villas and bungalows. . . .
> Everywhere in our Quarter washing was strung from windows, everywhere there were slatternly women. Yet this was a poverty proudly worn, a people ready to fight to the death for the things they cared for. Workers, and more precisely, carpenters, cobblers, blacksmiths, me-

chanics, mosaicists. And taverns, shops grimy or gleaming, cafés in the modern style.

The street. Florence. The Quarter of Santa Croce.

We were just ordinary folk. A simple gesture might arouse us to love or to hate. . . . It was after six o'clock when we finished work, and life and friendship had no existence for us until we were back in our streets and squares.

The story itself is somewhat loose. It concentrates upon the events of not one, but several, youngsters. The two main protagonists are Valerio and Giorgio, and we follow them from the time of their first naïve affection for girls to their eventual marriage; with them we become aware of their intellectual and emotional growth. Valerio, for example, after a puppy love with Luciana, takes a mistress. He then finds in Olga (another young girl of the gang) the woman he would like to marry. But the possibility is suddenly cut short by Olga's departure from the city: her mother, a former prostitute, has found a man willing to marry her and give her and Olga a decent home. Elements such as this make up the thin plot, but they are nicely complemented by the adventures, the conversations, the innocent escapades, of the members of the gang (Giorgio, Gino, Carlo), and of their vague, but modest aspiration: "We knew nothing. Perhaps we had no desire to learn. But we promised ourselves honest joys, to earn more at work, to become more skilled. And to have a girl friend, and if possible another after that, and then marry one in earnest, to lie with her in a wide bed, to make love to her with all our strength."

The driving force of the youngsters is objectively described; the characters themselves are at once more coherent and, because they are also far less pronouncedly autobiographical, they are more believable as fictional figures. The lucid descriptions of the Santa Croce Quarter are no mere adornment here: they are the elements enabling the writer to illuminate the life he depicts in a manner at times strangely suggestive of the nineteenth-century naturalists:

If I speak to you of our vice, of filth and brutality in our Quarter, what have you to say about that? We were poor.

. . . If you venture into our streets you'll find they stink, stink of tanneries and stables.

If I speak to you of vice, you may say it's to be expected in streets like ours. But come into our homes, in the year of grace 1932, after all the bunk* that's been written about us. Try stepping into our shoes. Get a bellyful of the poverty that grinds us down, day and night, that burns us like a slow fire or like consumption. For centuries we've been fighting back, unscathed and aloof. A man gives way, a woman falls—but for centuries they had been fighting back, for an eternity kept on their feet by a desperate hope. And suddenly this hope disappeared from their hearts. There is no escape, either we stand on our feet, desperately clinging to our rags, our cabbage soup, or we lie stretched out in the mud, never to rise again. We have no weapons to use against anyone; it wasn't us who made the laws that govern us. Our only defense is our inertia.

The book sets out to show how the youngsters overcome inertia through an irresistible allegiance to the spirit of their gang. Governed by unwritten laws, they possess an admirable amount of honesty and integrity. They stick together because they respect one another, a respect that is also affection. They want to grow up as responsible citizens, conscious of their limitations and their responsibilities.

"Indeed hope was something rooted in our Quarter," confesses the protagonist at the end of the book. Yet the boys are certain that "the world doesn't begin at the Arch of San Piero and end at Porta alla Croce." For them, just as it was for the Malavoglias of the Sicilian novelist Giovanni Verga, to leave one's home ground may mean to risk bitter disillusionment and failure. Pratolini attaches much of the same symbolic quality of Verga's book to the importance of being rooted somewhere, of having friends who give the feeling of a common condition, a fate that must be shared if we are to survive together. Those who drift away from Santa Croce are called traitors. In leaving the quarter, the traitor "has left behind our world of love and goodwill, where a timid handclasp, a geranium blossom in the hair, a simple word, is enough to bring happiness." Friendship is for the author and his adolescents the only

* In the original, Pratolini ironically uses the word *"lettera- tura."*

way to resist the adversities of life and bear the intolerable burden of their poverty, the lack of opportunities that forbid any change and force them to be what they are, now and forever. Gino, the sophisticated member of the group, decides to break the scheme of an inherited condition and prepares to eat the bitter fruit of his betrayal. Much like 'Ntoni Malavoglia, of Verga's novel *The House by the Medlar Tree*, he, too, obstinately refuses to accept Santa Croce as his whole world. Lured by the attractiveness of what lies beyond the Bell Tower, he leaves home. He becomes a pederast; after an involved affair with a wealthy bourgeois, he first robs and then murders him when he resists his threats of blackmail. Jailed, he dies "worn out by prayer and fasting," but not before he has written a long and moving letter to his friends explaining that his sin had been one of envy. His friends, in turn, read into his letter a reflection of their failure in letting Gino down, and of having been incapable of assisting him and seeing him through his difficult days.

The world of *Il quartiere*, finally, acquaints us more than casually with the working class with whose aspirations the novelist fully identifies himself. Their role is as conspicuous in Pratolini's fiction as Silone's *cafoni* or Moravia's bourgeois are in their work. The fate of the *popolani* is to remain poor: centuries of exploitations have made them what they are. They accept their condition stoically, as a matter of course. Their only solace is in the fact that they have friends, to whom they can turn for help, guidance, and advice. They respect those who, like Giorgio and Valerio, have intellectual aspirations. It seems to them that such people are capable of recasting man's important issues. In their case, they "must understand what to want and why," as Giorgio says at one point. His words anticipate by a full decade the focal experience of Metello and the novelist's central problem: how can the working class, burdened by centuries of social inferiority and cultural and economic backwardness, be made aware of its condition to the extent of rebelling against it? And how can the novelist, immersed in his own time, dramatize history in terms of social conflicts and class struggles without writing a tract? The principal ambition of Pratolini, from *Il quartiere* on, has been to study in depth the first such question in order to transport into an imaginary world the life and problems of the working class. Perhaps his achievement may be said to consist in having followed faithfully his plan, without falling slave to political ideologies.

*Cronache di poveri amanti,* written between February and September of 1946, is certainly Pratolini's best, if not his most important, novel. While it takes up many of the figures and themes of the previous books (especially *Il quartiere*), it is no mere extension or elaboration of those works. Through a technique similar to that of early Italian chroniclers, it dramatizes a crucial moment of Italian history. In an apparently casual manner, Pratolini gathers and recounts many of the incidents of the lives of several characters, and the tragic events in which they participated between the summers of the years 1925 and 1926. He reconstructs, both poetically and with meticulous attention to reality, the incidents that distinguish an era marked by the transformation of fascism from a poorly organized political movement into a ruthless dictatorship. Its grip on the internal administration of the nation is described as becoming firmer by the day, especially after having silenced the vocal opposition (Matteotti). The mere mention of historical events, against which the novel is set, does not make *Cronache* a historical novel. The book is primarily a story about people, a particularly felicitous re-creation of a cosmos through the invention of well-rounded, believable characters, an absorbing milieu, and a set of problems that are practical, political, and moral.

The cast of the novel is so imposing that the first page of the American edition wisely lists its characters—more than fifty in the slightly abridged translation. Their affinity with the lesser characters of the previous novels is evident. Yet, they are also more varied in temperament and sensibility, more responsive and mature to the ethico-politico-moral issues facing them. The historical and social situation of their time has been carefully reconstructed. The author has modestly confessed that his good fortune has been to "discover the testimonials of [his] characters"; his function has been limited to transcribing them in his novel.

The problem of the heroes of *Il quartiere* was primarily one connected with the search for a permanent, secure

job; for a decent place to live; for an understanding wife
with whom to share the little to which they could aspire.
Theirs was, fundamentally speaking, the problem of the
adolescent and the youngster struggling to find—and live
up to—his place in society. There was, to be sure, more
than a hint of the political responsibility one must assume
in modern society. This was dramatized by the attitude
the youngsters chose to assume toward the war just declared against Ethiopia. Their position was determined
by human consideration as well as by a genuine, if not
always firm, sense of patriotism. The heroes of *Cronache*
are placed in a different historical context and are afforded
an alternative with respect to their political posture. Their
choice is ultimately assessed in terms of the moral and
political commitments they are willing to assume, responsi-
bly and sincerely. Their decision as to whether they should
join the "Blacks" (the Fascists) is reached according to
their intellectual and emotional resources. The author's
sympathy unmistakably goes to those who have the courage
to resist the trend and remain faithful to their principles. A
stubborn refusal to join the party is interpreted as a moral
rejection of its principles and its methods. To come to terms
with the violent Fascists signifies for the "Cornacchiai"—
as the author calls those who live in Via del Corno—the
surrender of their dignity. It is certainly immoral (though
practical) to side with the dubious allies of the Church and
Capitalism in their attempt to stifle the opposition, to
extinguish the generous hopes to reform the antiquated
social structure of the nation.

As in *Il quartiere*, the story of *Cronache* is somewhat
loose. Its vastness makes any attempt to synthesize it
rapidly all but fruitless. Though the book does tell at least
one main story (whose hero is Maciste), which moves in
a rectilinear manner, with well-defined chronological and
geographical limits, it is structurally episodic. Its effects
are derived largely from the rapid alternation of its many
subplots, through which the novelist manages to keep us
interested and informed about what is going on in the
wildly incredible, and yet quite real, Via del Corno. The
focus shifts frequently, with the author moving from one
character to another and telling or showing us what they
are doing; at other times, in a technique reminiscent of

Dos Passos', he gives us a simultaneous view of what is taking place in two different places to two or more characters. By means of an accumulation of seemingly fragmentary insights we become intimately acquainted with the "Cornacchiai." The total impression emerging from the book is that of a frequently amoral society, which thrives on gossip but is deeply interested in the fate and improvement of the human race. As for the condition of the characters, they seem to accept the status quo with an almost callous indifference. In Via del Corno gossiping is equivalent to expressing a genuine interest in others, not for malicious reasons, but rather because it is an elementary manifestation and undeniable part of the people's rudimentary psychology and social habits. The narrative, proceeding in sustained sections, manages to conjure up the atmosphere of a nation in crisis. We acquire a distinct feeling for Via del Corno through apparently disconnected vignettes. To quote the critic Francesco Flora: "*Cronache* is a novel that gathers and orders in a powerful fresco all the human and literary experiences of Vasco Pratolini."

The story is told impersonally. But the third-person technique does not lessen the impression that the author is part of the milieu he describes. He is too well acquainted with its flaws and virtues; he knows too well the secrets of his characters. That he is at home in Via del Corno is proved by the frequent, privately guided tours of the street in which he takes his reader, pointing out the facts and people of interest. At other times he interrupts his narrative to indulge in a humorous, ironic, but always informative, disquisition about the traditional games, the *feste*, the celebrations of the *quartiere*.

When the novel opens we are in *medias res:* Via del Corno, "about fifty yards long and five wide. It has no pavement. One end runs into Via dei Leoni and the other into Via del Parlascio, as though it were enclosed between two streams." The year is 1925. The air, despite its surface tranquillity, is tense. The patrols make the rounds, checking up on parolees and keeping others under surveillance. Early in the morning the alarm clocks begin ringing. The street wakes up: with it, the novel begins to move. The times are difficult: some years before the Fascists had invaded the street "to settle accounts." Now everything seems to be under control: "the police force is an affectionate but stern mother." Fascism is gaining the upper hand elsewhere in Italy: soon the "Cornacchiai" will be forced to change their political views, with the help of the club and a generous dose of castor oil. Violence is being tolerated by the police, which benignly shuts its eyes to the bloody raids executed by the Fascists. Freedom is slowly being curtailed. Those who were once openly opposing the Fascists are being isolated, intimated, and eventually forced to give in. The three villains of the story are: Carlino Bencini, a public accountant; Osvaldo Liverani, a traveling salesman; and the Signora, a perverted, sickly old woman who, from her apartment up high, looks over the goings on assisted by the so-called "four Guardian Angels" (Aurora Cecchi, Milena Bellini, Bianca Quagliotti, and Clara Lucatelli), by whom, in her most critical moment, she will be abandoned to her destiny. It is she who secretly directs much of the fate of the "Cornacchiai," through her contacts with the Fascists and her influence in the *strada*. Those who oppose the Fascists are the heroes: Corrado Maciste, a blacksmith; Ugo Poggioli, a fruit vendor; and Mario Parigi, a printer's apprentice. Maciste's death occupies the central part of the story. The events leading up to the fateful evening of July 12, 1925 are anticipatory and necessary to the climax; what takes place after the slaying of Maciste is an appropriate anticlimax and denouement. Each of the three heroes represents a different kind of opposition to fascism in three slightly different stages and motivations. Maciste is the die-hard Communist who has joined the party less for ideological than for human reasons; Ugo personifies the Communist who, after breaking with the party after a personal quarrel with Maciste, recognizes its worth and returns to the fold in a critical moment; Mario, the youngest of the three, becomes a "red" quite late in the novel, principally out of sympathy for Maciste, whose disciple and protégé he has been. Similar fates await all three; Maciste is killed; Ugo is asked to carry on the secret activities of the cell until his eventual arrest; Mario is asked to organize and run the youth organization of the entire province. At the end of the story, he too is arrested.

The world of *Cronache* is far larger than its geographical

setting would indicate. Similarly, its gamut of characters
is vaster than it has been possible to indicate thus far.
Via del Corno, "the gutter," as the author calls it, is the
habitat of whores, pimps, shady political thugs, as well as
simple, generous people who, through will or selfishness,
have achieved something resembling temporary economic
security. All are implicated, however indirectly, in the
conflict that looms large on the horizon. The conflict forms
the thin ideological skeleton of the story; the daily doings
and the love affairs between one "Cornacchiaio" and another are its very flesh and blood. Happy, stable marriages
are rare on the Via del Corno. Illicit affairs are a daily
occurrence; bawdy escapades with the whores in the hotel
of the Via del Corno are frequent. At the end of the novel
we are bound to remember less the "normal" relations
between Maciste and Margherita or Alfredo and Milena—
whose honesty and uprightness are exemplary—than the
affairs between Egisto Nesi (the coal vendor) and Aurora
Cecchi, who eventually betrays her lover to marry his son
Otello. Aurora, in turn, is betrayed by her husband who,
just as his father had done, keeps his mistress (Liliana,
wife of Giulio Solli, a petty crook) in the very hotel room
where his father had once kept Aurora. "An eye for an
eye, a tooth for a tooth" seems to be the philosophy that
prevails in the street: through it, justice is meted out to
mankind. It is difficult for any "Cornacchiaio" to trust
another, either on the human or on the political level.
The thesis advanced for such a state of affairs has a familiar
ring: the milieu in which these people live is largely responsible for their ignorance, amorality, and irresponsibil-
ity. Every one of their actions comes under the close scrutiny of their neighbors. Every opinion or statement is
methodically discussed. Surprisingly enough the "Cornacchiai" can, in spite of all this, manage to live together without undue tensions. "We must remember," Pratolini writes
at one point stepping out of his story, "that life must be
lived hour by hour, one day after another, with the weeks
and months chasing each other. . . ."

*Cronache di poveri amanti* is not a minute-by-minute
description of the events of Via del Corno: its occasional
detailed accounts of characters and their behavior give us
a deeper insight into their temperament and, by reflection,

into the nature of the basic problems of the working-class.

In a larger sense too, the novel is a striking and accurate picture not only of the age-old poverty endured by the "Cornacchiai" but of their lack of social consciousness. Because of its skillful handling, the story of *Cronache* is a significant documentation of a society kept for centuries in a state of quasi-feudalistic servitude, a society forced to lead a life degrading to the human spirit. *Cronache* is also the most complete expression (until *Metello,* at any rate) of themes latent in Pratolini's previous works, but here masterfully executed for the first time. We discover that Via del Corno, human as it may be, is little more than a gutter of vice and degradation. Pratolini, born into a poor family, is well aware of its real existence and of the fact that, tolerable as it is thanks to the solidarity between its people as demonstrated in periods of crisis or sorrow, it should be erased from the human map. The world is presented with feeling, of course, but also with considerable detachment, which permits Pratolini to view it critically and to make some cogent comments about it. For him, the vice and poverty rampant in Via del Corno have been enforced by history and economics—nothing less than a complete change in historical and economic thinking will change the situation. This message is clear, though never explicitly stated.

The stress upon the socioeconomic condition of the "Cornacchiai" is, unfortunately, somewhat damaging in the sense that it prevents the characters from being "problematical." Their great issue is how to keep afloat in the perennial storms of life. Thus, much emphasis is placed on *what* they do for a living and *how* they are able to make ends meet. So great is the concern with the basic necessities of life and how to satisfy them, that the few characters who think of the issues in other than "practical" terms (they are Maciste, Ugo, and Mario) choose to find a tentative answer to the riddles obsessing them *outside* the limited world of Via del Corno. But their search is wholly devoid of any intellectual or ideological content. It is framed within the limitations of human reason understood in the sense of what experience tells them they can expect from life. This should serve to underscore Pratolini's most serious flaw: the inability to create human characters who can *think*—people who can rise above their practical needs without necessarily indulging in meaningless abstractions.

The novel's finest quality, its warm humanity, proves to be also a real source of weakness. In creating characters incapable of comprehending their plight in rigorously intellectual terms, Pratolini has made them incapable of rising up to their condition in historical and dialectical terms. As a result, we have a literary work that sheds much light upon the social situation of a people without necessarily illuminating the ideological struggles of history.

Intellectually not very stimulating, *Cronache di poveri amanti* is nevertheless a most satisfying reading experience proving to be an immensely effective work of fiction in which milieu and characters are fully realized. Its method of presentation, purposely a disconnected one, does not prevent our learning a great deal about the "Cornacchiai" (and by extension, about human nature) by the time we finish the book. The variety and diversity of the characters, the deftness with which they are handled, the atmosphere conjured up by the author, make of *Cronache* probably the most significant work written to this date about that particular era of Italian history. Fascists and Communists, prostitutes and honest workers, shopkeepers and hotelkeepers people the infamous Via del Corno: above them all stands the Signora, the silent accomplice of the Fascists, the tyrant who is alternately feared, detested, and admired. She is described in vivid, violent colors, in a manner bordering on the surrealistic. She is the source of much evil in Via del Corno: she is indirectly responsible for Nesi's premature death; she spreads discontentment and hate among the "Cornacchiai." When she unexpectedly comes into an inheritance running into millions of lire, she prepares to purchase every house on Via del Corno to evict her enemies and perpetuate her power. Fortunately her scheme is never carried out. A cerebral hemorrhage and partial paralysis force her to spend most of her remaining days in bed under constant medical care.

The end of the story describes the dawn of a new era, coinciding with the laying down of the rebellious "Cornacchiai's" arms:

> It was of course natural that they should eventually toe the line, for they were obliged to live and they were natu-

rally afraid. Staderini now felt his right hand raise itself
automatically, hammer and all, into a fine Roman salute
whenever Carlino passed his shop. Fidelma even agreed to
work in Carlino's house. . . . Leontina sewed the ribbon
of [Staderini's] decorations onto his black twill shirt for
him. . . . If however, we looked into the hearts of our
people, we should undoubtedly have found fear there. To
call it hatred is an active sentiment; so let us compromise
by saying it was rancor, like smoldering fires beneath ashes.
There was no vacillation about whether they ought to join
the Fascist party. Wear the badge? No! Give it public support? No! This was the only mute protest possible, and the
only way of distinguishing themselves from Maciste's mur-
derers.

With the surrender of the "Cornacchiai" and the beginning of a new historical period, the story comes to a close.
But it is clear that after *Cronache* Pratolini must return to
his major theme—history and the people. He must re-
investigate and re-create, with greater breadth and ideological content, the "real" story of modern Italy. The social
turmoils, the beginning of the labor movement, the scourge
of poverty that has always infected the country, demand
further treatment. Understanding our past, Pratolini states,
is the only way to understand our present. A clearer conception of our present problems and of their historical
causes should certainly help us in our constant attempts to
solve tomorrow's problems.

*Una storia italiana* (An Italian History), a trilogy that
will attempt precisely to tell the history of Italy in a "new"
manner, was conceived in those years. Before his vast
project was begun, the cycle begun with *Il quartiere* and
continued with *Cronache* was completed.

Before settling down to write what Pratolini himself re-
gards as his most important work, he published, in 1949,
a novel titled *Un eroe del nostro tempo* (*A Hero of Our
Time*). Not an entirely convincing novel, the tale is nevertheless one of the author's best constructed pieces of fiction.
Moreover, it represents Pratolini's first real attempt to move
away from the familiar world of his experience into one
created by his imagination. Its purpose is to "illustrate"
and shed some light upon what many would no doubt consider an appropriate subject for a novelist with Pratolini's

historical ambitions. It fictionalizes, with candor and strin-
gent realism, the decadence and amorality of Fascist Italy
in the years immediately following World War II. The
chief protagonist of the story, appropriately set in crucial
1946, is Sandrino Vergeri, a youngster who represents
(and is frequently either called or defined) the typical product of Fascist upbringing. We follow him in his various
adventures, in his love affair with Virginia, the widow of
a Fascist, and in his more platonic affection for a teenager,
Elena. The other characters of the story are Bruna and
Faliero Susini, the positive heroes of an otherwise negative tale. Both have played an active role in the underground; both have long been acquainted with Sandrino's
Fascist activities, especially during the short-lived Republic
of Salò. Both have been bruised, more or less permanently,
by the youngster. Yet out of their generosity and their
hope that he is worthy of being saved, they have become
his guarantors so that he will not be sent to a reform
school. When the story begins, Sandrino is a retail clerk
in a clothing store; soon afterward, he becomes Virginia's
lover, and a thoroughly spoiled one at that. Sandrino's
sordid behavior and his past criminal record are carefully
reconstructed through detailed description of his actions
and through retrospective discussions of his earlier life.
After three Fascist fanatics have swindled the youngster
of the money he had appropriated from Virginia's savings,
he returns to town to find that his mistress has suddenly
disappeared. Just when Sandrino is falling in love with
Elena, a student he has met shortly before, Virginia comes
back to tell him that he is the father of a child she is now
carrying. She pleads with him to marry her, offering him
her husband's money, which has finally been released by
the court. After a long walk in the streets of the town,
Sandrino murders Virginia by pushing her head into the
spikes of a steel fence.

The grim story makes abundantly clear the author's
intention. Sandrino represents the perversion, the cruelty,
and the immorality of a generation raised by fascism. In
this sense, the novel takes its place in the stream of the
so-called literature of the Resistance, which in Italy (unlike France) emerged only in the last months of the war
and concentrated on exposing the errors of the past.

The book leaves something to be desired, primarily on two accounts. In the first place, Sandrino is never explained in terms of what he has done but in terms of what he now is. Likewise, the "positive heroes" (Bruna and Faliero), with whom one does not find it difficult to sympathize, are presented as decent individuals through their utterances not their actions. Pratolini's novel has a thesis, but the thesis is too frequently explained rather than enacted. In the second place, since he created Sandrino as an exceptional youngster (who is emotionally disturbed), Pratolini should not have called upon him to represent an entire generation.

Despite its unfortunate weaknesses, *Un eroe del nostro tempo* is rich in highly dramatic scenes and succeeds in moving the reader, who instinctively feels some sympathy for Sandrino. There are fascinating passages describing violence and lust, sadism and arrogance. Vicious, sick with an impudent *arrivisme*, Sandrino is a convincing specimen of much that is bad in human beings. When he displays his worst qualities he is a tridimensional character. In the second part of the book the tale loses its initial impact, especially when Sandrino is allowed to fall in love with Elena in a manner that has none of the violence of his temperament. Indeed, the great bulk of the final section does little to give us further insights into Sandrino's character. He has been fully realized (and has lost his force) in his possessive love affair with Virginia. The final image of the novel is significant not only because it proves that Sandrino's rational power has been suspended throughout the whole story, but also because it demonstrates the inconsequential nature of his tender liaison with Elena and its irrelevance in the development of Sandrino as a character. Inspired by exterior circumstances, as the author privately acknowledged, *Un eroe* is significant primarily as Pratolini's first attempt to objectify a lyrical world by dealing with an observed, rather than a "lived," reality. The world of *Un eroe* has been intuited without ever being adequately investigated and patiently reconstructed.

After a brief return to the folkloristic Florence described in *Le ragazze di San Frediano* (*The Girls of San Frediano*), Pratolini attempts to sum up his vision and correct past artistic shortcomings by turning to a small Balzacian project, a trilogy entitled *Una storia italiana.*

*Metello*, the first volume of a projected trilogy, was completed in 1952 and published in 1955. The second volume appeared after the completion of this book. For the moment, however, *Metello* seems to me to be Pratolini's most controversial and important book. Though as a novel, it is in my opinion far inferior to *Cronache di poveri amanti,* it is nevertheless an interesting attempt by the author to fuse those qualities critics generally acknowledge he possesses— a keen power of observation, an intimate knowledge of Florentine life and its people, his profound lyrical vein— with an ambitious drive to become the "popular" novelist of modern Italy. By fictionalizing history, with an eye to accuracy in so far as its protagonists and events are concerned, he aims to arrive at an interpretation of history that is both poetic and realistic.

To understand exactly the plan of the project, it is necessary to record fragments from the dust-jacket blurb, reportedly prepared with the approval and collaboration of the author himself:

> *An Italian History* is the title of a cycle that embraces a certain period of time, from 1875 to 1945 . . . each novel will be [a] finished [work], autonomous and without any relation to the others, except for marginal circumstances. . . . From time to time there are different characters and milieux, typical of different social strata, from the proletariat to the aristocracy to the petite and middle bourgeoisie, which during those seventy years have characterized life in Italy. . . . The story of Metello Salani (the hero of the first book) . . . is based upon certain indestructible human values: man's origin, the training of his sensibility, the struggle for life, and afterwards his friendships, his love, solidarity and sin. [It is] a private, simple, obscure story which [set] in the Florence during the latter part of the XIXth and during the first years of the XXth century, synthesizes the major experiences of an entire class and takes its place in the process of the development of a society.

Clearly, the goal of the trilogy is to dramatize historically with a considerably greater perspective, the themes al-

ready present in Pratolini's previous novels. Its program
is broader, its design sharper, and each book is to begin
where the preceding has left off. When completed, the
work will no doubt amount to history written (as Pratolini
remarked) "from the perspective of a novelist." While it
is unfair to pass judgment upon the scope and achievement of the entire work until the last novel appears,
it is possible to consider each book individually since
each supposedly tells a single story.

The focus of *Metello* is once more the working class;
the milieu is Florence; chronologically, it covers the period
from 1875 to 1902, although the greater part of the novel
(over three fourths of it) is given to a close description of
events that took place in the spring and summer of 1902.
As in *Cronache*, there are two central episodes in *Metello*:
one is erotico-sentimental (Metello's affair with Idina);
the other is sociopolitical (the famous strike of 1902).
Together, the two episodes show the development of the
main hero. The book is divided into four parts. Part One
tells of Metello's birth; the death of his parents; his adoption by a family that emigrates to Belgium in search of
work and whom Metello refuses to follow, preferring to
stay in his native city; and his entrance into manhood
symbolized by sexual experiences first with a prostitute
and then with numerous other women, among them a
beautiful former teacher named Viola. Called to the army
and discharged after serving his three-year tour of duty,
he goes back to Florence, finds himself a job as an apprentice plasterer and bricklayer, and acquires his first friends,
most of whom are anarchists and socialists. Work is scarce,
however; after a hard winter and after being out of a job
for three months, Metello finds himself participating, almost unconsciously, in the riots of May 1898. Arrested,
he spends seventeen months in jail. By this time he has
met Ersilia Pallesi, the daughter of a fellow worker who
was accidentally killed while working. She goes to visit
him while he is in jail, and Metello decides to marry her.
Thus ends the first part of the novel.

Part Two describes Metello's new life, his marriage to
Ersilia, his job with the construction firm Badolati & Co.,
and the birth of his son, Libero. The labor movement is
becoming better organized and more articulate about its

demands, and Metello participates, without too much enthusiasm or conviction, in its frequent meetings. A growing dissatisfaction with the low salaries and with the fact that even minimum wage laws are frequently not observed, leads the bricklayers to decide to strike.

Part Three opens with the beginning of the strike of May 15, 1902, and goes on to describe the numerous hardships, frictions, and pressures it brings. During Metello's enforced idleness, he has an affair with Idina, who lives in the upstairs apartment.

Part Four describes the end of the strike which has lasted forty-six days, and the capitulation of the building industry to the demands of the masons. Metello's affair with Idina comes to an abrupt end (after it is discovered by his wife). He is promoted to foreman and forgiven by Ersilia. Together with several of his fellow workers, Metello is arrested for having instigated the strike and the riots and jailed for six months. The novel ends with his release from jail.

This brief sketch of the plot makes clear the substantial differences between *Metello* and previous novels; and while the protagonists of most of Pratolini's novels are workers, the conflict becomes in *Metello* less ethico-political and more social-economic. There is still an enemy to be confronted, to be sure, and in *Metello* it is symbolized by the building industry, the A.E.C. (Associazione Costruttori Edili). In *Cronache* the atmosphere, the historical events, and the conflicts generated were seldom directly represented but re-created, and quite effectively so, by the private stories of a large number of individuals, none of whom achieves the status of the major protagonist. In *Metello* the procedure is drastically reversed. Not only does the author describe history in the making, but he creates a major character who impersonates, lives, and reflects upon the manifold sentimental, social, practical, and economic issues that face him. Metello, a bright, curious, alert, and moderately articulate person is the medium through which the issues are dramatized and who supposedly embodies the ideological evolution of the working class. As a work of fiction, it marks, as Carlo Salinari pointed out, the passage from neorealism (where there are no major characters) to realism.

*Metello*, more so than any of Pratolini's previous novels, in its design and in the programmatic intentions of the author stakes a claim in historicity and attempts to describe, with accuracy and insight, certain historical events of the years at the turn of the century, dramatizing the ideological struggle between two socioeconomic classes. As such, *Metello* is a historical novel in the general tradition of Manzoni's *Promessi sposi*, whose deficiencies it tries to avoid. Manzoni, however, does not always succeed in blending the historical with the "inventive" part of his tale. The history of seventeenth-century Lombardy, absorbing in itself, frequently remains only a background against which Renzo and Lucia's story is placed. Pratolini, conversely, places his characters in the midst of history, not against it. Their adventures and conflicts emerge out of history and are rooted in true ideological tensions. One has the feeling that in *Metello* the characters create history and dramatize it, unlike Manzoni's *Promessi sposi*, where the two main heroes submissively accept their roles as *victims* of history to be saved only by their indomitable faith in Providence and God's mercy. The author is forced to step out of his book (as he frequently does) to point out the moral, the "lesson" learned by his characters. Even when his characters themselves tell the reader and each other what they have learned, we perceive the author speaking through them: "I have learnt," says Renzo at the end of the novel, "not to get into riots: I've learnt not to make speeches in the street; I've learnt not to raise my elbow too much; I've learnt not to hold door-knockers when there are excited people about; I've learnt not to fasten a bell to my feet before thinking of the consequences. And a hundred other things of the kind."

The lesson man learns from history, however, must be shown through his acts not merely recited. It is one of the most grievous flaws of Pratolini's novel that the character he creates to embody the gradual ripening of a socialist outlook and of the labor movement is one whose ideas and convictions throughout the story remain too vague and unsure. Indeed, Metello's eyes and thoughts are more regularly on feminine skirts than on the class struggle. His frequent sexual encounters do little to explain, except in a negative sense, the formation of his personality. Irony is added to this already awkward situation when we become aware (and Metello is the first to admit it implicitly) that he has become involved in socialism and the labor movement *malgré lui*. He is never a convinced, engaged worker—and if this is a good thing for the novel on a human level it is downright damaging in so far as its ideological content is concerned. Thus Metello, discussing the situation with some of his co-workers, sums it up by saying: "According to Del Buono, Pescetti, Marx and Turati and all those 'wise men,' it is a class struggle, let's call it that. The important thing is to snatch [from our employers] a little more bread. . . . But we also have to work, and on Saturday we have to collect our pay. Otherwise what is there to cook in the pot at home? Class struggle, mere satisfactions?" In the majority of cases, Metello is coherent in his attitude: he plays what should be his great role either unwillingly or unenthusiastically. He becomes involved in mass demonstrations and riots without really believing in what he is doing; thus, he turns himself into a victim of those agitations that should have awakened in him all the very feelings that motivate the novel. Even his "hate" for the capitalists turns out to be a mild affair indeed. He never comes to ideological grips with his situation as a worker and never reaches a clear understanding of the many issues confronting him. Like most of the other characters of the novel, Metello too remains satisfied to be "guided by [his] instincts," by the "natural force" steering the masses in the right direction.

It is not on the ideological but on the "sentimental" and emotional level that Metello turns out to be a convincing character. He is quite believable when he makes love to the numerous women who come under his spell, far more so in fact than when he engages in discussions of issues to be faced and solved by the working class. Slightly conceited, fortunate in having a combination of good looks and vocal persuasion, he is fundamentally what one may call a "good man without many problems." For him, as for many Italians he polemically mirrors, the education of his senses is superimposed upon and equated with the education of his mind, and the two are inextricably and hopelessly confused. Though a negative reading of *Metello* is hardly one the author would be likely to sanction, it is possible to see in his tale a portrayal in reverse of socialism and the labor movement, a picture of their failures rather than their victories. Such a tempting thesis, improbable as it ultimately must be, is supported here and there by the text. Metello is more than reticent in exercising the prerogatives and the duties of leadership: when his presence is urgently needed by his comrades to formulate policies or make decisions affecting the entire movement, he is busy making love to Idina in the fields near Florence rather than being on the scene. He refuses to assume the responsibility of speaking *as* a worker, *for* the workers. "There!" he exclaims at one point. "It's always the same story. You attach to me an importance I do not feel I have. I don't command at all, I haven't forced anyone's will!"

As a historical novel *Metello*, insufficiently enriched by historical events, is only sporadically convincing. As a social novel, it fails to dramatize the motivation of the tensions that bring about the clash between labor and capitalism. Although the two economic groups are set against each other in earnest they are never *shown* to be fighting with traditional rancor so as to impose their ways upon the losing side. The two forces are never clearly differentiated, except in a vague way, and the reader fails to "see" their ideological differences enacted. Personified by the engineer Badolati (the industrialists) and Del Buono and Pescetti (the labor movement), the two groups never generate the kind of antagonism toward each other that justifies—in the novel as well as in reality—the fierce partisanship traditionally associated with them. "In *Metello*," Arnoldo Bocelli has written, "there is no clash, no conflict, no dialectic of forces and ideas. The tale is lived only by one side, the workers'; and the writer descends deeply into that world that is congenial to him and is rooted in his blood and memory." Without conflict, Metello—indeed like many other Pratolini characters—is but an idyllic, lyrical figure incapable of rising to the status of a true hero. His actions are seldom lived (except his love affairs), rather they are summarized by the author, who is constantly striving to place him in the role that has been prepared for him but that he never accepts.

There are several parts in the novel that are thoroughly

enjoyable. The figure of Ersilia is drawn with considerable sympathy and understanding, as is almost always the case with Pratolini's women. She is a very human person, tolerant, serious, and intelligent—to the point of explaining the complex ideas of Marx and socialism to her husband. Although we do not see as much of her as we would like to, we feel that unlike Metello she matures considerably in the course of the story. Similarly, the scenes of the workers' meeting at Monterivecchi and the discussions that take place throughout the tale sound authentic and vivacious and recall the best pages of *Cronache*. Finally, the early section of the book, where Metello's youth and manhood are described, as well as the youngster's attachment to his native soil, is a moving experience of the finest order.

In the previous pages, *Metello* has repeatedly been called Pratolini's most important work. By inference the novel, together with the other volumes of the trilogy, may well determine Pratolini's final position in Italian literature. In view of the fact that the novelist's literary production is far from being complete, the comments that follow are a tentative evaluation subject to future revisions. Indeed, while Moravia, for example, is unlikely to surprise his readers, Pratolini has a considerably freer road before him.

The world of the novelist has been shown to be Florence and the working class. In all but one book (*Un eroe*) Pratolini has made his native city the center of the poetic map of his "limited" universe. Writing out of his life in his initial stage, he has narrated with feeling the small joys and frequent pains of adolescence. Not content with composing sensitive autobiographies, Pratolini has moved toward the point where he can speak of the sorrows of men rather than the sorrow of man. From *Il quartiere* onward (and significantly the turn coincides with the end of the war and comes after an important experience in the underground), he has explored a vast range of feelings, attitudes, and problems of a steadily richer cast of characters. He has placed them and their story in the context of the troubled years of modern Italian history, those years that lend themselves to effective dramatization. He has moved toward the point where he can observe, study, and narrate, with increased objectivity, the world he knows best and the sort of problems closest to his sensibility and interests. Concerned with the destiny of the working class and with its perennial struggle to better itself, he has projected his tales further and further into history in order to find a reason for the present. He has felt the need— and here may be an indication of his seriousness as a writer—to go back into the past to find in history itself what it is that moves men. It is in this sense that his projected trilogy, despite the weaknesses of *Metello,* assumes an importance few would deny. *Metello* is one of the few novels in contemporary Italian literature that has set its goal at a realistic re-creation and reinterpretation of the past viewed in the richness of the story of social struggles. As recaptured in the novel, the never-ending attempts and the ensuing failures of the people to improve their lot have been humanly depicted. One wonders, at this point, whether it is possible that Pratolini could conceivably turn out to be the Verga of our century. The question must not be pressed too far, because, except for an ambitious program, the two have little in common. Where the Sicilian novelist set himself the task of showing how man is fundamentally ruled and stifled by the environment in which he has matured and how he has no hope outside of it, Pratolini, who is far more optimistic, believes that somehow, in the foreseeable future, mankind in general and the working class in particular will fight for its rights, for a chance to ameliorate its condition, and, above all, to participate in the making of history.

Only the future work will provide a better answer to the unresolved questions asked here. Should Pratolini's trilogy fail to achieve its stated goal, it is at least certain that he will have answered the question of whether Italians can write novels at all. The fiction he has so far completed constitutes, for the time being, an eloquently coherent, if somewhat slightly distorted, image (as all fiction must be), in which modern Italy can, for better or worse, recognize herself.

# CHAPTER THREE

# Elio Vittorini

In the rich literary firmament of contemporary Italy, no one occupies as unique, and in many ways ambiguous, a place as Elio Vittorini. He is one of the few literary artists to have reached a truly international audience without becoming, in any way, "popular." Yet, every book he brings out—a rare event, for he is anything but prolific— is hailed as an exciting expression of avant-garde literature, as a new and bold attempt to turn into a finished literary expression the "one" truth Vittorini wishes to make articulate. His work forces the critics to take stock of their past appraisals of the writer and to come to new conclusions about a man whose work is as strange as it is confounding.

As some may know, Vittorini is more than a mere writer. The story of the important contributions he has brought to Italian culture is now a matter of established record, even though it is not as widely appreciated outside of his native country as it deserves to be. In the thirties he translated with brilliance and sensitivity the works of Poe, D. H. Lawrence, Faulkner, Hemingway, Steinbeck, Saroyan, Caldwell, and other, lesser Anglo-American writers, and with the late Cesare Pavese he pioneered American studies in Italy. For several years after the war he served as the editor of the original series of neorealistic fiction dubbed *I gettoni* ("Chips") authored by the younger novelists; between 1945 and 1947 he published a politico-cultural sheet, *Il Politecnico*, remarkable for its breadth and for the impact it had upon Italian readers at all levels; recently, in association with the novelist Italo

Calvino, he has been editing the Milanese quarterly *Il Menabò*, a review whose critical essays bear on the various problems presented by the poetry, drama, and fiction published in its pages. At present, he is head of the foreign literature division of Italy's largest publishing house, Arnoldo Mondadori of Milan.

Such activities have placed Vittorini in the intellectual limelight of contemporary Europe. As a creative writer, he has authored a book of short stories, seven novels and short novels (both terms are used here with reservations), and a fascinating big volume entitled *Diario in pubblico* (Public Diary), in which he has collected a generous selection of lyrical prose pieces, articles, notes, and aphorisms bearing on literature, the arts, politics, and life in general —all published by him since the twenties.

The list of Vittorini's work will seem quantitatively unimpressive. Yet no other Italian writer matches Vittorini's internal coherence, no one can boast of a similarly rich, or similarly erratic, progression toward "his" book. What he has written thus far, however the reader may consider it (allegories, realistic fiction, symbolic tales perhaps, poetry certainly) should be viewed as parts of a "work in progress." And there is the rub: despite their notable achievements none of Vittorini's books, with the possible exception of *Il garofano rosso* (or the work he has come close to rejecting completely), is a "well-made" novel, a truly finished piece of fiction. Hence the furious revisions (such revisions have prevented his *Le donne di Messina* from appearing in English translation), the dilemmas of technique and form, the inevitable dissatisfaction with the finished product. "I have never aspired to write books; I have always sought to write the book," he wrote recently. "I write because I believe there is 'one' truth to be said; and if I turn from one thing to another it is not because I see 'other' truth that can also be said, or because I have 'more' or 'something else' to say, but because it seems to me that something constantly changing in the truth requires that the way of expressing it be constantly renewed." To this end he has indeed dedicated the better part of his creative efforts.

But not in a regular, "disciplined" manner. It is, in fact, his *"acentricity"* (translations, editorial work, creative

writing, and so forth) that led one of his critics to comment
how ". . . his way of reasoning . . . is like a small jungle:
to confirm, to consolidate an idea that has just struck him,
Vittorini loses himself in other arguments, at first parallel
and similar, then always more disparate, always less probable, finally opposed to one another. . . ." "I envy," Vittorini wrote another time, almost as though he were in
effect answering his critics, "those writers who have the
capacity to remain interested in their own work while
pestilences and war are raging in the world. . . . A big
public event can unfortunately distract me and cause a
change of interests in my own work just as, no more no
less, can a personal happy event or a misfortune. Thus the
outburst of the Spanish Civil War, in July of 1936, made
me suddenly indifferent to the developments of the story
[*Erica*] on which I had worked for six months in a row."

Vittorini's rich curriculum, his complex personality, make
it abundantly clear that he commands our attention for
reasons not immediately restricted to his creative writing.
His perceptive interpretations of other literatures, his deep
and continuing interest in helping younger writers, his efforts to make possible the emergence in Italy of a truly
"modern" culture, have turned him into a force to be
reckoned with much in the same way as Silone, as R. W. B.
Lewis points out, may be considered a "moral force." As
an intellectual, he has never ceased taking part in the dialogue of his generation, addressing himself to the relations
between life and art, culture and politics, the paramount
issues of contemporary European artists. These points are
of importance, for they underscore the fact that for Vittorini, his writing and the many roles he has been playing
on the cultural scene are symbolic of his active participation
in the discovery of what he once termed "a way of life in
the world." Intensely involved in culture-in-the-making,
his creative-critical activities are part of the same process;
they can neither be disassociated from each other nor from
any other human commitment. A man of culture is, in
his view, highly conscious of his position in society, of
his duties not only toward himself and his fellow artists
but toward society itself. He must courageously accept
his share of commitments, political and human, no matter
how high the stakes or how great the possibilities of error

may be. For such reasons, Vittorini's "discovery" of American literature, for example, assumed a special relevance, since it responded to a need at once human *and* artistic. Translating the Americans meant for him purging himself of the rhetoric of his literary tradition and bathing in the stark naturalism of writers whose vision was fundamentally alien to the Italian view of the world. He identified himself not merely with a vision or an idea of freedom, appealing as they must have seemed, but with a way of writing and, even more, with a concept of literature. The meaning of American literature—of which he has been a regular reader since the late twenties—would become clearer as he matured. It ultimately led him, as the pages that follow will show, to visualizing creative writing as the ideal ground where man's moral search and sociopolitical interests may properly be juxtaposed.

His roles as translator and commentator of literature, his active participation in the underground, his work in the editorial field, his frequent polemical positions—attest to his fervent desire, as someone perceived, "to insert himself in the daily reality of his time." From reality and from his time he has drawn the subjects for his books. But he has transformed contemporary events into a timeless, mythical reality, discovered anew by his imagination. His manifold interests in culture coincide thus with his desire to communicate with his fellow men, urging them to follow him in an engrossing quest, and in his attempts to understand and depict those facets of man's condition that have struck the chords of his sensibility.

The rare richness of Vittorini's position in the broader cultural context makes an appraisal of his fiction all the more difficult, lest the reader is made aware of his extra-creative activity and projects it against a vaster canvas of a man's work. The difficulty is further compounded by the fact that with each new book Vittorini has tended to remove himself from the ranks of the traditional novelists like Pratolini and Moravia, whose first and perhaps only concern is, simply stated, "to tell a good story." The world he has created in his recent books, endowing it with a life of its own, has fewer and fewer connections with the "real" world as we know it. These books have something in common with at least the spirit of the American novels he has translated. They seek to dramatize not so much individual facts and events as universal states of mind, transporting the reader into an imaginary no-man's land, where people feel and suffer, to be sure, but don't work or play or make love. It is not for nothing that his finest tales take place in a mythical Sicily (*Conversazione in Sicilia*) or on a train (*Le donne di Messina, La garibaldina*) or anywhere in postwar Italy (but is it really Italy?) as in *Il Sempione strizza l'occhio al Frejus,* rather than in the realistic cities in which the action of *Il garofano rosso* and *Uomini e no* is placed.

Vittorini was born in Syracuse, Sicily, in 1908. His father was an employee of the State Railroad and, being a southerner and a worker, he wished his son to be a white-collar worker. Elio and his three brothers traveled daily to a nearby town where they completed their elementary schooling. He was then enrolled in a technical school to learn to become a bookkeeper. He did not succeed in winning the diploma however, realizing at the age of seventeen what he had long suspected: that studies did not suit him, and that it was better to give them up once and for all. Using his father's railroad pass, he traveled frequently, sometimes leaving his home for weeks at a time. One day he left—for the fourth time in three years—with his mind made up not to return. He had left "for the Continent," hoping to begin there a new life away from home. After a few years in Gorizia, in the extreme northeastern part of Italy, he moved to Florence where he associated intimately with the writers and critics of the review *Solaria.* "I became *solariano*," he wrote in *Diario in pubblico,* "and *solariano* was a word that in the literary circles of these days meant to be anti-Fascist, European, internationalist, anti-traditionalist." He had worked for some years as a linotype operator and typographer when he decided to earn his bread through intellectual activities and writing. His first book, published in 1931 with the title of *Piccola borghesia,* is a slim collection of eight short stories. They are exercises of a sort, competent tales in which the author has transcribed in a humorous, slightly ironical style the monotonous life of government bureaucrats.

*Viaggio in Sardegna* (Journey to Sardinia) followed in

1936 and was reprinted in 1952 with the new title *Sardegna come un'infanzia* (Sardinia as a Boyhood). A collection of poetic reportages of a trip to the island, the book is a flight from reality, the fulfillment of a desire to escape and wander off into a world recaptured through the recreation not of its concrete reality, but its broad spectrum of lights and colors. It is easy to sense throughout the volume how profoundly enjoyable the experience must have been for the author, who confesses that "few times [before] have I been as happy as now."

In the months prior to the publication of *Viaggio*, Vittorini confronted for the first time in any serious way the American writers, particularly William Saroyan. He was then at work on his first full-length novel, *Il garofano rosso* (*The Red Carnation*).

The events connected with the writing of the novel are the subject of a lengthy preparatory essay written in 1948 for the first edition of the work in book form. In view of the fact that the novel appeared some thirteen years after its completion, Vittorini felt obliged to discuss his own attitude toward it and its particular place in his work. The Preface is, in my judgment, one of Vittorini's most significant pronouncements on the art of the novel. It is also a pertinent personal document and an illuminating statement of his poetics.

*The Red Carnation* was begun in 1933 and finished one year later. It appeared in several installments in the magazine *Solaria*. Its unorthodox views of why some youths were attracted to fascism caused it to be censored, and one issue of *Solaria* was ordered withdrawn from circulation.

As a work of fiction, the novel is in the tradition of European narrative. It tells about a student, Alessio Mainardi, and his love for Giovanna, a schoolmate from whom he receives a red carnation, and for Zobeida, a mysterious prostitute who is involved in a narcotics ring. Intermingled with the narrative are several letters written by Alessio's friend Tarquinio and pages from the hero's diary. Nothing exceptional happens in the story. Alessio fails his courses, prepares himself for the October make-up examinations, but is not promoted. At that time he learns from Tarquinio himself of Giovanna's affair with him, and the book comes to an end.

The book's real interest lies not so much in the story as in the atmosphere re-created with considerable accuracy of tone by the author. The air echoes with familiar names and recent events: Matteotti's murder, Rosa Luxemburg, fascism and communism, Lenin, and ever-present in the background, Mussolini himself. The restlessness of the students, their uncertainties, their "ambivalent" political attitude (as Vittorini rightly defines it), are effectively dramatized.

When viewed against the work already completed by Vittorini, *The Red Carnation* is the novel that marks the division between his first and second period, that is to say, between one conception of the novel and another, accompanied by a different style that, though already mature in his early books, rapidly loses all connections with what had been the author's first "manner." Such change, to be sure, did not occur overnight. But certain events were to hasten and encourage it. It was precisely during the first months of writing *The Red Carnation* that Vittorini took a trip to Milan.

> If I ever write my autobiography, I will explain what a great importance this trip to Milan had for me. I came back enamored of places and names, of the world itself, as I had never been except in my childhood. This state of mind had not come of itself; I had sought it out. Yet it came in an extraordinary way, after a period of five or six years during which it seemed to me that only as a child had I had spontaneous relations with the maternal things of the earth. It came at a time when I looked only to the past, when I wrote with my eyes to the rear.

*The Red Carnation* had cost him "cold sweats of study." When confronted with the book as it was being written, he discovered its "technical mistakes," the incoherence and immaturity of its point of view, and, above all, his own inability to identify himself with the characters he had created or with the vision his book conjured up, or with its view of the world. "The power of contact, the passion I had recaptured in March '33 had little by little worked its way into every aspect of my environment, and now I could 'feel passion' for political events as well. I felt that the wrongs of fascism against others now offended me personally." His changed attitudes toward a world he had more or less accepted lessened his belief in his manner of writing. While engaged in writing his novel, he also began to feel uneasy and unhappy with the fundamental vehicle of expression of a writer: language, or better still, with the kind of language that was available to the contemporary novelist working within his tradition.

> Such a language constituted a century-old tradition that every novelist, Italian or otherwise, could bring up to date. One could bring to it those variations suggested by his sensibility as a writer . . . but in practice he had to respect its structure and no one could be called a novelist unless he did so. [Such a language] was excellent to gather the *explicit* facts of a reality, and to connect them with each other *explicitly;* to show them, explicitly, in their conflicts, but it is today inadequate for a type of representation in which someone wishes to express a total sentiment or a total idea, an idea that might synthesize the hopes and sufferings of men in general, all the more if [they were] secret.

This problem obsessed him and continued during the months following the completion of *The Red Carnation,* right to the next *novella, Erica e i suoi fratelli (Erica),* which was published in English in the volume *The Dark and the Light.* He wrote the tale between January and July of 1936, interrupting it because of external circumstances ("I envy those writers who have the capacity of remaining interested in their own work while pestilences and wars are ravaging the world. . . ."). He put aside the manuscript and forgot about its existence, until it was found by the author's late son, Giusto. One year later it was published in the Roman magazine *Nuovi Argomenti,* accompanied by a letter by the author addressed to the editors, Moravia and Carocci. In a note appended to the *novella,* Vittorini once again told why he had been both unwilling and unable to finish the work, even when the manuscript had been retrieved:

> The manner in which I have become accustomed to write from *Conversazione* on, is not exactly the same in which the present story is told. Today I have become used to refer to my characters' feelings and thoughts only through their exterior manifestations. . . . It no longer comes nat-

ural for me to write that such and such character "felt" that, or that "he thought" that. . . . But when I wrote this book it was still natural for me (as it had been in *Piccola borghesia*, or in *Sardegna*, or in *Il garofano rosso*) to say directly what one felt and what one thought. The book is, in fact, replete with "she thought," "she felt," "she used to think."

Traditional in structure, *Erica* is clearly Vittorini's first work not genuinely autobiographical, the first experience of handling the theme of poverty in a world of cruelty and hypocrisy. The story revolves around the experiences of a fourteen-year-old girl left in charge of her younger brother and sister by her mother, who leaves town to join her husband working in a distant locality. Erica shows her maturity and good sense by assuming the role of a mother, and the three manage well as long as they can subsist on the few provisions of pasta, coal, beans, and oil left by their parents. Even when she is under the pressure of repeated offers of help from her neighbors (whose real intention is to exploit her), Erica insists on living her own life. One day, however, when her provisions are exhausted, she realizes that she has reached an impasse. She becomes a prostitute, for it is the only thing she can do without feeling that she is begging others to help her. Her decision is readily accepted by her neighbors: "Indeed just because she was little more than a child, and because they had witnessed the long agony which debouched in this misfortune they were silent more than ever . . . in a certain sense, they also felt grateful to Erica for having freed them of their preoccupation about what she should do." Despite the numerous wounds she suffers—wounds that only time and affection can heal—she is proud of the fact that she can continue to take care of her little family and face life with courage and serenity.

The *novella* is left unfinished at the point when the young girl, in Vittorini's intention, was supposed to enter the world and find a partial solution to her problems. Simply written, the last of the so-called realistic works by Vittorini is especially notable for the depth with which the author explores complex feelings and social situations, reducing them to understatements in order to heighten their effect. The importance of *Erica* is clearly thematic rather than stylistic, in that it is the first work by Vittorini that searches for the meaning of the human situation.

In retrospect, and taking into account the position of the book in the context of Vittorini's production, we realize that *Erica* contains the first fruits of a seed planted in his earlier *The Red Carnation,* a seed that eventually blossomed into the author's total identification with the aspirations of the masses. The identification was to transpire through his lyrical concern for the "doomed human race" —a race divided into *"uomini e no."* At the time when Vittorini was writing *Erica,* however, he was still working within the limitations of those modes of expression and structure imposed by his native (and unoriginal) literary tradition. It is only in scattered sections of the *novella* that it is possible to find the first hints of a style soon to develop into a coherent, personal, poetic means of communication: only seldom in *Erica* does an attentive reader sense that it is endowed with a magical quality of myth and fable. By the end of 1936—the great year of the Spanish Civil War and of an intensive period of translation—Vittorini was no longer interested in the facts of the day and in a realistic diction and vision. He had reached a spiritual and artistic crisis, out of which he was to produce his truly significant novels.

*Conversazione in Sicilia* is to this date Vittorini's most significant book (even though the author prefers the later *Il Sempione strizza l'occhio al Frejus*), his most original contribution to the novel as an art form and to the solution of the problem of fiction as he sees it. Better than any of the works written before or since by the novelist, it recaptures in its own cryptic form not only the spirit of the years of fascism, but the anguish, expectations, and frustrations of modern man, fighting desperately to overcome despair. *Conversazione* is indeed a unique book: born out of hopelessness, it led its author back to hope.

I have mentioned in the previous pages how in the midthirties Vittorini had "discovered" Saroyan. He translated several of his short stories, especially from *Inhale and Exhale* and *Little Children,* in an omnibus volume with the suggestive title *Che ve ne sembra dell'America?* (What Do You Think of the U.S.A.?) Much has been made of Vittorini's careful reading of Saroyan and of such writers as

Wolfe, Faulkner, and Hemingway, as well as of his mimetic sensibility. It is appropriate to point out here that he approached the American writers because they, more than any of those of his own literature, strengthened his feeling of dissatisfaction with style and technique of the novel. Translating became for him not a mere mechanical labor of changing into his native tongue thoughts, images, and feelings of other writers, but a search for a style that would "repeat" the tone and poetry of the original text. Thus Saroyan, like Hemingway and Faulkner later on, proved to be helpful to his own artistic growth in suggesting certain effects possible in his own native language. The insistent repetitions of words and even sentences for which he became known were attempts to render Italian more plastic and musical. It was both extraordinary and fortunate that Vittorini's encounter with Saroyan should take place just as his dissatisfaction with "the way" he had written his books and with "the 'way' it was then thought novels should be written," had reached a critical stage.

Between 1936 and 1937 he began *Conversazione,* publishing it in installments in the review *Letteratura* and in book form in 1941 (in a limited edition) and again in 1942. This time, however, the censor could hardly be insensitive to the book's various implications and references and consequently ordered it withdrawn from circulation. For years copies of the work circulated freely among the partisans becoming symbolic of the intellectuals' opposition to fascism. Read in many of the Nazi-dominated countries, it reminded men of their elementary obligations to each other, the necessity of working for peace and justice; and it dramatized the great insults perpetuated by man upon mankind.

The book makes few concessions to the sort of formal structure we are accustomed to expect from a novel. Indeed, one cannot say much more than that *Conversazione* is a book about the "real" journey undertaken by Silvestro, a thirty-year-old linotype operator, who works in Milan, to his native town of Syracuse, in Sicily. He decides quite suddenly to take a trip: one day, as his mother's birthday approaches, he receives a message from his father announcing that he has left his wife and begging Silvestro not to forget her. Doomed by "abstract furies," Silvestro decides to deliver his birthday wishes in person; he wires some money to his wife, gets on the train, and leaves for Sicily. The events of the trip are few: Silvestro arrives in his native town and goes to his mother's house, where the two have a long talk, mostly about Silvestro's grandfather and father—in their discussion the qualities of the two men with all their faults are delightfully confused to the point where it is seldom clear about whom they are talking. Silvestro then follows his mother, who earns her livelihood by giving injections to the destitute townsfolk who cannot afford a doctor. He is given the opportunity to visit and become acquainted with a few ordinary people, including a knife grinder (Calogero) and a *paniere* (Porfirio). He talks at length with them (and surely their conversations make up the finest pages of the book) about the "doomed human race," gets slightly inebriated, and goes to the cemetery, where he meets the ghost of his brother who was killed in battle. Then he returns home to Milan, but not before having learned that his father has gone back to his wife.

These events, sparse and seemingly disconnected, allow the author to give vent to the "abstract furies" obsessing Silvestro at the beginning of his journey. The trip he undertakes to his native land proves to be a salutary spiritual experience: the things he sees, the people he meets, the landscape he takes time to admire, conjure up a vision of anguish—anguish that is loneliness and trepidation and sorrow for a mankind that has for centuries been vilified by man. But there is also a vision of hope, for it is only upon his return to the North that Silvestro is ready to face life once again.

Structurally, *In Sicily* resembles a great symphony orchestrated around individual and recurring subthemes, such as the motif of the "stink" (Chapter VI), the "dark mice" (Chapter II), the "oranges" (Chapter IV). Stylistically, there is a far subtler repetition of words, such as "cheese," "the medal," and "prickly pears," that contributes substantially to achieving an unusual rhythm. The entire action takes place in Sicily, with the author warning us that it is so called purely for accidental reasons, since "the word Sicily sounds, to me, more harmonious than Persia or Venezuela." No passage exemplifies the mythical quality of the tale's milieu more than the description of Sicily near the end of the book:

> It was night in Sicily and in all the still world. The out-raged world was shrouded in darkness; the living had shut themselves up in their rooms with the lights on, and the dead, all those men who had been killed sat up in their tombs, meditating. . . . Those lights below and above, that freezing darkness, that glacial star in the sky, were not a single night, but an infinite number; and I thought of the nights of my grandfather, the nights of my father, the nights of Noah, the nights of man, naked in drink and defenseless, humiliated, less a man than even a child or a corpse.

What gives the book its unity and is the element that forms the leitmotiv of the entire journey is Silvestro's "abstract furies." Beginning with the masterful opening passage, and running right through the tale, "the abstract furies" are not the dominating force but the motivating reason that induces the hero to undertake his trip and regain contact with life, incarnated with considerable perception and simplicity in the mother and his own native Sicily.

> That winter I was haunted by abstract furies. I won't try and describe them, because they're not what I intend to write about. But I must mention that they were abstract furies—not heroic or even live; some sort of furies concerning the doomed human race. They had obsessed me for a long time, and I was despondent. I saw the scream-ing newspaper placards, and I hung my head. I would see my friends pass an hour or two with them in silence and dejection. My wife or my girl would be expecting me, but, downcast, I would meet them without exchanging a word. Meanwhile it rained and rained as the days and months went by. My shoes were tattered and soggy with rain. There was nothing but the rain, the slaughters on the news-paper placards, water in my dilapidated shoes and my taciturn friends. My life was like a blank dream, a quiet hopelessness.
>
> That was the terrible part: the quietude of my hopeless-ness; to believe mankind to be doomed, and yet to feel no fever to save it, but instead to nourish a desire to suc-cumb with it.
>
> I was shaken by abstract furies, but not in my blood; I was calm, unmoved by desires. I did not care whether my girl was expecting me, whether or not I met her,

glanced over the leaves of a dictionary, went out and saw my friend, or stayed at home. I was calm, as if I had not lived a day, not known what it meant to be happy; as if I had nothing to say, to affirm or deny, nothing to hazard, nothing to listen to, devoid of all urge; and as if in all the years of my life I had never eaten bread, drunk wine or coffee, never been to bed with a woman, never had children, never come to blows with anyone: as if I had not thought all such things possible; as if I had never been a man, never alive, never a baby spending my infancy in Sicily, among the prickly pears, the sulphur mines and the mountains.

But the abstract furies stirred violently within me, and I bowed my head, pondering mankind's doom; and all the while it rained and I did not exchange a word with my friend, and the rain seeped through my shoes.

One of the qualities of the style of this novel is that it is at once dramatic and poetic. Its strange cadence—which may seem forced at times—is achieved not only by the constant repetition of words or even sentences, but by the elliptical form in which the author reports a conversation: "I," "the soldier," "I." The characters themselves have no names, or when they do it is likely to be a historical or biblical one or one denoting some particular physical or regional peculiarity: Moustache and No-Moustache, the Great Lombard. One feels, after completing the book, that *In Sicily* is not a novel in the sense that it tells a story in which the various characters have a chance to develop. It is more a romance, in the manner brilliantly defined by Richard Chase, in his study *The American Novel:*

By contrast [with the novel] the romance, following distantly the medieval example, feels free to render reality in less volume and detail. . . . The romance can flourish without providing much intricacy of relation. The characters, probably rather two dimensional types, will not be complexly related to each other or to society or to the past. Human beings will on the whole be shown in ideal relation —that is, they will share emotions only after they have become abstract or symbolic. . . . Character itself becomes, then, somewhat abstract and ideal. . . . The plot we may expect to be highly colored. Astonishing events may occur, and these are likely to have a symbolic or ideological, rather than a realistic, plausibility. Being less committed

to the immediate rendition of reality than the novel, the
romance will more freely veer toward the mythic, allegorical, and symbolistic forms.

*Conversazione,* as indeed all of Vittorini's succeeding
novels, is quite likely a romance in the sense Chase describes. The characters, however alive and believable, have
the function of incarnating a state of mind, certain political
positions, or attitudes toward and interpretations of human
problems. In the Preface to *The Red Carnation* Vittorini
has discussed what must be considered his most interesting
"problem"—technique. He has directly tackled the problem
with which he has concerned himself for more than two
decades by making certain parallels between the novel
form and opera. He writes that after his first experience of
seeing an opera performed, he became aware that the
novel, unlike opera, does not have "the power . . . of
expressing through its complexity some splendid general
emotion, indefinable by nature and independent of the
action, the characters, and the emotions portrayed by the
characters. As a matter of fact, while the opera is in a position to resolve its problems of scenic representation
poetically, the novel is not yet in a position to solve poetically all its problems of the novelistic representation of
reality. . . . The novel, at least in the hands of the realistic novelist of today, cannot without turning into philosophy, transcend its own preoccupation with a reality of a
lower order." Opera, with its special combination of action
and music, offered him the example of a fiction still possible to a writer who, like himself, "had to express himself without actually saying it."

The problem to which Vittorini is referring is familiar to
novelists everywhere, especially in western Europe (Thomas
Mann, Jean-Paul Sartre, Albert Camus, Graham Greene,
et al.). Ever since it was created, the novel genre has
gradually been absorbing philosophy, psychology, sociology, history, politics, economics: hardly any form of
man's intellectual or creative activity has escaped being
used in fiction. However, unlike opera (which also has
accepted subjects other than music), the novel has failed
to assimilate and reabsorb nonfiction elements, re-express-
ing them in its own particular mode.

*Conversazione* demonstrates, perhaps more brilliantly

than any other book written by the novelist, how fiction can be made more poetic and still dramatize at the same time those facets of the human reality dealing with certain intellectual and spiritual problems. The style created by Vittorini, and achieved only after a careful reading of the American novelists, was most appropriate to the allegorical type of fiction the author wrote between 1940 and the immediate postwar years. The novelist, in short, was resorting to what Glauco Cambon has correctly defined "the heightening iteration" in order to avoid trouble with the censor. His postwar work, such as *Il Sempione* and *Le donne di Messina*, has continued the method initially put into practice in *Conversazione*. This is creditable indeed, as it demonstrates the coherence of Vittorini, dedicated to a refinement and an extension of literary language in order to fill the abyss left by so-called realistic fiction. His method, assuming that it has been correctly pinpointed, inevitably engenders new problems. Many of his recent books, including *Conversazione*, frequently have this much in common: they tend to transform human beings and human actions (the raw materials of fiction) into abstract symbols that live for and by themselves without firm relation to the concrete reality from which they supposedly spring. One can understand why the critic Giovanni Cecchetti complained that in the distant future *Conversazione* will have to be accompanied by footnotes and explanations clarifying some of the allusions to events that, although clear to us today, will no longer be clear to tomorrow's readers. The criticism is legitimate if we insist, as some do, that a novel must mirror a certain historical era, rather than man's eternal condition. For this is the point: Vittorini is interested in the latter, not in the former. For him history may provide no more than the background against which he can unfold the eternal saga of mankind. There have always been wars, and there has always been despair; but there has also always been something in the world that has enabled man to regain confidence in his ability to shape life and the world in his own image. If we accept these premises, then *Conversazione* is far more valid than *Il Sempione strizza l'occhio al Frejus*, despite the author's attempt to show the "truthfulness" (or accuracy) of his representation of contemporary conditions by appending a final note giving essential statistics on the cost of living in Italy in 1945-6.

*Conversazione* is more than a good book. It is the work that provides the themes that the novelist has been re-working in his more recent works, as the motif of the "doomed human race," and of the duties that somehow have become worn and no longer matter. During his trip to Syracuse, Silvestro meets the Great Lombard who, look-ing at Moustache and No-Moustache busily talking to each other in the train's corridor (they are secret-police agents), says:

> I believe that man is ripe for something else. . . . Not only for not stealing, not killing, and so on, and for being a good citizen. . . . I believe he's ripe for something else, for new and different duties. It is this that we feel, I be-lieve, the want of other duties, other things to accomplish. Things to accomplish for the sake of our conscience in a new sense.
>
> Ah, I think it is precisely this. . . . We feel no satis-faction in performing our duty, our duties. . . . Perform-ing them is matter of indifference, and we feel no better for having performed them. And the reason is this: those duties are too old, too old and they have become too easy. They don't count any longer for the conscience. . . .

The opportunity to participate in a more active way in shaping the destiny of his nation came with the outbreak of the last war; Vittorini joined the underground. Out of his experience he wrote *Uomini e no* (Men and Non-Men), a title probably inspired by Steinbeck's *Of Mice and Men*. *Uomini e no* exasperates the technique of *Conversazione*, whose themes it takes up again, briefly expanding on them.

Structurally, the novel represents something of a drastic departure from the previous books. It is divided into one hundred forty-three extremely brief chapters that narrate the events of the tragic months of the winter of 1944—one of the mildest winters in Milan's history. But the mildness of the winter is contrasted with the bloody action that rapidly unfolds. We witness the exploits of the parti-sans, the cruel German reprisals, and the slaughter of in-nocent women and children.

The narrative does not flow in a normal fashion: it is interrupted eight times by passages written in highly lyrical language. The function of these passages, printed in italics, is to break the "monotony" of the narrative, almost entirely made up of dialogue, as well as present certain events in the narrator's time that are glossed over without regard to their true chronology.

As in *Conversazione*, the last name of most characters is seldom given. They are called by monograms (Enne-2) or with a simple first name. Little or nothing at all is told about their lives. More than in *Conversazione* Vittorini experiments with the poetic effects created by repetition of the same phrase, with slight variations, in a manner that reminds one of Gertrude Stein rather than Hemingway, whose *For Whom the Bell Tolls* may have served as a model for *Uomini e no*. Examples are quite abundant, but the following is representative of Vittorini's technique:

—He does not have much to do with many companions.
—Has he much to do with other companions?
—He has nothing to do any more with many companions.

Unfortunately—and here it is not difficult to agree with the severe criticism leveled at Vittorini by Mario Praz—the technique used is not subservient to poetry but it seems to be the author's dominating concern. What could have served him well, if used with moderation, to increase the ever mounting tension of the tale becomes something that detracts from the story, distracts our attention, and eventually degenerates into a mannerism. Nevertheless, it is unfair to stress with Praz that Vittorini's partisans talk "like the shepherds in Theocritus's *Idyls*," since that would mean that the author's expression has been restricted to a realistic or mimetic technique. Vittorini's procedure is generally legitimate in that the effectiveness of his novel consists in the simple way in which the protagonists explain themselves; indeed, it is possible to see that their constant repetitions may well have been thought and are expressed only to reinforce their agreement with their companions and thus become an expression of solidarity. *Uomini e no*, like *Conversazione*, is not a novel: it is a lyrical affirmation of man's right to a certain dignity, to happiness. As Selva proclaims at one point, speaking with Enne-2, "We work in order that men may be happy. What good would it do to work if it didn't serve to make men happy? That's why we work."

The discourse begun in *Conversazione* about the "insults" endured by the "doomed human race," "the sorrows of the outraged human race," are partially erased by the active struggle of *Uomini e no*. But the fundamental question posed by that book is somewhat more universally urgent: "How can man be happy?" Or, given the present conditions, how can man fulfill himself?

*Il Sempione strizza l'occhio al Frejus* (*The Twilight of the Elephant*), published in 1947, is a book written, in Vittorini's words, "*con piacere.*" Much like *Conversazione,* this book, too, seeks to recapture universal problems and feelings rather than to recount a story. There is, of course, a story to be told, but it is made up of small events that do not by themselves hold our attention. *Il Sempione* is about a man and his family. The man (never named) used to be, in his younger days, unbelievably strong. He had helped build the Semplon, the Frejus, the most imposing buildings the world over. Now he is old, tired, silent. Beloved and respected by his family (his daughter, her husband, their children), he is the cause of additional hardship. A voracious eater, he consumes more than three pounds of bread every day—a mere trifle when compared to the twenty-two pounds he could eat when he worked! The family is forced, therefore, to purchase bread on the black market (bread is still rationed) and is deprived of all other necessities. The only member of the family who works is the son, and what he earns is barely sufficient to purchase the bread which, along with some chicory, picked in nearby woods, serves to satiate their continuous hunger.

One day a man with a smutty black face (he is thereafter called *Muso-di-Fumo*, Smut-Face) walks in. Grateful for the welcome extended by the family, he shares with them their poor supper. But what was ordinarily a meager meal is transformed into a sumptuous dinner when everyone agrees, without even thinking about it, to "make-believe" that they are to have chicken and wine and other delicacies. The money Smut-Face gives the father will purchase some real wine and chestnuts and even anchovies, and the feast may be repeated all over again, without having to "make believe." They are provided with the occasion to talk about man's poverty and wretchedness, and they listen to Smut-Face talk of how he wanted to be a sorcerer. Having obtained a fife, he had found a tune. But the tune, he explains, is not yet perfect and in order to perfect it he goes every day into the woods to practice. With the perfect theme he will some day be able to enchant elephants. When he shows them the fife, they notice that a piece of red rag hangs from the end of the instrument. The music apparently is quite effective, for the grandfather, who has been a silent witness to what has been taking place before him, begins to mark time to the music with his fingers. After telling the amazed little audience how elephants die (they go to a secluded place, which man never sees, to lie down and die), the man departs. The next morning, the grandfather, who is called "the elephant," disappears into the forest, presumably to die, although the mother states calmly that the workers will no doubt bring him back home.

The book's message, strangely enough, has never been commented upon by Italian critics. Vittorini is interested in dramatizing a human situation in terms of its social and political problems. In *The Twilight of the Elephant* he hints that a greater awareness of the issues of ideologies and of the various methods of struggle will inevitably help the proletariat to overcome the ruling class. Yet the *novella,* for all its allegory and suggestiveness, cannot be read as a political tract heralding the coming of communism. There is, of course, some naïveté in the symbol of the fife played by Smut-Face, the red flag hanging from it, and the overt declaration of a future revolution. What I find more significant is the human attitude of the author who is actually pleading for a new condition that will bring dignity to mankind. Such a condition can only mean the death of those ideologies and social divisions that are out of step with modern times. Thus, Vittorini has great feeling for the grandfather, the old man who incarnates the accomplishments of unorganized, exploited labor. The fact that he is now old, worn out, and silent (he never speaks in the story) means little, for he can, when the real opportunity presents itself, respond to the call of history. When Smut-Face plays the fife the grandfather suddenly comes to life again and ceases being a mere spectator.

Never are we allowed to forget that he built, after all, "tunnels and buildings, bridges and railroads, aqueducts, dikes, power plants, highways, and, of course, the Duomo, the Colosseum, the Wall of China and the Pyramids!" The trouble with him is that he is heavy, burdensome, and inert. No one is trying to minimize his past accomplishments. But what of the present, or what of the future? they ask. Has he, per chance, outlived his usefulness, becoming in the last years of his life an additional burden to his family?

The sociopolitical implications of *The Twilight*, written during the time when Vittorini was a Communist sympathizer, are extended in *Le donne di Messina* (The Women of Messina), a long, turgid work that has cost its author "cold sweats of study." *Le donne di Messina* is the first work written since the war to bear the subtitle "novel." It, too, is to be linked with the previous books and brings Vittorini's story one step further. Having depicted mankind as being "insulted," the author shows how it could retrieve its dignity by actively fighting against any and all tyrannical governments (*Uomini e no*). *The Twilight of the Elephant* dramatized how certain ideologies were clearly superseded by others and that society was in dire need of transforming itself and of accepting a system that will not tolerate people being forced to live on a standard of living that borders on starvation. *Le donne di Messina* proposes to show how, after a period of conflict and destruction, mankind may settle down in an old territory to found a new community. As Ines Scaramucci has aptly stressed, Vittorini's previous novels underscored the fact that man was ripe for something else, for "things to be done for our conscience"; *Il Sempione* looked forward to the time "when men would really be like elephants, serene like elephants. . . . But they must be free and not belong to somebody else, not from a menagerie. . . . Such a time can never have been. But perhaps it may come. And when it comes I don't want be alone." *Le donne di Messina*, written between 1946 and 1949, even with its flaws, is, by virtue of its themes, its structure, and its organization, Vittorini's *summa*. Indeed, the book exemplifies in a lucid manner the direction in which the novelist has been moving since the time of *In Sicily*. It may also be taken as the best specimen of the sort of fiction possible from a writer with Vittorini's ideas about the novel, politics, ethics, and art.

The setting of the novel itself is interesting: the greater part of the story takes place on a train. Its ideal hero is the pleasant Uncle Agrippa, a retired employee of the State Railroad who is making full use of his pass to travel constantly.

In his chapter on Faulkner, R. W. B. Lewis, commenting on Steinbeck, describes *The Grapes of Wrath* as "a picaresque novel in the modern manner, an episodic long tale of encounters along the way of a harried and difficult journey —the journey of dispossessed Oklahomans toward and into the deceptively promising land of California." These comments apply well, *mutatis mutandis,* to Vittorini's *Le donne di Messina,* which tells of the search by "dispossessed" Italians for a land on which to settle. The war is barely over and there is much pioneering work to be done. A nation has been defeated—that is tragic enough. Yet the people are intensely conscious that the material reconstruction of their country must be accompanied by a moral reconstruction. As Uncle Agrippa travels up and down Italy (and his traveling gives the novel its particular rhythm and controls its movements) and as he goes by the new town founded by the pioneers (the new version of the pilgrims who left for America), we feel that two worlds, a new one and an old one, are brushing each other without ever coming to a full confrontation. It is the same sort of feeling, indeed, that one gets from *Il Sempione* and especially from the unresolved meeting between the pensive, old, mute grandfather "elephant" and the fife-playing worker, Smut-Face. Uncle Agrippa's travels have a purpose: he is trying to locate his daughter, Siracusa, whom he has not seen since she left home. His constant travels give him a chance to meet many people, to whom he becomes friend, counselor, and sympathetic listener. His life has been devoted to what is clearly his last "search." Alone in the world, he has no other purpose for living than to look for his daughter, who is presently among the settlers of the new village founded in the Apennine mountains. The two never meet, although at times Uncle Agrippa has heard several people talk about his daughter without really being sure that it is she they are discussing. Siracusa has become

attached to a man named Ventura, a former Fascist who
has joined the settlers and who is trying to make a new life
for himself. He is a dedicated and hard worker in the new
colony. But one day the "hunters" come to town, after having finally traced a man wanted for horrible crimes committed during the years of fascism. Siracusa tells Ventura
that they are looking for him, and for a while Ventura
plays with the idea of escaping and evading justice. Terri-
fied by the news and unable to bear his girl's condemnation, Ventura kills Siracusa in a stable. One half of the
third part of the book consists in the reconstruction of
the murder and the events that follow it—the actions of
the members of the community—and how Ventura is
finally shot by the "hunters." The tale ends when the author
realizes that the actions he has just described have taken
place in the village almost simultaneously with his writing:
"we have arrived in an identical present: the village and
myself. . . . And to want to continue writing would mean
to continue our story in the guise of a diary." And so the
tale is finished without a "conclusive word" either about
the uncle or the village. What of the town, or its people,
or of their struggle against the lawful owners of the land,
which they have cleared of mines, cultivating it and giving
new life to it? What of the freedom of the individual citizen
of the community? And what of the possibility of a society
capable of leading an orderly life without the supervision
and control of a merciless, bureaucratic government? These
questions are left unanswered: Vittorini is too aware that
the poet may touch upon and delve into human problems
and human possibilities. But man alone must try to resolve
the conflicts inherent in life; he alone has the supreme
potential ability to bring about any improvement in his
social or spiritual life.

   *La Garibaldina* (the last full-length work completed
and published by the author in book form) reads much
like an extension of, or a concluding note to, *In Sicily* and
*Le donne di Messina*. Written between December 1949
and May 1950, *La Garibaldina* was originally brought out
in installments in the Florentine review *Il Ponte*. It is
appropriate and revealing that the *novella* should have
appeared in the same volume with *Erica,* written fourteen
years earlier, as we are thus offered a valid yardstick to

measure the long road Vittorini has traveled in his poetic quest. It becomes even clearer, too, that the novelist's *sense* of, and *feeling* for, reality has increased at the same pace as his *interest* in contemporary reality has decreased.

Structurally and stylistically, the affinities of *La Garibaldina* with Vittorini's previous works are numerous and easily recognizable. There is hardly a plot in this story, and much of it takes place on a train. Likewise, *La Garibaldina* is an effective tale less for what it says than for what it succeeds in evoking. Its style is typical of the linguistic agility we have come to expect of Vittorini, and the feeling for situations and sentiments is, as always, profound and amazing. And one can always rely on the amusing combination of encounters and confrontations as an instrument of aesthetic pleasure. There are many wonderful scenes in the book: the meeting of the eccentric Signora, Baronessa Leonilde, with Innocenzo, the *bersagliere* on his way to Terranova on leave; their meanderings in the town after the two have gotten off the train; and the strange finale itself. What is most instructive, however, is the author's method used with considerable subtlety to fuse the real with the unreal, the present with the past, the immediate with the timeless, as in the description of the town and the impact it makes on the unsophisticated soldier:

> The tolling of a bell whose tone fell suddenly, reverberating against the paving stones, reminded them both of the task they had in common, but it frightened Don Carlos who ran out of one of the alleys. They looked back at the dark town whose bronze throat had given voice. Was it one o'clock or did the sound mark a quarter after an unpredictable hour?
>
> The town too had something that was undefinable. There were wide-open doors, dark wells of emptiness, wide-open windows, wells of emptiness too: and there were other doors and windows closed as if they had been blacked out for centuries upon centuries in a far distant age, before the flood.
>
> The walls were covered with cracked dust and the northwest wind, blowing full strength, raised a yellowish clay of grit from the façades; even the houses with some sort of attempt at a style appeared shapeless with their outlines

grayed, their corners rounded and their cornices nibbled away.

The town might have witnessed the coming of Abraham, the pilgrimage of the Three Kings, Roland's passage on his way to Roncesvalles, and Garibaldi's passing. . . . The soldier and the old woman were somehow reconciled. They stopped and decided to rest.

The tone of the entire book is constant as in this passage. Things are made to speak for themselves and questions are made to contain the answer to what is being asked. And that answer, in the last analysis, is the truth of the great Lombard of *In Sicily:* "I believe that man is ripe for something else. . . . Not for stealing, not killing, and so on, and for being a good citizen. . . . I believe he's ripe for something else, for new and different duties." Hence the insults in *La Garibaldina* heaped upon the train conductors who insist that the poor soldier traveling on the wrong train pay the difference in fare; hence the heroine's magnificent rebellion and condemnation of old and useless rules, and of human folly.

People speak in this extraordinary *novella:* but so do houses, smoke, and ghosts! And after we are through reading the tale, and manage to find stillness again (after so much, and such astonishing *coralità*), we realize that it was not a "novel" we had been reading all along: it was a cry against despair, or a hymn to man's dignity and hope, and to the vitality, courage, and humor of a race not yet totally doomed and certainly not yet ready to surrender.

The foregoing has sufficiently explained why Vittorini, as original an artist as he undoubtedly is, has been said to present considerable difficulties if considered exclusively a novelist. He is, of course, original on many counts. His unusual mastery of language is coupled with a considerable feeling for it and an extraordinary awareness of its flexibility. I can think of no other contemporary writer who can match the poetic intensity of his prose, with the possible exception of the late Cesare Pavese. Like many other novelists and poets of modern Italy, Vittorini has a strong conception of the effects that can be produced through a skillful handling of words. A comment he once made about Eugenio Montale's *Le occasioni* is entirely applicable to his work. "A fact counts only when, in some way, it is new for man's consciousness. Only in this circumstance is a fact truly a new fact: if it enriches the [human] consciousness; if to the long chain of meanings of which such a consciousness is composed, it adds a new meaning." Vittorini has devoted his creative work precisely to the discovery of new meanings in new words; he has been concerned with illuminating "new," or hitherto unexplored, facets of the human condition. "A word," he wrote in the same article, "may give to a fact not new a *new* meaning" (italics mine). With words, enriched with simplicity, he has created a landscape where the eternal feelings of man have not only a life of their own but a real relevance to contemporary situations. Beginning with *In Sicily*, he has attempted—often with considerable success—to make the novel come close to matching the achievement of opera. Words, and the situations they describe, must in his view create a larger reality, larger because they do not only reflect the actual reality of things and people. Devoid of realistic paraphernalia, such re-creation is applicable to all times however much it may require and expect an understanding of the historical circumstances that inspired it. He has managed to achieve wonderfully new effects through his own peculiar mixture of a highly allusive, melodious language with slang, gauche expressions, and familiar words ordinarily eschewed by traditional writers.

The road Vittorini has chosen for his own quest for a "new" novel is not an easy one, as the flaws of his method and language clearly attest. "Vittorini's style is all tricks, fanciness or fancy over-simplicity, ponderous whimsy, half-formulated statements, false poeticism," commented Diana Trilling in her front-page review (in *The New York Times Book Review*) of *In Sicily*. Such a devastating criticism of Vittorini's style should be rejected. It would have been sounder to have projected the whole matter of the linguistic and structural problems presented by Vittorini's novels against his experience as translator and reader of American fiction. If the artist has the right to begin somewhere, he should hardly be censured for having chosen a literature other than his own as his point of departure. Throughout the years, Vittorini has eloquently demonstrated how a writer with sufficient intelligence and sophistication may employ a language rooted in a foreign example and eventually free it of its foreign aspect, making it a highly personal manner of expression.

Few can deny the originality of Elio Vittorini, not only as a writer but as a man of culture, all the more if one bears in mind the literary tradition of which he is part. He is one of a small nucleus of writers who have attempted to give the meaning and force of myth to contemporary history. Despite the final notes appended to *Uomini e no* and to *Il Sempione strizza l'occhio al Frejus*, the worth of both books, and of the latter in particular, rests in their depicting, in a highly mythical manner, something toward which mankind has long been groping. Finally, Vittorini is one of the few writers to refuse to accept the novel form handed down by the nineteenth century, so that he may continue to experiment, as every artist must do, with new ways to express the "human comedy." No better example may be cited here than *Le donne di Messina*, where he has avoided some of the flaws marring his earlier works. The novel's fascinating features—its mixture of straight narrative with passages made up exclusively of dialogue, the choral effects in the last part of the book, where the minor characters take turns in recounting the events of Ventura's homicide—can be appreciated easily by any attentive reader. This novel in particular, and Vittorini's work in general, is eloquent proof of the maturity and seriousness of practitioners of fiction in Italy. Among them, Vittorini may be considered the one who has most consistently and coherently strived to rejuvenate the form of his expression. The changes he has brought to the novel have made the genre more interesting, to be sure, but they have also emphasized the constant need for the artist to commit to a form not merely fictitious incidents and events but the thoughts and feelings, as well as the changing sensibility, of a society on the threshold of becoming modern.

# CHAPTER FOUR

# The New Writers

Each generation produces its own share of novelists and poets, few of whom are fortunately destined to be read one hundred years after their death, except by specialists and writers of dissertations. In dealing with contemporary letters the temptation is strong to be either too generous or too critical. Frequently we tend to disparage contemporary literary artists, in support of our negative view, by comparing them with the so-called classics, which also (as we conveniently forget) undergo periodic reassessment not always to their advantage. How, we ask ourselves, does such and such a writer compare with the giants of fiction— Flaubert, Melville, Manzoni, or Dostoevski? Without adequate historical perspective, it should be clear that all the critic of contemporary letters can possibly hope to achieve is the formulation of an approximate, incomplete judgment subject to frequent revisions both during and after the completion of a writer's work. The greatness of a writer, the significance and meaning of his work, its impact upon both his own and world literature, may be evaluated only after his death, although it is frequently acknowledged during his lifetime. Even then the critics will argue over the very meaning of greatness, for our concept of what constitutes greatness in art inevitably undergoes changes brought about by a combination of factors. We may become more refined through intellectual maturity; or we may discover the meaning of a literary work through sustained study and meditation; or we may simply be influenced or distracted by the changes of fashion and taste that distinguish every cultural period. These problems notwithstanding, we may agree that the classical (the term being synonymous with "great") work of literature is, first of all, one that has survived the crucial test of time and has withstood constant close analyses by critical minds (which need not be those of the critics). Its formal and internal perfection enables it to epitomize and transcend its own time. It can instruct and amuse us at the same time, illuminating in mysterious ways many truths about life. A work of art challenges us to "define" it; yet its meaning grows every time we confront it. The gap that separates the reader and the literary work can never, for all our efforts, be closed completely.

The postwar years in Italy have already distinguished themselves as being extraordinarily rich in imaginative novelists and poets. The most prominent and widely admired feature of recent Italian writing has been the lucidity and courage of the artist's vision. The younger writers, unlike their elders, no longer seek to escape reality or, much less, have any illusions about it. If anything, they understand its bitterness and emptiness. Though in the majority of cases the outlook presented is far from being optimistic, it is on the whole encouraging precisely because it takes full cognizance of our present difficulties. The insights found in postwar fiction enable us to understand the nature of the human predicament without fostering despair. It is through the work of the younger novelists, born between the end of the first decade of this century and 1930, that Italy's literary status has been immeasurably increased. The maturity of such works has impressed the world, which has recognized itself and its problems in Italian novels. Alberto Moravia, Elio Vittorini, Italo Calvino, Carlo Levi, are just a few of the many writers whose work has frequently become as familiar outside of Italy as it is in their native country. Through them we have gained new insights into the tragic character of our generations; in them we have seen reflected some of our disturbing preoccupations. But in them, too, we have—to paraphrase in the affirmative a verse of Eugenio Montale—discovered "what we are and what we want."

It is impossible in the present context to give any more than a general picture of the contemporary Italian literary scene, and to mention briefly some of its outstanding novel-

ists. Few periods in the history of Italian literature (with
the exception of the Renaissance) have been as productive
and as rewarding as the present. None, except the decades
between 1860-1900, matches its surprises, promises, and
even disappointments. Someday, when the historian of literature will have the necessary detachment and impartiality
to write a complete account of the literary events of our
century, he may well conclude that the first fifteen years
following the Second World War constituted something
more than just the fascinating but essentially amorphous
period it seems to today's critics. He will then proceed to
examine the works produced within this particular span of
time, sifting the wheat from the chaff and judging accord-
ingly.

From the present vantage point a few general observations on the state of contemporary Italian letters may be
helpful in orienting the reader. First, it should be pointed
out that one of the most important and fruitful trends of
postwar Italian fiction has been the pseudo-documentary
one. Such fiction has concentrated on the themes of war,
the humiliations endured under fascism, the social and
political problems faced by the nation on the verge of, and
after, defeat. In the five or ten years after the end of the
war, many novels have stood out for the forthrightness of
their message and the clarity of their vision: among them
are Fenoglio's *I ventitrè giorni di Alba*, Rigoni-Stern's *Il
sergente della neve* (*The Sergeant in the Snow*), Berto's
*Il cielo è rosso* (*The Sky Is Red*) and *Guerra in camicia
nera*, Lunardi's *Diario di un soldato semplice*. In these
books, which are novels only in a limited sense, real experience plays a larger role than fantasy. There is no
attempt to hide the historical reality of the experiences they
narrate, although sometimes reality itself is enriched by
imagined events as the whole is woven into a coherent,
well-developed plot.

Some writers and critics, such as Italo Calvino, for example, hold that Italian literature today "cannot be said
to have any real school or current, but only complex personalities of writers who are [ever] so different" from each
other. The remark is true to some extent. Literary schools,
or *cénacles*, have always had considerable difficulty existing
in Italy, a country where, culturally at least, creative artists

try to hold steadily onto nonconformist positions if only to assert themselves as individuals. Unconsciously perhaps, today's writers are joined less by schools than by common interests. An attempt to describe them according to such interests can be made without minimizing their originality.

Another prominent trend is one ordinarily referred to as *costumbrista*, the novel of manners and customs. The writers of distinction who have authored such novels are numerous: sufficient to mention, among them, Moravia, Pratolini, Silone, Rea, Levi, the late Vittorio Brancati, the younger Prisco, Cassola, and Quarantotto Gambini. They have described, colorfully and sympathetically, life as is lived in a particular region in Italy. Their work is not, as one might assume, a static, photographic representation of reality. It is, rather, a critical, at times even severe, interpretation of actual conditions tempered by a measure of compassion. The social, political, and moral problems they study are only in a limited sense "provincial." Their timeliness and universality are illustrated by contemporary international events.

There are also other writers, for instance, Franco Fortini, Guglielmo Petroni, Oreste del Buono, Elémire Zolla, whose fiction reveals above anything else a precise, uncommitted stand toward reality. These writers are more intellectual than the rest, interested in ideas rather than facts and in feelings more than sentimentalities. The interest of their work is also one of psychology and philosophy: they dramatize problems that have been felt acutely by the generation born at the end of the first decade of this century. Their themes are man's loneliness, his inability to communicate at a rational and an emotive level at the same time. Their heroes strive to achieve an internal coherence that may permit them to watch, objectively and serenely, and participate if need be, in the obscenities and cruelties of contemporary existence.

The end of the war has also marked the final decline of tendencies to which reference has been made throughout this volume, namely, *rondismo* and hermeticism. The postwar fiction seems to have been written all too often with a vengeance against the *bello scrivere*. The writers strive to communicate what is in their hearts, in violent language, if necessary. The situation need not evoke special surprise,

as part of the customary reaction of a period of social and
political turmoil is the desire to break with the past as
completely as possible. The revolt of the young writers
(few of whom can, however, be called "angry" after the
British) is directed primarily against the idols of the past
generations (Fogazzaro, D'Annunzio, Papini, and Panzini)
as well as against the aesthetics promulgated with im-
placable logic, and perhaps too much inflexibility, by the
late philosopher Benedetto Croce. The new writers, with
few exceptions, are not interested (as were the literati of
the twenties and thirties) in writing well; they are interested in writing. They wish to write something with an
ideological or human content. This has caused cries of protest: some claim it is impossible to find in recent Italian
fiction what Italians call "a page worthy of being included
in an anthology." To be driven by a compulsion to transmit a message is not, one would agree, the ideal condition
in which fiction may be written. It may well be an awareness of this that has persuaded some of the promising writers to eschew the novel genre altogether and test their
creative power in the essay genre or the essay-novel
(*romanzo saggistico*). Still others, like Enno Flaiano and
Romano Bilenchi, perhaps out of an incapacity to be inspired by the "new" conditions have temporarily given up
writing fiction and have devoted themselves to journalism
of a highly sophisticated kind, or books of travel, or
*réportages*. The quality of their writing—their range and
penetration—is in the finest tradition of Italian letters.
They write for a limited audience that demands not only
competence but a sense of style and intellectual sophistication. Their public, more than wanting to be entertained,
wants to be challenged by the writer's imagination to
meditate about national and international problems and
issues.

Carlo Levi's *Cristo si è fermato a Eboli* (*Christ Stopped
at Eboli*) marks, as it were, the beginning in the postwar
period of a literary genre that has always had considerable
fortune in Italy: a hybrid of history and autobiography,
sociology, politics, and philosophy. Levi's book is a refined
document of the encounter of the civilized North (Levi
was born in Turin, the city of gentility and manners) with
the primitive South. The work's success is due to the con-

siderable understanding with which Levi, forced to live in the backward region of Lucania, discovered the humanity and problems of people whose very existence had barely been acknowledged during the prewar years. Indeed, even Christ never went that far south: "No one has come to this land except as an enemy, a conqueror, or a visitor devoid of understanding." A similar interest in the underdeveloped or "new" nations has yielded several other documentary books, whose chief merit is their maturity and the breadth of the views expressed. Guido Piovene's masterful study of the United States (*De America*), Moravia's recent *Un mese nell'URSS*, Curzio Malaparte's *In Russia e in Cina*, Carlo Bernari's *Il gigante Cina*, Ezio Bacino's *America bifronte*, and Levi's *Il futuro ha un cuore antico* belong to the category of interpretative analyses.

It is understandable that in a world that is shrinking more and more each year people should naturally be interested in faraway nations, exotic lands and customs. In Italy, such interest has extended to its own regions. As a matter of fact, one of the prominent trends of these last years has been made clear by numerous books (both fiction and nonfiction) dealing with certain Italian cities and regions, particularly those situated in the South. The excellence and pertinence of such works is attested by the solicitude with which numerous political leaders have tried to tackle the vast socioeconomic problems of the South. Numerous steps have been taken in an attempt to correct, or at least alleviate, a situation that was barely short of being disastrous. New, bold programs have been launched, partly with American aid, to help make the South an integral part of the nation and a decent place to live in. Along with the purely documentary books (as the outstanding *Report from Palermo* and the recent *Outlaws,* by Danilo Dolci), there has been a genuine revival of the southern imagination. The impressive character of such a trend has led the critics to speak of a "southern renaissance," comparable to the renaissance American literature has been enjoying for some years now, thanks to such "southern writers" as William Faulkner, Eudora Welty, Robert Penn Warren, Flannery O'Connor, and others.

"The depth and intensity of the problem of the South must be seen to be believed," the historian Umberto Zarotti-

Bianco recently wrote. Describing the ills affecting the large section of Italy comprising one third of its total area and known as the *Mezzogiorno,* the eminent author neglected to point out the vital role played by fiction in the story of the slow reawakening (at the "official" as well as at the popular level) to the southern problem.

The Italian South's striking similarities with our own South have seldom if ever been noted. Both regions have an extraordinarily rich cultural heritage: novelists, poets, philosophers, and critics (from Allen Tate to Cleanth Brooks in our country and from Vico to Croce in Italy) have brought a handsome contribution to the letters of their respective countries. Frequently they have not only written with intensity and feeling about their native soil but have founded, or given new direction to, philosophical, critical, or creative trends. The *Mezzogiorno,* despite its awesome social and economic backwardness and the lack of educational opportunities, has produced a crop of novelists and poets second only to Florence's: Giovanni Verga, Luigi Capuana, Salvatore di Giacomo, Grazia Deledda (born in Sardinia, but considered a southerner just the same), Luigi Pirandello, Salvatore Quasimodo (the last three winners of three of the four Nobel Prizes awarded to Italy), Corrado Alvaro, Elio Vittorini, Eduardo de Filippo —are the first names to come immediately to mind.

Both Souths are primarily agricultural; both have often felt "estranged" from the rest of the nation, to the point of shutting themselves in their unbelievably out-of-date "obscurantism" and in an obstinate and naïve faith in the status quo. Both regions have frequently been in the vanguard in matters of foreign policy and in the retrogradation in internal affairs. The temperament of the southerner is quite similar in both countries: his warm-blooded, violent, proud, and jealous character is so widely known as to have become a commonplace. The hot and sultry weather has no doubt influenced their disposition. It is likely that the various degrees of exploitation to which he has been subjected throughout history may have significantly contributed to his alienation and deep-seated resentment.

Ever since the last century numerous and unusually talented writers have dramatized the social and economic predicament of the South of Italy. The fiction they have produced has not, to be sure, been written out of a secret wish to rebel against the oppressions of their sophisticated countrymen from the North. Nevertheless, it has often accomplished a positive function when it has been read as an objective indictment of a society unwilling to recognize the dignity of man, his inherent right to a life higher than an animal's. No sensitive reader can have failed to see in the tragic existence depicted by the *narrativa meridionale* the life really led by the southern peasant but also the depiction of a human, "real" situation in dire need of being changed. On no other occasion, save for the latter part of the nineteenth century, has Italian fiction succeeded in illuminating the tragic quality of life in the regions. Seldom before has literature become such an irresistible power demanding concrete action.

The "school" of southern novelists has always had a coherent and articulate narrative tradition. Verga is the recognized master and the writer most would like to emulate. The example of Verga has been understood not by southern writers alone. Like all great novelists, he eloquently demonstrated by his example the limitations of the mere regional novel. With a unique single-mindedness and imagination, he showed how writers could dedicate themselves to the "invention" of a language patterned in its rhythm and structure after the dialect, through which they might express the passion and torment of man.

It is interesting to note here how the literary renaissance of the South coincides with the beginning of a period of industrialization. As Piero Bigongiari writes, in an excellent essay entitled "Roots, Language and a Style of Fiction," "the South is reawakening to fiction just at the time when it is losing its characteristics as an all too typical region; it is precisely in this trend toward equality of life (when oil wells are taking the place of the abysses of its haunted and sulphurous land), that the South feels the need of a voice, as if men had begun again to speak, having rejected the idea that silence was still part of an ancient sense of dignity."

"Books, like people, die; only a few of them have a persistent life," Malcolm Cowley wrote in his prefatory note to the somewhat revised edition of Ignazio Silone's novel

*Fontamara*. Silone (b. 1900) himself, in an essay entitled "Fiction and the Southern 'Subsoil,'" reminded his readers that "books are like trees; they do not grow for nothing." Of all novelists writing about the South, few have, in our days, the special place and significance of Silone. *Fontamara* has now become a kind of classic, a book that illuminates its own time and man's condition. Silone composed it in 1930 in Davos, Switzerland, where he had found political asylum from Fascist Italy. After several years of militant communism, he had grown disillusioned with the party; he was sick and restless. As he wrote in *The God That Failed*, it was then that "a time came when writing meant, for me, to free myself from an obsession"; writing, he recently stated, "became my only means of defense against despair." *Fontamara*, after several rejections, was finally brought out in German by a Zurich publishing house. But the story Silone felt compelled to tell demanded that he continue writing. In 1937 he produced another remarkable novel, *Pane e vino* (*Bread and Wine*), and two lesser works. He returned to Italy in 1944, after a fifteen-year exile, an internationally known and respected writer whose work had been translated into a score of languages but had been read only by a "happy few" of his countrymen.

*Fontamara* does not, of course, surprise the reader as it did in the thirties. Few people today lend much faith to the worn legend of the Italian South as a land of music, sunshine, heady wines, and sensual passions. Yet, despite the three decades that have elapsed since its original publication, *Fontamara* (Bitter Fountain) has lost little of its power and none of its relevance. Indeed, in its new slightly revised form, it is less the sociopolitical document it was, and more a profoundly human story about people and their immense capacity for suffering.

It seems to me that this is the point of the book. Although *Fontamara* tells one main story and several incidental ones, it hardly has a well-developed plot in the traditional sense. The effect and poetic quality of the novel are in the incredible simplicity with which Silone depicts his *cafoni* ("peasants," with a distinct derogatory connotation), raising them to symbols of mankind in a perpetual state of suffering. The *cafoni* are the exploited farmers of the section of the Marse, in the Abruzzi, who carry on the burden

of "a misery received from their fathers, who had inherited
it from their grandfathers, and against which honest hard
work had never been good for anything." They are the
"men" in Steinbeck's sense; they are the "doomed human
race" of Elio Vittorini's *In Sicily*: "a man who is sick or
starving is more than a man; and more human is the race
of the starving." In *Christ Stopped at Eboli*, Carlo Levi
wrote about the southern peasants: "We're not Christians,
we're not human beings; we're not thought of as men but
as beasts, as beasts of burden, mere creatures of the wild."
But if neither Christ nor reason ever reached Fontamara,
a little village forgotten by civilization, history certainly
did. Silone's tale recounts how history, and the vicious
political system it produced, made the *cafoni's* lot still
more miserable by adding physical violence to century-old
injustices.

The story is told by a father, a mother, and their son.
Through their narrative, stylistically and philosophically
consistent, we learn of the extraordinary events of their
town. Through them, we relive the eternal cycle of life
and death at Fontamara, where the young become old
and the old die without ever experiencing the end of life-
long exploitation. The hero of the story is young Berardo,
a peasant, who goes through the various stages of rebellion
against vested authorities. His final acquiescence results in
disappointment and bitterness. His hope, lost momentarily
when he realizes that the odds against him in his fight
against tyranny are too great, is reborn in jail where he has
been placed on a charge of vagrancy. There he meets the
"Solitary Stranger," a legendary underground figure who
has been fighting for the people's cause against fascism.
His brief contact with him persuades Berardo that he *must*
resume his battle and his militant opposition against a tyrant who has allied himself with the Church and the rich
landowners to exploit the peasants further. Willingly, almost happily, he confesses that he is the Solitary Stranger
wanted by the police and sacrifices his life so that the
struggle may continue. In jail, he comes to understand not
only the meaning of suffering but its necessity. Even death
has, in its own absurd way, a positive meaning: "If I
die . . . it shall be the first time that a peasant has died
not for himself but for someone else." The present version

of *Fontamara* no longer speaks of the necessity "to unite," but ends with the same haunting question: "WHAT CAN WE DO?" The question, as recent international events eloquently demonstrate, is still awaiting an answer; but it has become even more urgent.

Silone represents a special segment of the "southern school," and his work is more understandable when projected against the author's particular politics. From the time Silone first began writing and up to the end of the last war, he made no mystery of the fact that his fiction had a message that was human, social, and political. His stories dramatize the need for action; but they are also fascinating fictional stories revolving around ideologies.

In fact, despite some notable exceptions, the bulk of fiction authored by southern writers has in the past been one-dimensional, betraying an excessive preoccupation with a photographic-documentary technique, and frequently limiting itself to treating those aspects of life that may be called, *tout court,* folkloristic. The genuinely original books about the *Mezzogiorno* have often not been works of fiction, but the essays and autobiographies authored by Carlo Levi, Danilo Dolci, Giovanni Russo, Dante Troisi, and other writers who have justly perceived that it is better (at least for the time being) to study the nature and origins of the present social structure in the South than to "narrate" a pathetic and deplorable facet of the Italian reality.

There are, to be sure, a few writers whose work strives to achieve simultaneously recognition of, and insight into, southern life. Leonardo Sciascia, for instance, deserves to be singled out for his seriousness of purpose and his depth and objectivity of observation. His *Le parrocchie di Regalpetra* is a penetrating report of the social deficiencies of southern life written without concessions to the present or past governments. Likewise, his fiction (the short stories collected in *Gli zii di Sicilia* and the more recent *Il giorno della civetta,* soon to appear in English) succeeds in presenting believable stories that unmask the tragedy as well as the farce of local traditions. The characters of his books endure their reality (and endure they must, true repressed citizens that they are), but they also manage to find in their painful experiences something that enlightens them. Their suffering, in short, has not been totally in vain, for it has made them more aware of their "condition," and thus better able to cope with life, more eager to prepare themselves for a day of change that is sure to come.

By contrast, Domenico Rea, probably the leading and most intelligent exponent of the new generation of southern novelists, is concerned with the need for social reform while remaining aware of the fact that his stories are first and foremost fiction. Rea was born in 1921 in the town of Nocera Inferiore, near Naples. Although he aspires to be a novelist, he is really a short-story writer. His tales have often been described as superb, if distorted, sketches of Naples: but the Naples of his fiction is clearly symbolic. Naples, to any Italian and to a *meridionale,* means the city where poverty is most conspicuous, a blatant reminder of how backward certain sections of Italy still are despite the progress made by other regions. In Naples, however, wretchedness has traditionally been hidden by folklore. There are enough songs and festivities in that city to make the occasional visitor happy and unconcerned with the dramatic, tragic poverty that can easily be observed through the shallow veneer of holiday spirit. For Rea, indeed, "poverty is the cause of all evil." In an essay appended to his volume *Quel che vide Cummeo* (What Cummeo Saw) the author confessed his ambition to depict a "real" Naples more real than the Naples apparently surrounded by happiness. For him, poverty has been subjugated to color and a new myth has been born: "among Neapolitans and its most accredited interpreters there may be a pact: they must feign, even to themselves, their very nature." His stories have the smell of Neapolitan life; reading them one hears the idiom of Naples. It is the language of people condemned to an eternal state of social inferiority, but it is also the language of proud human beings for whom poverty is part of their personality, the element that makes them at once different from, and in some ways better than, the others. Rea is captivated by what he considers another essential quality of his people, that of wanting to seem and be judged more "a Pulcinella than an unbeliever; a man without dignity more than a cuckold; a 'sentimental' more than a total man lacking a sense of reality." Witness a story, *"Gli oggetti d'oro"* ("The Gold Items"), in which Rea gives a masterful description of a provincial who comes to Naples, meets an old friend who comes from the same town, and accepts his hospitality. Impressed at first by his affluent condition, he soon realizes that his friend is riddled with debts and lives an existence more wretched and provincial than his own.

Rea has written only one novel, *Ritratto di Maggio* (May Portrait), whose theme and treatment is more like that of a *novella*. The book, well received by the critics, has with considerable justification been called one of the most impressive inquiries into the state of education in the South.

One of the results of the intense awareness of and interest in reality that distinguishes a large share of postwar Italian fiction is that creative writing has taken on the quality of a "document." In a recent interview, one young novelist expressed what has largely been felt by the generation born and brought up under fascism. "We began writing at the end of the war," he said, "with an abyss behind us. We had to start anew." The young writers sought then to depict reality, the burning reality of their experience, so as to draw a moral lesson from the chaos of their years and the blunders of their elders. The themes and techniques of recent novels do not always point to a bolder, more experimental creative age. Yet, no one would deny that it has been terribly important for the young novelists to undergo the experience of "neorealism," just as in nineteenth-century France literature was able to produce a Proust and a Gide after realism and naturalism. As the French critic Fernandez has astutely written:

> The crisis of collective conscience causes two kinds of reactions: either a desire to distract and evade, or a wish to understand and overcome. It is in Germany and in Italy, the two nations most harshly marked by contemporary history, that the desire to understand and overcome [history] has inspired, with the greatest amount of joy, the most disparate writers, who are joined by a ferment and a lucid spirit of inquiry.

The need to understand, analyze, and criticize the human situation, especially as it prevailed in postwar Europe, did not always produce a strictly "realistic" literature. After an impressive, prolonged outburst of novels of "revolt" or of "the war," the situation settled somewhat: and if the experience of fascism and of World War II is not easily erasable from Italian consciousness, it has been sufficiently explored or even exploited in the period dating from the middle forties to the early fifties. The better writers who lately have produced novels dealing with the war (as in the case, for instance, of Giorgio Bassani) have demonstrated that they have completely assimilated that experience and are interested in going beyond their point of original departure so as to comment upon universal conditions. For purposes of clarification, I have chosen three lesser novelists who represent three different tendencies and yet have, at one time or another, dealt with the war in one of their novels. They are: Guglielmo Petroni, Natalia Ginzburg, and Italo Calvino. The first two were born around the time of the First World War; Calvino is their junior by several years but is also a more versatile creative writer. Individually they exemplify, by their style, orientation, and technique, the intellectual, the psychological, and the fantastic novel. All three, while relatively young (so far as Italian writers go), have demonstrated an unusual seriousness of purpose, a rare skill in handling the novel form, and substantial intellectual and creative maturity. Like many of their contemporaries, they have frequently set their tales in recent history: but they have shown themselves to be uninterested in making history serve an ideological cause, or in exploiting it because it is fashionable to write about historical events. It is impossible to predict accurately what they may have in store for us, or indeed whether they will ultimately succeed in achieving a permanent place in the history of Italian literature. At this time all that can be said is that the sobriety of their work, their lack of pompousness, their inventiveness, and their sense of style persuade me that their work is worthy of our respect and critical elucidation.

Guglielmo Petroni, the oldest of the three, was born in

Lucca in 1911. He spent his adolescence and youth working in his family's store, and he educated himself by reading the classics. After a brief period of painting, he began
writing poetry, the first of which appeared in the early
thirties. His official entrance into the world of fiction was
in 1949, when his first autobiographical volume, *Il mondo
è una prigione* (The World Is a Prison) appeared. It was
followed, in 1950, by his first novel, *La casa si muove*
(*The House Has Started Moving*), and, in 1953, by *Noi
dobbiamo parlare* (We Must Speak).

His first book, although described as an autobiographical
account of the months spent in the German jail in Via
Tasso in Rome, is really a hymn to man's greatness and
courage. Moreover, it is a foundation upon which the
following novels rest. Written in an extremely moving style,
*Il mondo è una prigione* has been called, and justly so,
today's equivalent of Silvio Pellico's *Le mie prigioni*. There
are many notable episodes, but I shall recall only the one
where the author-protagonist visits a friend, a resident
psychiatrist in a Lucca hospital. At one point, having observed the wretched state of the patients, the author comments: "In order not to be mad, one must be either
semiconscious or more or less a hypocrite." To which the
doctor replies: "If, with all this, we could succeed in for-
giving one another, even madness might be overcome."

Two passages introduce the reader to Petroni's world.
One relates the author's difficulty, while in jail, in communicating with his fellow prisoners:

> "You never talk," one of them would say to me; and I
> suffered on that account. "You never talk" did not mean
> that I was silent, but rather that I never recounted any-
> thing. And it was true. It was true and I felt humiliated by
> it, especially when one of them, precisely because of his
> situation, precisely because of the absolute necessity of
> it, would talk like an open water tap that lets the water
> run out interminably, monotonously, but which is pleasant
> to listen to and is capable of distracting those who have
> something on their mind.

Once out of jail, where he had been treated like an animal and repeatedly beaten, the author experienced a profound loneliness that made him wish that somehow he

might be able to return to the place where he had suffered so much. The "moral" of the book, however, is to be found not in the final pages but in the opening paragraphs of the story:

> At that exact moment I felt all that in the ensuing months was to appear to me as the simplest truth: that the immense whirling of wars, social tragedies, was not merely around us but within the most secret part of our lives, in the midst of our innermost interests . . . that the first steps toward life cannot be taken unless one starts from the depth of one's own soul, one's own culture, of the experience that in each one of us the secular feeling of our tradition and our history represents; [they cannot be taken] if not by discovering in ourselves the meaning of things that arise around us, of the feelings that take place and evolve.

After *Il mondo è una prigione* Petroni set himself to search for a possible meaning of things and of man's place in the world. The result was *La casa si muove*, one of the most bizarre books to have been written in postwar Italy. The story begins with a man getting up from his bed and calmly dressing himself. There would be nothing exceptional about his doings were it not for the fact that the hotel where he is staying had been hit by a huge bomb the night before. Its entire façade has, as a result, been sliced off, leaving its front rooms exposed to public view. Before a curious, amazed crowd gathered in front of the hotel, the man thanks the fireman who helps him reach the ground by means of a stepladder, tips his hat, and leaves.

The man is the hero of the story. He is Ugo Gattegna, a wealthy landowner who leads a secluded life in his farmhouse, assisted only by his old, faithful woman-servant, Cesira, who has been with the family for many decades. Gattegna, as we soon find out, is a strange man indeed. He has not only withdrawn from life altogether, but he does not have any friends. Although he has attended the university he has no outside interests. He spends his time reading and meditating, in monastic silence and tranquillity. Frequently, he scribbles on pieces of paper obscure, disconnected words or strange phrases that possess a peculiar rhythm but are otherwise meaningless: "It will come, it will not come, what difference does it make. Certainly, everyone, come, comes, will come, will come without doubt." Needless to say, his farm manager, Baccelli, protests frequently that the situation is absurd, all the more because Gattegna refuses to make any decision whatsoever regarding the handling of his affairs.

One day the protagonist receives a letter from an old friend begging him to offer hospitality to a young man named Gianni who is in some kind of undisclosed trouble, presumably of a political nature. Gattegna accepts the request, but although he makes Gianni as comfortable as possible, he does not establish any kind of rapport with him. By this time the war is drawing closer to the household with each day. Gattegna refuses to prepare to save either himself or his property or to take refuge in the nearby hills. The retreating German troops finally arrive at the farm and order complete evacuation of the territory. Gattegna refuses to follow the orders and is shot by the officer in charge of the German patrol. When the Americans arrive, shortly afterward, there is nothing they can do to save his life.

Gattegna's personality and psychology do not undergo any change or development in the story. He remains, to his death, forceful and strangely coherent. Gattegna is an extension of the author-hero of *Il mondo è una prigione*. In that book the issues of life have been posed in these terms:

> What about prison and freedom—aren't they truly like a real prison, and a real true freedom? Is the world itself a prison? Are we ourselves perhaps our own prison, or is our freedom only within us? What of the others: are *they* your prison? A prison that one may love, perhaps, just as one loves that *real* prison left behind with an obscure regret?

The question was asked directly in that book, as a document or a diary requires. In *La casa si muove* Petroni fictionalizes the condition of solitude to which mankind in general, and the intellectual in particular, is condemned. But the enigmatic personality of Ugo Gattegna becomes clear just before and after his death. As he prepares himself for the Germans, he experiences an inner peace, and "his thoughts about the future were nothing but fleeting flashes, whereas he would live every instant that passed and sink back into it as though it contained all eternity." He himself confesses to Cesira that he has failed to understand people and their aspirations, and that he has never sympathized with them sufficiently: "Perhaps I should have been able, somehow, to understand what one gets out of one's own life if one has the courage to enter into the life of other people." After his death, Gianni, who has returned to the farmhouse, finds several sheets of paper on which Ugo used to jot down his notes. He reads only one of them—but what he reads is sufficient for the reader to grasp the meaning of Ugo's life, a life only apparently desiccated by his inability to become involved in life, a life spent preparing himself for death: ". . . nothing to resolve, no problems. To know how to wait is the most difficult task, no one knows how to do it; but there is an end for those who don't know how to wait. Toil, patience, toil, toi, to." There is a considerable measure of strength in Ugo's obstinate preparation for the final moment, and for all his unwillingness to live with and for others, it is difficult not to feel sympathetic toward him.

*Noi dobbiamo parlare* is Petroni's last published work of fiction. It examines, once more, a problem that is central in the world of the novelist. Here too the plot is quite uninvolved. A young peasant, Venturino Frateschi, by sheer manipulation and unscrupulous deals, has become a successful businessman and has amassed a large fortune. He lives in a handsome villa, not far from where his parents live. Unlike him, however, they are quite destitute and spend their last energy trying to earn their livelihood by tilling the soil.

One day a girl comes to the villa: she is Natalina, the daughter of Frateschi's brother, who has come to beg her uncle to help his parents in their distress. Venturino thrashes her and throws her out of his house. The girl meekly promises to return. And return she does several times without succeeding in moving her uncle's obstinate egotism.

Venturino's mistress, herself a prosperous business-woman, decides to adopt the young girl. Even though Natalina is eventually able to help her grandparents without Venturino's help, she returns to him and persists in her vain attempts to make him realize his obligations. Her life is devoted to the proposition that "we must speak," whatever the cost. To speak means, for her, to utter a human truth; to speak also means to break the solitude surrounding us and to define ourselves through our acts and words.

Her perseverance is not unrewarded. At last Venturino is converted and becomes more charitable to his neighbors. He has been tamed by his docile niece. Yet something tragic happens to Natalina: in the fierce and prolonged spiritual and physical struggle of trying to turn her uncle into a decent human being she has exhausted her own energy and capacity to love. Her life is ruined when she becomes aware of this and breaks off her engagement with a young man who is deeply in love with her.

Petroni's novels are traditional in terms of structure. He seldom seeks to rejuvenate the novel form or experiment with new ways of expressing his vision of the world. In the last section of *La casa si muove*, where Gattegna prepares for his inevitable death and the dictation of his will to Cesira, the author resorts to a technique appropriate to dramatic art. The conversation between Ugo and his old servant is as pure dialogue, wholly without interruptions or intrusions on the author's part. Everything in these pages— the tensest and quietest in the book—is dedicated to emphasizing Ugo's extreme desire to "communicate" his last message to mankind.

"In Italy," Petroni recently wrote in the essay "The Fate of the Novel," "the most burning things, once uttered, come back to their speakers much like an echo resounding in a vacuum." Amidst so much realistic or purely documentary fiction of postwar Italy it is refreshing to find a writer who is concerned with spiritual and intellectual questions that arise from, and are part of, our present climate, and who points out that these problems must be resolved by each individual through his personal experience, sensibility, and beliefs. They can never be resolved by ideologies.

Petroni has written a very short story, entitled *"Il ricevimento"* ("The Party"), where at least one of the themes of his fiction is strongly declared. The story tells of a social-literary reception in a Roman bourgeois house and the various comments made by people there. The protagonist, a writer named Gianziro, returns home and goes to

his study. He carefully puts away the many things that
have always been part of the personality of his room.
Then he begins to feel a violent headache, and he asks himself: " 'What am I looking for? What on earth are we looking for?' He felt a sharp pain enter his head, but in his
mind he was constructing happiness, since he knew that
soon his thoughts would be more painful than his headache
and this, too, could have some sense, if one could at last
understand whether something, among us, *has* a meaning."
Petroni's fiction is, in a large sense, an attempt to achieve
a clearer understanding of suffering: intellect has failed by
itself, and love alone (as Natalina dramatized) is insuffi-
cient to overcome it. There is something noble about
Petroni, however, because unlike many of his contemporaries, he has refused to concede that "isolation" (understood in the special sense of dedication to meditation) is
necessarily an evil that must be avoided. Writing about
such a condition among creative artists, he has stated:

> I believe that the isolation of these few [writers] is the
> only expression of participation. The moral disinterest with
> which they accept all the disadvantages of a still longer
> solitude . . . will, in time, be the clearest indication of
> how the writer must understand the meaning of freedom
> of expression, individual freedom and of the disinterested
> participation in all problems, in expressive research, with-
> out which he may be many things, but never a "poet."

The nucleus of Italian writers who have achieved substantial literary maturity of late includes a large number
of women. Their increasing popularity with the public and
the critics represents a significant cultural phenomenon
that may well herald a new era.

It is not surprising that relatively few women should
attain intellectual distinction in a country where the social
order is shaped exclusively by men. The tradition of a
feminine literature in Italy is, therefore, a relatively recent
one: it began with the unification of the nation and with
the first steps toward social emancipation. There is evidence that even then the woman had achieved greater
cultural refinement than was ordinarily suspected; witness
the impressive number of women authors who wrote with
perception not only about feminine problems but about
human nature and social problems. Neera, Matilde Serao,

Grazia Deledda—novelists of different range and talent, to be sure—won immediate esteem as competent and serious artists. Croce himself, usually unsympathetic to modern letters, proved to be lenient to the point of being uncritical when he assessed women writers: his excessive sympathy for such a minor figure as Annie Vivanti is one of the factors that make his survey of *La letteratura della nuova Italia* somewhat puzzling.

Italian women writers, despite their occasional popularity, have never wielded the literary influence of their English or French counterparts. There is no Italian equivalent of Mlle de Lespinasse, George Sand, Colette, Gertrude Stein, and Simone de Beauvoir. With few exceptions, no woman author in Italy has been deemed worthy of receiving the sort of critical comment to which the works of Jane Austen, Dorothy Richardson, or Emily Dickinson have been subjected. Frequently this is due less to an objective question of artistic merit than to critical negligence or a pronounced prejudice against feminine talent.

The situation has changed considerably over the past years, and women authors are at last receiving a share of critical attention proportionate to their literary merit—as is only right. The imposing body of fiction produced by women writers with considerable cultural refinement and exquisite sensibility has vindicated their right to be admitted into the circles of adult and serious novelists. In a way, the war itself has given further impetus to this trend. While the men were away, busy slaughtering each other in a long conflict, the women were left free to devote their time to cultivating their intellect and to brooding about their situation.

Out of the experience of sensibilities repressed for centuries, for a variety of reasons, several powerful tales authored by women have emerged during the last two or three decades. The majority of such works, as might be expected, deal primarily with feminine problems. Their major theme is often the stark reality confronting the woman who as a rule (at least in Latin countries) is the victim of man's whims, forced to lead an existence with little freedom, few choices, and even less hope for the future. Several novelists have insisted on presenting characters who lead lives robbed of emotional, intellectual, and even physical, satisfaction. Infidelity—and at times, even violence—seems to provide the sole means of escape from an otherwise meaningless, boring existence. Whenever novels describing the gray, monotonous life led by the average woman are successful, they are far more than mere documentary evidence of woman's perennial subjugation to the desires, passions, and follies of men. They are indictments of the failure to permit other human beings to realize themselves as people. The novels written by women often become haunting appeals for a genuine understanding of the difficult role often imposed upon the woman against her will—a role she must play with skill and diplomacy in modern life.

Today the names of Anna Banti, Anna Maria Ortese, Gianna Manzini, Alba de Céspedes, Livia de Stefani, Elsa Morante, Milena Milani, and Natalia Ginzburg have become quite familiar to Italian readers and frequently to the international reading audience as well. Their works have achieved a distinct resonance: through them we have been made far more sensitive to the drama and "situation" of the woman in Italy and elsewhere. It would be grossly unfair to identify these women novelists, through a study of their themes and style or their common interests, with any particular tendency in Italian fiction, just as it is unjustifiable to lump them together merely because they happen to be women. Each of the novelists mentioned has a definite artistic personality and a unique vision of the world that make a general treatment impossible. My favorite among them is Natalia Ginzburg.

Few good writers in contemporary Italy have been as unprolific as Signora Ginzburg. To this date she has authored three *novellas, La strada che va in città* (*The Road to the City*) in 1942, *E' stato così* (*The Dry Heart*) in 1947, and *Le voci della sera* (The Voices of the Evening) in 1961; a long novel, *Tutti i nostri ieri* (*A Light for Fools*) in 1953; and a volume of three long short stories, entitled *Valentino*, in 1957. Her talent has already received official recognition primarily by way of three distinguished literary prizes, the Veillon International, the Viareggio, and the Chianciano, awarded to her in 1954, 1957, and 1961 respectively.

Signora Ginzburg was born in Palermo in 1916 and began her literary career by writing some short pieces for the Florentine magazine *Solaria*. Viewed in its entirety, her fiction shows an interesting stylistic development as well as a progression toward the more sustained genre of fiction, the novel. As for her stories, there is little in the way of events to interest the reader; moreover, they are frequently quite similar to each other in that there is little or no concentration on the construction of an involved and carefully resolved plot. Similarly, her heroes and heroines appear as though they were brothers and sisters afflicted by similar ills and marred by common emotional and intellectual flaws. It is not unusual for her protagonists to be engaged in fighting what the reader suspects to be a hopeless battle. The world they live in is surely a strange one: although the action acknowledges the existence of an external world, little or no attention is paid to it. For this reason, Ginzburg's heroes give the impression of living in a glass bowl unhappy with their condition and yet doomed to it. But, unlike the fish in a bowl, they lead an unharmonious life, never showing a capacity to come to grips with what they are, perhaps because they feel too intensely the fact that they are dismal failures as people. It is not unfair to apply to them a lucid observation made by Ginzburg in a commemorative vignette to her friend the late Cesare Pavese: their error lies in their not wanting "to demean themselves to love the ordinary course of existence that flows with an even rhythm and apparently without secrets."

Her themes are the solitude and anguish of life as well as the impossibility of communicating our despair to other humans. The situations depicted in her fiction are quite stark. Life is not only a wretched thing but a meaningless business. Her characters live in a self-enclosed world only dimly related to the world of people and things. Emotionally and intellectually they are not strong enough to understand the world and to adjust to the demands made by society. As a result, their lives come to a sudden, violent end, usually brought about by suicide or homicide. In a world where they are unable to solve, on a psychological or philosophical level, the basic problems of life, death is considered a more satisfactory alternative to an incongruous "drifting."

On the basis of what has been said thus far, Signora Ginzburg's heroes would seem to have something in common with the existential protagonists of Camus and Sartre. Like them, her characters sense the fundamental absurdity of life, although they never rationalize or intellectualize their posture; similarly, they show through their actions the impracticability of commitment to anything material or, much less, spiritual. Unlike Camus' heroes, however, Ginzburg's do not find in human solidarity a sufficiently positive factor capable of redeeming them from isolation. They never pose to themselves the question of man's purpose and direction while on earth: for them the human struggle has ceased being an essentially economic one (as it was in the last century) and has become a metaphysical and a psychological one.

At the core of Natalia Ginzburg's fiction there is the story of a marriage that failed—a failure brought about by its having been conceived without a clear understanding of its meaning. It is significant that Ginzburg should be so intimately concerned with such a situation. The failure of marriage is reflective of other equally serious failures at all levels, which are eventually responsible for a more thorough personal estrangement—to the point that the reader is led to devastating conclusions about the state of our "civilized society."

Relatively little happens in her novels: Signora Ginzburg relies for her effects less on a story rich with incidents and surprises than on a subtle manner of relating a tale. We are usually presented with a limited cast of relatively static characters, through which the author projects her own personality and ideas. Whatever tension there is, is generated by the careful manner in which the author depicts the emotional or psychological state of her heroes and moves them slowly toward the climax. Her rare gift is to make us see and hear what she describes, thereby involving us in the human drama. The events are usually recounted by the narrator-protagonist, purposely a naïve, simple girl. Nothing ever stands between the reader and the characters; the perspective is never allowed to become blurred by fancy technical devices. Thoughts that another writer might be tempted to give indirectly are given here as simple confessions.

Her short fiction is conspicuously devoid of anything even remotely resembling a plot. Her stories are told from the point of view of the heroine, who, despite a deep yearning for happiness and companionship, fails to find understanding or spiritual or emotional fulfillment. In a sense, her first two *novellas*, which are published in the little volume *The Dry Heart*, are two different pictures of a single problem—the disillusionment life brings to human beings. In *La strada che va in città*, the sixteen-year-old Delia, dissatisfied with life, is attracted by the false glitter of the city and allows herself to be seduced by a law student named Giulio. The young man is ultimately forced to marry the girl to save his face and her reputation. During the ceremony, duly performed in church, Delia realizes what she had probably never considered: she understands absolutely nothing of what the priest is saying and is even more perplexed by what has brought her to marrying a man with whom, deep down, she is not in love. Such a predicament is shared by several of Signora Ginzburg's characters. They never truly comprehend how they have gotten themselves into their predicaments, although they have a clear awareness of how entangled humans can get with each other. Whether Delia is really in love with her cousin Nino, who dies toward the end of the story from a combination of drinking and frustration, is ultimately irrelevant. Since Delia is pregnant she knows that people expect her to do the "decent thing." Nino's death is in all likelihood a symbol of physical and spiritual erosion, as he has been presented as an intelligent young man with more than a hint of intellectual aspirations. His death serves to heighten the bitterness of the melancholy evaporation of an adolescent dream of happiness. The end of the tale finds the heroine resigned, bored, and no longer as free as she once was: she is, in fact, substantially worse off than when she was an untroubled, purposeless individual.

Not very different is the case of the unnamed heroine of *E' stato così*, a murder story with various implications which will be discussed later. At the very start of the story the reader is given the central incident of the tale: in a

moment of utter despair, the protagonist has murdered
her estranged husband, Alberto. She procedes to relate
the events that led up to this—an unhappy love story that
began with her belief that marriage might bring her the
companionship and affection she needed to continue living and ends instead with a complete, bleak refusal to
believe in life. The heroine is a former teacher who, after
meeting Alberto at the house of some friends, marries him
but is unable to make him love her. Alberto persists in
maintaining his ties with his former mistress, an older
woman who is herself married and has a child. Even the
child the heroine gives her husband cannot keep him away
from Giovanna, nor does she succeed in drawing the two
closer together. The situation is aggravated by Alberto's
frequent trips away from home, when he goes to stay with
his mistress; by his incapacity to give of himself; and by
his gradual withdrawal from life. Here, as in the previous
novelette, the background is purposely left vague: what
happens here could happen anywhere. Local color, so common in recent Italian fiction, is lacking: we are isolated
in time and space. Stylistically both stories are "realistic."
Yet, it is clear that the term overused of late *ad nauseam*
has lost most of its critical usefulness. Nevertheless, ambiguous as it is, it fits Ginzburg's case if one uses it to describe a definite frankness, bordering at times on crudeness,
a freedom with words that occasionally betrays a distinct
effort to be antirhetorical. The function of such a style is
to make us perceive the immediacy of things *as* they have
occurred and, by its confidential tone, bring us closer to
a fuller realization that people have become inextricably
involved with one another. Her style does not attempt to
depict a material, tangible reality—as does most recent
Italian fiction—but a more fascinating psychological and
emotional reality, about which Signora Ginzburg has written her finest pages. The focus of her attention is always
upon the way in which the interior life of her characters
is reflected externally, by way of acts, gestures, and words.
The interior analyses to which the novelist subjects her
heroes is but another way for her to give an impression of
the character. Lastly, the author and the narrator are one
and the same person: the tale is therefore told in the first
person, in an indirect, discursive manner.

Natalia Ginzburg's achievement is primarily a stylistic one. Her prose has a rhythm of its own and through it the author projects, with unusual simplicity, her conception of how people act, think, and behave. The texture of her style is replete with past descriptive indicative tenses; one sentence is joined with another by means of the conjunction "and." Through such deceptively simple techniques Ginzburg recaptures the rhythms of human discourse and elevates it from trifle to poetry. The elemental character of her prose makes her stories fully accessible to the reader who has only the barest acquaintance with the Italian language.

Signora Ginzburg has tried to give a fuller body to her manner of expression and vision. Her most recent published novel, *A Light for Fools*, is told in the third (and presumably more detached) person in a more complex language than that of her former novels. The book's subject is more ambitious in that it fictionalizes the time of fascism and of the last war. The focus is on the young generation and its illusions and delusions, the strength and weakness it demonstrated during a crucial era.

Fundamentally, the heroes of what is to date her most sustained work are strange and alienated from the rest of society, although they have become personally involved in the destiny of their generation. But here their unhappiness and estrangement is social and political, rather than psychological or metaphysical. Nevertheless, they too find it difficult to adjust to society: thus, some either kill themselves or actively seek death; others, undismayed by the fear, insecurity, and persecution prevailing in their country, choose to live. The range has been substantially broadened. *La strada che va in città* undoubtedly reads well as a pathetic account of how a simpleton of a girl is attracted by the false glitter of city life and falls victim to it; *E' stato così* has a real meaning not on its literal plane (it is a murder story) but as a striking depiction of what it means to be alone. *Tutti i nostri ieri*, on the other hand, represents the author's noblest attempt to bring together the various themes close to her sensibility: love and anguish, courage and fear, dedicated love and spiritual and emotional desiccation. Such themes have been treated in a single, long story that moves from the former personal, "limited" reality of a small group of individuals to a personal reality that symbolizes the complex curriculum of an entire generation. The action moves from Turin to a small village in the Abruzzi region, San Costanzo, so that the reader may witness what is in a final sense the end of one era and the beginning of another: old problems are disposed of, but they in turn generate new ones. Will the young people of today, born and brought up in an era of dictatorship, conformity, and moral degradation, be able to resolve the day-to-day problems of life? Has the war, the destruction it has brought to nations and human beings, the meaning people intended it to have, that of a final liberation from spiritual and physical enslavement? These are some of the questions the story poses. One senses, too, that over and beyond the personal rapports of one youngster with another there is mankind's dominating concern to find, at long last, a more harmonious and just way of life.

In the novel the figure of the intellectual receives special treatment: indeed, it seems to me that ultimately he is depicted as incapable of rising above the turmoil of his time and helping shape his nation's destiny. In *E' stato così* the two male characters, Alberto and his friend Augusto, are illustrations of the intellectual who has never succeeded in knowing himself and is, in this sense, a tragic figure. Ippolito, in *Tutti i nostri ieri,* may be considered an inevitable, but far more human reworking of the same figure, obsessed by the same preoccupations, unable to bear the burden of his shortcomings and the cruelty of his world.

Cenzo Rena (the real hero of this tale, supported in his role by his wife-to-be, Anna) articulates the profound need to go back to certain traditional notions about life to avoid getting lost in dramas that have not the slightest connection with the reality in which we all must live:

> Emanuele muttered that these were commonplaces. Commonplaces, cried Cenzo Rena, of course they were commonplaces, but why not repeat commonplaces if they were true? For fear and shame of commonplaces they had lost themselves in vain and complicated fancies; they had lost themselves in fog and smoke. And gradually they had become like a couple of old children, a couple of very old,

wise children. They had created around themselves, as children do, a complete dream world—but it was a dream without joy and hope, the arid dream of a pedant. And they did not look at women, they never looked at women; they passed numbers of women on their country walks and did not look at them, lost as they were in their pedantic dream world.

The failure of not only some of the characters of *A Light for Fools*, but of Augusto and Alberto (*The Dry Heart*) and Giovanni (*The Road to the City*) could not have been more explicitly pointed out than it is here. It is an intentional ironical twist that Cenzo Rena, presented throughout the tale as the one person who, while capable of identifying himself with the *contadini* and through them with mankind, is a wholly passive man, is the character who utters words that synthesize the central problem of their story. It is the same Cenzo Rena who, having shown through his utterances how man may regain touch with reality in its completeness, sacrifices his own life so that others may live. In giving up his life for his friend Giuseppe, who has accidentally killed a German soldier, Cenzo rises above the practicalities of everyday life to a plane of self-sacrifice and noble idealism. His act represents not merely a superb deed but the finest answer Cenzo can offer to counteract the arid dreams of the intellectuals. It is the war, terrible and devastating as it always is, that makes his friend realize that the spirit of man endures even in war and enslavement. Emanuele, who has been writing for anti-Fascist sheets, says:

> Producing secret newspapers was easy, oh, how easy and splendid it was. But newspapers that had to come out every day with the rising of the sun, without any danger or fear, that was another story. You had to sit and grind away at a desk, without either danger or fear, and out came a lot of ignoble words; you knew perfectly well that they were ignoble and you hated yourself like hell for having written them, but you didn't cross them out because there was a hurry to get out the newspaper for which the people were waiting. But it was incredible how fear and danger produced not ignoble words but true ones, words that were torn from your very heart.

Through Cenzo Rena we see the essential predicament of the modern intellectual and the most serious personal flaw of Ginzburg's strange heroes. Because he understands himself, and his frailty, he can live his life to the fullest extent of his possibilities.

Natalia Ginzburg's tales, simple documents of human flaws and human capabilities, stand out for what they say and for how they say it. Signora Ginzburg has managed to give us a few worthwhile books about ourselves by creating a cast of unforgettably strange characters, longing for a compassion and love that remain unattainable. An accomplished writer gifted with a remarkable style, a perceptive novelist capable of distilling so much of our own anguish in simple and unusually poetic stories, she deserves to be read. Her future work is certain to warrant far more sympathy and attention than it has received in the past. If one is to judge from what she has already written, one can only conclude that the future has much in store for us.

Of the small group of writers chosen to illustrate some of the tendencies and problems of contemporary fiction in Italy, Italo Calvino is not only the youngest member but the most productive and versatile. Despite his relative youth (he was born in 1923 in Santiago de las Vegas, near Havana, Cuba), he has already authored four *novellas*, an intriguing two-volume collection of fables (which he has elegantly editorialized from documents), and an imposing collection of short stories, published first in separate books and then in the omnibus volume *I racconti*, which won for him the coveted Bagutta Prize in 1959.

His first published *novella*, *Il sentiero dei nidi del ragno* (*The Path to the Nest of Spiders*), was at first appraised by the critics as another sample—less crude and more literary, to be sure—of neorealistic fiction. The assumption seemed to be justified particularly by the fact that it is a story of the exploits of the Italian partisans during the last war. His ties with Cesare Pavese and Elio Vittorini, the two writers under whose tutelage he took his first steps in the world of letters, further buttressed the suspicion of neorealism. The books Calvino has written since 1947 have clearly demonstrated not only his double interest in reality and a fantastic world of fairies and knights but his increasing concentration on the latter at the expense of the former. His is a peculiar manner indeed that has led him to conquer the novel form, believed perhaps mistakenly to have been rejuvenated by realistic depictions of recent historical events. For Calvino, as a matter of fact, looks forward to the time when other literary forms—the essay, the travel book, the imaginary story, the philosophical and satirical tale, the "dialogue," and the *operetta morale* (a genre practiced with considerable success by the poet Giacomo Leopardi during the early 1800's)—"may occupy once again the place of protagonists of literature, of the historical intelligence and of social battle."

In a long, polemical essay, *"Il midollo del leone"* (The Lion's Marrow), Calvino has articulated his poetics with conviction: "We believe" he has stated, "that political engagement, partisanship, self-involvement is, more than a duty, the natural necessity of the writer of today and, even before the writer, of modern man. Ours is not an era we can understand by remaining *au dessus de la melée.* On the contrary, we understand it all the more when we live it, when we situate ourselves even close to the front line." His words, however, must be taken with much caution. Few writers have successfully demonstrated how a writer can be *engagé* and yet not subservient to political ideologies. (It may be worth noting at this point that Calvino withdrew from the Communist Party in 1957 after several years of militant activity in it.) Indeed, in a later passage of the same essay, he wrote:

> The novels we would like to write or read are novels of action, but not because of a residue of a vitalistic or energetic cult: what interests us above all are the trials man undergoes and the way in which he overcomes them. The mold of the most ancient fables: the child abandoned in the woods or the knight who must survive encounters with beasts and enchantments, remains the irreplaceable scheme of all human stories, the pattern of the exemplary novels where a moral personality is realized by moving amidst a cruel nature and a cruel society.

Faithful to his poetics (formulated only in 1955), even his first work, *The Path to the Nest of Spiders*, is not a realistic *novella*, although it has real people, real situations, and real actions. The merit of the tale is not in any photographic depiction of the life and the coups of the band of partisans but in the wonderful whimsicality and vivaciousness with which the protagonist, Pin (a mere boy), is treated; it lies also in the lightness of the author's touch, especially in the descriptions of nature, the same nature that becomes in Calvino's later books a veritable treasurehouse of inspiration. Significantly, Calvino almost invariably chooses a youth as his main hero. Only a youngster possesses a real sense of enchantment with nature, a sense of tranquillity and perennial discovery of the mysteries of life. Typical of such confrontation is the short story *"Un giardino incantato"* (*"An Enchanted Garden"*), so characteristic of Calvino's deftness and elegance. In the tale, two youngsters, Giovannino and Serenella, find themselves by chance in a marvelous garden:

> There were big, old, flesh-coloured eucalyptus trees and winding gravel paths. . . .
> Everything was so beautiful: narrow turnings and high, curling eucalyptus leaves and patches of sky. There was always the worrying thought that it was not their garden, and that they might be chased away at any moment. But not a sound could be heard. A flight of chattering sparrows rose from a clump of arbutus at a turn in the path. Then all was silent again. Perhaps it was an abandoned garden?

The story proceeds with the same rhythm. Nothing much happens, and indeed little need happen. The youngsters play, swim, have some tea and sponge cake (thoughtfully put on a table by the servant of the household), and then leave. It is a delicate, poetic story, which exemplifies how little action or plot Calvino needs to render his tale interesting.

Calvino's vein is not always as light as this. In the short story *"Dollari e vecchie mondane"* (*"Dollars and the Demi-Mondaine"*) he concocts a vision reminiscent of a modern ballet or a surrealistic painting. Another, rather long tale, *"La formica argentina"* (*"The Argentine Ant"*), has some of the spine-chilling power and suspense of Dino Buzzati and Franz Kafka (but without the latter's metaphysical implications). It is about a family, a husband and wife and their child, who move to a house, despite having been warned that the place is riddled with ants. Soon thousands upon thousands of ants invade their home, and no remedy, however intelligent, can stop them from coming. There is no solution to their plight. The tale ends as the couple takes a stroll to a nearby beach where there are no ants and where they can once again enjoy themselves. There is probably an allegorical meaning to the story: the ants may well represent the insidious, devastating elements of modern life that rob man of his privacy and tranquillity. Perhaps it is because he is driven by a desire to express his disgust with certain social phenomena that Calvino has composed short stories like *"La speculazione edilizia"* ("The Speculation of the Building Constructors"). This long tale is in the realistic vein of *Il sentiero dei nidi di ragno,* but without its humor and vivacity. It tells of a constructor named Caisotti, a *nouveau riche* of Italian postwar society, who entices his friend Quinto, an impoverished intellectual, to become his partner in a real-estate venture that should prove to be quite profitable. Quinto feels deeply committed to his "speculation." A former Communist (and as such he may well, as some critics have noted, reflect the uneasiness experienced by Calvino himself after his own repudiation of communism), he does not feel the need to live among comrades. Rather, he is tremendously attracted to the business people, to the smart entrepreneurs with "their guns always aimed," and he identifies himself with "all that was new, in contrast, with all that caused violence." "He felt himself taken by something that resembled a scientific interest: 'We are witnessing an important sociological phenomenon, my dear. . . .'" The tension of the *novella* is strategically built up by the slow progress made by the construction company, by Caisotti's deliberate procrastinations, and by Quinto's approval of the new rising class, an antibourgeois society, corrupt, amoral, and equivocal. The climax is reached when, after numerous *coups de scène,* Quinto discovers, in the chaos of the situation, that Caisotti has once been a partisan. Some ten years before "two partisans, a peasant and a student, had rebelled together with the idea that Italy should be entirely remade; and now look at what they have become: two men who accept the world as it is, who shoot for dough, without even the virtue of the middle class of yesteryear, two bunglers of the building industry who have become (and not by sheer chance) partners. . . ." There is considerable criticism of the degeneration of society in postwar Italy, and it is fictionalized skillfully and intelligently. Calvino may be a realistic writer here (in more than one way), but he succeeds in making his points without polemics or cries for social reform.

The richer side of Calvino, nevertheless, is to be found in his fantastic tales, of which he is one of the few practitioners in contemporary Italy. He has written three works —recently collected in a large volume entitled *I nostri antenati* (Our Forefathers)—which may be read as a trilogy or enjoyed individually: *Il visconte dimezzato* (The Viscount Cut in Half); *Il barone rampante* (*The Baron in the Trees*); and, quite recently, *Il cavaliere insistente* (The Knight Who Did Not Exist). Of these three supernatural tales, the best is probably the second one.

The story is most unusual. It is about a twelve-year-old boy, Cosimo Piovasco, who on the fifteenth of June 1767, having been severely scolded by his father for refusing to eat a dish of snail soup (to be followed by more snails as a main course) prepared by his sister Battista, decides to climb a tree and live there. What ordinarily would have been regarded as a child's prank turns out to be a tenacious and diverting plan to live in the trees, cut off (if only in a special way) from the rest of the world. Not that Cosimo refuses to have anything to do with the world: quite the contrary. He goes on living (taking his usual shower, building an extensive library in his hut, and even attending Mass with his family) without ever descending from the giant holm oak—and is considerably helped by the fact that, since the forest in his garden is very thick, he can travel from tree to tree without renouncing his vow not to descend to earth. That Cosimo is "up there" means very little as far as his own activities are concerned. He grows up, studies, loves, and even fights from the trees, successfully demonstrating that the kind of fantastic life we no longer believe feasible *is* possible and contains the adventurous flavor our own, "real" life too frequently lacks. For his life is a rich one, replete with encounters not only with ordinary people (and even a noblewoman, Viola), but with soldiers (both French and Austrian and finally even Russian) and leaders—Napoleon among them! But Cosimo, being after all human grows old: "Youth soon passes on earth," Calvino wryly remarks, "so imagine it in the trees, where it is the fate of everything to fall: leaves, fruit." At the age of sixty-five, his end is near. Suddenly, some English aeronauts who were experimenting with balloon flights unroll their anchor to try to' grip some support. "When the anchor rope passed near him [Cosimo], gave one of those leaps he so often used to do in his youth, gripped the rope, with his feet on the anchor and his body in a hunch, and so we saw him fly away, taken by the wind, scarcely braking the course of the balloon, and vanishing out to sea. . . ." The inscription on the tomb erected in his honor reads simply: "Cosimo Piovasco di Rondò—Lived in trees—Always loved earth—Went into sky."

This brief account of the story is sufficient to give the reader an idea of the richness of Calvino's imagination. The novelist has no doubt been influenced by his family's professional interest in botany and by his own interest in science and folk tales. His work recalls the Grimm brothers and Swift, or, especially to the Italian reader, Boccaccio, and, above all, Ariosto. It is with the great poet from Ferrara that Calvino has closely identified himself and has confessed an admiration that goes well beyond that felt by every youngster and adult for the *Orlando Furioso*. In a lecture given at Yale, he said:

> Of all the poets of our tradition, the one I feel nearest to me and at the same time most abstrusely fascinating, is Ludovico Ariosto, and I never tire of rereading him. This poet, so absolutely limpid and cheerful and problemless, and yet, at bottom, so mysterious, so skillful in concealing himself; this unbeliever of the sixteenth century who drew from Renaissance culture a sense of reality without illusions and . . . persists in creating a fable.

Calvino, much like Ariosto, abstracts from our historical time certain verities that he weaves into fantastic stories about knights and their adventures. Like Ariosto, Calvino sits in his laboratory (his study in Turin) and dreams of a world created by the novelist's fantasy. Unlike Ariosto, however, Calvino holds that his fables are not, *in fondo*, flights from reality, but come from the bitter reality of our twentieth century. They are the means—perhaps the only means left to a writer tired of a photographic obsession with modern life—to re-create a world where people can still be people—that is, where people can still dream and yet understand; flee from the world (as the young Cosimo does) and yet never sever relations with it; where man's aspirations are fulfilled through his intellect rather than through his physical power. However, there is a passage in which Calvino mocks the pure use of reason. When Cosimo's brother (who is the narrator of the tale) goes to France, he visits Voltaire, the great French sage.

> The old philosopher was in his armchair, surrounded by a court of ladies, gay as crickets and prickly as a porcupine. When he heard I came from Ombrosa he addressed me thus: "Is it near you, *mon cher Chevalier,* that there is that famous philosopher who lives in the trees *comme un singe?*"
>
> And I, flattered, could not prevent myself replying: "He's my brother, *Monsieur, le Baron de Rondeau.*"
>
> . . . "But is it to be nearer to the sky that your brother stays up there?"
>
> "My brother considers," answered I, "that anyone who wants to see the earth properly must keep himself at a necessary distance from it." And Voltaire seemed to appreciate this reply.
>
> "Once it was only Nature which produced living phenomena," he concluded. "Now it is Reason." And the old sage plunged back into the chatter of his theistic adorers.

Through the fable, told in an ironic, amusing style, Calvino manages well to recapture much of the silliness and the seriousness of life. But one wonders where his fiction leads. Calvino himself seems to have become aware of this issue, for in the closing pages of *Il cavaliere inesistente* he formulates it explicitly: "Lately I have started writing furiously. From one line to the next I jumped from nation to nation and from sea to sea and from continent to continent. What is the fury that has overtaken me? One would say that I am waiting for something." He may indeed. And the future work, now in progress, should best answer the question.

# CHAPTER FIVE

# *Poetry*

Why does modern Italian poetry continue to be little read and all but ignored by the international public, studied only by the informed specialists? This question, puzzling as it may seem in light of the favorable reception accorded to recent Italian fiction and films, should not evoke surprise. In discussing the numerous problems in translating a literary work, Edward Sapir, in his book *Language,* states: "All the effects [of the literary artist] have been calculated, or intuitively felt, with reference to the 'formal' genius of his own language; they cannot be carried over [into another tongue] without serious loss or modification." This comment pertinently illuminates the situation, since the problem of communication is of course always a central one in literature. Gone are the days when Italian was a language spoken by many and understood by all cultured men; gone too are the days when the nation, thanks to the brilliant life at the courts of the Medicis, the Estensi, and other illustrious families, was a cosmopolitan center of culture at the forefront of artistic creativity and even criticism. When Italy was invaded by foreigners, and subsequently divided into several states, its literary importance began suffering a steady decline that was to continue through the following two centuries. It is not as if no artist of stature emerged in those years. Although few in numbers, the writers of the post-Renaissance period are among the greatest of all times. Recent studies and translations (especially in England) of the work of Manzoni, Foscolo, and Leopardi, among others, provide sure indications of their worth—recognized at last after a period of unjust neglect. With the loss of political unity, the country began experiencing an isolation that was to have serious repercussions in its literature. Cut off from the mainstream of European literature, many writers (except those who, by luck or circumstances, were able to maintain contact with foreign artists) resigned themselves to working strictly within their native tradition, seldom taking notice of what was occurring in other countries. Although this situation was partially modified toward the end of the nineteenth century, when Italy at last achieved political unification, it was only with the end of the Second World War that the cultural isolation (aggravated by a political provincialism for which the dictatorship of Mussolini was wholly responsible) finally came to an end.

It was inevitable that the poets, immersed in and vitally conscious of their times, should be affected by their "situation." They longed for freedom, but their dream of a united country was frustrated time and again. As Renato Poggioli acutely observed, "the shock of the new world of European reality, made of power politics and historical necessity, turned Italy back to the other world of her ideal dreams. Incapable of rejecting forever the ancient vision of a fatherland, she found escape from the nightmare of history in a patriotic myth of her own."

A study of the themes and forms of poetry from its beginning to the latter part of the nineteenth century would in itself be conducive to a wider understanding of the problems peculiar to Italian literature. Traditionally, for instance, the main motifs of Italian poetry have been love (for a woman or for the country) and religion. Nearly every poet has worked to a considerable extent within this tradition. The early poets, those usually grouped together in the school of the *Dolce stil novo* (Sweet New Style), made of the object of their love something resembling an angel, a *donna angelicata,* as she was aptly called. Dante himself, in the closing lines of his youthful autobiographical book, *La vita nuova* (*The New Life*), promised to praise his beloved Beatrice "by saying of her what had never been said about any woman"—a promise he more than handsomely kept by writing the immortal *Divine Comedy.* Francesco Petrarch, who belongs to the generation after Dante, wrote out of his love for Laura several hundred poems. He then proceeded to order them in a carefully calculated manner, establishing in his *Rerum Vulgarium Fragmenta* (Fragments of Vulgar Trifles, thenceforth known as the *Canzoniere,* or Song Book) a dramatic conflict between love of the spirit and love of the flesh.

With Petrarch we get a first inkling of the difficulties Italian poetry was to face in the following centuries. In one of his *Epistolae seniles* (xiv, 4) the author confesses the fascination he has always had for words and how enchanted he is by their sounds. Petrarch's extreme alertness to the sonority of an unusually musical language was transmitted to other poets. A genuine artist and a craftsman of the highest order, Petrarch was able to master his language and exploit both its subtle and less lofty expressiveness. His poems cover a wide spectrum of emotions, making use of a diction that penetrated the innermost secrets of his heart and intellect. Other poets, however, either misread Petrarch's intention or misunderstood his technique: for them language became something to be adulated because, if properly mastered (at least in a technical sense), it could lead to an artistic perfection that, being only formal, was really meaningless. The history of Italian letters tells us substantially more about this story and its rich cast of characters, its long record of achievements and failures. It is sufficient to stress here that after Petrarch poetry was no longer the same. Few poets escaped his influence or were not indebted to him, in one way or another. Both Dante and Petrarch became models as well as specimens of a literary perfection that, however often imitated, was never matched. As one literary historian remarked, "until modern times neither the changes in cultural substance nor the individual experiences of talented poets were able to emancipate the poetical consciousness from the mastery of Petrarch."

Contemporary poetry begins in Italy with a different awareness of, and a different emphasis upon, the aural value of poetry, and with a more intensive attention upon its content. Perhaps because of this change of attitude, the writer of modern times, while acknowledging the greatness of Petrarch, recognizes his true *maestro* in Giacomo Leopardi (1798-1837). Leopardi, the poet from Recanati, a hunchback, timid, extremely sensitive, and a learned philologist and scholar (by the time he was sixteen he had mastered several modern and classical languages so well that he composed a work in Greek that stunned the critics, who thought it to be a newly discovered work of antiquity), was a man who was doomed to be supremely unhappy throughout his life. He never experienced the affection of his family, which was tyrannical and unsympathetic to his yearnings, nor did he ever know the love of a woman. Although he wrote several patriotic poems, he was one of the first artists of his time to transform poetry from a form that describes a patriotic or autobiographical occasion (although his poetry *was* his life) into a vehicle that expresses the eternal condition of man. While he himself entertained the firm belief that life was nothing if not boredom and pain, he kept writing about it with a secret sense of exaltation and hope. An atheist, he recaptured the humanity of people better than some of his devout confreres. His lyrical imagination rises often to the contemplation of the vicissitudes, but also of the perennial beauties, of life, the mysterious beauty of the infinite:

> *Così, tra questa*
> *Immensità s'annega il pensier mio:*
> *E il naufragar m'è dolce in questo mare.*
> (*"L'infinito"*)

> So, among this
> Immensity my thought is drowned:
> And sweet is to me to be a shipwreck in this sea.
> (*"The Infinite"*)

Stylistically, his achievement is no less impressive. He moved from a traditional twelve-syllable verse to blank verse (*verso libero*); he used a vocabulary which, after the first attempts, consistently eschewed high-sounding words, preferring instead indefinite, suggestive, archaic ones, which he thought to be more poetic because of their allusiveness. His compositions, collected in a single volume entitled *I Canti* (*The Songs*), are among the precious gems of poetic creation of all times. Written in what is often an unbelievably simple style, often committed to memory by school children, they are appreciated only with maturity: they grow larger with age, so meaningful and relevant are they to all life.

The unification of Italy, and the secularization of culture in a country of strong religious tradition, posed more problems than it solved, especially as poetry began losing an equilibrium it had only by extraordinary luck succeeded in maintaining. There were poets who, to be sure, continued writing, apparently undisturbed by the "new" times, among them Giosuè Carducci (1835-1907), Giovanni Pascoli (1855-1912), and Gabriele d'Annunzio (1863-1938). Their work, massive and widely read in Italy and even abroad, is still quite impressive from the point of view of traditional inspiration handled in orthodox and nontraditional metrical schemes, rejuvenated at times by Greek schemes. This poetry did, of course, speak to those who, having cherished the idea of unity, were busy trying to make it a living reality; just as it appealed to those who held that poetry must express content and structure. But, although every poet who wrote after them liberally helped himself from the vast storehouse of words, images, and even themes of the great "triad," there came the time when serious readers and poets realized that after the experience of French Symbolism their sensibility must be trained to respond and recapture the subtler, more complex "life" of a poet. Poetry became, then, a means to reach a purity denied to other genres, a purity no longer concerned with physical reality but with its essence. The new poetry found its themes not in history or religion or even love, but in the vast layers of the human subconscious and in the inner spirit of man projected into reality. "In other words," as Oreste Macrí wrote, "twentieth-century poetry begins with a new speculation of things. . . . By objectifying himself and his own historical inertia, by accepting alienation, enjoying the bitter flavor to the very end of the curse of living, man placed himself in the condition of putting an end to the fall."

But here is where the history of the revolution in poetic taste, its ensuing poetics and visions of poetry, follows in Italy a path parallel (even if not chronologically) to that of England and America. And this is the critical juncture where culture realizes that it can be national but not nationalistic. Ezra Pound left his native United States and settled in Italy; T. S. Eliot left the United States and became an English subject; Ernest Hemingway and the expatriates lived in Paris, where Soffici, Ungaretti, Rea, Papini, and others spent much of their time. But now we are in our century, and with the First World War (or better still, with the year 1907) a new era begins.

The years preceding World War I represent, from the political point of view, a period of adjustment to the new role Italy was ready to play after having achieved national unification. Yet Italian life and politics were far from tranquil; indeed, restlessness and uncertainty ("anxiety" is a later term) were the dominating moods of those years. On the cultural scene, for example, a growing dissatisfaction with the dogmatic positivism inherited from the nineteenth century led to its gradual rejection in favor of new philosophical positions heavily impregnated with, when not completely shaped by, idealism, of which the main theorist and self-appointed custodian was the Neapolitan philosopher Benedetto Croce. In literature particularly, a kind of revolt against the nineteenth century and romanticism was slowly emerging. The clearest evidence of an antagonism that was to become progressively more polemical and even bitter (as in Papini's work) could be found in the opposition to the poetic triad—Carducci, Pascoli, D'Annunzio—who had dominated Italian poetry, establishing themselves if not purposely certainly willingly as "literary dictators."

One of the most dynamic contributions to the development of a modern culture was that of the many literary magazines that sprang up in Florence and Rome between 1902 and 1919. Around these reviews, often hastily organized by fertile and imaginative but undisciplined minds, there gathered young intellectuals who felt that the time had arrived to bring their country into a more meaningful rapport with European culture. The most important of these "little magazines" was published in Florence and called La Voce.*

The intellectual activities of the reviews were balanced with the activities of several artists both before and after the inception of the Roman little magazine La Ronda (1919-23). These writers, without any special allegiance

* The extraordinary story of the Italian "little magazines" is discussed in Chapter Nine.

to literary schools, strove to test anew the potentialities of the written word and to discover its hitherto unknown dimensions. Their efforts to rebuild a literary language that for centuries had resisted the ever-changing demands continuously made upon any medium of self-expression led to disparate results. One of the first groups to test the validity of using common themes and words, long excluded from a poetry traditionally austere in form and aristocratic in content, was one dubbed by the critic Giuseppe A. Borgese the *Crepuscolari* poets (the poets of the Twilight school).

The group was a small one; its life span was by all standards comparatively brief—1903-14—and its products, although often distinguished by a gentle touch of irony and nostalgia, were on the whole quite tenuous. The label of *Crepuscolari* was a felicitous one. But with time the term itself changed its original meaning: Borgese had used it to describe those poets writing at the sunset of a glorious era; later on it was employed to describe not so much their chronology, but their content. *Crepuscolare* became then a poet whose compositions focused on the grayness of life, on its loneliness (devoid, however, of the controlled anguish and the alienation of the later hermetics), on its provinciality, and its boredom—the latter without the power and universality of Leopardi. For their inspiration the *Crepuscolari* turned to a past infinitely mellower than the present, and sang—in a language never brilliant but rather "monotonous," colorless, humble—of the Sunday promenades, the uneventfulness of life, the sameness of their existence, their adolescent loves.

Three of the five poets usually associated with the group in its initial stage died when still quite young: Fausto Maria Martini (1886-1931), Sergio Corazzini (1887-1907), and Guido Gozzano (1883-1916); the other two, Marino Moretti (b. 1885) and Aldo Palazzeschi (b. 1885), were soon to turn their talent in other directions, and became prominent and prolific fiction writers.

The literary antecedents of the *Crepuscolari* are not hard to find: Verlaine, Maeterlinck, Jammes, Laforgue, Rodenbach, Samain, and Pascoli were the poets who by their example established a climate conducive to the technique employed by the *Crepuscolari*. The life they viewed was observed through a small window, through slightly foggy lenses that caused the vision to be softened and even sentimentalized. Hospital corridors, gentle beggars, vignettes of home life, rainy afternoons, the sun—but never in its full radiance or intolerable heat—were the themes with which the poets became associated. Both Moretti, by calling one of his collections of poems *Poesie scritte col lapis* (Poems Written with a Pencil), and Corazzini, by asking,

> Perchè tu mi dici: poeta?
> Io non sono un poeta.
> Io non sono che un piccolo fanciullo che piange.

> Why do you call me a poet?
> I am not a poet.
> I am just a small child who is in tears, crying.

managed to define and synthesize the dominant mood and level of their poetry, understood as an artistic experience easily erased from the reader's memory.

The most talented member of the lot was probably Guido Gozzano, whose tenderness and humor infuse many of his poems, such as *"L'amica di nonna Speranza," "Paolo e Virginia,"* and *"La Signora Felicita."* The last poem is particularly effective since, quite aside from its intrinsic merit, it reveals Gozzano's style—a style that was narrative rather than poetic. Thus his lyrics abound with descriptions of objects, persons, milieux; and frequently, the poet makes a definite effort to create live dialogues through which the characters' temperaments are exposed, much as in fiction. Unlike the other *Crepuscolari* who make habitual use of a colloquial, everyday language, Gozzano alternates and intermingles a literary style with a spoken one.

If Marino Moretti had, by his title *Poesie scritte col lapis*, placed an accent on a poetry that had neither the hope nor the ambition to resist the test of time, Gozzano, with the single line *"le buone cose di pessimo gusto"* ("the good things of horrible taste"), came closest to defining the nature of the poetry of the Twilight school. Yet, for all the negative criticism of the *Crepuscolari*, it can hardly be denied that the contribution they brought to poetry was not a slight one. In exposing the inflated musicality and sensuality of D'Annunzio, the magniloquence of Carducci, and the post-Romantic sentimentality of Pascoli, the Crepuscular poets found a way to reduce poetic language to its lowest possible denominator: not word-as-music, not word-as-symbol, but word as an instrument to communicate, even at the risk of being prosaic, the simplest kind of life and feelings.

If it was not clear then, it became increasingly more certain that contemporary Italian literature (poetry as well as fiction) was long to feel the subtle, persistent influence of this trend (it could not be called a school, since it had no banner, no leader, no manifesto). However, by the end of the first decade *Crepuscolarismo* had lost its momentum and was definitely on the decline, no longer attracting new sympathizers or even critical attention. (It was to receive the latter in the twenties and mid-thirties, with the appearance of Montale.) It was just at that moment, February 20, 1909, to be precise, that Futurism made its noisy debut on the cultural scene through the Futurist Manifesto, published in the Parisian newspaper *Le Figaro*. Written in French and conceived mainly by Filippo Tommaso Marinetti (the official spokesman and high priest of this movement), the manifesto announced a program that in its violence and exuberance surpassed anything that had ever before, or has since, been written in Italy. Because it damned the past and all those institutions committed to the preservation of a cultural heritage, because it declared boldly that a break with the past and with all existing traditions was necessary before anything worthwhile could be produced, Futurism became for a limited time the rallying point for the rebel artist. The important writers and artists who joined its ranks, however, did so more to register their utter disappointment with the past and express their hope for a different, and possibly more vigorous and challenging, future, than because the cultural program Futurism offered or the kind of life it promulgated had truly caught their imagination. By the same token, however, the contribution of Futurism to an open discussion of certain literary questions ought not be slighted. Even before the publication of his manifesto, Marinetti started a "Referendum on Blank Verse" in the review *Poesia*, in which many of the well-known Italian and French poets and critics (Pascoli, D'Annunzio, Jammes,

and Verhaeren) took an active part. The outgrowth of that
symposium was a rich, curious volume—The Poetic Reason and the Program of the Blank Verse—written by a
man who soon became an ardent Futurist, Gian Pietro
Lucini. Later on, when the "Technical Program of Futurism" was published by Marinetti (on May 11, 1912), some
of its violent suggestions for a "new" literature were explicitly clarified: Marinetti openly predicated the destruction of syntax (placing the nouns at random, without
any effort to arrange them logically or rationally), the use
of the verb in the infinitive only, the abolishment of the
adjective and the adverb, as well as of punctuation, the
introduction into literature of three elements he felt to
have been unjustly neglected: noise, weight, and smell.

> Courage, audacity, rebellion, are to be the essentials of our
> poetry.
>  Literature hitherto has exalted pensive immobility, rap-
> ture and sleep: we shall exalt aggressive movement, hectic
> sleeplessness, the quickstep, the somersault, the slap, the
> blow.

These are the words most regularly quoted by commentators and historians of Italian literature. It is clear
today that in the last analysis Marinetti, for all his violence,
was dramatizing the issue of a literature freer from tradition, more consonant with the spirit and the exigencies
of modern man. Although Futurism produced far more
important painting than it did poetry, it did bring about a
reorientation of creative writing, permitting greater liberty
from rules than had hitherto been possible.

The multifarious activities that have been enumerated
did not produce a respectable corpus of genuine poetry;
nevertheless they were responsible for creating a climate in
which a "new" poetry—a poetry ready to recognize existing literary traditions without being subservient to them—
could be written. It was through the teachings of the little
magazines that many a young poet rediscovered certain
nineteenth-century masters, notably Ugo Foscolo and Giacomo Leopardi, and sought in their stylistic example and
in their poetics a solution, achieved by a process of ex-
clusion if necessary, to formal problems that had become
all the more urgent after D'Annunzio. The little maga-

zines, too, performed an especially valuable function not only in helping the new writers to mature intellectually, but in publishing them and thus bringing their work to the attention of the public much sooner than would otherwise have been possible.

The reader with a good knowledge of classical poetry who comes in contact with the poetic texts of the period previously described is apt to be struck by certain differences between *this* and previous poetry. Classical (viz., mythologic, patriotic, humanitarian) themes are consistently eschewed; the new poets work less with the traditional hendecasyllabic verse than with blank verse; interior, not exterior, rhyme is their goal. Structurally, their compositions are often simpler than those of many of their predecessors, but they are difficult to understand at first reading without an extensive background in modern European poetry. That the overwhelming part of these poets' work should revolve almost exclusively around personal incidents and feelings, hence becoming a sort of spiritual autobiography, will not surprise the reader well aware of a tradition that goes back in time to the *Stilnovisti*, Dante, and Petrarch. The traditional poets conceived of poetry as a way to achieve a sensitive elaboration and clarification of complex personal problems and were therefore less interested, in abstract moral problems and issues, unless they were treated indirectly. In this sense, as a commentator intelligently noted, "[they] realize in a personal manner the contents of a high moral experience which is identified with the goals of a poet's work." One of the most significant things about them is that they always write with an extremely alert critical awareness, bearing in mind what Valéry once wrote about Baudelaire: *"classique est l'écrivain qui porte un critique en soi-même et qui l'associe étroitement à ses travaux."*

In trying to identify some of the general characteristics that distinguish the new poetry from that of previous years, one must not forget that if the polemics around the "formal" literary problems form a colorful chapter in the history of contemporary Italian letters, as *causal* reasons for the rise of this poetry, they are somewhat marginal. It is because of a certain climate that a poet is often impelled to seek new ways to express a personal vision.

Indeed, it is this very climate that places the sensitive person on a different vantage point from which new, unexpected light is thrown upon his problems. Because the spiritual atmosphere prevailing today is largely an aggravation of that atmosphere existing at the turn of the century, it will not be necessary to consider its familiar characteristics at length. Suffice it to say that it was a spiritual opposition to the artificial and outdated modes of the past, the renewed awareness of man's feeling of inadequacy in respect to certain problems, his bewilderment before a reality that resists coherent and precise explanations, the rejection of positivistic and deterministic positions assumed in the second half of the nineteenth century, the loss of religious faith and the loss of belief in traditional myths that had long given the poet working material with which to mold his creation, that forced the artist, in whatever field he may have been working, to undertake a personal search for new ways to express an ever-changing reality and arrive at a personal vision of truth.

It is not unfair to say that the compositions of the major poets of our century as well as those of the greater part of their contemporaries (in Italy and elsewhere) are firmly rooted in a moral anxiety and a spiritual crisis that is traceable to the Renaissance and emerges in full force at the beginning of the twentieth century.

## UMBERTO SABA (1883-1957)
### Autobiography as Poetry

> *Esser uomo fra gli umani,*
> *io non so più dolce cosa.*
>
> To be a man amongst men,
> I know of no sweeter thing.

Umberto Saba, *"esperto di molti beni e molti mali,"* is a poet whose work staunchly defies any critical attempt to label or neatly classify it, in spite of the fact that he had much in common with the great and minor poets of his generation and with the lyrical tradition of his native country. His uniqueness consisted not in revolutionizing the genre by resorting to a new vocabulary or new metrical schemes, but, on the contrary, by making use of the most ordinary language and of those schemes provided by the examples of his predecessors, from Petrarch to Leopardi. For over half a century he sang, in a style that was never beyond the grasp of his audience, the joys and torments he had experienced in his long life. Although he called himself "egocentric," he nevertheless succeeded, especially in his later work, in divesting his lyrics of any and all autobiographical vestiges and in charging them with a meaning and a relevance without and beyond chronological limitations.

Self-educated, Saba was with Papini, Prezzolini, and several other mature contemporaries fortunate in reaching literary prominence during his lifetime. In 1933, shortly after he had published his collected poems, the Florentine review *Solaria* dedicated an entire issue to his work. But, unlike Ungaretti and Montale, he never had any intellectual pretensions, nor did he try to dazzle his audience by means of his creative gifts or critical intelligence. He was content to write poetry: *"Io seggo alla finestra e guardo, / guardo e ascolto, però che in questo è tutta / la mia gioia: guardare e ascoltare."* ("I sit at the window and I look outside, / since in this is all / my joy: in looking and listening.") His greatest pleasure was to observe and to listen; his most coveted ambition was to record by means of delicately simple images what he felt and what he saw, but above all what he loved.

Saba was born in Trieste of a Jewish mother and a father whom he was not to know until he was twenty and about whom he was to write: *"Mio padre è stato per me 'l'assassino,"* / *fino ai vent'anni che l'ho conosciuto. / Allora ho visto ch'egli era un bambino, / e che il dono ch'io ho da lui l'ho avuto."* ("My father has been for me 'the murderer,' / until I was twenty when I met him. / Then I perceived that he was but a child / and that the gift I have [viz., to write] I received from him.") In his native city and in his conscious acceptance of the Jewish faith (Saba tried to convert to Catholicism during his last months but was dryly turned down), one may perceive two vital facts of his humanity. First of all, living in

Trieste meant, as the poet never tired of explaining, to be at least thirty years behind the times; to choose to be a Jew inevitably meant to assume the burden of centuries of persecution and to accept by choice being on the side of the "insulted and the injured." As a boy Saba went through the agony of living in a hostile environment clearly unsympathetic to his yearning to breathe and understand the great classical writers of his literature. His lack of education (he never went beyond the fourth year of classical high school) and his family's lack of understanding had a strange effect upon the young Umberto, for he was brought to the point of despising those very things he had once cherished, and, for a while at least, he was even alienated from his teachers. As Saba once had the occasion to confess, he "burned in a bonfire of joy the texts of the classical writers which had become, for lack of love, too difficult, indeed almost impossible [for me] to understand." For a limited time he attended the local Commercial and Nautical Academy, hoping to become a "good honest, and reputable businessman." Immediately after the First World War, Saba became first the manager and then the owner of a bookshop called Libreria Antica e Moderna. His Libreria soon acquired a national reputation not only because of the interesting items it offered for sale, but also for the honesty of its wise and literate owner.

Saba's first poems were written between 1900 and 1910. The first slim volume was followed, at irregular intervals, by several others, until in 1921 the Libreria Antica e Moderna brought out Saba's collected works in a single volume bearing the title *Il Canzoniere* (reprinted in 1945, 1948, and again in 1961 to include all the poet's work written after 1921). His frequent borrowings from Petrarch, Tasso, Metastasio, Alfieri, and Leopardi, as well as his adoption of Petrarch's title for his own collected work, may be taken as evidence of a subconscious desire to be linked to a tradition and a culture from which various circumstances had cut him off, and toward which he had felt much indifference in his younger days.

When Saba began publishing his verse, the *Crepuscolari* first and the Futurists soon afterwards were managing to attract the attention of the critics and the readers. At the same time, sophisticated sensibilities were attracted by the French Symbolist poets, whose high priest, Stéphane Mallarmé, spoke of a poetry that must "suggest," not indicate, things. In the provincial salons of the capital city, as well as in the austere halls of the academies, people still talked (or shouted, when necessary) the names of Carducci, Pascoli, and of course that of the *enfant terrible*, Gabriele d'Annunzio.

It was therefore almost inevitable that in such literary climate Saba should at once be compared to, and linked with, the *Crepuscolari*, with whom initially—despite all his denials—he did have something in common. His first compositions stunned those critics who held that only a revolution of a technical nature could bring new vigor and beauty to poetic expression and give it hitherto unknown dimension. In an unassuming language, which soon became his trademark, Saba set out to describe his world, the world of the bourgeoisie. In his later years he remarked that "the *Canzoniere* is the story of a life relatively poor in external events, rich at times in torture, of feelings and internal echoes, and of people whom the poet loved during his long life and out of which he created his 'characters.'" One of the things that never fails to amaze the reader, and which perhaps is the spinal cord of the *Canzoniere*, is precisely how rich Saba's poetry is in people and objects and living beings, all endowed with a life of their own, seen and understood in their deepest meanings and interrelationships by a poet whose goal was to be "a man amongst men."

The themes of the hundreds of poems Saba wrote were not only the melancholy and the hardship he experienced, but the numerous people, his mother and father, his "sweet wet nurse," the country house, the stores, the hidden cafés, the inns and the streets of Trieste—which in the magic of his verse ceased to be a geographic entity and became a poetic city—and finally, the animals: from the goat of his early poetry to the mockingbirds of his later compositions.

As a craftsman he lacked the severity of such contemporaries as Ungaretti and Montale or the *engagement* of a Quasimodo. He was perhaps too frequently prone to be uncritical about his verse simply because it responded to a deep urge to give form to a particular moment of his life. But even in those moments when Saba does not reach the stylistic perfection of an artist, we know that without the weaknesses inherent in his poetry, the *Canzoniere* would not be what it is. When set side by side with Petrarch's lofty, and perhaps overlabored and therefore unspontaneous, perfection, the *Canzoniere*, with its ingenuity and occasional naïveté is the more human and moving document.

One of his early critics, the Triestine Scipio Slataper, once remarked acutely: "Saba belongs to a group [of poets] who, in order to be understood, need to create around the reader a particular atmosphere. . . ." Saba invites a close, intimate contact. Every time one reads his poems, one senses a kind of secret invitation to gather around the poet and allow him to recount in a sad, soft-spoken tone, the story of people he knew and the experiences he underwent. Every page of *Il Canzoniere* is filled with scenes that at once become quite familiar and which, together with the "protagonists," have long endeared Saba to his public. Woven out of the human threads of his life, Saba's poetry may be regarded almost as a long episodic novel, the effects of which derive not from the unfolding of a single story, but from the rapid succession of vignettes, sketches, impressions.

Structurally, the *Canzoniere* is divided into three major parts, each of which is subdivided into shorter sections. All such parts are chronologically arranged, and through their particular disposition in the context of the collection we can follow not only Saba's growth as a poet, his increasing ability to handle different metrical schemes, but his personal curriculum, the satisfaction, horror, and even hate he knew during his lifetime. Thus, from his youthful and adolescent poems, we move on to his life in the army (he served in the Twelfth Regiment in Salerno) and we go back to Trieste with him—the city that was to be, with brief exceptions, his established residence.

One of the difficulties presented by Saba's poetry has to do with the manner in which it should be read. An articulate body of critics holds that a cumulative, or "bloc," reading of the *Canzoniere* is the only relevant way to measure its freshness and its artistic achievement. There is considerable truth in this view, since an extensive reading of Saba's poems does enlarge considerably the vast canvas patiently painted over the time span of five decades, giving to it a tone definitely lacking when the poems are read individually. For here, too, is much of the beauty of the impressive array of Saba's poems: in the variety of tones, in the amazing alternation of moods, now pathetic, now happy, now humorous, now serious. Taken as a whole, however, his poems are quite instructive in that they succeed so well in presenting the image of a young man, alternately lonely and happy, embarked in a never-ending process of trying to break the solitude to which every artist is condemned and to establish human contact with the world by way of the written word. His falling in love with Lina, who is destined to become his faithful wife, marked the end of a trying period and the beginning of a richer one. Just as his love for his wife injected new warmth into his work, so did his rediscovery of his native city, which is ever present spiritually and even physically in the *Canzoniere,* and which became the symbol of a world in miniature. Significantly enough, he named this particular section *Trieste e una donna* (Trieste and a Woman).

A work of art derives a good share of its power from the tensions generated among its various parts and between itself and the reader. In Saba's Song Book, such tensions do exist and are lyrical—not, as in Montale's poetry, metaphysical. Such tensions do not impede a wonderful internal coherency from existing. Few poets have been as faithful as Saba to a manner of self-expression that can undergo few changes and yet always appear spontaneous. No other man of letters has been equally stubborn in rejecting fashionable poetics for the sake of appearing an avant-garde poet.

Aside from a personal style, every poet needs a symbol that stands for his strongest passions and embodies his subtlest feelings about life. Saba's poem *"La Capra"* (*"The Goat"*)—celebrated to the extent of being memorized by school children and unanimously chosen as one of his most representative lyrics—is a composition that for many signifies the perpetual suffering of man. Like animals, human beings are destined to suffer; like animals, they too need their share of lasting affection, often denied to them. Such conditions impelled the poet to make use of an idiom that, for all its modernity, has a distinct biblical flavor. Frequently, as the critic Giacinto Spagnoletti remarked, Saba's attitude reminds one of Saint Francis of Assisi, as exemplified in the often-quoted verse: *"La sua gattina è diventata magra. / Altro male non è il suo che d'amore: / male che alle tue cure la consacra."* ("His kitten has become thin. / Her ill is no other than one of love:, / an ill which consecrates it to your cares.")

He believed in simplicity, to be sure, but a strange kind of simplicity that was not to obfuscate the difficulty of its subject matter. *"Amati trite parole che non uno osava. / M'incantò la rima fiore amore, / la più antica difficile del mondo."* ("I loved trite words no one dared [to use]. / I was enchanted by the rhyme flower-love / the most ancient and difficult in the world.") *"Amai,"* "I Loved," in *Mediterranee.*) He loved but also endured much: during the war years, he was forced to flee from his native Trieste and take refuge with friends in Florence. In one of his longest and bitterest poems, "Avevo" ("I Once Had"), he tells of all the things that were so dear to his heart, and which fascism and the war took away from him. Five out of seven stanzas end with the identical lines, *"Tutto mi portò via il fascista abbietto / ed il tedesco lurco"* ("The base Fascist and the greedy German / took everything that was mine"), reinforced in the last line of the last stanza with the words, *"anche la tomba"* ("even the tomb"). But his pain and sorrow never prevented him from loving the world:

> *Per divertirti apro una scatoletta*
> *musicale. Il dolor del mondo n'esce*
> *in un suono così mite che riesce*
> *a commuovermi quasi.*

> To amuse you I open a small music
> box. The sorrow of the world comes out of it
> in a note so mild that it succeeds
> almost in moving me.

His verse, tender and unpretentious, remains the striking testimonial of a poet for whom life was poetry, and who made of poetry his life.

## GIUSEPPE UNGARETTI (1888-    )
### The Quest for Innocence

*La poésie seule peut récupérer l'homme.*
GIUSEPPE UNGARETTI

Giuseppe Ungaretti, born in Alexandria, Egypt, in 1888, has woven the greater part of his poetic work around his life, entitling his collected poetry *Vita d'un uomo* (*Life of a Man*). He was first introduced to readers by Giovanni Papini in 1917; since the twenties, when the critics began writing earnestly and seriously about his work, he has received more attention than any other living Italian poet. The fact that he lived in Paris for several years, his excellent mastery of the French language (some of his first poems were in French), and his having taken an active part in the well-known little magazine *Commerce* have endeared him to the French audience and literati who, on two separate occasions, have honored Ungaretti by translating his *opera omnia* into their own tongue—a rare honor for an Italian poet.

Like Saba, Ungaretti often works with a simple vocabulary and a deceptively simple metrical scheme. But there the similarity between the two poets ends. Unlike Saba, Ungaretti had the advantage of a sound academic training at the Sorbonne, studying under the renowned scholars Bédier, Lanson, Hauvette, and the philosopher Bergson. He also became an intimate friend of the brilliant critics, philosophers, and artists of Paris at the turn of the century, Picasso, Apollinaire, Salmon, Braque, Jacob, Sorel, Péguy, Valéry—"qui a été mon maître," as he recently confessed. Unlike Saba, he never experienced cultural isolation, never knew what it meant to be on the periphery of Italian letters. Through his friends Papini, Soffici, and Palazzeschi, who divided their time between Paris and Florence, and most of the painters and writers of his own country, Ungaretti has always remained in close touch with the creative writing of young and old alike. In his mature years, he continued an intimate association with the young minds by teaching modern Italian literature at the University of Rome.

Shortly before the outbreak of the First World War Ungaretti left Paris to return home, where he joined the interventionist groups. When Italy declared war against the Austro-Hungarian Empire, he enlisted in the army as an infantry soldier and spent several months in the front lines.

His first volume of poetry, which contained thirty-three extremely brief compositions, was entitled *Il porto sepolto* (*The Buried Port*). It made its debut in 1916, thanks to the assistance of Ettore Serra, an intimate friend, who printed a limited edition of eighty copies. It was reprinted in 1919 as part of a somewhat longer collection of verse entitled *L'allegria di naufragi* (*Gay Shipwrecks*), and then several years later, in 1931, with the simpler title *L'allegria*. It was accompanied by a short note in which the author stated: "This book is an old diary." To write a diary of his inner torments, of his sorrows and crises intimate and human at the same time, became one of Ungaretti's chief ambitions. He went on to remark that he "did not have any ambition, and I believe the great poets have none, other than to leave a very beautiful autobiography."

The period Ungaretti spent in France was for him one of great intellectual stimulation, for he plunged into the reading of those great poetic voices of nineteenth-century French literature, Mallarmé in particular, which had such profound influence upon his creative and critical sensibility. But it was the war, with its misery and tragedy, that was to become one of the central experiences of his entire life, matched only by the grievous loss of his brother and of his young son, Antonietto. Living in the trenches for days on end (those trenches became symbolized by the image of the "buried port" forgotten by civilization) created a dramatic state of loneliness in which the poet could live intensely with his own thoughts. The man, recording his fears and trepidations in a diary that bore at the foot of each page the time and place of composition (usually a battlefield), sought to find an illusion of a religious faith that might give him the inner strength and the courage to live. The artist, forced to live from day to day never knowing whether his life would come to an end, destroyed by a bullet or a bayonet, realized that the "concentration in the single instant knew no bounds. The instant contained eternity." Because he experienced emotionally the fact that immediacy must be projected into eternity to assume its fullest significance, Ungaretti became increasingly aware of a problem of expression that he, like all other poets before and after him, would have to solve in his own unique way.

His first lyrics bear eloquent witness to his attempt to find a "new" language capable of expressing the anguish of modern man; in them, language was carefully taken apart, to be "reconstructed" in a patiently subtle manner. As Ungaretti's English translator, Allen Mandelbaum, has perceptively stated, "Ungaretti purged the language of all that was but ornament, of all that was too approximate for the precise tension of his line. Through force of tone and sentiment, and a syntax stripped to its essential sinews, he compelled words to their primal power." How the poet achieved all this is still a miracle that dazzles even his most severe critics. He was able to find a language that was poetical without being rhetorical, and he then proceeded to isolate its component parts; he controlled the flow of rhythm of his poems not by traditional means (punctuation, caesuras, etc.), but by a special typographical arrangement by which each word achieved its original "virginity." The Futurists had also attempted to give new meaning to the written word by mixing it with unusual symbols and numbers, by abolishing punctuation, by introducing bold, revolutionary typographical technique that succeeded, if anything, in shocking the reader and making him aware of the different meanings made possible by the association of words with numbers and printed symbols. But the Futurists, however cultured or gifted, seldom had either the critical control or the poetic fire necessary to literature: they were mere rebels, not artists. Ungaretti, on the other hand, slowly elevated every single word he employed to a poetic purity by placing it in a single line, and hence stressing all the more its individual worth. The constant revisions to which he has subjected his work amply demonstrate the superb craftsmanship and critical intelligence of the poet. To read the various editions of his poems is to see his lyrics transformed, solidified, often relieved of possible sentimental nuances or of the realistic touches of the first phase. Some critics, notably Giuseppe de Robertis and Leone Piccioni, have made extensive studies of the variants seeking to demonstrate (not always convincingly, however) that Ungaretti's poetry improves with each successive recasting, reaching in its later stages a perfection frequently denied to the earlier ones.

The poems collected in the volume *L'allegria* make clear that Ungaretti's achievement is primarily a stylistic one. Even without his being able to free himself from particular influences of his own tradition and of certain French poets, Ungaretti restored to the word much of its allusion and power of suggestion. Without falling into oratory, he gave poetry an unknown "essentiality." A reading of the first edition of *L'allegria* can be quite instructive: the poems are uniformly brief (in the successive editions they have not only been thoroughly revised, but reorganized and structurally regrouped), and one single image or thought or feeling is, as a rule, their sole focus. The compositions of *L'allegria* are less poems, in the conventional sense, than rapid illuminations, flashes of intuition, poetic perfection achieved suddenly and briefly. The most celebrated (and controversial) example is the poem *"Mattina"* (*"Morning"*), made up of four words separated into two lines:

> *M'illumino*
> *d'immenso.*
>> (*"Mattina," L'allegria,* 1914-19)

> I illuminate myself
> with immensity.
>> (*"Morning," The Joy,* 1914-19)

Unsustained as these two lines may seem, they illustrate, first of all, the particular period Ungaretti was undergoing (one should point out here that the poem was written on January 26, 1917, at Santa Maria La Longa) and his particular attempt to "put into contact all that is most distant. The greater the distance, the better is the poetry. When such contacts generate light, poetry has been achieved. Briefly, I use, perhaps I abuse, elliptical forms." Silence, long pauses, and insistence, all the more impressive when one is privileged to see the manuscripts of the poet, and the numerous corrections that testify to the continuous reworking of the original poem to the poet's satisfaction. *"Mattina"* represents the lyrical expression of a contact between Ungaretti the poet and the immense universe, an experience that, as has often been remarked, renders the poet exuberant and exhilarant.

*"Mattina"* is also typical of Ungaretti's first phase, in which the reader was given a number of isolated signals that he was supposed to link together with his own sensibility before arriving at a total, coherent poetic image— a process that required constant co-operation between the artist and the reader and to a greater extent than in the traditional poetry of the romantic period. Ungaretti's initial method made for considerable difficulty, and much scorn was heaped upon his first work by those who, accustomed to the pomposity of Carducci and the verbal fireworks of D'Annunzio, were naturally suspicious of any artist experimenting with language and revolutionizing metrics.

In a poem dedicated to his friend Ettore Serra (his first publisher) Ungaretti wrote:

> *Quando trovo*
> *in questo mio silenzio*
> *una parola*
> *scavata è nella mia vita*
> *come un abisso.*

> When I find
> in this silence of mine
> a word
> it is dug out of my life
> like an abyss.

His particular poetics, his personal attitude toward poetry, encouraged certain critics to hold that to be understood Ungaretti's poetry (dubbed *poesia-baleno*, flash-of-lightning poetry) should be read in a certain manner, not aloud, however, since "its tonal poverty and the lack of warmth" forbade it, but silently—as a prayer, almost, or a suggestion. The critic De Robertis went on to compare this situation with that of a musical score that must be played in order to become realized and yet paradoxically can become unintelligible when played.

*Il sentimento del tempo* (*The Feeling of Time*) appeared in 1933. Its poems, especially those in the final part of the book, show the poet's conscious efforts to reconquer the full measure of the hendesyllabic verse, the classical verse form of Italian poetry, and witnessed the introduction of a careful punctuation. More objective than the early *Allegria*, it also is far more difficult and obscure. It was this volume that germinated a long and important polemic in the field of literary criticism, and caused Francesco Flora to write biting essays later collected in a volume entitled *La poesia ermetica.* "Hermetic," meaning literally "sealed," "mysterious," "cryptic,"—an adjective still useful in literary criticism—assumed at a later stage the derogatory connotation of a poetry which, because it was enclosed in a world of its own and stubbornly obscure, was inaccessible to anyone without a "key" to unlock its meaning. Historical perspective has done much to correct that view, and *Ermetismo* has lost its formal meaning of "school," and describes instead a special kind of poetry written by a small nucleus of artists. Hermeticism, indeed, became a particular way to combat the rhetoric and propaganda of fascism, a manner of preserving the dignity and honesty and integrity to which every artist clings; as Alessandro Pellegrini carefully pointed out, it was "founded on an effort to isolate a poetic tradition from the influences of politics and vulgarity, and keep it safe from any corrupting contrast."

*Il sentimento del tempo* paved the way for the collection written between 1937 and 1947 entitled *Il dolore* (*Sorrow*). Ungaretti, soon after the publication of *Il sentimento*, had left for South America to attend a cultural convention. Subsequently, on the invitation of the Brazilian government, he accepted a chair of Italian literature at the University of São Paulo, where he was to remain until 1943. It was in South America that he lost his son Antonietto and it was there that he composed a good section of *Il dolore*. While in the earlier volume Ungaretti had attempted to find a meeting point between traditional Italian meters and contemporary expressive necessities, he wrote *Il dolore* primarily to give vent to the anguish experienced during those years. From a purely stylistic point of view the poems of this volume are indeed marginal; and yet they are, from the human side, the most touching of Ungaretti's poetic production. Divided into several parts, each made up of one or more poems, the lyrics of *Il dolore* dwell on a pain that is not merely autobiographical. It springs from the death of the poet's son and brother, from the Nazi occupation of Rome, from the mass deportations he witnessed, from the gloomy, desperate atmosphere of those years—perhaps the most tragic of modern times. The poet's desolation reaches different intensity at various points in the book, but it always remains calm, controlled, severely resigned, and, thus more virile. "*Roma occupata*" ("Rome Occupied"), for example, is one of Ungaretti's most pessimistic pieces, less lyrical than others and yet written in a language vibrant with questions, moving because of the fear and trepidation experienced by the poet. The losses suffered by Ungaretti are sung in a subdued tone: lonely, but strong in his acceptance of man's fate, the poet finds in his work the only possible salvation from the oblivion to which man is ultimately condemned.

Of Ungaretti's recent published work, perhaps none is as important as the dramatic poem *La terra promessa* (*The Promised Land*). The work was begun in 1935 and was originally inspired by a visit to the poet's native Egypt and to places dear to his imagination, and reminiscent of many myths.

It appeared for the first time in the little magazine *Alfabeto* in 1948 (with the simple title "*Frammenti*"), then in 1949 in *La Rassegna d'Italia* ("*Trionfo della Fama*"), and, substantially revised in *Inventario*; once more corrected, and with numerous additions, it was published in 1954 as part of the poet's collected works. The poem, however, is still to be considered a "work in progress," with the poet occasionally adding (as he did in the special issue of *Letteratura*, Nos. 35-6, which was dedicated to him) additional fragments, another part of that impressive mosaic which, when completed, could well turn out to be one of the milestones of contemporary Italian poetry. The poet himself has written about this work. Some of his comments are well worth quoting at length:

Perennial beauty (bound inexorably to death, to images, to earthly vicissitudes, to history, and thus but *illusively* perennial, as Palinurus will stress) assumed in my mind the aspect of Aeneas. Aeneas is beauty, youth, ingeniousness ever in search of a promised land, where he makes his own beauty smile and enchant in the fleeting and contemplated beauty. But it is not the myth of Narcissus: it is the animating union of the life of memory, of fantasy and of speculation, of the life of the mind; and it is, too, the fecund union of the carnal life in the long succession of generations.

Dido came to represent the experience of one who, in late autumn, is about to pass beyond it; the hour in which living is also about to become barren; the hour of one from whom the horrible, tremendous, final tremor of youth is about to depart. Dido is the experience of nature set against moral experience (Palinurus).

*La terra promessa*, in any case was—and still is—to begin at the point at which Aeneas, having touched the promised land, the figurations of his former experience awaken to attest to him, in memory, how his present experience and all that may follow will end, until, the ages consuming, it is given men to know the true promised land.

From a long and elaborate period of creativity, a new fruit has blossomed that is richer and more rewarding than anything written before it, since it synthesizes and injects new power into a work that is truly sustained. The lyrical tone of *L'allegria*, the objectivity of *Il sentimento del tempo*, the autobiography of the *Poesie sparse* ("Scattered Poems")—all converge upon the experience of *La terra promessa*. But in the last work, Ungaretti's intention to "elevate his biographical experience to [the level of] ideas and myths" seems to have come much closer to realization than in any of his previous works. Notable in the dramatic poem is the increased importance attributed to memory—understood not as the elegiac, nostalgic means to recapture past events, nor as a tool to evade the past and avoid the present anguish, but as a process of recreating in our minds the *élan* that gives either a person or an event a life of its own, as though either one were really living *now*. The reality of the past has become the reality of the present, capable of surviving time only because the poet has transfigured it into words.

Recitatives, choruses, and *canzoni,* terms customarily employed when speaking of music, are most appropriately chosen by Ungaretti to head the pieces he has thus far finished. Of these, the *"Recitatif of Palinurus"* is the most successful. The story of Palinurus (*Aeneid,* V, 833-71; and VI, 337-81) is well known. During a storm at sea, Palinurus, at the helm of Aeneas's ship, is thrown into the sea by Sleep. Faithful to the end, the young man (who is innocent), when he sees his master again confesses that while desperately trying to fight off Sleep he had clutched the helm of the ship and had looked fixedly at the stars. When he was finally thrown into the sea, he feared not for his own life but for that of his ship, left without a pilot. In *La terra promessa* Ungaretti has continued his work, begun more than four decades before, in making the word the very thing that transmits not so much images but sensations, feelings, something that may explain why his work is so conspicuously devoid of the images one usually find in poetry. His ultimate purpose is to transmute the single instant into symbol or myth, with cosmic applications. A good share of the poem is one continuous song, an extremely melodic, lyrical composition that succeeds in making alive the poet's deep states of spirit. In a brilliant essay on his own poetic works, Ungaretti has reminded his readers how, during a period when everyone was clamoring for the prose poem (those were the years of the First World War and the time of *La Ronda*), he felt, deep within, that the memory was "an anchor of salvation." Faced by the central problem of his creative activity, the re-creation of a language that changed along with his poetic experiences, he has always been aware that language "is a Babel today . . . it will be for the artist a source of great pain to resign himself to work exclusively *by* himself." But Ungaretti's long poetic itinerary points to the fact that his conquest is not a mere linguistic one. He has constantly moved from one stage to the next, from a poetry of innocence to one of memory to a supreme co-penetration of the two with a mythical poetry. In *The Promised Land* Palinurus declares himself to have remained faithful, not only to life but to a remembrance of life made eternal by the memory. No longer close to life, or to the events of life, he is able to re-create and hold in a state of perennial "presence" his life and his feelings.

No one in our times has felt as Ungaretti has the gravity of the poet's task and has so fervently and brilliantly
dedicated himself to making his readers conscious of the
beauty of the written word. But he has also created, with
a style probably unmatched to contemporary Italy for its
sheer melody, a vast landscape of dreams, of feelings, and,
in spite of its pain and sorrow, peace. His is, indeed, the
promised land toward which we may all aspire, here and
now, to retrieve that part of us only poetry can recapture.

## EUGENIO MONTALE (1896-    )
### The Quest for Meaning

Eugenio Montale, born in the seaport of Genoa in 1896,
acute literary critic, journalist of wide interests, and translator of English and Spanish poetry, is an intellectual whose
complex style demands an unusual concentration from his
readers. While Montale shares the position of poetic leadership with the older Ungaretti and the younger Quasimodo, he is considered by many of his contemporaries
both the spokesman of the generation born at the turn of
the century and its sternest conscience. His poetry has reflected, especially in its initial phase, the anxiety of our
century, the contemporary faithlessness and hopelessness.
Paradoxically, his poetry is also distinguished by an indomitable confidence in the individual and in his ability
to meet his fate.

Montale's biography is perhaps one of the least "interesting" of contemporary writers. He attended school in his
native city and, at the outbreak of the First World War,
received a commission in the Infantry. He served with the
troops fighting on Mount Corno and the Lòner. Unlike
Ungaretti, however, he never felt the impact of the war
to the extent of writing about it—even if some of his compositions have some striking images of the war. His intellectual curriculum is, once again, quite simple. With
Sergio Solmi and Giacomo Debenedetti, he founded a
little magazine (*Primo Tempo*), which ceased publication

less than a year after his inception (1923). From 1927
until 1938 he was the head librarian in Florence (at the
Scientific-Literary Library Vieusseux), a post he relin-
quished for political reasons. In 1948 he joined the staff
of the Milanese newspaper *Il corriere della sera*, as editor
in chief of the third, "literary," page.

Montale's vision may strike the reader as stifling and
oppressive. Historical circumstances are to a degree responsible for the gloominess of his work. The poet belongs,
after all, to a generation that witnessed the breakdown of
recognized values, experiencing more than its share of
disillusionments and chaos. Three major revolutions, two
world wars and a series of lesser armed conflicts, the temporary triumphs of a score of dictatorships, the horrors
of the concentration camps and the gas furnaces extermi-
nating millions of innocent victims—such is the balance
sheet of a society that prides itself on being quite "civilized." Amidst so much destruction and hate, in an era
when man, to survive, is constantly forced to make countless concessions and compromises, it is comforting to
realize that there are still a few writers (Montale among
them) who are able to preserve their artistic and human
integrity. Montale was never lured into joining the Fascist
party at a time when it was *de rigueur* to do so. He paid
the penalty for his nonconformity and liberalism by being
fired from his position in 1938. Likewise, he has never
injected political ideas into his poetic work, however fashionable this may be. There is in his poetry a unity of
thought, inspiration, and, above all, of style that is certain
to commend him to the most demanding readers. In this
sense, too, it is not surprising that several years after the
proclaimed death of hermeticism, Montale should still be
writing in a hermetic vein. For him hermeticism has never
been anything but a label, useful perhaps only to critics
who wish to categorize poetry. The success achieved by
his volumes, all of which have gone through numerous
reprintings, testifies eloquently that Montale, for all his
difficulty, has a real and faithful audience.

By all accepted standards, Montale's literary output is
almost disconcertingly small: barely four short volumes,
*Ossi di seppia* (Cuttle-Fish Bones), first published in 1925;
*Le occasioni* (Occasions), 1939; *Finisterre*, published in

Switzerland in 1943; and *La Bufera e altro* (The Storm and Other Things), published in 1956 and incorporating the poems of the previous volume, out of print and generally unavailable. The unimpressive quantitative output of Montale—a total of about one hundred and fifty short poems—cannot but underscore most dramatically the miraculous poetic achievement of a writer whose verse has yet to reach the international audience.

The high quality of Montale's poetry has made him the focus of much attention and subtle exegesis, some of them from the finest contemporary Italian critics: Gianfranco Contini, Alfredo Gargiulo, Francesco Flora. The pessimistic character of his work has compelled several intelligent readers to speak of the poet as a man without ideals, a singer of life in a wholly negative sense—a view certainly supported by a first reading of his poetry. "Having felt, from the day of my birth," Montale recently stated, "a total disharmony with surrounding reality, the matter of my inspiration could hardly be anything else if not *that* disharmony. . . . Fascism and the war gave to my sense of isolation the alibi which it needed perhaps." It might be best for the reader to approach Montale without expecting any explanation of the incongruity of life, or even without any hope that he may be helped to master what the late Cesare Pavese once aptly called *"il mestiere di vivere"* (the business of living). As Montale writes,

> *Spesso il male di vivere ho incontrato:*
> *era il rivo straziato che gorgoglia,*
> *era l'accartt occiarsi della foglia*
> *riarsa, era il cavallo stramazzato.*
> (*Ossi di seppia*)

> Often I have met the evil of living:
> it was the strangled stream that gurgles,
> it was the shriveling of the dry leaf,
> it was the horse fallen, battered.
> (Cuttle-Fish Bones)

Images such as these cannot but remind us of the debt Montale owes to his tradition. For a long time several of the younger critics have been concerned with tracking down the influence of Pascoli, Gozzano, Camillo Sbarbaro, and even D'Annunzio on the early poetry of Montale. It is undeniable that many of the metaphors and images (particularly in *Ossi di seppia*) are "derived" from the tradition, for the poet is extremely conscious of the literary texts of his and of the previous century. But if these are "borrowings" they are so only in a limited sense. For Montale has transformed them, almost always bringing them to an unusually striking and unforgettable perfection. The poetry of Pascoli and of the *Crepuscolari* has carefully filtered through a highly critical mind that has reworked it for his own purposes. There is a power in Montale that is totally lacking in the compositions of his *maestri;* there is a masterful synthesis of the human condition that is truly unique.

From his very first, unforgettable lyrics, his attentive readers have always been made aware of a sensibility so unusual that it captures the conflict of man and his environment, the dramatic struggle to survive and understand the suffering of life. Throughout such an experience (and here is at least one side of Montale's intricate poetic personality), the poet looks on without any emotional participation that can be easily individualized. He is a silent witness, whose feelings are clear but toned down, whose vision is rendered in an intellectual manner, dry and without rhetoric. In one of his early poems Montale defined, once and for all, the relationship between himself and his reader:

> *Non chiederci la parola che squadri da ogni lato*
> *l'animo nostro informe, e a lettere di fuoco*
> *lo dichiari . . .*
> *Non domandarci la formula che mondo possa aprirti,*
> *sì qualche sorta sillaba e secca come un ramo.*
> *Codesto solo oggi possiamo dirti,*
> *ciò che non siamo, ciò che non vogliamo.*
> > (*Ossi di seppia*)

> Do not ask us for the word hewing from all sides
> our formless soul, and with letters of fire
> declare it . . .
> Do not ask us for the formula apt to open up the
> > world to you,
> but only for some crooked syllable, dry like a withered
> > branch.
> Only this can we say to you today,
> what we are *not,* what we want *not.*
> > (Cuttle-Fish Bones)

Such is his poetry, and the reader will do well to accept it with its limitations. Elsewhere, Montale has written that his "poetry was born spontaneously in the woods . . . it was born out of the desire, a need, to be expressed in *certain words*, with words that would suggest, that is, a certain physical and moral world. It was then a meeting of sensuality (of a verbal kind) and asceticism. Music and ideas, or better still co-penetration rather than addition." His poetry makes abundantly clear what this world is. It is a brutal place, merciless even, where the poet seeks in vain to find the fundamental reasons for death and suffering. Truth is what Montale seeks, truth which is always ungraspable, elusive. He is committed to giving us a disquieting picture of a society that has reached a critical juncture in history—one of its greatest torments is its inability to awaken from a metaphysical nightmare. It is a life that promises nothing beyond what mankind has always endured. But if such is the human fate, Montale does not relent from his passionate quest. He seeks everywhere *"il male che tarla il mondo"* ("the evil that eats away the world"), *"la piccola sortura d'una leva che arresta / l'ordegno universale"* ("the slight twist in a lever that brings to a stop / the mechanism of the universe"). Both verses, taken from the volume *Ossi di seppia*, spell out the position of the poet with respect to the world. The hero of all his poetry is, however indirectly, Montale himself, at odds with life because he cannot penetrate its mystery but only its desolating reality:

> *talora ci si aspetta*
> *di scoprire uno sbaglio di Natura*
> *il punto morto del mondo, l'anello che non tiene,*
> *il filo da sbrogliare che finalmente ci metta*
> *nel mezzo d'una verità.*
>
> ("I limoni," Ossi di seppia)

> sometimes one awaits
> to discover an error of Nature
> the dead point of the world, the link that does not hold,
> the thread to disentangle, that may at last place us
> in the middle of a truth.
>
> ("The Lemons," Cuttle-Fish Bones)

Struck by divine indifference and by the nothingness of life, Montale sees in nature an appropriate symbol of man's condition. True, nature does resist time and man does not—yet both are exposed, so to speak, to gradual erosion and are ultimately condemned to be the victims of a constant, never-ending process of consumption, decay, and eventual disintegration. It is in this personal vision of the world that Montale drastically differs from his contemporaries, whose sensibility is closer to the French Romantics and Symbolists, while his is more akin to that of the English poet T. S. Eliot, whose poems Montale introduced to the Italian audience in 1929, in his own brilliant translations and whose "objective correlative" has found in the Genoese a successful practitioner. Back in the twenties, in fact, Montale described an obscure poet as one "who works with his own problem as though it were an object, accumulating in it instincts, meaning, and *soprasensi;* conciliating in it the irreconcilable to the point of making of it the staunchest, most unique, most difficult correlative of his own expression." His own tendency, after his early poetry, has been, to use his own words once more, "toward the object, toward an art clothed with, incarnated in, the expressive medium, toward a passion that has *become* a thing." Like Eliot, he made of the reality surrounding him, and in particular of the rugged Ligurian region, living poetic symbols of a vision devastatingly devoid of sentimentality and emotionalism.

It is in the descriptions of his native Liguria that Montale particularly excels: his compositions are re-creations of a real geographical place made universal because it contains those elements that, for the poet, stand for life itself: static, fluid, dynamic, cruel, inconquerable, and yet—it is important to remember—never hopeless. His compositions abound with extremely effective descriptions, not infrequently replete with highly technical or scientific terms. Probably no artist more than Montale has made poetic such a large part of our geographical and living universe: rocks, flora, animals, birds, the strangest and rarest elements of nature have been recaptured by the attentive eye of the poet. Montale's poetry is very much one of *things,* of emotions *made* things, never seen and described for the aesthetic joy they may yield, but as valid symbols of our condition. There may be, to be sure, other reasons for what has been termed the "emblematic objectivization." One of his recent critics has pointed out that "the essential difference between Montale and his contemporaries is that they are at peace with reality . . . while Montale has no certitude of reality." Things and nature offer the poet rich opportunities to reveal the sterility, the vacuum, the terrible and uncontrollable flux of life. His insistence on a strident vocabulary has earned him the title of "rocky," "scabrous," "arid": the very adjectives he himself uses adroitly in his own verse.

> *Avrei voluto sentirmi scabro ed essenziale*
> *siccome i ciottoli che tu volvi,*
> *mangiati dalla saledine;*
> *scheggia fuori del tempo, testimone*
> *di una volontà fredda che non passa.*
> > (*"Mediterraneo," Ossi di seppia*)

I should have liked to feel myself rough and fundamental
like the pebbles you are turning over,
eaten by salt tides;
a splinter out of time, an evidence
of a cold firm will that abides.

> ("Mediterranean," Cuttle-Fish Bones)

Montale's poetry is, to a large extent, written in that constant tension between a present reality and metaphysics that stops short on this side of despair. Firmly rooted in the harsher part of the day, it evokes the sense of stifling, the unbearable heat, the profound aridity of Montale's geography. "To rest at Noon, Pallid and Absorbed" (*"Meriggiare pallido e assorto"*) forces us to another confrontation with a stillness that is of a most dramatic kind: *"Meriggiare pallido e assorto / presso un rovente muro d'orto"* (To rest at noon, pallid and absorbed, / next to a scorching garden wall"): from there, the opening lines of a striking poem, Montale continues through a series of images that are strictly visual. He tells of how he hears the cackling of blackbirds, the stirring of snakes; of how he watches the files of red ants first scattering and then reuniting with each other; of how he sees through the foliage of a tree the throbbing of sea shells; to conclude, in a magnificent last stanza:

> *E andando nel sole che abbaglia*
> *sentire con triste meraviglia*

*com'è tutta la vita e il suo travaglio*
*in questo seguitare una muraglia*
*che ha in cima cocci aguzzi di bottiglia.*
(*Ossi di seppia*)

And walking in the dazzling sun
to feel with melancholy wonder
how all of life and all its labor spent
in this following a wall
with bits of broken bottles on its top.
(Cuttle-Fish Bones)

In more ways than one, Montale's poetry echoes the tradition, sometimes of even such a distant cousin as Leopardi, but especially of the author of the *Idilli* (Idyls). Like Leopardi, Montale has a pessimistic vision of life. But unlike the poet from Recanati, Montale, in his attempt to "deromanticize" his verse, makes use of a diction more consonant with his goal to depict the *contemporary* condition. In technique (as in the poem "*Meriggiare pallido e assorto*") the two are quite similar, moving from a series of images of surrounding reality to a final philosophic statement on life.

*Il mondo esiste . . . uno stupore arresta*
*il cuore dei vaganti incubi cede,*
*messageri del vespero: e non crede*
*che gli uomini affamati hanno una festa.*

The world exists . . . a stupor stops
the heart of the wandering nightmares yield,
messengers of the evening: and does not believe
that hungry men have a holiday.

Hope is not entirely denied to the poet, who finds the sea, with its power and magnitude, its foam and music, a source of salvation: "*Con le barche dell'alba / spiega la luce le sue grandi vele / e trova in cuore la speranza.*" ("With the morning boats / the light unfolds its large sails / and finds hope in the heart.") Esterina, the young girl threatened by her youth, finds in the sea "the force that tempers you / in the water you find and renew yourself." But the sea can also be destructive and, as he writes in "Eastbourne" (*Le occasioni*), the sea "rises to destroy the marks of horse hoofs damp in the sand of the shore line."

*Le occasioni* is a continuation, and a refinement, of the central experience of *Ossi di seppia*. But the book also has a meaning that transcends its artistic perfection, for it represents the distillation of the anxiety, the fear, the gloominess, of the decade immediately preceding the last war (the volume is a collection of the lyrics written between 1928 and 1939). To read the poems of *Le occasioni* is to read a record of those years, of so great a share of what people thought and felt: *"Cerco il segno / smarrito, il pegno ch'ebbi in grazia / da te. / E l'inferno è certo."* ("I seek / the lost sign / the pledge redemptive I received / from you. / And hell is certain.") Montale remarks, *"La vita che sembrava / vasta è più breve del tuo fazzoletto"* ("Life which seemed / so vast is a tinier thing than your handkerchief"). The world is tottering on the brink of the war. Destruction is approaching rapidly: the very survival of mankind is questioned.

> *Tu non ricordi la casa dei doganieri*
> *sul rialzo a strapiombo sulla scogliera*
> *("La Casa dei doganieri," Le occasioni)*

> You do not remember the customhouse
> on the edge of the steep cliff overlooking the reef
> ("The Customhouse," Occasions)

The poem from which I have quoted the memorable first lines is one of the finest compositions of Montale at his best. There is so much in it that to speak of it in detail would be critically frustrating, because its symbolism is very rich and its images concise. There is the wind, the sea, the "sound of a laughter no longer merry," as there are the famous lines *"la bussola va impazzita all'avventura / e il calcolo dei dadi più non torna"* ("the compass turns madly at random / and the reckoning of the dice no longer comes out"). There is the tragic passing of time —a most disturbing Montale theme—as there is, as Glauco Cambon stresses, "the strong intimation of loss of sense, loss of direction, madness itself." And there is also the tragic last line, "and I do not know who leaves and who stays." But what is really "new" about the collection *Le occasioni* is that it represents a distinct moving away from the epigraphic poetry of Montale's first phase toward a more articulate and sustained effort to synthesize the human condition in a fresher form. And as a result his poetry achieves new breadth, both structurally (his verse tends toward the hexameter and the hendesyllabic) and also from the point of view of content. There is also a new measure of courage: *"il domani velato che non fa orrore"* ("the veiled tomorrow that does not make us shudder").

The poetry of Eugenio Montale, its power and suggestiveness, is in the themes and in the confrontations I have briefly described. Man, for the poet, is a being aspiring naturally to a condition of unachievable harmony within and without. He longs to "know," yet he is fully aware that *the* reasons of existence will always escape him. Hence his resignation, which has nothing to do with the romantic and languid resignation of the earlier poets: his is virile, stronger, a product not of sentiment but of a rigid, rational knowledge that all man can do, in such circumstances, is to try in his humble and limited way to continue his long journey to understanding.

For himself and his contemporaries, Montale has created a striking world, reflective of the reality of our times without being "realistic." He has created a new diction, a new music. He has conjured up a world where "isolation" is the only condition that enables the artist to communicate with his reader. Strange as it may seem, in an era in which lack of communication is proclaimed as one of the crucial problems, Montale has asserted lucidly and convincingly, in his poetry and criticism, that "even tomorrow the most important voices will be those of the artists who, through their voice of isolated people, will let [the world] hear an echo of the fatal isolation of every one of us. In this sense, only those who are isolated speak; the others—the people of mass communication—repeat, echo, vulgarize, the poets' words, which are today not words of faith but may someday perhaps be so."

Consolation is the last thing we should expect of Montale. Glauco Cambon put it succinctly when he wrote: "Montale will never give us programs, only 'occasions.' Occasions of wonder, sorrow, and dream; unexpected colloquies with reality, lightnings of revelation not to be reduced to dogma; his limit is also his worth. What else should we expect of a poet? Faith in our world, or rather in the possibility of living in it and improving it, is something we shall have to find in ourselves."

## SALVATORE QUASIMODO (1901-    )
### Engagement as Poetry

There is little doubt that the award of the Nobel Prize for Literature in 1959 to Salvatore Quasimodo will long be remembered as one of the truly memorable and controversial events of recent times, matched only by the international furor provoked by the 1958 Nobel award to the late Russian poet-novelist Boris Pasternak. Quite aside from the controversies it stirred, the 1959 award has a significance that transcends the recognition of a truly poetic voice in that it marks the first official awareness on the part of the international audience of the worth of Italian creative writing.

In Italy and elsewhere the announcement was received with a mixture of exaltation and regret, the latter caused by what seemed to many to have been an unjust neglect of the elder Giuseppe Ungaretti and Eugenio Montale. The press was quick to add its own share of confusion to an already unclear situation by presenting Quasimodo as a poet whose work is inaccessible to the greater part of his audience (as though the same was not true of other poets, as T. S. Eliot and Ezra Pound sufficiently demonstrate) and hardly known outside of his native country. Finally, the wording of the citation itself, which singled out Quasimodo's postwar production which "expresses with classical fire the tragic feeling of our time," contained its own share of irony. For it is this particular part of Quasimodo's poetic work that is quite accessible to the general reader but which, strangely enough, has failed to win the admiration of his critics—most of whom prefer the prewar, hermetic verse of the Sicilian.

Current views on the poet can stand partial correction. Quasimodo has been translated into several languages (although the volume of his *Selected Writings* did not appear until several months after he had been awarded the

Nobel Prize) and Russian, Swedish, and German translations have appeared during the last few years. As for his
stature in his native country, only gross ignorance of the
contemporary literary scene would lead anyone to claim
that the poet is less than fully esteemed by critical opinion
in Italy. The poets and critics who have written on him
are too numerous to be listed here, but they include
Eugenio Montale, Oreste Macrí, Sergio Solmi, Luciano
Anceschi, Giuseppe de Robertis, Gianfranco Contini, and,
more recently, Francesco Flora. As early as 1943, barely
a decade after he had begun publishing, his position in
Italian poetry was deemed sufficiently important to warrant a monograph and an interesting chapter in a volume
on hermeticism. In the postwar years additional volumes
(of which Natale Tedesco's is the latest) on his poetic work
were authored by young critics. Yet, such distinguished
English critics as Sir Cecil M. Bowra and Herbert Read
have obfuscated the picture first by maintaining that "not
a single work of art of universal significance . . . nothing
but bombast and vulgarity" had been produced in Fascist
Italy, and then by presenting Quasimodo as a postwar
poet, disregarding entirely the fact that by the beginning
of the war he had already completed his first important
(and, in the opinion of several qualified critics, best)
poetic period. The pages that follow are offered to those
who wish to take the opportunity presented by recent
events to become better acquainted with a generous poetic
voice whose words have meant so much to so many in
tragic and hopeless times.

Salvatore Quasimodo was born in the small city of
Modica, near Syracuse, Sicily, on August 20, 1901. His
father was an employee of the State Railroad. The stillness
of the valley, rich in sulphur mines, was interrupted frequently by the constantly ringing bell that announced the
trains passing through. He learned to read and write at
an early age, and was at once attracted by poetry: though
he did not understand what he was reading, he was greatly
struck by his readings.

He began his formal education in the schools of nearby
Gela. After the famous earthquake of Messina, in 1908,
his father was transferred to that city. Quasimodo continued his education in Palermo, where he enrolled in a

technical school. His ambition was to become an engineer,
as he was particularly attracted by mathematics. In 1918
he left Sicily for the "more civilized North"—thus continuing a tradition of other Sicilian intellectuals, like Verga,
Capuana, and Pirandello, who, blessed and cursed at the
same time by their Sicilian birth, left the island for the
more cosmopolitan air of the Continent. He took up residence in Rome where he continued his studies. It was
there that he met Monsignor Rampolla del Tindaro, who
was responsible for persuading the young man to study
closely and seriously the classical authors of antiquity in
the original. Quasimodo's interest in his profession stopped
there and then. For the next several years engineering was
to be only a means to earn his livelihood. His friends
wanted him to accept a position offered to him by a newspaper, but he refused, preferring to join the Ministry of
Public Works, which assigned him (another irony of his
life!) to the southernmost city of Reggio Calabria.

He had written some poetry when he was still an adolescent, and although he had never stopped writing, he had
given up the hope of ever being published. In Reggio he
again took up his pen, this time more seriously. He was
twenty-seven then and his Sunday pastime consisted in
crossing the Strait of Messina and spending the day on
the island with his friends Elio Vittorini, Pira, Glauco
Natoli, and Salvatore Pugliatti.

In 1929, following the example of Vittorini, Quasimodo
left the South once again and settled in Milan. He visited
Florence regularly, for that city was the cultural seat of
the nation, where the avant-garde writers and poets lived
and met, and where the important little magazines were
published. It was there that Quasimodo met and became
part of the group of *Solaria:* Montale, Manzini, Loria,
Bonsanti, Vieri Nannetti. One day, as the train was pulling
out of the station, headed for Milan, Quasimodo handed
three sheets of paper to Bonsanti: they were his first poems
earmarked for publication. The issue of *Solaria* that appeared a few weeks later carried the first samples of a
genuinely new poetic voice. The editors and readers received those poems quite favorably and a volume of verses
was subsequently commissioned by the subsidiary pub-
ishing house, Solaria. It appeared a few months later,

with the title *Acque e terre* (*Waters and Land*), a collection of the best compositions the poet had written between 1920 and 1929.

The book opened the first period of Quasimodo's poetry, one which lasted until 1942 and that takes its place in the general stream dubbed by the critic Francesco Flora "hermetic." The tone of Quasimodo's early poetry is subdued; the metaphors strange; the language at times obscure. The principal force of such poetry is understatement, thanks primarily to a linguistic texture not studded with numerous adjectives. Its rhyme structure is freer and less committed to "repeat" the classical twelve-syllable verse. Its motifs are no longer religious or patriotic (though Quasimodo is, for all his dedicated opposition to religious authority, quite religious). The poet's efforts were bent, from his earliest lyrics, to finding a language that could be poetic without being either subservient to the tradition or rhetorical, a language which, through its being sensitively handled, might gain new dignity and meaning. In a brilliant essay written in 1938 by Oreste Macrí (a critical piece that is a real landmark in the understanding of our poet) one finds the following observation: "the word of Quasimodo is at the basis of the poet's technique, the beginning of a conscious worth, the final desideratum, the cathartic meaning in which the entire current of inspiration and pathos is brought to a focus. In the problem of the word the new character of our poetry has become defined: a movement of poetic fancy, antiromantic, controlled, geometrical, eschewing the external, the fact, the preordained." It may be accurate to state here that Quasimodo was by no means the first to give a new emphasis to the written word. It should be readily conceded, however, that it was he who brought what was aptly termed "the poetic of the word" to some extreme positions.

The reader coming into contact with the poetry of *Acque e terre* is invariably struck not merely by the delicacy of the images, the quiet, unassuming melody of its verse, but by the suggestive attempt to re-create the illusion of ancient art of communication: communication suggested and heard, as the words "sound," "voice," and "speech" indicate. It is always a continuous source of amazement and aesthetic joy to read the poet and witness how words themselves, subtly employed, become through sheer magic poetic power light and yet profound images:

> *Desiderio delle tue mani chiare*
> *nella penombra della fiamma:*
> *sapevano di rovere e di rose;*
> *di morte. Antico inverno.*
>
> *Cercavano il miglio gli uccelli*
> *ed erano subito di neve;*
> *così le parole.*
> *Un po' di sole, una raggera d'angelo,*
> *e poi la nebbia; e gli alberi*
> *e noi fatti d'aria al mattino.*
> ("Antico inverno")

> The desire of your hands transparent
> in the penumbra of the flame:
> they smelled of oak and roses;
> of death. Ancient winter.
>
> The birds were looking for millet
> and they were suddenly of snow;
> so with your words.
> A little sun, an angel's halo,
> and then the mist; and the trees
> and us made of air at morning.
> ("Ancient Winter")

Slowly the poet was beginning to move in a direction opposite to that followed by his predecessors, who lived, as he perceived, in an era far too different from his own. For this reason, he earnestly studied the various poetics of the tradition only to reject, not out of an emotional impulse but out of a secret wish to "improve" the tradition, those theories that had been formulated in the past, the various theories that presented themselves fully equipped with rhyme schemes and with lists of "occasions" deemed worthy of poetry. Thus, in an essay published in the review *Letteratura* (1939) in a special issue devoted to the poet Gabriele d'Annunzio, Quasimodo made his position unmistakably clear. His particular opposition to the poet from Pescara was not to be interpreted as an expression of a lack of love for an artist whose contribution to poetry could never be denied, but as an indication of a personal belief in a different, individual search for an expressive instrument. It is in this light that *Acque e terre* is essential to a finer appreciation of the Sicilian poet, as his first sustained attempt to write a poetry based on different concepts: poetry, that is, far less committed to the articulation of traditional motifs than to a restoration of language through serious re-creation of a personal condition in itself reflective of a contemporary-timeless situation. A first reading of the poems of *Acque e terre* may thus give the impression, unless read with less than a naïve superficiality, that we are faced once again by artful, unusually mature evocations of the poet's birthplace, which become immortalized by the poet's powerful images. A closer reading dispels such a notion. Quasimodo makes use of the elements of nature and of his native Sicily to re-create for himself and for us the condition of anguish that in his first period of creativity is the prevailing theme of his work. When the compositions are especially felicitous, the result, from the artistic point of view, can hardly escape the reader. It is a compelling synthesis of life that is contained in the often quoted three-line poem *"Ed è subito sera"* (*"And at Once It's Evening"*):

> *Ognuno sta solo sul cuore della terra*
> *trafitto da un raggio di sole:*
> *ed è subito sera.*

> Each alone on the heart of the earth,
> impaled upon a ray of sun:
> and suddenly it's evening.

Quasimodo, though intensely aware of the fact that the world he lived in had been stripped of much of its meaning and was tottering upon the brink of destruction, aspired nonetheless to an ideal condition of peace and serenity. His ultimate goal, as in the case of his elder Ungaretti, was to achieve the "land of innocence," or better still, "the promised land." Quasimodo's Garden of Eden, as has frequently been said, is idealized in a Sicily half land, half water, drunk with the scent of the oranges, lemons, and eucalyptus, stunned by the heat, home of a glorious civilization whose remains are eternal reminders of a time that is no more. Expressive of this particular feeling is the beautiful poem *"Vento a Tindari"* (*"Wind at Tindari"*):

*Tindari, mite ti so*
*fra larghi colli pensile sull'acque*

Tindari, I know you mild
among broad hills, above the waters

Much has been made of this extraordinary poem, certainly one of Quasimodo's finest. Its superb musical rhythm is achieved by the skillful disposition of words and images. "*Onda di suoni e amore*" ("Waves of sounds and love")— sounds are followed and preceded by movement, if only of a figurative sort: "*e ti chini in cuore*" ("and bend into my heart"); "*Salgo vertici aerei precipizi*" ("I climb peaks, airy precipices"). It is a sweet climbing and a sweet, but more mellow, descending: "*Tindari, serena torna*" ("Tindari, serene, return"). Quasimodo is indeed a poet who is best enjoyed when read aloud, in contrast to Eugenio Montale who is, at least for this reader, more rewarding when read silently. "*Vento a Tindari*" also illustrates the dramatic conflict between what is and what the poet would like life to be, symbolized by the antithesis between North and South—a recurring theme with the Sicilian, who insists on the bitterness of his "exile" ("*aspro è l'esilio*") and speaks of the bitter bread he is earning by his work in the northern regions of Italy (Milan) "*amaro pane a rompere*." Again and again, in too many ways indeed for me to list here, the South captivates his imagination. An interesting and sensitive anthology of his "southern" pieces could be usefully compiled, and in such a collection "*Strada di Agrigentum*" and the "*Lamento per il Sud*" would soon appear as among the most moving lyrics of our time. Quasimodo's compassion for his people, like that of all southerners, soon sharpened his concern with mankind in general—mankind striving to achieve what seems to be denied to it: peace, bread, love.

The poetry produced after *Acque e terre* belongs not only to a "moment" already defined but arises out of a particular inspiration. Such is the case of *Oboe sommerso* (*Sunken Oboe*), published in 1932 and defined by Vittorini as the book in which the poet "succeeds in defining the sense of aquatic and vegetable decay"; and such is the case, too, of *Odore di Eucalyptus* (Scent of Eucalyptus), *Erato e Apollion* (*Aerato and Apollyon*), 1936, and of his collection titled *Poesie* (Poems) published in 1938 and representing the first critical anthology and the ideal yardstick to measure the trajectory of the poet and his achievement.

*Oboe sommerso*, for example, strives to make alive, with greater clarity and depth, the sense of suffering, the feeling of loneliness that had already become poetic matter in the earlier compositions. The poem that gives the title to the collection is, in this sense, a conscious effort to confess and restate the poet's isolation:

> *Avara pena, tarda il tuo dono*
> *in questa mia ora*
> *di sospirati abbandoni.*
>
> *Un òboe gelido risillaba*
> *gioia di foglie perenni,*
> *non mie, e smemora;*
>
> *in me si fa sera:*
> *l'acqua tramonta*
> *sulle mie mani erbose.*
>
> *Ali oscillano in fioco cielo,*
> *làbili: il cuore trasmigra*
> *ed io son gerbido,*
>
> *e i giorni una maceria.*

> Miser pain, delay your gift
> in this my hour
> of longed-for abandons.
>
> Chill, again an oboe utters
> joy of everlasting leaves,
> not mine, and disremembers;
>
> in me, evening falls:
> the water sets
> on my grassy hands.
>
> In a dim sky, fleeting
> wings sway; the heart migrates
> and I am fallow
>
> and the days, rubble.

Sicily is the central image in the poems of *Sunken Oboe*, Sicily as a suggestive island not only because of its quality of dream and myth that, after all, are the central qualities of Quasimodo's own sensibility, but because, as someone recently suggested, "it is so much like an Eden, the mysterious place buried in the heart, into which the poet has miraculously succeded in injecting new life." Sicily is the place that evokes sweet memories of childhood, the years and sentiments every poet, at one time or another, strives to recapture. Youth, for the poet, just like water, the sky, the air, the sun, and the wind, symbolizes the freedom of that uncorrupted part of our lives which, for him and for so many of us, represents at once the "real" point of departure and the "ideal" point of return: "In my beginning is my end."

While thematically the various volumes published after *Acque e terre* contain few substantial innovations, linguistically they show a development worth noticing. One can hardly refrain from pointing out at this point (and T. S. Eliot is our constant reminder) how the poet *is* very much concerned with "the preservation and restoration of the beauty of language," and how he is committed to "help language develop to be just as subtle and precise in the more complicated conditions and for the changing purposes of modern life as it was for a simpler age." Quasimodo's diction readily accepts archaic words, freely borrowed from old Italian texts, and uses them in a contemporary context to create what he once termed, in one of his poems, "makeshift images." Archaic words, so employed, yield a striking linguistic timelessness, a sense of a tradition that would otherwise not exist.

Time, meanwhile, was passing slowly for the poet: 1932, 1933, 1934 . . . new books, slim collections of lyrics. They did not, it is true, partake of the emptiness and futility prevailing in the sociopolitical climate of those tragic years. To the contemporary reader, exposed to those poems *here* and *now*, they transmit an electrical feeling of expectation, of anxiety, as though the wire of human existence, already stretched to its utmost, were about to snap. It was in the mid-thirties that Quasimodo undertook an important activity that soon began yielding its own fruits. I am referring to his study and eventual translations of the Latin and Greek classics. In many ways, indeed, his translations enabled him to achieve a truly personal voice. Like

T. S. Eliot (studying and translating from Dante, Laforgue) or Ezra Pound (translating from the texts of Provençal and Italian literature and from the Chinese), Quasimodo's renditions of some of the masterpieces of classical civilization sharpened and perfected his own poetic idiom. Faced by a poetry, metrically, thematically, and linguistically, far different from his own, the poet measured his own ability as a craftsman and an artist by how successfully he could enliven old texts in Italian. His translations, by common consensus, have proved to be masterful re-creations imbued with a personal fire that, despite the antiquity of the original texts, makes them particularly meaningful to the modern reader.

Quasimodo's second poetic period begins with the slim volume *Giorno dopo giorno* (*Day After Day*), published in 1947 and accompanied by a perceptive testimonial written by Carlo Bo. The poetry of this period differs in tone, content, and style from earlier verses. Linguistically, it is a good deal easier, to the point indeed that some critics spoke of a degeneration of Quasimodo's language. The poet employed the language of everyday use, willingly and purposely sacrificing a diction he felt to be inconsistent with themes that are more "dramatic," heavier, and realistic. For another thing, this segment of the Sicilian's poetry deals consistently with real life, real issues, real people. Such a change, undergone by several Italian writers and artists, was brought about by the war. The visions of the water, the sky, the passing of time, the world of antiquity —still and secure—give way to a more concrete world of utterances, searchings, questions. The poet becomes at this point less concerned with the written word as such in order to focus on the word that will enable him to engage in a vibrant dialogue with the people. His dialogue is of the "engaged" variety and displays a formidable concern with the fate of mankind and that of the individual living in a world of perennial, increasingly more serious crises.

A reading of Quasimodo's critical essays of this period would prove to be quite instructive and would certainly illuminate his seemingly drastic change from a position of "retreat" to one of participation: "The poet, in so far as he is a man, participates in the formation of a society, indeed he is a necessary individuality in this formation."

These words were followed by a calmer observation: "The poet cannot console anyone, cannot accustom man to the idea of death, cannot decrease his physical suffering, cannot promise an Eden, nor a milder hell." "Today, after two wars in which the hero has become an immense number of dead people, the poet's commitment is still more serious, because he must 'remake' man. . . ."

Looking back in time, Quasimodo wrote in 1947 in a poem entitled "*Alle fronde dei salici*" "*On the Branches of the Willows*"):

> *E come potevamo noi cantare*
> *con il piede straniero sopra il cuore?*

> And how could we sing
> with the alien foot upon our heart?

Yet one remembers, he has indeed sung some of his sweetest and memorable songs. But the experience of the war, the sociopolitical problems of the postwar period, the remembrance of the blood and of death and misery of the last catastrophic war, could not leave the poet untouched. Since 1945 Quasimodo has become involved in a polemical debate with his critics and has often (and quite brilliantly, one adds) justified his poetics by projecting his work and that of his contemporaries in the context of universal and contemporary letters.

> We are witnessing [he wrote in the "Discourse on Poetry" appended to his volume *Il falso e vero verde*] the growth of a social poetry that addresses itself to various aggregates of human society . . . the poetry of the new generation, which we shall call social in the sense indicated above, aspires to dialogue rather than monologue. The new poetry may become dramatic or epic (in a modern sense) but not, I repeat, gnomic or sociological. Civil poetry, one knows, is beset by deep traps, and sometimes has toyed with "aestheticisms" . . . the new generation is truly *engagé* in every sense of the literary field. The new "contents" are heavy at times, but the content is conditioned by the course of history. The poet knows today that he cannot write idylls or horoscopes.

History, the social conditions of the people, the yearning of people everywhere—these have been made, once again, worthy poetic subjects by Quasimodo. At the same time, however, one is struck by how the production of the postwar years is a strange mixture of poems seemingly inspired by bygone themes (and as such they "repeat" the moods of the first, hermetic period) and poems of the "second" manner, socially and politically conscious. The latter yields a large share of haunting compositions, inspired by timely occasions and events: the slaughter of a handful of partisans, the launching of a new moon, a letter to an "enemy poet." It is fitting that in such poetry the recurring words should be war, tears, blood, sirens, death and the dead, rifles and rifleshots, dust, fear, iron, more iron—still more blood. One poem, *"Colore di pioggia e di ferro"* (*"Colors of Rain and Iron"*), closes with the stark question:

> *E dimmi, uomo spaccato sulla croce,*
> *e tu dalle mani grosse di sangue,*
> *come risponderò a quelli che domandano?*
> *Ora, ora: prima che altro silenzio*
> *entri negli occhi, prima che altro vento*
> *salga e altra ruggine fiorisca.*

> And tell me, man cleft upon the cross,
> and you with hands thick with blood,
> how shall I answer those that ask?
> Now, now: before another wind does rise,
> another stillness fill the eyes, before
> another rust flourishes.

The personal poetry of the first period has clearly been superseded by an intense poetry that sings not of the anguish and sorrow of man but of the sorrow and anguish of mankind. Sir Cecil M. Bowra summarized the new situation correctly when he wrote that "Quasimodo's poetry was born in these years of agony and reflects his attempt to master circumstances by understanding them in their full significance for the imagination as well as for the intellect." For once, one is tempted to say, here is true poetry, poetry that succeeds in being understood before it can communicate.

In Italy, unfortunately, the later Quasimodo has enjoyed little favor with the critics: it is hoped that the recent award of the Nobel Prize may force them to read Quasimodo's postwar production again, and as carefully as they once read his hermetic verse. It is hard to imagine how they could fail to be moved by *"Al padre"* and *"Lettera alla madre"*—two of the most perfect and moving compositions that have been written in modern days. Let them reread, too *"Visibile, invisibile"* and the other lyrics of the postwar volumes. They will be struck by the poet's simplicity, his power, his restraint.

An unpredictable poet, Salvatore Quasimodo is, unlike his elders Giuseppe Ungaretti and Eugenio Montale (who have a long time ago "completed" their self-definition), far from having written the work that will consign him, so to speak, to posterity. An alive and productive poet, Quasimodo is going through an important phase of his career out of which, I predict, he will emerge as one of the most enduring poets of our century. An extremely courageous man is he, for he possesses an unshakable faith in the power of poetry. In a discourse delivered before the Swedish Academy, and again at Yale University, he declared: "The loyalty of poetry becomes clear in a presence that is beyond justice and beyond the intention of death. The politician wants man to be able to *die* with courage; the poet wants man to *live* with courage." Unafraid to renew himself, he has dared to make use of polemical themes and unorthodox forms without regard to how the critics may interpret them. He has employed a classical, limpid, and sensitive idiom to confront the social themes of our time. In a tradition-ridden society he has spoken boldly of a new conception of poetry and of the poet's ideal and *new* responsibility. However one might disagree with his *prise de position*, with his intellectual stand, one cannot but admire him. A poet of the highest integrity, Quasimodo has made his readers, the men of his own era and those who will read him in the future, still more conscious of our condition, the tragic condition that is man's. He has spoken with firmness and kindness to people the world over about life, with words that are beautiful but also replete with meanings.

Not an optimist in any sense of the word, Quasimodo has never despaired. He has sought with words that are the very tools of the poet to be not an orator nor a literary despot but a "workman of dreams." With all the intellectual resources at his disposal he has sought to illuminate for himself and for all of us the meaning of life and of man's condition in the universe. Discreetly, but convincingly, he has taught us to be a little stronger and a little braver, to be above the pettiness of everyday life, and to rise above the cruelty of man. He has rebelled against tyranny and death, against wars and man's destructive impulses, teaching us, in his own superb way, *to be* ourselves and never ask for either "grace" or "confusion."

## THE YOUNGER POETS

If statistics indicate that the last decade and a half has seen an imposing number of books of poetry published, a more serene assessment is bound to reveal that the truly "new" voices are relatively few. Perhaps no one deserves our attention more than Pier Paolo Pasolini, who, among the younger poets, stands out for his intelligence and personality. His age (he was born in Bologna in 1922) is quite deceptive, for he is a prolific writer indeed. His work is diversified enough to include philological and critical essays, several anthologies of poetry in dialect (of which he is an astute and competent commentator), and two novels, the dialogue of which is largely in Roman dialect, *Ragazzi di vita* (Children of Life, easily the most controversial book published in 1955) and *Una vita violenta* (A Violent Life, 1959). Critical recognition has come to him early in life. In the summer of 1957 his slim volume of poetry, *Le ceneri di Gramsci* (Gramsci's Ashes), was awarded the coveted Viareggio Prize. The numerous debts Pasolini owes to the tradition and to the poets of the nineteenth century, Carducci and Pascoli, as well as to the moderns (Saba, above all), in addition to his special usage of traditional forms and meters, are sufficiently indicative of his attempt to blend a new tradition with an older one, while simultaneously striving to lower "the language to the level of prose, that is, of the rational, the logical, and the historical." Certainly the reference to Gramsci, the founder of the Italian Communist Party, is more than a mere tribute; it is an acknowledgment of his nonpolitical teachings and his ever-growing stature in Italian literary circles. It was Gramsci who, in the late twenties, writing from the jail where he was to die, encouraged the rise of a new culture that to become "popular" must reflect the

aspirations of the people. It is particularly in this sense that
Pasolini has done much to narrow the gap that has always
existed in Italy between life and literature. Whatever
flaws one may find in Pasolini's poetry, it does represent, in
its curious and often happy amalgamation of traditional
and contemporary features, a passionate desire to further
man's understanding of reality in a more than merely
technological sense. It is for this reason that Pasolini has
intellectually defined his position in the central section
of the long poem "*Le ceneri di Gramsci*":

> *Vivo nel non volere*
> *del tramontato dopoguerra: amando*
> *il mondo per odio—nella sua miseria*
> *sprezzante e perso . . .*

> I live in the apathy
> of the twilight of the postwar year: loving
> a world I hate—in its wretchedness
> contemptuous and lost . . .

One of his most effective pieces is "*Terra del lavoro*,"
in which he looks at his southern companions in a third-
class train compartment, and relives with them all the
bitter experiences that make the southern peasant the new
"alienated" class.

Pasolini is not, it should be stressed, the only poet who
has succeeded in finding a language more in keeping with
the exigencies of the postwar years. Indeed, many of the
little magazines published in recent years have publicly
renounced the heritage of hermeticism. In one of the
literary manifestoes (published in *Situazioni*) one reads:
"It is evident that those [features] that seem to many
people to be the shortcomings of realism . . . are not
always a return to the rhetoric of the past, but may become an opening toward the future that may allow our
literature to cease being academic and arcadian. No one
today can believe any longer in a formal literature that
does not have human ideas and interests." There is, of
course, no artist worthy of the name who does not have
real human interests: but the manifesto, critically hazy
and fundamentally without a solid aesthetic basis, is interesting for its articulation of what has been felt by many
poets to be a real problem: "to extricate oneself from
the individualistic isolation so as to understand and rep-

resent other contents: those of society and history." Perhaps no one succeeded better in accomplishing a mission as did the late Rocco Scotellaro, who died when barely thirty, in 1953, and whose book *E' fatto giorno* (Day Came) won the Viareggio Prize, posthumously. Scotellaro was, for all his lack of academic training and literary sophistication, an unusually gentle, sensitive peasant (he served for some time as mayor of his native town in Lucania) who could capture the life in the fields, and the poverty of the South, in striking images:

> *Le ragazze dagli occhi più neri*
> *montano altere sul carro che stride,*
> *Marzo è un bambino in fasce che già ride.*
> ("Le viole sono dei fanciulli scalzi")

The girls with the deep black eyes
climb haughtily on squeaking vans,
March is a child in swaddling clothes who already laughs.
("The Violets Are Barefoot Children")

The majority of the mature poets, however, still cling to hermeticism, and recognize as their masters Ungaretti and Montale, as well as some of the late nineteenth-century French poets. The consistently high caliber of their work, the inventiveness and technical resources they have displayed, make them something more than minor figures. Among them are Libero de Libero (b. 1906) and Sandro Penna (b. 1906), winners of the Viareggio Prize in 1950 and 1957 respectively. They are the oldest members of the group and they are widely read and highly esteemed. Libero de Libero has produced a body of work that, while it initially drew its inspiration from the Roman countryside (he was born in Fondi, near Rome), has become precious, subtle, and elegiac. But while his native Ciociaria is ever-present in his poetry, most of which is in the octave form, he can at times transform the earth and country life into powerful and nostalgic images:

> *Sul mio corpo*
> *secca ormai è tutta la terra.*
> *Non la madre mi scorderà*
> *nè vecchio padre mi piangerà*
> *toccando l'erba o il sasso.*
> *All'amico diletto*
> *ignota è la sorte mia.*

*Mandate cavalli*
*a pascere quest'erba.*

Upon my body
dry is the earth now.
My mother will not forget me
nor will my old father lament me
touching the grass or the stone.
To my dear friend
unknown is my fate.
Send horses
to graze this grass.

Penna, on the other hand, is almost totally divorced from the regionalistic preoccupations of De Libero and eschews the metaphysical themes of some of his contemporaries. His poems are written in a simple and extremely graceful style. His subject matter is provided by his own life. As in the case of Saba, to whom Penna has often been compared, his work shows hardly a trace of any substantial change. The poet writes today, as he has always, about his deeply felt joys and sorrows:

> *Sandro penna è intriso di una strana*
> *gioia di vivere anche nel dolore.*
>
> Sandro Penna is sodden with a strange
> joy of living even in sorrow.

His compositions have become increasingly more epigrammatic (in the modern sense of synthesis and lyrical illumination), to the point that the entire poem's image is expressed in as few as three or four lines. Yet, however brief they may be, Penna's poems do captivate the reader with their elegant, almost feminine language, their haunting rhythms, and the dreamlike manner in which people and objects become blurred and marvelously transformed into delicate sensations.

Has the war, with its ensuing tragedy and wretchedness, changed in any important way the course of Italian poetry, as it has in France or Holland? Even Salvatore Quasimodo (who represents the avant-garde for a certain generation of younger poets) and the critic-poets E. F. Accrocca and V. Volpini (editors of an anthology of poetry of the Italian Resistance) have answered the question with strong reservations. "But this fact," write the editors, "does not seem to us sufficient to deny the possibility of establishing the authentic participation of the poets in the liberation of our country." Like many others, I too would find it difficult to make a strong case for a literature of the Resistance in Italy. By the same token, it is necessary to take cognizance of the select group of poets who have been directly inspired by the war: and here the situation can be more easily documented, thanks to the spadework done by Accrocca and Volpini. Among such poets, Franco Fortini, Alfonso Gatto, and Vittorio Sereni are recognized as the most mature, and have produced a work that stands out for its authentic personality and forcefulness. Franco Fortini (b. 1906) has devoted several of the lyrics of his *Foglio di via* (1946) to social polemics, conjuring up the horrors brought about by the war. In his poems he sees Italy, his native land, as a prison and as a prisoner at the same time:

> *Ora m'accorgo d'amarti*
> *Italia, di salutarti*
> *Necessaria Prigione.*

> Now I realize that I love you,
> O Italy, and greet you
> Necessary Prison.

He concludes by affirming that,

> *Ora non basta nemmeno morire*
> *per quel tuo vano cuore antico.*

> Now it is no longer enough to die
> for that ancient name of yours.

The emphasis is obviously on the adjective *"vano,"* on the rapid disintegration of a myth that is no longer valid or useful.

Alfonso Gatto (born in Salerno in 1909) is a more complex and purer poet, who owes a debt to D'Annunzio's rich vocabulary and images. Gifted with a great sense of style and a colorful and vivid imagination, he has relived some of the intensely dramatic moments of the war, the days of the Liberation, in his memorable *Il capo sulla neve* (The Head on the Snow), published in 1946. One of the most poignant poems of that rich collection is entitled *"Anniversario"*:

*Oh, l'Europa gelata nel suo cuore*
*mai più si scalderà: sola coi morti*
*che l'amano in eterno, sarà bianca*
*senza confini, unita dalla neve.*

Oh, Europe frozen in her heart
will never again grow warm: alone with the dead
who love her eternally, she will be white
without boundaries, united by the snow.

Although the literary output of Vittorio Sereni (born
in Luino in 1913) is quite limited, he has established a
firm place for himself with his *Diario d'Algeria* (Algerian
Diary, 1947). Like some of his contemporaries, he has
been heavily influenced by Ungaretti and Montale: the
first has taught him the lyrical purity of the word, while
from the other he has inherited a realization of the significance of the focal point of a poem, thus clearing the
creative ground of irrelevant details and excessive tenderness. There is something startling in his poem "*Non sa
più nulla . . .*" ("He knows nothing any more . . ."),
and yet the composition is tender without being sentimental; it is supremely compassionate:

*Non sa più nulla, è alto sulle ali*
*il primo caduto bocconi sulla spiaggia normanna.*
*Per questo qualcuno stanotte*
*mi toccava le spalle mormorando*
*di pregar per l'Europa*
*mentre la Nuova Armada*
*si presentata alla costa di Francia.*

*Ho risposto nel sonno: E' il vento,*
*il vento che fa musiche bizzarre.*
*Ma se tu fossi davvero*
*il primo caduto bocconi sulla spiaggia normanna*
*prega tu se lo puoi, io sono morto*
*alla guerra e alla pace.*
*Questa è la musica ora:*
*delle tende che sbattono sui pali.*
*Non è musica d'angeli, è la mia*
*sola musica e mi basta.*
*(Campo Ospedale 127, giugno 1944)*

He knows nothing now, is high on wings
the first man fallen on the Norman beach.
That is why someone last night
touched my shoulder whispering

to pray for Europe
while the New Armada
appeared on the coast of France.

I answered in sleep: It's the wind,
the wind that makes strange music.
But if you were really
the first man fallen on Normandy beach
pray, if you can: I died
to war and peace.
This is the music now:
some tents shaking on the poles.
This is the music now: it is my
only music and it will do for me.

(Hospital Field 127, June 1944)

The number of poets who have devoted at least a part
of their work to describing the anguish of the war, and
how it felt to be engaged in a conflict more useless than
any previous one, is too great to be discussed here completely. To the names already mentioned, it may suffice
to add those of Sergio Solmi (who shared with Gatto the
St. Vincent Prize in 1948), Giorgio Caproni (born in
Leghorn in 1912), and Giorgio Bassani (born in Ferrara
in 1916).

Leonardo Sinisgalli (b. 1908) has often been called the
most versatile member of the hermetic group. He has written perceptively on architecture, interior decorating, the
plastic arts, geometry, design, dance, and optics. He is
a mechanical engineer, mathematician, and student of
metallurgy and electrical sciences. He began his diversified career in 1936 with a little volume entitled *18 poesie*
(Eighteen Poems). His initial collection has grown considerably during the past two and a half decades, and he
has kept up his vitality throughout the following volumes,
the most noteworthy of which are *Vidi le Muse* (I Saw
the Muses, 1943) and *Tu sarai poeta* (Thou Shalt Be Poet,
1957). As a poet he is quite difficult to define. Often accused of being too cerebral, too detached from reality, he
has nevertheless written some fine poems about his native
Lucania, his family, and the monotonous, hard life his
parents and brothers lead in the fields—thus turning his
eye toward a reality he had previously avoided. His latest
verse (*Tu sarai poeta*) reveals a more intimate fusion
of the two tones, the elegiac and the epigrammatic, which

prevailed in his early period. As he has grown older, Sinisgalli has become concerned with life and death, trying to recapture the meaning of all things past without losing sight of the present.

The last of a group of poets who, while not "major," have shown considerable talent, is Mario Luzi (b. 1914 in Florence), winner of the Marzotto Prize in 1957 for his *Onore del vero* (Honor of Truth). Luzi combines his interest in creative writing with a professional criticism of French and Italian letters (he is a teacher in a Florentine *liceo*). Learned, perceptive, frequently obscure, Luzi has been able to create a poetry replete with allusions to Mallarmé and Montale. For him, too, the war has been an important experience. But, as he wrote recently, "After the experience *ab ovo* which the war has been [for me] both in so far as the identification of the real, of the living continuum, and its moral dramatization are concerned, I felt the need of giving my work a more elemental substance and aspect, founded more firmly upon the experience of man and the nature of his language that expresses it; I felt, in fact, the need to write in a way that such should be the very object of poetry, and would occupy it in an ideal identity between subject and object."

*Un Brindisi* (A Toast) and *Quaderno Gotico* (Gothic Notebook) are his most representative works. Perhaps not quite as allusive and metaphorical as his previous books, they are, especially the latter, powerfully evocative. *Quaderno Gotico* dramatizes in a particularly skillful and moving manner the spiritual and carnal torment experienced by the poet, thus justifying the remark recently made by one of Luzi's critics that "to the travail of the mind, the full and tumultuous travail of the heart has now been added."

It might be interesting to point out that Luzi is still anchored to hermetic positions abandoned by many of his fellow poets and has strongly denied the validity of a "realistic" poetry. Such intelligent poets as Pier Paolo Pasolini take an opposite position. Answering a referendum conducted by the literary magazine *L'approdo* (1959, No. 6), Pasolini affirmed that, first of all, "the present moment seems ripe for the writer, for the poet, to try to ascertain with accuracy the nature of the rapport of his poetic activity [*fare poetico*] with the society that has expressed him. The historico-rational act must now preside over his [creative] work, substituting for the rationalizing intellectualism [of the past] that has prevailed up until now. . . . Society around us no longer demands . . . evasions toward the inner part [of man]. To practice such evasions now is a vain prolepsis of the absolute, a gratuitous ascetic act." Pasolini, following the logical reasoning of Gramsci, claims that "a new poetry cannot be born except from a new culture, or at least from the moral and rational consciousness of its own culture." Mario Luzi, on the other hand, firmly believes that

> a true realistic poetry seems highly improbable. Poetry has, in my opinion, only one chance to survive, only one justification in the modern world, which is lost after the little episodes, divided into many small and primitive mythologies that have arisen as a consequence of the absence of a myth, a faith, a conviction. [Such justification is] its own force of synthesis. . . . The great adventure of modern poetry consists, in fact, in its attempt to reconstruct through language that unity lost by the ideal, practical, expressive world. Such has been, in substance, the effort of Italian poetry of the past decades, of hermetic poetry. . . . The wind has shifted or the seasons have advanced, it is evident: but can that synthesis be performed today in reality, when . . . there is no serious premise to conceive integrally the world as a reality with a beginning and an end in itself?

The comments made in the course of this brief survey of the state of contemporary Italian poetry, and the numerous quotations given to document the views expressed, might well be sufficient to give an idea of the complexity and the richness of the landscape of Italian poetry. "The poet is alone," said the Nobel Prize poet Salvatore Quasimodo in his speech delivered at Yale. "The wall of hate is raised around him, [a wall] built of stones thrown by literary marauders. From this wall the poet observes the world without going to the squares as the minstrels did or in the mundane world as did the literati. Precisely from that ivory tower, so dear to the torturers of the romantic soul, he arrives amidst the people." "Poetry," recently wrote that acute literary critic, Carlo Bo, "remains, in spite of everything, a limit of salvation, at least as ransom, as the least corruptible image of life, of *our* life."

# Existentialism

The reader who has the slightest acquaintance with Italian letters is well aware that, unlike France, Italy does not have in its roster of writers' names matching those of such novelist-philosophers as Jean-Paul Sartre, Simone de Beauvoir, Gabriel Marcel, and the late Albert Camus. It is through the fiction and the philosophical essays of these distinguished writers that existentialism has achieved an unusual popularity in recent years—both in Europe and elsewhere.

In the last decades only a handful of Italian writers have successfully incarnated some of the vital aspects of this philosophy in believable fictitious characters. Similarly, few philosophers of prominence have written sympathetically about a philosophy symptomatic of the anxieties of our century. The distortion to which existentialism has been subjected, and the scorn heaped upon it by Benedetto Croce and Guido de Ruggiero, who once defined it as "a philosophy in the manner of a 'thriller,' " has not prevented intelligent analyses—of both the specialized and popular variety—from appearing in various publications. A typical illustration of the frequent symposia on existentialism appeared in 1955 in the Roman review *Nuovi Argomenti* with the participation of writers and scholars.

The Italian interest in existentialism is not a postwar phenomenon. Heidegger was translated in the early years of this century, and since then the bibliography of studies on existentialism has grown richer by the year. Paradoxically, however, at a time when in most countries of western

Europe it has captured the imagination of the younger generation of writers, existentialism has produced in Italy neither a philosophical school of international reputation nor, as in France, Germany, and even the United States, an existentialist novel, as such.

The situation may be partially explained by pointing out that Italian fiction was traditionally lacking in psychology and philosophy—two necessary ingredients of existentialist creative writing. Exceptions to this statement are not hard to find, to be sure: and here one could profitably mention the names of Svevo, Tozzi, Bontempelli, and Moravia. As a rule, however, the writer in Italy has traditionally been preoccupied with the "social" reality of the life in his country, a concern recently enriched by an acute awareness of economic and political problems peculiar to the postwar years. The fact that Italy was ruled for over two decades by fascism is also useful in realizing that a nation whose dictator insisted that the will of the individual must be subjugated to the good of the state could hardly be receptive to a philosophy with an unusual stress on personal freedom.

Existentialism has thus far eluded a strict definition, as demonstrated by the disparate interpretations that keep appearing every year. This notwithstanding, or perhaps because of the flexibility of this philosophy, many novelists, without regard to cultural background or national barriers, have assimilated several of its insights, without necessarily adhering, on a strict intellectual level, to existentialism. As in other European countries, several novels reflecting what may broadly be classified as existential preoccupations have appeared since the end of the war. The change of political climate and a renewed awareness of problems of apparently insurmountable magnitude have intensified a latent disposition toward a reappraisal of life in the light of recent tragic experiences.

One of the positive features of existentialism is its courageous confrontation with the starkest facts of human life. Recent Italian fiction has been particularly applauded for the honesty with which the new writers deal with death, hunger, the loss of faith, and with such a fundamental and crucial contemporary problem as the difficulty experienced by people who wish to communicate with each other, on the intellectual or on the emotional level. Such fiction, as one commentator remarked recently, attempts "to relate poetry to human activity in such a way as not to destroy poetry and to make life itself poetic. This restores to philosophy some of its original significance and mythical preoccupation, serving thus to compensate for the failure of semantics to cope adequately with the necessary and valid emotive and irrational constituent in all languages." The Italian imagination has been particularly attracted by existentialism's emphasis on the *concrete* existence of the individual, as it is lived from day to day, from one moment to the next, and on the personal choice as the most relevant criterion with which to assess man. Jaspers once wrote: "So far as I choose, I am; if I am not, I do not choose." It is in this postulate that some of the contemporary Italian writers have seen the possibility of new conflicts and hence new dramatic situations, more consonant with contemporary conditions.

Since existentialism has been preoccupied with studying the moral and intellectual postures of the individual as they are translated into acts, it follows that fiction (and in some cases, even poetry) should be its appropriate vehicle of expression. Fiction is, of all creative activities, the one that offers the writer the chance to give dramatic substance to his sensibility in a way that can reach the general audience without difficulty. By his ordering experience and by a careful revelation of the psychology of his characters, the novelist is able to succeed where the philosopher might well fail. Thus, while there is general agreement that it is in the work of the Dane, Kierkegaard, the Germans, Jaspers and Heidegger, the Frenchmen, Sartre and Marcel, that we find a theoretical foundation of existentialism as a philosophy, it is through the fiction and drama of the early Malraux, or St. Exupéry, Sartre, and Camus that the principal tenets of the philosophy are dramatized with a vividness that permits them to be perceived readily by the lay reader. Indeed, it has been the novelist who has brought philosophy from the academic halls to the people.

The phenomenal rise of existentialism has been commented upon by several scholars. It seems certain that the numerous changes in the social and economic structure of society are responsible for the rise of a philosophy whose major idea takes the form of a protest against the gradual loss of freedom incurred by the human personality and against the ever-increasing power of the machine over its creator. The existentialists are therefore violently opposed to the technological aspects of our civilization which, in their opinion, have robbed man of a substantial part of his freedom. They similarly place little faith either in enlightenment or in positivism. They hold that since the aim of philosophy is to study the principles by which man lives so as to test the validity of values or to propose new ones, it should be cognizant of the inescapable realities man must face, irrespective of the time. One such reality goes under the name of alienation. It is easy to see how in a highly mobile and technological society man should no longer cherish those human rapports that were ordinary in a more static and, in a real physical sense, provincial society. Until a century ago, life was conducted in a manner that permitted and encouraged intimate contacts between people living in the same geographical area. There were fewer distractions, and wealth was unevenly distributed—these conditions were conducive to people spending time with each other. The advent of the steam engine and the subsequent invention of the airplane, the radio, and television eventually broke down normal geographical barriers. The world has shrunk to the point where no more than a few hours separate any two points on the globe. As geographical distances grew smaller, human rapports reached new, unexpected crises. The dilemma arising out of a society with overwhelming technological problems centers on the fact that man, once the focal point of life and all human activities, has turned into an adjunct of the machine he has created, becoming estranged from his environment. As Heinemann succinctly puts it in his excellent study *Existentialism and the Modern Predicament:*

> The facts to which the term "alienation" refers are, objectively, different kinds of disassociation, break, or rupture between human beings and their objects, whether the latter be other persons or the natural world, or their creations in art, science, and society; and subjectively, the corresponding states of disequilibrium, strangeness, and anxiety . . . the belief of a preceding unity and harmony has been transformed into disunity and disharmony.

Alienation, the supreme importance of personal choice, political and intellectual freedom to act in accordance with ones own desire "to be"—these are some of the main ideas fictionalized by the existentialist novelist. The important questions being asked today by the creative writer are: "What am I?" and "What is the order within which nature and people may achieve a more meaningful and understandable relation than the one they have?" Having discarded the notion of a universe created and governed by the laws of God, we must, he insists, seek other answers to the haunting riddles of existence.

It is not strange that the questions posed by contemporary Italian novelists were also asked by Luigi Pirandello, through his characters and situations. Eric Bentley, in his stimulating essay "Pirandello's Joy and Torment," advanced the provocative suggestion that the vision of the Sicilian playwright has much in common with that of contemporary existentialist novelists:

> Perhaps it would nowadays be called an existentialist vision; life is absurd; it fills us with nausea and dread and anguish; it gives us the metaphysical shudder; yet, without knowing why, perhaps just because we are *there*, in life, we face it, we fight back, we cry in pain, in rage, in defiance (if we are Sicilian existentialists), and because all living, all life, is improvisation, we improvise some values. Their Form will last until Living destroys them and we have to improvise some more.

To begin the present discussion by mentioning Pirandello is more instructive than one may anticipate. I do not wish to imply that he was directly influenced by existentialist thinkers, although there is ample evidence that he was thoroughly familiar with, and often sympathetic toward, certain ideas of Bergson and Nietzsche. If some readers correctly see in him an existentialist *avant la lettre,* it is mainly for his having dealt effectively, after much "realistic" and decadent fiction, with the dilemmas of man who, thrown into the world, suddenly discovers the twofold nature of reality—the inner and the outer—and begins a long reflective discourse about the crucial problems of his existence. His heroes, struggling to find solidarity needed to survive the painful business of living, find instead that they are faced by an essentially malicious society, which in a manner strangely similar to that of Kafka's world, conspires against their well-being and peace. In Pirandello's fiction and theater, the heroes seem to be looking for an unattainable peace, understood not merely as a solution to the conflict between Life (which is always changing and moving) and Form (which fixes life in an immutable way), but as a preservation of that freedom envisaged as man's most valuable possession. Take, for instance, *Right You Are—If You Think You Are,* one of the better known plays by Pirandello and a classical illustration of what, refined and intellectualized, was later to become known as *Pirandellismo.* The play concerns a strange situation, about which everyone in town wants to know "the truth": Is the wife of Signor Ponza, a civil servant who has just taken up residence in town and who leads a very secluded life with his mother-in-law, the daughter of Signora Frola, or is she, as Signor Ponza claims, his second wife whom Signora Frola has been allowed, out of charity, to believe to be her daughter (who presumably died in an earthquake)? And if she *is* Signora Frola's daughter, why does Ponza force her to live alone in a small flat on the outskirts of town? Right up to the last scene, the author plays with great skill upon the intricate question, always bringing up new evidence that supports now one, now the other, version of the same story. Finally the whole town, after listening to the explanations of Signor Ponza and Signora Frola, requests that Signora Ponza tell which of the two versions is true.

We have seen in this drama a kind of play between illusion and reality, with the author trying to demonstrate that truth is very fluid and at best an extremely subjective affair. By extension, too, we have perceived that Pirandello wanted his audience to realize that society deals with human beings in bizarre and cruel ways. Lately, however, we have come to understand that what gives Pirandello's plays a contemporary relevance is his insistence that mankind must devise other ways to deal with each other. How else could we explain why Pirandello's characters should so persistently turn to deceit and trickery, both of which amount to an open, if cerebral, revolt, against a society that, dehumanized to the point of meanness, persecutes people who fail to conform rigidly to pre-established patterns of behavior? As the playwright himself stressed in his little-known essay *L'umorismo,* "the simulation of force, honesty, sympathy, prudence—in short, of every virtue, and of that greatest virtue, veracity—is a form of adjustment, *an effective instrument of struggle*" (italics mine). His characters rebel against a cruel society that is forever interfering with their lives but also against the popular notion that rationalism holds the key to the solution of the irrationality that pervades so much of modern life. Thus, Signora Ponza, summoned by the townspeople so that she may solve once and for all the riddle of her "situation," calmly admits to an astonished audience that she is *both* Signora Frola's daughter *and* Signor Ponza's second wife. "As for myself," she concludes, "I am what people think I am." Her contention constitutes what is probably the central point of Pirandello's vision: life is nothing but what *we* think it is, and what we make of it. After a man has accepted the fact that he "is," he must then proceed to "define" himself through his acts and words; his personality is seen as being nothing if not a "creative" process. If we ourselves are no longer what we think we are, but many different persons according to the multifarious interpretations of other people, then let us make life a project per se, an act of perennial invention and improvisation. Indeed, in one of his later plays, Pirandello said: "Life is nothing. 'To be' means to build oneself." In this statement, uttered by a character appropriately called *I' Ignota* (the Unknown), there is the essence of Pirandello's existentialism and intellectualism. For if the Sicilian playwright did conceive of human existence as a continuous project, he also dramatized the complete breakdown of the human personality without suggesting how this might be overcome. While Sartre's characters define themselves through their acts, through which they achieve a deeper consciousness of their being, Pirandello evades the whole problem by illustrating the fact that life is so infinitely absurd that it discourages or frustrates the man who wishes *to be.* Most of the tension of Pirandello's world is generated by the friction between our freedom to act, think, and speak as we wish, and the fact that our words and actions will reveal us to be frail creatures. Our freedom is, in the last analysis, both a blessing and a curse. Yet the playwright entertains a view that, for all the pessimism of his plays, is basically positive: in the not-too-distant future man will learn to have the courage and strength to face life stripped of his masks, naked (*Naked Masks* is, appropriately enough, the title of his collected plays), and will learn to respect, understand, and love not just himself but his fellow men. Only then, after much anguish and pain, will he begin to live humanly and see that his traumatic experience has not been in vain: life, in spite of its thorns, can be a source of joy. Had Pirandello lived, he might well have agreed with Sartre that "life begins on the other side of despair."

Pirandello died in the mid-thirties, when existentialism had neither met its public nor found its teachers and preachers. If his literary production deals with certain ideas that only the next generation was to acknowledge as being vital to a more complete understanding of modern life, it was because he was imaginative and bold enough to venture into regions comparatively unexplored by writers of his time. He dealt with problems and issues in a personal manner, thanks to his extraordinary sensibility. He wrote with intensity about the instability, and what was later known as the "anxiety," of the years following the First World War. But in this he was not alone. While he had been concerned with fictionalizing the splitting up of the human personality into a million different personalities, other European writers, disheartened by the deep social and economic unrest, turned elsewhere for any possible sign of hope—only to be confronted with a sick world that was slowly crumbling apart, a world that, having lost most of its perennial greenness and beauty, had been turned by man into a desolate wasteland. T. S. Eliot's poem of the same title, Montale's *Ossi di seppia* (Cuttle-Fish Bones), Thomas Mann's *The Magic Mountain,* James Joyce's *Ulysses,* and Alberto Moravia's *Gli indifferenti* (*The Time of Indifference*) express, either thematically or linguistically, a similarly disjointed vision of the world, each focusing in its own way upon the vacuum and alienation that were to become almost overnight the symbols of an over-mechanized and dehumanized twentieth century.

Alberto Moravia is a pertinent example of a novelist whose sympathy for certain existentialist ideas, latent in his early work, has become explicitly and intentionally articulate in his more mature fiction. Carlo Falconi has tried to trace what he terms the existentialist undercurrent in Moravia's work, and the reader may be referred conveniently to his essay for a detailed analysis of an interesting problem. Yet the article fails to do justice to the subject, as it limits itself to citing a number of passages bearing on the feeling of anguish and dread that Moravia's characters repeatedly experience. It does not point out that their true tragedy lies in the inadequacy of the actions they take to extricate themselves from their predicaments. Michele's anguish, in *The Time of Indifference*, for example, is quite intense. He knows that there is little hope in his playing the double role of the accuser and the accused and that he will never get out of the mess he is in. All Moravia's heroes have this much in common with Michele: they engage in feeble attempts to change their world and, when they fail, they "choose" to be what they are out of fear, turpitude, or "indifference"—and in this sense we may speak of existentialism of a negative kind. Michele chooses to be indifferent, for he discovers that often there is more to be gained by maintaining the status quo than by trying to upset it; Pietro (*Mistaken Ambitions*), a second-rate journalist, decides out of sympathy (or is it personal convenience?) to make a "good woman" of Andreina, and yet he himself behaves like a hypocrite when he tries to convince himself that his beautiful plans for redemption are not motivated by selfish reasons; the youngster Luca (*Disobedience*), out of his unhappiness rooted in his parents' apparent lack of understanding, feels lost and lonely and eventually, believing that the world is a disgusting place, revolts against it, if only in an extremely passive manner. Marcello Clerici (*The Conformist*) wants to conform, however naïvely and superficially, and so rid himself of a pathological and psychological "abnormality." Moravia's imagination is indeed haunted by the awareness of a universe no longer governed by traditional morality. His heroes, having privately acknowledged the death of God, are left with little to guide them in their social actions besides their senses and their instincts: hence the confusion of their world, their alienation, and despair.

The vision is not always as turbid as this. Moravia has attempted to reach some sort of reconciliation between the discordant elements of contemporary life by writing *The Woman of Rome*, the story of Adriana, a young Roman prostitute, and of her lovers. One of these lovers is Mino, a university student who is active in a clandestine movement working to overthrow the Fascist party and who may be seen as the antihero of the story. When, toward the end of the book, he is arrested and questioned by the secret police about his underground activities, he betrays both his friends and his cause because he suddenly discovers that everything in which he had once believed has mysteriously ceased to have any importance or meaning for him. His loss of faith in life is brought about by his loss of faith in his very ideas. Surrounded by a vacuum, Adriana, who is but a meek prostitute, suggests that life is, of course, "nothingness, obscurity and weakness," but at the same time our spiritual drought and desolation may be overcome. She herself, in her daily experience as a prostitute, exemplifies a love that is charity, the only sentiment that will attenuate and soothe the many cruelties man has been inflicting upon man since the beginning of time: "I understood that everything was love and everything depended on love. One had this love or one did not have it. And if you had it, you loved not only your own lover, but also every person and every thing. And if you did not have it, you could not love anyone or anything." This view, simply stated by Adriana and held by other Moravia characters who belong to the working class, represents the novelist's only genuinely positive answer to the problem of the incoherence and senselessness of life. The solution is yet to blossom into a broader and deeper vision. With the exception of *The Woman of Rome* and *Two Women*, Moravia is tormented by a vision of nothingness and irrationality. For all his penetrating insights, the novelist has yet to present a possible resolution (which need not be positive, to be sure) of the existential problem of man, who finds himself confronting a world in which no rational pattern seems to exist but who is nevertheless forced by his ontological structure to "choose" and "act" without a strong moral code or universally respected principles.

While Moravia's interests are largely metaphysical, those

of another important novelist, Elio Vittorini, are socio-political. The solution he proposes, as demonstrated in his tales, is largely derived from his concern with solidarity and action as effective antidotes against all forms of tyranny. Vittorini's best novel to date is still *In Sicily* (1941) for no other reason than, aside from its lyrical beauty, it represents the author's discovery of his big theme: "Not every man is a man. One persecutes and the other is persecuted. Similarly, a man who is sick of starving is more than a man; and more human is the race of the starving." Yet, Vittorini felt that the discovery of this basic truth about mankind was in itself not enough. If life must be understood backward it must also (as Kierkegaard rightly contended) be lived forward. One can achieve such a posture by thrusting oneself toward the future, after an initial movement of reflection, so as to create and shape life out of the numerous possibilities offered us in our daily living.

The opportunity to become "engaged" in a more active resistance was not late in coming, for in the summer of 1940 Italy entered the conflict against the Western powers, and shortly afterwards Vittorini joined the Resistance movement. His experiences with the underground sharpened an already acute political sensibility, and his vision became rich in political implications that made his books significant documents as well as polished literary expressions. Out of the war came *Uomini e no* (Men and Non-Men), a terse and highly unorthodox account of a man's struggle to preserve his freedom and dignity; *Il Sempione strizza l'occhio al Frejus* (*The Twilight of the Elephant*), which was inspired by the lamentable standards of living the Italian worker had to endure in the postwar years; and finally, *Le donne di Messina* (The Women of Messina), in which Vittorini attempted to sing in a highly lyrical prose the admirable solidarity displayed by a group of people working together to rebuild life out of chaos and destruction.

As in the case of certain French and American writers, existentialism has been a valuable, if indirect, influence upon Vittorini's literary production in that it has pointed out that meaningful human actions are still possible in to-day's chaotic world, so long as the writers, who are the conscience of their age, urge their readers to cope with those social or political problems that society can no longer afford either to ignore or to underestimate. Most of Vittorini's novels bear witness to the fact that, following Sartre, he believes that the mission of the literary artist is not only to illuminate life and broaden our experience and knowledge of it but to reflect the constant changes registered in his society. To be sure, the multifarious activities in which Vittorini has become involved buttress once more the present argument: in his view no writer can afford to separate life from literature, for one *is* the other; the novel is a product, and hence an experience, of both the imagination and life. It has to be lived, imaginatively and concretely, for only in this way will it enable us, the readers, to "live" the problems of our age.

During the last decade or two, existentialism has gained a particular resonance in the creative arts. Such a development is not unexpected, for existentialism has proved to be an effective world view appropriate to our time. It may be argued that every period in human history contains its share of crises, and that each has been marred by wars, revolutions, social and economic upheavals, and by some kind of general restlessness—all readily recognized as characteristics of the twentieth century. Yet few would deny that in no other historical period has man endured such horrifying and catastrophic experiences of unbelievable magnitude as those of the concentration camps, the atomic bombs, or the possibility of a nuclear holocaust. Never before has mankind faced the prospect of total extermination by hydrogen and atomic weapons. Never before has mankind witnessed the slaughter of millions of innocent victims, burned in the furnaces of Buchenwald and Auschwitz—where man's cruelty reached an unexpected, infernal perfection.

Existentialism, although defined as a philosophy of crisis, arose in times of great experiments and discoveries: Einstein and Fermi, to be sure, but also Freud, Picasso, and Joyce. It has become a way of looking at the world and at man that—however traceable it may be to writers and thinkers of the past—is strikingly modern in its assumptions.

The anxiety generated by the conditions of our era, the

sense of loss, the intense anguish experienced by man—suffering in the concentration camps or fighting a war in which he has no faith—the deep probings of certain issues of contemporary life, these are the dominating themes of much recent Italian fiction. A rapid survey of the novels published since the end of the war would show that the younger writers are obsessed, haunted it seems, by the futility of life and by an awareness that for all man's courage in confronting reality, there results a feeling of absurdity or confusion or indecision that permeates the intellectual climate. The collapse of moral values experienced by many a novelist at a young age has been aggravated by the enormous destruction brought about by the war.

The significance of such a novel as Oreste del Buono's *La parte difficile* (The Difficult Role) is in its effective dramatization of some of the sociopolitical, moral, and intellectual issues faced by the hero, Ulisse. Told in a retrospective manner, the story narrates Ulisse's return from the war, his unhappiness in his family, his love affair first with Giulia, the former mistress of one of his friends, and then with Dora, the wife of Ulisse's own brother, whose return from the war, although announced repeatedly, never takes place in the novel. At the end of the book, Ulisse murders Dora and then tries to take his own life.

The hero bears a striking resemblance to Moravia's Michele (*The Time of Indifference*), to the narrator-hero of Petroni's *Il mondo è una prigione*, and to Natalia Ginzburg's existential heroes, particularly Alberto (*The Dry Heart*). Much like several other characters of contemporary fiction, Ulisse is unable to find any justification for his continuing to play what, deep in his heart, he considers to be a senseless farce. He yearns, of course, for love and political commitment. For a while he thinks he has fallen in love. He joins the Communist Party and is elected leader of one of the cells. Soon enough, however, Ulisse realizes that it is impossible for him to be aroused by his own actions, since they are performed without conviction and sincerity.

It is particularly important to note here that the hero of the novel is himself a writer and an intellectual, and as such he symbolizes to a large extent the typical situation of the Italian intelligentsia in the years immediately following the war. Nothing gives meaning to Ulisse's life: not his love for Giulia, not his infatuation for Dora, not his own work, and much less his political activities. He feels that his life is just like a prison:

> Once, when I was a prisoner of war, another youngster had insisted on reading my fortune. . . . He told me . . . that I would always remain in a prison. At first I was insulted, but then we all laughed, because the prison was what was all around us. But as I thought of that past episode it seemed to me that that youngster had read correctly [into my life]. He had not been speaking of *that* prison, but of *my* prison. A prison that I had succeeded in building for myself, and that has always surrounded me, ever since I was born.

When Giulia tries to pick up the thread of her affair with him, Ulisse confesses that he "experienced a feeling of emptiness in my work. . . . If I tried to write something about my own feelings of solitude, the certitude that I could only be writing for myself would stop me."

Slowly the hero withdraws into the loneliness he despises. Communication with other humans is denied to him, and in vain he seeks affection and sympathy from either his family or his friends. He comes dangerously near total estrangement from the world. No longer capable of bearing the intellectual mediocrity and the emotional isolation to which he feels he has been relegated, he tries to take his own life, and by that act attempts to make clear his total denial of life itself.

The case of Franco Fortini, poet, critic, and novelist, is once again a pertinent illustration of how certain existentialist ideas pervade many postwar Italian novels. His sole work of fiction to date is *Agonia di Natale* (Christmas Anguish), a novelette written alternately in the third person and from the hero's own, more personal and direct, point of view. The typographical arrangement of the two perspectives helps considerably in distinguishing what is told objectively and what is in essence a lyrical narration of the story.

Structurally and thematically the works of Del Buono

and Fortini could hardly be more different. The former tells of a hero who is unhappy and alienated from a world with which he is rapidly cutting his ties; the latter centers on an astutely philosophical characterization of a young man, Giovanni Penna. Del Buono's novel has a well organized, coherent story to tell: everything leads to a final crisis that forms the real climax of the book. Fortini's story, on the other hand, reaches the climactic point not by the conventional method of making one incident illuminate the previous ones and foreshadow the following ones, but by intensifying the chief theme of dread and fear already stated in the opening lines of the novel.

As the book begins, we find Giovanni Penna, a white-collar employee, in the doctor's laboratory. He is told that he is sick, and that he must remain under the constant care of a physician. His disease is never revealed, although he is told (and we with him) that it is entirely possible for one to survive if he disciplines himself to follow exactly the diet and cure prescribed by the doctor. It is, however, inconceivable that he should even consider marriage, since his illness is a communicable one.

Penna decides to visit his fiancée—who lives in a foreign country—and tells her that he is unable to marry her. Upon his return home (after a nightmarish stay at the hotel where his fiancée is temporarily residing), he becomes increasingly more aware of his illness. Disheartened by the prospects before him—by now he has lost his job— he goes to a doctor recommended to him by a prostitute. The doctor has lost his license for political reasons, and lives in the house of the prostitute, a hovel in a squalid section of town. Persuaded at last that Giovanni is not a government investigator, the doctor consents to speak to him about his illness. Not only does he fail to offer any cure but in the course of his conversation with him he makes abundantly clear the fact that mankind as a whole is sick. The only difference between Giovanni and mankind is merely the degree to which they are conscious of their condition. Man, states the doctor, is but a "pilgrim" on earth, and as such he soon tires and understands the "futility of his wanderings." The only encouraging advice he is able to give Giovanni is the following:

No one is certain of his own health, as yet there are healthy people and there are sick ones, there are illnesses that are so-called fatal, but there are no illnesses from which it is impossible to recover. . . . Some people succeed in freeing themselves of their diseases only a few hours before dying. There are some people who pass from sickness to health without becoming aware of it. But in general the others are those who become aware of their recovery.

The author has evidently used Giovanni's mysterious disease to symbolize a sickness that pervades the whole of mankind—thus echoing in more than one way Franz Kafka's existentialist vision of the world. Like Kafka, Fortini leaves many of the details vague. We know neither the milieu in which the story takes place, nor the nature of Penna's illness, nor his occupation. As in Kafka's fiction, we are continuously under the shadow of death and we accompany Penna's slow, unavoidable decay until (as the book ends) he approaches death. Throughout the story we are also reminded not only of the hero's strange malaise, but of the sense of guilt and of the anguish and fear it generates. His perceptivity tells him that he is surely "guilty" of either a crime or a sin committed by himself, by his parents, or perhaps by the world at large. He therefore feels compelled to expiate it, without his ever being fully certain of the nature of the sin.

The work of Natalia Ginzburg and Guglielmo Petroni has been discussed elsewhere in this volume. Along with the fiction of Dino Buzzati, Cesare Pavese, Giuseppe Berto, Arrigo Benedetti, and others, it shows that many novelists have been preoccupied with existentialist themes. On the other hand, it is necessary to add that despite the interest the Italian intellectual has shown in the philosophy, and for all the intelligent discussions and polemics it has provoked, it has not given rise to a purely "existentialist" novel such as those of Sartre or Camus.

The importance of existentialism in the mainstream of Italian fiction is still difficult to pin down and define exactly. The fact that several novelists in Italy have absorbed and integrated existentialist ideas in their work is only indicative that this philosophy is very much a part of the general climate in which we all work and whose influence we can hardly avoid. Perhaps the genuinely important contribution made by existentialism at the creative level is its urgent plea that man reconsider his values, reappraise his predicament, and remember that only through a personal choice, made with a full awareness of its import, will he reach a valid, if lonely, decision as to where he stands and what he "is."

In an age in which science has all but drowned out the arts and threatens to destroy mankind by means of impersonally efficient machines, few would deny that any philosophy that, like existentialism, deals with problems of existence and survival in a world of crises is bound to be particularly influential.

If the novels that have been reaching our shores from Italy in recent years have met with considerable success, no small share of well-deserved acclaim may be attributed to the fact that, aside from their intrinsic merit, they have spoken with eloquence and humanity about the meaning of today's existence. Someday, when we achieve a better perspective of the history of postwar Italian letters, we shall perhaps come to the conclusion that for no small measure of this awareness many Italian novelists owe a distinct debt to existentialism.

# CHAPTER SEVEN

# The New Cinema

The postwar years have witnessed an extraordinary and well-justified interest not only in Italian letters but in Italian cinema. Since Roberto Rossellini's *Open City*, in 1945, Italian films have achieved a position of singular prominence, winning critical praise and several important international awards. Indeed, it has been primarily the Italian cinema that has brought about a much needed re-evaluation and a deeper understanding of Italy and her problems.

A favorite topic of conversation in cultured circles has been for some years the "Italian success story." There is no denying that the attention Italy has received of late can be attributed in part to the films that have been presented to American audiences. In investigating the causes for a complex cultural phenomenon that has turned what might be called the "balance of cultural power" in Italy's favor, the term "neorealism" is heard most insistently; irrespective of the individual views expressed, the term plays a large role. Yet, seldom before in the history of criticism have we been at such a loss to define not only what neorealism purports to be but what it ultimately means within the large frame of contemporary Italian art. Not that definitions have been lacking. Quite the contrary; if anything, we have been drowned in a sea of conflicting reports and interpretations, many entirely plausible and all equally attractive. Every critic has had his say, to the point where the term "neorealism" profusely and loosely used in a variety of contexts has been employed to describe the style of such diverse literary artists as Vittorini or Moravia or the

younger *engagé* novelists, and to indicate the highly polemical sociopolitical themes prevailing in the majority of
postwar cinematic productions. In common practice neorealism, as used in cinematographic criticism, has come to
mean a representation of realistic situations by certain
traditional methods—filming on location, faithful reproduction and study of customs and traditions, historical
accuracy, and so forth. A less vocal group of critics, on the
other hand, has dismissed the whole question of neorealism
by simply treating it as a catchword, a slogan, at best a
kind of useful orientation within which many prominent
Italian artists have readily found their place.

## A Background of Parochialism

There may be a grain of truth in all these contentions.
However, my chief objection is that this sort of reasoning
distorts the problems confronting us. Overemphasizing
the mechanics of neorealism or denying its existence have
gotten us nowhere. Gradually, as we achieve a larger perspective on this question, we begin to see that neorealism
considered as a tool, or a bag full of tricks ranging from
the adoption of local dialects to the use of nonprofessional
actors, is not of great consequence to the artist struggling
to communicate with his public. One does not strait-jacket
a certain theme in a certain form, and more exactly, in the
type of form that has the widest possible popularity in
terms of practical results or box-office receipts. The creative artist intuitively finds *the* style that makes his subject
a living and independent work with a definite relevance
to timeless and universal situations.

In our efforts to pin down the technical peculiarities
of neorealism, we have thus far failed to consider the
problem in a broader manner. As a result, we have over-
looked the fact that its important achievement—publicly
acknowledged by now—has been its focusing attention
(either with words or the camera) on a variety of *real*
Italians, with their aspirations and hopes and anguish, by
moving against a truly Italian background—therefore
substantially, even if unintentionally, contributing to the
formation of a genuine *Italian* cinema.

To be sure, one of the problems we should have grap-
pled with long ago was *why*, in spite of having produced

several significant films, Italy could never claim a truly "Italian cinema." The logical question that should have been asked was, to paraphrase the nineteenth-century critic Ferrini, "*Esiste un cinema italiano?*" In 1875 Ferrini asked precisely this question about the Italian theater, and even without his ever having explicitly stated what he meant by an "Italian theater," it is fair to assume that he visualized it as one drawn from Italian life, written from an essentially Italian viewpoint, and one which, while preserving the local flavor and color, would be equally appealing to people of all walks of life the globe over.

If it is impossible to discuss briefly and then casually dismiss the complex reasons for the nonexistence (to this very day) of an indigenous theater, it may be said that two traditions are generally responsible for the critical state in which the theater (and, for many years, the cinema) have found themselves in Italy.

The first such tradition is one that is deeply embedded in the nation's social conditions, in a religious and philosophical outlook through which the Italian has come to accept things as they are, in a painfully stoical manner. Until recently, there was no "literature of protest," no "beat generation," in Italy. Even today's youngsters prefer to be called "the cheated generation." It may also be that, as Nicola Chiaromonte aptly pointed out a few years ago, "in a deep sense good drama and good farce are always moral ordeals, and simply a certain willingness on the part of the audience to undergo a test of how much truth it can stand; and on the part of the playwright, a certain boldness in going as far as he can in submitting his contemporaries to such a test. It would almost seem as if we moderns were too oppressed by real life, too concerned that our problems be solved in practice, to enjoy having them tested in a purely moral sense on the stage."

The second tradition is more purely a literary one and dates back to Petrarch and the Renaissance—a tradition that has always looked with repugnance upon any attempt to make life an integral part of literature. Even taking into account such writers as Boccaccio, Machiavelli, and Verga, the cleavage between life and literature is a predicament which until recently was never truly alleviated by time.

It is impossible to explain *logically* how the first tradition came into being and became rooted in the very fabric of Italian life. As for the second tradition, it is feasible to speculate that it was made possible by a long record of failures on the practical level of life. It was such failures that prompted the Italians to compensate (with a pride that with time metamorphized into vanity) for their disappointing military and political performance by resorting to an exaggerated glorification of their rich cultural heritage.

As this pride which every Italian instinctively felt for the artistic achievements of his country turned into adulation, it became less and less possible for the artist to work outside his native tradition. In literature, and later in the cinema and many other areas of creativity, few nonconformist or experimental works made their appearance in the first decades of this century. Gradually, as Italian artists gained the conviction that it was both desirable and profitable that they work within the tradition, their work became progressively more rhetorical, falling back on self-imitation and losing whatever urgency it might have had under more normal circumstances. If a poet has the right to depart from tradition, there is not much evidence that many artists elected to exercise this natural privilege. Having refused to express themselves in a unique, personal manner, and unwilling to look elsewhere for ideas that could readily be assimilated in their cultural pattern, their product became not only ultraregionalistic in content but downright parochial in form and scope.

However severe this judgment must seem, it is made here because past failures and our awareness of them can often be used as convenient yardsticks to measure the extent or to predict the probable durability of today's triumphs. Indeed, these preliminaries should make it clear that to a large extent the success Italian artists are enjoying today must perforce imply not only the discovery of a new *maniera* in which to articulate a national condition with universal applications, but also an unburdening of the personality of whatever was conducive to a highly distorted view of life—a calculated rejection, therefore, of certain attitudes and traditions that had long been an intrinsic part of the artists' intellectual and emotional baggage.

## Shackles Old and New

It was generally against the background described that the movie industry came into being in Italy at the beginning of the century. Thus, rather than being accepted as a *new* medium that, unhampered by existing traditions, could start afresh to explore and dramatize in a visual manner feelings, passions, and problems of a country that had at last found its independence, the movie camera was used to exploit, as literature had done and continued to do, a glorious past that, having lost much of its glow, had been turned from a living reality into a shallow myth.

Shortly after producing some insignificant, sentimental movies, the Italian cinema entered a very important phase. The years 1910-19 were, in fact, quite promising. It was in those years that dozens of historical films, many of the "spectacular" variety, were made. And if they attest to the wish to "play up" the greatness of Italian history, it is also true that they represent significant conquests in the new medium of expression. *Nerone*, *The Last Days of Pompei* (1913), *Cabiria* (1913), *Quo Vadis?* (1913), are impressive contributions to the technique of movie making. They also showed how rising production costs inaugurated a new set of economic problems. It was during those years that the cinema stopped being an infant art and began walking, a fact vividly demonstrated by the new flexibility allowed the camera when it was placed on a dolly. Sets and costumes, made on a fantastic scale, were designed with an eye to historical accuracy and realism. The masses were used effectively (for the times, at any rate) to convey the enthusiasm, the anger, the restlessness, dominating them. The important writers of the day (from D'Annunzio to Gozzano, Lucio D'Ambra, and Luciano Zuccoli) joined the bandwagon and signed contracts to prepare scenarios or dialogues for captions. Thanks to its overwhelming initial success, the Italian movie industry achieved a position of leadership in the newly born but still not overcompetitive world of the cinema.

Crises always test the real strength of leadership, and the crisis provoked by the First World War, at first political and then economic, and the ensuing chaos proved eloquently that the leadership of the Italian film industry was only temporary. There were an infinite number of problems that the Italian movie makers, interested less in the cinema as an art than in its attractive earning possibilities, had failed to consider. Their lack of organization, their unwillingness to be inventive, and their weak economic position forced them to take a back seat, with the entrance of the American producers into the world market.

The invention of the sound track caught the Italians, already noticeably behind the new techniques and refinements of the medium, by surprise. Several years had to pass before they could afford, much less master, the new equipment. Thus, while the sound film was revolutionizing the theaters all over the world and while the camera was being used with increasing flexibility to explore in depth the facets of the human sensibility, the situation in Italy reached an impasse. Most of the equipment had been damaged or destroyed during World War I. Raw materials could not be purchased without a stable currency, and credit was not extended to a country that gave every sign of being on the verge of economic and political collapse. The quantity and quality of Italian films experienced a decline which was to stop only in the twenties. Meanwhile, as economic and political unrest plagued the country, American and German movies flooded the nation and were well received by an audience that, after having become conditioned to historical extravaganzas, at last found a new escape in the musical comedies and the Westerns that arrived daily from the United States.

It became clear that it was necessary to start all over again. The process of reorganization and reconstruction made giant strides in the thirties, especially with the opening, in 1935, of Cinecittà Studios, the largest and most modern in Europe. Two years earlier, a new Centro Sperimentale della Cinematografia had been opened. In this center, directed from its inception by Luigi Chiarini, designers, technicians, writers, and actors studied, worked, and discussed in serenity and with enthusiasm the problems of film making, achieving a new understanding of the function of each individual and the part each was to play in the complex project of realizing a film.

It was at that crucial point that the Italian cinema actually could have been rejuvenated by new concepts and imaginative action—had it not been for the fact that a dictator firmly held power. The new order he inaugurated became known through a series of clichés, painted in large white and black letters on the façades of buildings from Piedmont to Sicily: their stern reminders that "Mussolini is always right" left no doubt that a new era had truly begun.

Mussolini, a leader of limited vision, did not grasp immediately the possibilities afforded by the cinema to his regime. When he finally took an interest in the fate of the industry it was not because he was sensitive to any art expression but rather because he decided to demonstrate to a skeptical world the numerical superiority of Italian film makers.

Gradually a new, strange relationship was established between the state and the industry—a relationship based, as is usually the case in totalitarian countries, on favoritism, special interests and concessions, and frequent offers to finance new projects. Credit, of course, was obtainable at a "price," and only those studios that agreed to submit their scripts in advance and to accept suggestions and instructions regarding the cast and the content of the film were given financial support. Eventually the state discovered other ways to "regulate" the industry: it agreed to set up a scale of rebates to be given to those films officially "approved," a scale based not upon the artistic merits of the film but on the success it obtained at the box office. The more successful the picture the higher the rebate, which ranged from twelve per cent to twenty-five per cent of the costs. Clearly such a policy could only encourage the studios to produce only those pictures that pleased the government and were certain to be financially successful. The story by no means ends here: reluctantly at first, but less so as the years passed, the state became the controlling shareholder first of the studios and then of the Banco del Lavoro, whose specialty was film financing, and, finally, of E.N.I.C., the organization that distributed the films and through which *all* movies had to be booked.

The mediocrity of the films produced in those years is, therefore, directly attributable to the continuous interference of the government and to the corruption such interference fostered and encouraged. The best films that could be produced under such circumstances were those that, like *Scipione l'Africano* (made in 1936-7 at the cost of several million lire, an extraordinary sum in those days), exalted a glorious past but were almost completely devoid of any human content; or like *Squadrone bianco, Sentinelle di bronzo,* and *Bengasi* (all three of some artistic merit), which tended to reaffirm faith in Fascist ideals and goals.

By the late thirties the cinema began feeling the stifling impact of censorship. It became first hazardous, then altogether impossible, to deal with suicide, moral or political aberrations, social or religious themes, sabotage, discontentment. Italy, so dictated her bureaucratic bosses, had to be depicted as morally and physically sane, clean, happy. Tourists and diplomats, if at all aware that Italy had been steadily losing her freedom, could derive satisfaction only from the fact that, at last, trains were running on time, the streets were clean, and beggars had disappeared (at least from the prominent tourist landmarks). It was a pleasant sensation, they thought, to be faced everywhere with a picture of order and respectability!

Because the Italian screen writers were neither free nor willing to deal with the raw stuff of life, they became lax and shallow, allowing the cinema to degenerate in the hands of the Fascists into an inefficient and puerile instrument of propaganda. The rest of the world could well be undergoing one crisis after another, but with a few rare exceptions, it is difficult for the student of contemporary Italy to find in the movies produced between 1920 and 1935 a sharp reflection of those crises. In 1934, Count Galeazzo Ciano, then Undersecretary of the Press and Propaganda Office, openly declared in the Senate: "The movie industry must be placed under strict control, and under an even more careful and efficacious vigilance. . . . Action on the part of the state is therefore necessary—the state which alone can discipline, promote, and whenever necessary, create the initiative."

The thirties soon acquired the name of "the period of the white telephones," which, conspicuously ever-present on the sets, had assumed the symbol of a false modernity and of a particular type of comedy characterized by sentimentality and an astonishing absence of human problems.

One of the most typical products of this era was *Una dozzina di rose scarlatte* (A Dozen Red Roses), a film partially redeemed by the pleasant interpretation of Vittorio de Sica, and *Mille lire il mese* (One Thousand Lire per Month), the ideal representation of the mediocrity of ideals allowed to permeate Italian society during the glorious years of fascism.

## Stirrings

Yet the waters were not altogether stagnant: a number of writers, without special allegiance to any particular school, disgusted by the emptiness prevailing in the culture of their day and the rhetoric of its form, began a crucial search for a "style" through which they might express once again some of the problems that had been drowned by the fanfare of official propaganda. In literature this quest led to such disparate results as Alberto Moravia's *Le ambizioni sbagliate* (1935), Corrado Alvaro's *L'uomo è forte* (1938), Romano Bilenchi's *La siccità* (1940), Elio Vittorini's *Conversazione in Sicilia* (1941), and the difficult poetry of the hermetic group (Montale, Luzi, Quasimodo), which produced lyrics charged with strange, obscure images and metaphors that made their "message" hardly comprehensible to anyone without an extensive training in modern poetry.

In search of what was soon termed "the national style," it was almost inevitable that scenario writers and directors should turn to the works of the late 1800's, which more than any other had given a serious, colorful, and intensely human depiction of mores and happenings of a regional character. Critics of literature and cinema began to re-analyze and re-evaluate those styles and contents that had left an indelible imprint upon modern Italian art. As part of this spirit of inquiry of the thirties, a new orientation took place in the cinematic world. Among the factors that gave further impetus to this trend was the publication of *Cinema* (1936) and *Bianco e nero* (1937), two excellent cinematographic reviews, edited respectively by Umberto Barbaro and Luigi Chiarini, which emphasized the need to turn to reality—and not to literature—as a source of scripts. The war in Ethiopia (1935-6) also contributed to a revision of traditional techniques, in that it forced the Italian film directors to work outside the familiar geographical and cultural context that had always been available to them. Working far away from their homeland, forced to use untrained actors and to rely on improvised methods, they were challenged by the possibility of discovering an approach that would give them the opportunity to shed some light upon the life of a strange people long considered barbarians but with a civilization that warranted careful scrutiny.

Through this experience the focus underwent a shift. It was not necessarily the conventional situation of the Italian middle class that needed exploring, but the very nature of man in general and of the Italian in particular. Such a man, living in a given socioeconomic-political milieu, obsessed by certain desires and ambitions, afflicted by peculiar longings, had almost been slighted by Italian film makers. In dramatizing his situation the artist was not to lose sight of the fact that this must be done in such a way as to draw ultimately the moral issues involved in living that particular life, and thus be concerned with the overriding questions of good and evil that are the proper concern of any serious artist. Frivolity, light comedies, superficial situations, seemed to belong to a past that could be no more. A cinema was required that would reflect the seriousness and the grimness of the times.

This general climate made possible such films as Francesco de Robertis' *Uomini sul fondo* (1941), Mario Soldati's *Piccolo mondo antico* (1941), Luchino Visconti's *Ossessione* (1942), and Vittorio de Sica's *I bambini ci guardano* (1943). Far from representing special tendencies —as the titles may indicate—these films are samples of the personal approach adopted by individuals of different background, endowed with different sensibilities, to give form and meaning to their products. Whether they operated within a school that tended toward the documentary style (out of which was to emerge the neorealistic school of the postwar days) or one that held that the cinema must draw its subjects from masterworks of literature, they all tacitly agreed that in cinema, as in poetry, one must explore universal themes. The cinema of the thirties had been shallow and provincial because, with few exceptions, it had restricted itself to Italian life, and the kind of life with the least possible emotional or intellectual appeal to non-Italians. Each one of the mentioned directors brought a new measure of realism to the screen after he became conscious that cinema by being first of all an art of people and facts could contribute to a more complete knowledge of life. What had marred the productions of the thirties was the apparent inability to come to grips with fundamental human motives and emotions. Film makers had placidly been content with describing the outward manifestations of human behavior and had thus created the image of man with no inside. *I bambini ci guardano* was, in this respect, a promising beginning of a new direction in film making. Directed by De Sica, it was carefully thought out and artfully created. It dared to take the traditional triangle situation, and by presenting it from the vantage point of a youngster who lives through the experience of adultery and suffers from it, change a prosaic theme exploited by literature and the cinema alike into a poignant indictment of the moral values of the Italian bourgeoisie. The film also presented a radically "new" De Sica. Ever since his first movie roles in the early thirties, De Sica had unanimously been considered a talented and popular actor. Tall, handsome, simple, and gentle, with a pervasive shyness and kindness, he seemed to embody the best features of the ideal Italian male. A little sentimental and always somewhat ironical, he had fortunately never been cast as a bold, courageous Fascist hero, a part played *ad nauseam* by Amedeo Nazzari and Fosco Giacchetti. His career included several years on the stage, as well as intensive experience as a motion-picture director. Although his first performances as a director were less than distinguished, *I bambini ci guardano* was a real technical and artistic milestone.

Similarly, such films as *Piccolo mondo antico* and *Ossessione* accomplished far more than demonstrating the value of shooting on location. Their achievement consists perhaps in their having vividly and concretely presented, for the first time in many a decade, a slice of the Italian landscape and life—in its misery, brutality, and humanity —that previous film directors had carefully avoided because it was in direct contradiction to the teachings of fascism.

It was only in the summer of 1943 that the various tendencies were brought together and almost incredibly found some sort of unified direction. As the government fell, an editorial published in the review *Cinema* denounced in no uncertain terms the clichés, the grotesquerie, the rhetoric, and the conventionality that had characterized so large a share of Italian movies under fascism. In the latter part of the same year, Luchino Visconti declared, in what was to be a rare autobiographical reminiscence, the reasons for his working with the cinematographic medium: "What brought me to the cinema, first of all, was a need to recount stories of living human beings, of men living in things and not of things themselves. . . . I would shoot a movie of a man standing before a wall, if I could find in so doing the qualities of a true humanity, if it were necessary to put men before simple sets so as to better find them and express them. . . ."

## The Breakthrough

The time was ripe for a reawakening of the national conscience and a re-evaluation of values precariously upheld by fascism. If Italy was ready to seek its place in a continent devastated by a war that had left scars everywhere, then the nation had first to give an indication that it had reached moral maturity. Many works of poetry and fiction had already foreshadowed this reawakening: Montale, Moravia, Vittorini, Pratolini, and several other artists forced to live under the yoke of a dictatorship that had always mistrusted any free, unorthodox expression had depicted in their work what it was like to live a life that, humiliated time and again by violence and moral decay, had lost its dignity.

It is irrelevant to discuss in the present context why Italy was brought into a war when the nation and its people were neither ready to bear its consequences nor believed in its necessity. Suffice it to say, however, that for the young intellectuals (whether they happened to be film directors or creative writers) the war, in the words of Renzo Renzi, "meant, we thought, the fracture of the boredom and the ridiculous conformity of the revolution betrayed by the leaders."

When the war was barely over, the first signs of a

blossoming maturity began appearing as miraculously as the broom flower grows in arid lands. Carlo Levi's *Christ Stopped at Eboli* and Roberto Rossellini's *Open City* made their appearance almost simultaneously. That they belonged to two different genres made little difference. What did matter was that they were the creations of artists who, liberated from a life without freedom, were now ready to express in an eloquent and passionate language how much Italy had suffered in the disorder that had been at the base of an intolerable way of life for twenty "black" years.

With the films and the books that found their way into print, in circumstances that are hard to believe and under difficulties surmounted only through genuine stubbornness and enthusiasm, came a new view of what art in general and cinema in particular could be. In the words of Cesare Zavattini, a scenario writer who has become one of the most articulate spokesmen of the new generation of *cinéastes*, "the true function of the cinema is not to tell fables, and to a true function we must recall it. . . . The cinema must tell a reality as though it were a story: there must be no gap between life and what is on the screen." This poetics, so polemically stated, revolutionized a tradition that had been passively accepted for decades.

With this new conception of the role of cinema came new films and new visions. Italy was being re-explored and reanalyzed with objectivity and lyricism, as were the war and the suffering Italians had endured. The Italian artist learned to confess his fear and his poverty and his wretchedness. He pledged that the economic poverty of his people would never prevent him from exploring the mystery of existence, the social and political injustices, the mistakes of the past and of the present—so as to grow and help others grow. It is not without special meaning that Rossellini declared that his film *Open City* "is the 'film of fear,' of everybody's fear, but mine above all. I too had to hide; I too fled; I too had friends who were captured and killed. My fear was real: a fear that meant my losing thirty-four kilos, perhaps because of my hunger, perhaps because of that same terror I have described in *Open City*."

Rossellini's film marks the beginning of a truly fruitful

period in Italian cinema, a period distinguished by its neorealistic films. The script of *Open City* was hurriedly prepared: the manner in which the film was shot, the continuous interruptions caused by the war and the shortage of raw materials and equipment, and finally the lack of funds are all part of the story of the making of a picture that is almost as fascinating as the final product itself. Rossellini was no newcomer to the cinema: he had held a number of jobs in the industry and had even been encouraged by the Fascists, who never succeeded in buying him out. Rossellini dedicated himself to a search for the spirit that moves man in a period of crisis. In the story of two priests (Don Pappagallo and Don Morsini, joined in the film in the single figure of Don Pietro, masterfully played by Aldo Fabrizi), in their work with the underground and in the untold heroism of the partisans, fighting against the Nazis, he saw a real opportunity to depict, in a human and realistic manner, the pains of his own people as well as man's great spiritual resources and unending courage.

The validity of his masterpiece is to be found less in the astonishing special effects than in the superb manner in which the cast of professional and nonprofessional actors realized their parts. The camera caught the fear and the courage, the hesitation and torment, the corruption and brutality, of Rome under the Nazis in a manner that makes the city and its people live again every time the film is shown. Everywhere in the film—in its photography and in its acting—there is a sense of participation and an integrity that are both rare and extraordinary.

*Open City* is a monument to its director, the cast, the cameraman, and the technicians. The films that followed told with varying amounts of artistic integrity of the trials and tribulations of a nation oppressed but never fully subjugated by the enemy. Like *Open City, Paisà* (with its six unconnected episodes), which delved into the behavior of the American troops who, after invading Sicily, were moving north, gave a new measure of Rossellini's art and his ability to show the manifold problems faced by a people at war. But whereas in *Open City* Rossellini had been concerned with showing the story of a heroic priest and of an obstinate group of partisans, in *Paisà* he displayed his perceptivity unhampered by past restrictions, and showed the meaning of war, the pathos and tragedy of those caught in it. The second episode, in which a drunken Negro soldier, Joe, allows a Neapolitan *scugnizzo* (street urchin) to steal his boots, is typical of man's confrontation with the grim reality of the war. A day later, Joe wakes up, discovers what has taken place, and sets out to find the little boy. Upon finding him he threatens him and follows him to a dark, humid, wretched hovel where the boy, along with dozens of other Neapolitans, has found temporary shelter. In disgust and horror Joe feels deeply ashamed, tremendously shocked and moved by what he has seen.

The war, the great necessity to know each other better, the profound desire to tear off the mask of respectability and comfort that had been imposed upon the people by the Fascist regime, contributed to an atmosphere most propitious to making films that would reflect the agony the nation was undergoing. Alberto Lattuada expressed his views with conviction in these words:

> Our screen is Europe's screen, not to say the world's, and all appraisals must standardize themselves to this concept. This does not mean a renunciation of a clear Italian character, but pursuing the search for a character of such depth as to extract from it a universal interest, which is man's. Much boldness is necessary for this, especially on the producers' part. Are we in rags? Let us show everyone our rags. Are we defeated? Let us meditate upon our disasters. How much do we owe the Mafia? how much to a hypocritical bigotry? Or to conformity, to irresponsibility, to bad upbringing? Let us pay all our debts with a fierce love of honesty, and the world will participate, moved, in this big game with truth. This confession will illuminate our mad secret virtues, our belief in life, our superior Christian fraternal instincts.

The excellent films produced in the years following the war (1944-50) did much to create a new image of Italy. The world responded immediately to the honesty of the new vision by applauding and bestowing prizes on Italian film productions. The international audience understood such realities as the meeting of a soldier with a girl in a liberated town, his falling in love with her to find her, months later, a prostitute, without being aware that she is the same girl (*Paisà*); the man who finds a job only to lose it when his bicycle is stolen from him, a bicycle without which he cannot carry out his assignment (*The Bicycle Thief*); the isolation and pathos of a retired teacher who is about to be evicted from his apartment because he is unable to meet the increase in his rent (*Umberto D.*), along with many other little episodes of common daily Italian life. These episodes were transformed through the magic of De Sica, Zavattini, Rossellini, Visconti, and other able film directors into larger reflections of the boundless sorrow of mankind.

During the postwar years, Italy, through the films and books produced by its artists, conquered the hearts of millions of people everywhere. It was not hard to find in the compassion of its products the reasons for the enthusiasm that greeted every new arrival from abroad. Italy had lost the war—but through the genius of its artists had won the peace. Any men who could bring to the screen or the printed page such poignant syntheses of the anguish experienced by a whole nation were certainly worthy of the respect and admiration people everywhere (and in the United States in particular) felt for their work.

The traits of neorealistic cinema were its complete disregard for the conventions of the medium, the astonishing flexibility of the scenario writers and the directors, the plasticity and the craftsmanship of the professional and the nonprofessional casts. Its artistic goal was to achieve, with the help of the camera now "humanized" by the Italian genius, a fresh understanding of the reality of the new times. The Italian cinema reached its peak when it showed how a defeated nation burdened by numerous past mistakes and by the insoluble problems of the present, tackled and capsulized, with a new approach, pressing timely issues.

Neorealism became then not a school, or an organized movement with an explicit aesthetic or technical program, but a "state of mind" that permitted the film makers to broaden, first of all, the cinema's spiritual horizon and that took definite moral positions with respect to the social, political, and economic issues facing the nation. To realize their vision fully, the directors and scenario writers naturally became inclined to use nonprofessional actors and to shoot on location, often without rehearsals (so as to seize the most spontaneous behavior of human beings) and even without a script. The products were almost invariably genuine expressions of *prises de position*, polemical postures clearly calculated to make the audience aware of present conditions and of the necessity of action. To be sure, such was not always the case: a case in point is that of Federico Fellini, who after several years of training in the movie industry (working particularly under Rossellini) has emerged as one of the most gifted and original directors anywhere. While many of his fellow artists devoted their attention to the problems of the working class, Fellini concentrated at first on the small bourgeoisie, caught in a situation that fostered hopelessness and an unwillingness to participate in the moral regeneration of the nation. Fellini first came into his own in the early fifties with a picture entitled *I vitelloni* (whose connections with Brancati's *Gli anni perduti* has strangely been missed by the critics). The milieu of the movie was a small, provincial city: its heroes were a band of young men living the normal life of such a city, with its petty intrigues, its false illusions, its shabby morality. The disquieting part of the film was the stark depiction of the absence of any goal toward which the young men could work, their absolute lack of direction, their "indifference" toward themselves, their families, and their country. Fellini's subsequent films have shown a partial departure from the provincial milieu of his first films: *La strada,* for example, memorably interpreted by Giulietta Masina, Anthony Quinn, and Richard Basehart, focused on the wretched life of an itinerant circus performer and on his love affair with a waif. But what might well have been a trite story was turned by Fellini into a powerful film, rich with tragic overtones, whose main theme is the solitude of man. Fellini's more recent movie, *La dolce vita,* interpreted by a cast amazing because of its background and resemblance to the role each enacted in the film, was praised and condemned by the critics and even the politicians, who recognized in the portrait of decadence and corruption of Roman upper middle-class and aristocratic society (but, one wonders, is it truly Roman?) a clear reflection of their own miserable corruption. Beginning with the scene of a gigantic Christ being flown by a helicopter to its destination in the Vatican, the story moves through a series of brilliant episodes to its final denouement. The many remarkable features of *La dolce vita* range from the structure of each of the episodes to the poetry of movement and the blocking of scenes that surely must go down in the history of the cinema as among the most perfect ever filmed. In the immorality photographed without concessions to the ordinary tradition, there is something shocking that makes one wonder just how long Western society can survive without recasting its social and moral structure—a situation of despair, one is tempted to say, redeemed only by the final image of the young girl waitress beckoning the journalist-hero back to a purer and simpler and kinder life.

In the early fifties, it was customary to insist that neorealism was associated with the underground movement and with its struggles against the totalitarian governments. Anna Banti, in a penetrating essay entitled "*Neorealismo del cinema italiano*," defended precisely the validity of this thesis. Recent events have substantially contributed to rebutting her contention. Films like *Miracle in Milan, La strada, Umberto D.*, and *Il tetto* are irrefutable indications that old positions have been abandoned for new ones that are richer in social content and more ready to polemicize with official policies. If the cinema of the days immediately following World War II was largely preoccupied, and justly so, with documenting the suffering of Italy, different trends begin to be discerned today. The partisan hero and the soldier are no longer at the center of the stage: their parts have been played, their roles are almost over. If a certain amount of political slant characterized the films of the middle and late forties, the cinema that followed showed that its interest was to provide a testimony of its high degree of critical and moral consciousness by giving a truthful picture of Italian life, which needed more understanding and less apology. The novelist Alberto Moravia once remarked that Italian literature could claim neither a national novel nor a national theater because the people had never applauded or welcomed the healthy notion of self-criticism. Italians, so it seems, were not sufficiently reminded of, or taught to appreciate, the exhortation of the literary historian Francesco de Sanctis. In the final pages of his monumental *History of Italian Literature* (a work still woefully neglected outside of Italy), he wrote: "We must examine ourselves, our customs, our ideas, our prejudices, our qualities, both good and bad. We must convert the modern world into a world of our own, by studying it, assimilating, and capturing it. . . . We live a great deal on the past and on the work of other people. There is no love or labor we can call our own. And from our boasts, one can perceive the awareness we have of our own inferiority." As an antidote, he suggested "an art resharpened in the jargon of the people, closer to nature, an art with more alive passions, immediate impressions, deriving its language not from rules, but from impressions." Painfully and almost regrettably, the Italian artist has begun to understand, in the middle of our century, the wise synthesis of the Neapolitan teacher.

## New Times

Neorealism, as can be seen from today's limited perspective, was perhaps the only way to realize De Sanctis' hope. The new manner of seizing the meaning of reality has produced, among other things, a crisper language, which will undoubtedly survive our times. Neorealism was inducive, too, to forcing the Italian intellectual to reconsider and test in the light of new experiences the validity and meaning of yesterday's values in terms of today. The lesson drawn was that only that which lasts because it is truly close to "reality" is worthy of preservation. Thanks to the new mood, and the understanding achieved after a shattering experience, poets and *cinéastes* alike found the strength to recognize their weaknesses and the fortitude to hope and work—if not for the betterment of society, at least for the fullest realization of man's possibilities. Indeed, among the most memorable events of Italian culture of the postwar years was the fact that the arts were partially freed from the rhetoric by which they had been plagued for centuries.

The picture in the late fifties and early sixties was not as encouraging as one might assume from the present survey. Like all other sides of Italian life—politics, religion, economics—the arts presented to the informed observer their share of paradoxes. In the cinema, for instance, the early auspicious beginnings of the films made in the immediate postwar years have not produced the thorough stylistic and thematic rejuvenation one might have anticipated. Technical improvements (such as a finer handling of color film, a higher quality of sound and photography, a greater precision of details in the sets, and so forth) have, to be sure, enhanced the Italian product. However technical advances cannot compensate for a severe crisis that has gradually become more acute in the Italian film industry. Despite the notable and well-deserved success achieved in the United States by the better imports from Italy, it seems clear (as geographical distance is erased) that even a sustained interest in reality is by itself no longer sufficient as a source of inspiration for many films. It might be argued that the photographic, documentary depiction of the Italian reality, often flat and too faithful in its details, is more than redeemed by the warmth and humanity of its message. True as this may be (and it is upon such "quality" that most American critics have based their evaluation), one wonders whether the time for bolder interpretations of a nation still suffering from medieval social conditions may not be upon us, especially if new techniques are employed. In the case of the cinema one may well repeat a remark made some years ago by the critic Renato Barilli about fiction: Conditioned by what is essentially a conformist milieu, the Italian artist cannot experiment with techniques that are plainly, unreservedly, "subversive, revolutionary, avant-garde." This observation does not take anything away from the impressive achievements of certain recent neorealistic films. One need only recall that Luchino Visconti's *Rocco e i suoi fratelli* (*Rocco and His Brothers*), 1960, is another example of a consummate artistry that revealed itself as early as 1942, with *Ossessione,* and again in 1948, with *La terra trema* (adapted from Giovanni Verga's masterful novel *I Malavoglia*). The fact remains, nevertheless, that the greatness of *Rocco* does not conceal the limitations of an artist who insists in using his product as an *excuse* to investigate important facets of contemporary Italian life, principally the conflict between an agricultural South and an industrial

North, between two different types of humanity holding on fast to different conceptions of life. Through the descriptions of simple facts, which have been charged with a symbolic significance beyond the ordinary, for they take into consideration man's "feelings, the law and the taboo of personal honor," Visconti has dramatized the cruelty of modern society. His films have "exasperated"—as he put it—a real conflict: and such he visualizes to be the artist's function.

Far more interesting, and substantially more obscure, are the films of another director, Michelangelo Antonioni, who has rapidly become one of the most respected artists of the Italian cinema. Although his official entrance in the world of the cinema as a director is barely a decade old, he has behind him a long apprenticeship in the movie lots. His first works were of the documentary sort, and, as he later discovered, the first phase of his artistic creativity was extremely valuable as it enabled him to unburden himself both of technical preoccupations and of an obsession with studying (as is the case in the overwhelming majority of neorealistic films) the rapports of an individual with society. Antonioni's mature period began, in fact, with the decision to investigate less social problems (and thus run the risk of making another film of social protest) than individual problems, that is to say, the psychological, moral, and human problems of an individual vis-à-vis himself. For precisely such a reason, Antonioni's heroes are neither anxious nor interested in identifying themselves with a social class, and much less in defining their relations with it. The two films that embody such attitudes are *L'avventura* (1959) and *La notte*. From the technical point of view, both are distinguished by a superb photography and a sound that recapture not only the reality of their milieux, but their poetry. *L'avventura* may be classified as a sort of detective film with a twist (as in Natalia Ginzburg's *E' stato così*, where at the very beginning we know that there has been a murder and we know the murderer's identity). Initially, in fact, the film focuses on the disappearance of a beautiful girl who has tried, in vain, to extract some meaning out of life through a purely sexual love affair. The element that has caused most objections on the part of the critics, and has inevitably baffled all viewers, is that shortly after the disappearance of the girl (who has gone to one of the islands of Lipari in the company of friends whose corruption she shares), the characters lose all interest in trying to find out what has happened to her. Has she gone back, perhaps on another boat? Has she committed suicide? No one knows, and what is more curious, no one cares, for the event has lost all importance.

The theme of *L'avventura* is the desiccation of feelings to the point that little that happens between two individuals makes much sense. *La notte* develops the same theme in another direction: the problems of communicating with another human being, the necessity (and difficulty) of reciprocal love, the emptiness of contemporary life, are studied from a different perspective. Antonioni develops the action within a twenty-four-hour span and analyzes the anguish of two people whose sexual love is never redeemed by the supreme act of Love. Giovanni and Lidia, the two heroes of *La notte*, repeat the farce of Sandro in *L'avventura*, who after having had an affair with Anna, becomes the lover of her friend Claudia when Anna mysteriously disappears. But Claudia's destiny is to be betrayed in turn by Sandro, whom she discovers making love to a stranger, on the divan of a hotel where a party is being held. Antonioni's films have a definite literary, "intellectual" flavor that makes them surprisingly rewarding: their rhythm follows, in its very unevenness, the "natural disorder of human nature." But Antonioni represents a true exception to the rule; the majority of Italian directors are still obsessed by a persistent need to recall the reality of deplorable social conditions by showing the tragedy of wars, by describing the shocks of those "acts" which symbolically represent the passing from a state of grace to a condition of sin. Such is the case of De Sica's recent films, *Il tetto* (*The Roof*), 1956, and *La Ciociara* (*Two Women*), 1960, from the novel by Alberto Moravia. Thus, a persistent concern with social problems, be they the miserable conditions of the southern peasantry or the delinquency of the new adolescent, remain the exclusive focus of Italian scenario writers.

To attribute the present crisis of Italian cinema to the fact that the first phase of postwar activity may have reached the end would be only a partial explanation. This brief survey could hardly be concluded without pointing out another serious problem that is being fought, day by day, by a small nucleus of intellectuals: censorship. The work of Italian film makers is continuously being harassed by governmental pressures which, in one form or another, are either limiting or suppressing the freedom to which any artist is entitled in a democratic society. In no area of creativity is such a formidable threat being felt as in the movie industry. In a nation still painfully struggling to become modern in every sense, the repeated attempts either to censor or to deny the *nulla osta* (the official permit without which no film may be shown in Italy) are incompatible with the rights of a free society and inconsistent with the repeated promises of fair play, laconically but regularly made by the bureaucrats in the Ministero dello Spettacolo. In the name of decency, honesty, and morality (qualities the Italian government would do well to cultivate in its own garden before preaching to others), any film attacking or questioning the established social order, or conventional morality, is being harassed and frequently delayed from receiving a hearing in the courts, to which it must take its case before it can dispose legally of its particular status.*

Moreover, the economics of the industry are such that some studios have realized that there is no choice between bankruptcy and prosperity other than to remain silent or compromise with "official culture." Finding it difficult to withstand the competition of Hollywood (today no longer as intense as it was before the last war), the studios have opened their doors to American film makers who find it both convenient and ideal to shoot their films in Italy.

One redeeming factor in this picture is the recently published statistics that show that the public in Italy, previously apathetic toward the home product, is applauding the new national productions, though these are often but pale imitations of second-rate American comedies. Here, too, one is forced to realize that the cinema is an-other avenue of escape, an amusement and not only an

---

* A recent example of such ridiculous censorship was provided in 1961 by Autant-Lara's anti-military film, *Do Not Kill,* which Florence's liberal Mayor La Pira ordered shown in one of the venerable *Palazzi* designated as administrative offices.

art. The masses may be excused, temporarily at least, if occasionally they wish to inject a happy note in their dull, gray life by turning their attention to a gay comedy. In the long run, however, the drastic change visible in a situation that had been replete with possibilities is bound to be discouraging, to say the least. Italian cinema has slowly been turned into a medium less interested in encouraging meditation than in amusing. Thus, the original idea of using nonprofessionals has been discarded, and voluptuous females have replaced the ordinary, human faces of "real" people. The Italian nation would find it difficult to recognize itself in the clownish figures of Totò, Peppino, Titina de Filippo, and Macario. The images on the screen have changed considerably over the past years: the rags and hovels of *Paisà* and *Sciuscià* have been replaced by pictures of poor but happy-go-lucky, exuberant characters whose immaturity and frivolity are easily seen through their thin smiles. As times have changed, so have the stars and the criteria for choosing them. If recent films are sufficiently indicative of this trend, we may perceive that the Italian cinema, too, is in a way making the same kinds of mistakes for which Hollywood has already paid its heavy price. Of course there have been exceptions: statistics, however, warn of the dangers ahead. Thus, *Don Camillo,* a humorous, pleasant, but otherwise slight picture, topped all records in 1951 with a gross take of 1,469,000,000 lire, while the neorealistic productions of the same year hardly earned their cost. Since then, the Italian audience has shown greater interest in some of the more spectacular films, and the percentage of gross takes for Italian films has slowly risen, through the years, from a mere 28.4% to 42.03% (as against the current 43.11% earned by American films) of total earnings.

But what, one may ask, of neorealism itself? The leftist critic Giuseppe Ferrara, in his book on the Italian cinema, wrote recently:

> Neorealism meant, in 1945 as it does today, a rediscovery of the human dimension, a revolution where the total transformation of taste and contents did not take place in the internal discourse of culture, of that culture operating on the fringe of history, toward which [Elio] Vittorini had already significantly felt disgust, underscoring its inactu-

ality. Rather, it formulated with great power the regeneration [of society] to the point of going into the very heart of that society from which it had sprung.

Perhaps the time is ripe to consider the past as past and to make full use of its lesson to elevate our standards, our taste, our conceptions of the arts. If that moment should really come (right now it exists in the minds of many a critic as an unfulfilled wish), then we will realize that the mechanics of neorealism may or may not survive. Yet this is relatively unimportant. The question to be considered by tomorrow's observer of the cultural scene will be: has the Italian genius, so rich and so capable of surprising the world, been able to learn to look at reality honestly, and has it learned to view it in such a manner as to give us more than timely insights into its problems and significance? The movies we will view next year, and in the future, will alone help us answer that question.

# CHAPTER EIGHT

# Literary Criticism

The end of fascism and the freedom afforded to the
Italian intellectual by a moderately democratic form of
government has had its salutary effect not only upon creative writing but upon that branch of the cultural activity
which, in the words of T. S. Eliot, is concerned with "the
elucidation of the work of art and the correction of taste"
—namely, criticism. Through intensive contact with the
critical work of Europe and in the United States of the
past thirty of forty years, Italian critics have become informed of those methods which, because of Croce's widespread influence in literary criticism and aesthetics and
the continuous if indirect opposition of fascism, had not
received an adequate chance to be tested and objectively
evaluated. Since the death of Benedetto Croce (1866-
1952), the towering figure of Italian letters during the first
half of the present century, it has been possible to engage
in a realistic and detached consideration of the validity
(the genuine insights and the less tenable positions) of
the aesthetic theories of the Neapolitan thinker.

Only time will tell how effective a role has been played
by the Institute of International Education and the United
States Information Agency. Both organizations have enabled several young and mature scholars from Italy and
the United States to visit each other's nations for extensive
periods, and thus to acquaint themselves with the critical
disciplines practiced in various academic institutions. Moreover, through special grants and indirect subsidies, they
have been instrumental in making available, in Italian,
texts of theoretical and practical criticism, which because

of the language barrier had been inaccessible to the majority of students of literature. As a result, the works of Henry James, T. S. Eliot, Allen Tate, René Wellek, Austin Warren, Edmund Wilson, Erich Auerbach, Alfred Kazin, and numerous other critics have reached a wide audience, receiving at last the consideration they properly deserve.

For some years after the last war, there were few significant changes in the state of criticism. But as we observe the more recent developments of literary criticism, we perceive that the end of the war has meant, for some at least, if not a radical about-face and a clear rejection of the work of Croce, Gentile, and others, certainly an attempt to encourage a "changing of the guard." Croce has been replaced, too hastily perhaps, by Antonio Gramsci, or in the more radical cases by the Hungarian literary historian George Lukács. There is a tendency in contemporary cultural circles to group critics according to their political orientation. The two great classes are the Marxist (large enough to include critics of different personality and positions, such as Carlo Muscetta, Carlo Salinari, Giansiro Ferrata, and others) and the Catholic (subdivided, once again, according to the degree of political liberalism with which each critic is endowed, into various subgroups that include Carlo Bo, Leone Piccioni, Renato Bertacchini, Mario Petrucciani, and others). Between these two particular nuclei it is almost too painfully evident that the former outdistances and overshadows the latter in brilliance, scope, and range.

The Marxist critics show an intelligent awareness of the achievement of Benedetto Croce. But the respect they give the work of the great *maestro* is substantially detached and reserved, as opposed to the generally faithful and affectionate attitude of such scholars as Francesco Flora and the late Luigi Russo, both of whom (in spite of their leftist leanings) have kept political views and literary criticism in their respective places as distinct intellectual attitudes and activities that need not infringe upon each other's domain. The Marxist critics, incidentally, feel particularly proud of their attempt to "historicize" poetry, something they feel was denied to the followers of Croce because of their inherited negative attitude toward most, if not all, modern creative writing.

The limitations of Marxist criticism are too well known to be discussed at length in this context. Anyone even barely acquainted with the positions of a Lukács, for instance, need not be reminded that his view of literature is perforce an essentially narrow and limited one. Creative writing is frequently disparaged when it does not meet certain specifications set up a priori by the Marxists, for whom literature (and all art) must be committed to representing reality understood as a combination of social and economic phenomena according to the poetics of nineteenth-century bourgeois realism.

Lukács in his volume *The Contemporary Meaning of Criticism,* one of his many books to have been translated into Italian, writes:

> The struggle between socialism and capitalism is the fundamental problem of the age we live in. It is therefore obvious that literature and literary theory should also reflect this fact. . . . It is . . . impossible to operate with energy and conviction for the continuation of peace without a firm persuasion that the power of reason can in some way affirm itself in the social reality, that human action, and not merely that of the great masses, but also the decision of the individual, can somehow influence the course of events, etc.

According to Lukács' views, many of the classical authors have been reinterpreted according to the needs of our time—a procedure understandable enough, but as practiced by the Marxists, one that inevitably leads to distortions of the meaning of contemporary or past literature. It is impossible, and indeed rarely desirable, to understand and interpret past authors in the light of contemporary ideologies.

Gramsci, on the other hand, primarily because he lived in a different era, never embraced such a position in the writings collected and published only in the postwar years. His notebooks, filled with absorbing comments on history, literature, politics, and life in general, have proved to be a real treasury of information and insights, and have been widely read and assimilated by liberal critics of recent years. Gramsci did plead for a deep knowledge of the historical context, but only to the extent that it should illuminate the work of art and be in turn illuminated by it. His attitude was more in line with the thinking of the twenties and thirties than with the more orthodox and programmatic thinking of the recent past.

It must not be assumed from what has been said thus far that the political orientation (or rather the politics) of Marxist critics prevents them from producing some astute analyses of literature, especially in the case of those who may be said to belong to the socialist wing of the group (for example, Pier Paolo Pasolini, Angelo Romanò, and Giacomo Debenedetti). Debenedetti himself is perhaps the outstanding example of a refined critic steeped in the culture of his own time. Although his range is vast indeed, in his criticism he has limited himself to considering only modern and contemporary figures. His pages on the Italian classics of the eighteenth and nineteenth centuries, and on Proust, Svevo, and Valéry, are replete with insights and observations that show the author's remarkable intuition. Literature, for Debenedetti, is the occasion to stage a drama in miniature, through which he brings out the meaning of the texts he examines by way of carefully worked out psychological interpretations that bring into the picture names, ideas, and works of every age. He has pursued this method, which is hardly surpassed by other living Italian critics, in his study of Alfieri, Pascoli, Verga, and the more contemporary Albert Camus and Alberto Moravia. His great authors, however, have been three: Proust, Svevo, and Saba. To them he has dedicated his finest pages. It is worthwhile to remember here that Debenedetti also took an active part in the creation of literary reviews in the twenties and thirties. Together with the poet Sergio Solmi and Mario Gromo, he founded the literary review *Primato*, and he was among the first critics to recognize the importance of the poets Eugenio Montale and Umberto Saba, and to introduce them to the reading public.

For the more orthodox specimens of Marxist criticism one must inevitably turn to the pages of two reviews, *La rinascita* (primarily political, edited by Palmiro Togliatti) and *Società*.

A prolific, intelligent, and scholarly exponent of the less reactionary wing of Marxist criticism is (or rather was, since he recanted from his political position in October

1956, after the Hungarian Revolution) Natalino Sapegno (b. 1901), who presently holds the Chair of Italian Literature at the University of Rome. While his most impressive work, from the point of view of completeness and depth, is *Il Trecento* (a literary history of the fourteenth century), the project that has stirred considerable criticism and which is representative of his method is the *Compendio di storia della letteratura italiana,* a well-planned history of Italian literature, published in 1947. There is no denying that Sapegno's political view of culture, about which he had much to say in an essay entitled "Marxism, Culture and Poetry," published in the August 1945 issue of *La rinascita,* makes his interpretation of literary texts inadequate at best and distorted at worst. Literature, in fact, is examined by Sapegno not for its formal significance and as an expression of timeless feelings and universal aspirations, but as a constant mirror of the development of the social consciousness of the masses. For this reason, the author devotes much attention to and is particularly sympathetic toward the regionalistic fiction of the latter part of the nineteenth century as well as the work of the neorealistic school of recent years. As frequently happens with Lukács and the Marxist critics, the "content" of the literary work receives the largest share of consideration and is ultimately the factor that determines whether the final judgment should be a positive or negative one.

It is a matter of common agreement that if contemporary Italian criticism stems from Croce, who dominated the cultural scene for several decades, the revered and beloved master is still, to this very day, Francesco de Sanctis.

De Sanctis was born in 1817 in the vicinity of Naples. Throughout his life, he considered himself a teacher and not a literary theorist or a philosopher of art. Indeed, the better part of his life was spent in the halls and classrooms of the university. His special field was Italian literature, although he also wrote on certain French figures that particularly interested him. The bulk of his writings and lectures (*lezioni*) was published posthumously by his faithful students and admirers, who were perceptive enough to keep a faithful record of his lessons. They have been reprinted numerous times, and as in the case of the

*Storia,* they have long enjoyed much success. Arranged chronologically, they cover the whole span of Italian literature, from the *Dolce stil novo* to the end of the first half of the nineteenth century.

De Sanctis began his career teaching in his own private school in Naples until 1850 when he was given a three-year jail sentence for having taken part in the Neapolitan uprisings of 1848. At the end of his prison term he was exiled, and taught first in Turin (1853-5) and then at the Polytechnic Institute of Zurich, where he was named Professor of Italian in 1856. He returned to Italy in 1860, and after serving briefly as Minister of Education, he returned to teaching as Professor of Comparative Literature at the University of Naples (1871-7). The work for which he is particularly remembered is the *Storia della letteratura italiana,* written between 1868 and 1871. The work is hardly a history in the conventional sense. It is rather a series of essays ranging from the early poets of the Sicilian school to Leopardi and Romanticism. Through an original study of the literary figures, De Sanctis traced the development and manifestation of the Italian genius in its various cultural and historical phases. He interprets the masterpieces of Italian literature as symbols —concretely realized in artistic expressions—of the cultural awareness of a nation. His analyses are written in a warm, direct, unassuming style: he was the first to employ the *tu,* or familiar form of address, with his reader, to convey the sense of intimacy he felt should exist between a critic and his audience. His essays manage to be informative and challenging. At times, as in the case of his study of Petrarch's *Canzoniere,* they amount to fundamental interpretations of texts that have remained unchallenged for decades. Disagree as one may with De Sanctis' method, irritated as one may feel by his small factual errors and by the absence of that biobibliographical apparatus considered essential by contemporary scholars, it is difficult to deny that his *Storia* is a most fundamental contribution to the understanding of the Italian creative spirit and its achievement.

It is strange that our New Critics have shown complete unawareness of De Sanctis (and of Croce, for that matter), for they have more than a number of coincidental points in common. De Sanctis, for instance, was among the first critics to assert the autonomy of art. While he acknowledged that art is created by man endowed with his own religious, ethical, political, and literary views, he felt that it must ultimately be evaluated not for *what* it says but for *how* it says it. De Sanctis firmly declared that art should not be confused with science, philosophy, or religion. Its aim is truth, but truth of a special kind, not of reality, but of the artist's special world (a concept that recurs frequently in his writings). In short, De Sanctis advocated the perfect independence of the work of art from its historical causes and morality. It follows that to create such a work the artist must enjoy the fullest possible freedom. His final product is to be judged on how successfully it re-creates an independent world, a world that has no necessary connection to the world of reality as we know it.

Not a believer in what may loosely be called "comparative criticism" (a concept to be pursued with greater logic and force by Benedetto Croce), nor in the stylistic analyses so ably practiced in our day by the late Erich Auerbach and Leo Spitzer among others, De Sanctis stressed the necessity of considering the literary work purely as an artistic experience. He thus denied the validity of studying the antecedents of poetic creation, since he was of the opinion (later rejected by the Freudian critics) that no study of sources or influences and much less of the artist's private life could reveal the secret of his creation or help us understand it more intimately. De Sanctis was, of course, ready to acknowledge the need for historical, linguistic, philosophical, and literary preparation, as necessary prerequisites to the final total act of critical evaluation and synthesis. He was not persuaded, however, that any of these approaches should ever be allowed to be practiced at the expense of what soon became formalized in the academies as "the aesthetic method." The critic, much like the poet, must be born for his task, and to be worthy of the name, must strive to communicate with his audience at a highly intelligent level in a clear and understandable language. "Criticism," he proclaimed, "is to the work of art what philosophy is to the work of nature." The only relevant method to assess literature is on the basis of its form, understood as the personal (and therefore, unique) way in which the artist expresses his vision of the world.

As for criticism itself, again De Sanctis' ideas are not too alien to those held by the recent critics. For instance, his claim that the critic must surrender himself to impressions and submit himself to the work itself is close enough to T. S. Eliot's precept of "suspension of disbelief." De Sanctis pleaded for a more thorough knowledge of the poetic text, which alone could make possible a more thorough understanding of the poetic world of the artist. The final act of assessment could take place only then: it is important to remember here that De Sanctis' primary concern was to seize "the intrinsic value of a work." He was interested in the supreme individuality of that work, and not at all in whatever it might have in common "with the times, a school, and with its predecessors."

His method made it imperative that the critic identify himself closely with the work of art, to the point that he could define criticism as "the conscience or the eye of poetry." As for art itself, he never admitted that it could be anything else but "alive or dead; there is the poet or the non-poet, the eunuch brain." (Once again, this concept was to be taken up and expanded by Croce, in his argument for *poesia* and *non poesia*.)

De Sanctis' many shortcomings were readily recognized even by his faithful disciples. He was at times factually imprecise and given to impressionistic and psychological interpretations. His adversaries disparaged his failure to engage in "purer" research. They complained that he had never collated manuscripts, that he treated all too briefly the lesser figures of Italian literature, and that he seldom gave just prominence to methods of critical activity other than his own. A recent scholar, Dr. E. H. Wilkins, remarked that "its [viz., *Storia's*] verdicts, explicit or implicit, are not always just; its generalizations are not all acceptable." Some have raised objections on other grounds: De Sanctis' style is too ornate, to effusive, too "personal," repetitious, and highly involved. "The neglect of De Sanctis," wrote Professor Wellek recently, "must be due to the real difficulties of his position, the ambiguities of his terminology, the very complexity of his thought." He added, however, that "his achievement is . . . unique and great." All critics would, I believe, share that judgment. However opposed they may be to his method or interpretation or approach to literature, they have repeatedly paid tribute to his stature and his intelligence by assimilating a large share of his critical insights.

The death of De Sanctis, in 1883, coincided with a sharp turn in the general direction of literary criticism—a turn paralleled in France by the rise of a group whose main exponents were Taine and Brunetière and whose theoretical and philosophical views brought criticism dangerously close to a sterile pseudo science. In Italy the activity of such respected scholars as Giosuè Carducci (1835-1907), Pio Rajna (1847-1930), Alessandro d'Ancona (1835-1914), and Rodolfo Renier (1857-1915) was guided by new concepts. Facts, sources, influences, biographical studies—the very areas De Sanctis had pronounced secondary at best in the evaluation of literature —became so important that they overshadowed the fact of creation itself. Their contribution must not be minimized, for they were responsible, along with the many scholars that may be grouped under the heading of "the erudite-historical school" (the method they followed was the "historical") for producing an impressive number of excellent critical editions of literary texts of antiquity and the classical age. They centered around the widely respected *Giornale storico della letteratura italiana*, founded in 1883 and still in existence; their most typical and representative work was Rajna's *Le fonti dell' Orlando Furioso* (1876). It was only with the publication of Benedetto Croce's *Estetica*, in 1900, that a new synthesis of the various methods, tendencies, and aesthetic theories was achieved. And it is with Croce that a new period of critical activity begins in Italy.

Benedetto Croce was born in 1866 in a small town in the Abruzzi region. He began his intellectual activity by writing on Marx. Throughout his life he was to move from history to philosophy to aesthetics to literary criticism. He studied intensely Vico and Hegel, Kant and De Sanctis, of whose work he became the best disciple and the ideal

continuator. His brilliant edition of De Sanctis' *Storia* and
other works was responsible for bringing the Neapolitan
critic to the attention of young and old alike, and by the
power of his own intellect, added more prestige to a
critic who had suffered considerable neglect after his
death. Needless to say, many were the ideas Croce felt
he shared completely with De Sanctis. With him, he
firmly believed in the autonomy of art, in the concept of
form and content, and in the need for the critic to identify
himself with the work of art. Croce, however, used
De Sanctis' concepts to build a far larger, more intricate
and coherent edifice of aesthetics. It is important at this
point to remember that Croce's position was determined in
its first stage by polemical reasons. He wrote out of a
reaction against the positivistic tendencies of the latter part
of the nineteenth century, directing his attacks against that
group of academic critics who treated literature as a gal-
lery of ghosts, to be taken apart, with method and care to
be sure, but without ever striving to answer the basic question of its worth. Personal circumstances, in addition to an
immense intelligence, enabled Croce to prevail over his
critics and to maintain a strategic position of detachment
and independence. He was a man of means and never felt
either the need or the desire to become directly involved
with teaching or with the daily demands of scholarship,
although he himself produced some of the truly scholarly
contributions in his special fields of interest. He was further
successful in controlling his own writing and preserving
his views with the maximum freedom by having his essays
and books published either by a review he had helped
found (*La critica,* 1903-44) or by the publishing concern
Laterza of Bari, of which he was an important shareholder.

Croce's major contribution to literary criticism was his
definition of poetry, which for him was "neither feeling,
nor image, nor even the sum of the two, but 'the contemplation of feeling' or 'lyrical intuition' or (which is the same
thing) 'pure intuition'—pure, that is, of all historical and
critical references to reality or unreality of the images of
which it is woven, and apprehending the pure throb of
life in its actuality." He thus proceeded to identify intuition
and expression as parts of the same process.

His concepts owe a good deal to De Sanctis, and he

never forgot to acknowledge this debt to him. But he was aware that De Sanctis had not given a formal unity and order to his thought, something which he himself proceeded to do. He published his views on aesthetics in the long and fundamental article in the *Encyclopædia Britannica* (14th ed., pp. 263-72), expanding them in later works. For a more complete statement, one should read his volume *The Essence of Aesthetics*. In his article in the *Encyclopædia,* Croce progressed from one point to the next by a process of elimination: *Art,* he wrote, *is not philosophy* ("because philosophy is the logical thinking of universal categories of being and art is the unreflective intuition of being"); *nor is it history* ("because history implies the critical distinction between reality and unreality: the reality of the fact and the reality of fancied world: the reality of action and the reality of desire"); *nor is it natural science* (which is "historical fact classified and so made abstract"); *nor is it the play of fancy* (which "passes from image to image, in search of variety, rest or diversion, seeking to amuse itself with the likenesses of things that give pleasure"); *nor is it Feeling in Its Immediacy* (for feelings "in their immediacy are 'expressed' "); *nor is it instruction or oratory.* Finally, art must not be "confused with other forms directed to the production of certain effects, whether they consist in pleasure, enjoyment or utility, or in goodness and righteousness."

Like De Sanctis, Croce was not taken seriously in the United States, even though his work was translated and widely commented upon. In recent years, however, through the efforts of several scholars, his views have been reexamined in the light of the contribution of the New Critics. It is largely inconsequential to pursue, at this point, the question of whether Croce's thought in any way exerted an impact upon the younger critics, all of whom are in agreement in recognizing the "impractical" nature of poetry, and all of whom (from T. S. Eliot to Allen Tate, Cleanth Brooks, John Crowe Ransom) have underscored the autonomy of art. There is, I dare say, universal agreement with Tate's words that poetry "is neither the world of verifiable science nor a projection of ourselves." Recently Lienhard Bergel, in his essay "Croce as a Critic of Goethe," has stressed the validity of Croce's effort to show how the critic's function is to "separate in each work the 'poetic' from the 'practical.'"

Croce did not stop at theory: indeed, for several decades he was engaged in an intensive examination of Italian and other European major and minor writers. He authored a history of Italian literature (writing it in what he believed the only way possible: a series of essays devoted to single figures). He published the first four volumes before the end of the First World War and the last two in the early thirties, thus contributing unintentionally to a disturbing disunity of tone. Sentimental reasons often compelled him to revise and recast some of his negative judgments (as in the case of Fogazzaro, for instance) and to make them less biting. On the whole, however, his evaluations of modern and contemporary texts have not been accepted by the vast majority of his critics, who have repeatedly complained of Croce's basic unreceptive views (or even misunderstanding) of modern art. The negativeness of Croce's assessments are perhaps traceable to certain demands he made on the authors he studied: he found Giacomo Leopardi wanting, for instance, because of his philosophical inconsistencies; he rejected parts of Manzoni's *I promessi sposi* because of its realism; and he refused to recognize the worth of the symbolist and decadent poets. In the case of Dante (on whom he wrote a controversial book, *La poesia di Dante*, in 1921), he was guilty of leaving the reader with the impression that he wished to separate the lyrical parts of the *Comedy* from the intellectual (or theological, philosophical, historical, etc.) parts. Recent critics have accused Croce of performing an "anthologizing surgery" and of having failed to stress the unity of Dante's poetic inspiration throughout the poem.

As for the function of criticism, Croce never formally discussed or suggested a methodology, although he made it explicitly clear that a critic ought to be concerned with singling out the individuality of a work of art, which invariably meant to separate what is true intuition (poetry) from that which has not been molded by the poet into a concrete, living, autonomous image (non-poetry), a concept that led him to title one of his works *Poesia e non poesia*.

While Croce held that a knowledge of history (in its

broadest meaning) was essential to an understanding of a work and to what he termed "the aesthetic judgment of the art of that time," he also felt that the individuality of each work of art made impossible a study of a genre, a school, a theme, and thus he denied the possibility of literary history. He himself demonstrated by his writings that the only acceptable way to study poetry was the monographic one, a possibility that he extended to all other arts, since for him the arts had an indestructible unity. Lastly, he felt that once the critic had reached the point of recognizing the work of art his mission was accomplished, since he could say nothing about beauty.

It has been observed often before that Croce could put into practice many of his postulates because of his extraordinary erudition, his philological and philosophical *rigueur* and range. Others who followed in his footsteps did not always (indeed, only rarely) succeed in maintaining the proper balance between theory and practice. The negative part of Croce's role in literary criticism in Italy was that he created, through his authoritative positions, dogmatic assertions that went unchallenged for decades. As has recently been pointed out, Croce's teachings did much to bring about a way of approaching poetry that was partial, in that it forced the critic to divide carefully poetry from the non-poetry (as in Flora's criticism), thus taking rigid positions more and more remote from the texts examined. No critic in Italy has escaped his influence, even those who found themselves in direct opposition with him. It remains to be seen whether his theories will be expanded and modified further by his disciples.

During Croce's time there were several other critics who, though they began under the direct influence of Croce's theories, soon abandoned these and pursued their own direction. Giuseppe Antonio Borgese (1882-1952), fiery and articulate essayist and novelist (*Rubè*), began his career as a critic by writing a work that won the praise of Benedetto Croce, *Storia della critica romantica* (A History of Romantic Criticism). Distracted by other interests, he turned to militant criticism and for several years wrote for the daily *Il corriere della sera*. It was his merit to discover two of the most fascinating and important novelists of this century, Federigo Tozzi and Alberto Moravia.

Renato Serra (1884-1915) was a militant and sympathetic critic of contemporary literature (*Le lettere*). His premature death at the front lines cut short a brilliant and promising career: in the opinion of many he was the one critic whom all those opposed to Croce could have rallied. Although he did not bring to criticism many innovations, he tried to reconcile the scholarship of Giosué Carducci with a more adequate understanding of contemporary writing. In spite of his age Serra inspired and indirectly influenced several of his contemporaries. Giuseppe de Robertis, Emilio Cecchi, and the late Pietro Pancrazi continued, in their own way and with different emphasis and intensity, the *rapprochement* of the critic with the literary text promulgated by Serra.

Giuseppe de Robertis (b. 1888) began his critical activity during the years immediately prior to the First World War, first as a contributor and later as the editor of the Florentine magazine *La Voce*. Spiritually, culturally, and intellectually akin to Renato Serra, he was led by his unshakable faith in the written word to a meticulous aesthetic method of textual analysis. He tends to study with infinite care the development of the artist through a subtle study of his variants. (It is important to bear in mind here that De Robertis has devoted his attention primarily to texts of poetry, not fiction.) Not a founder of a "new" method of literary criticism, De Robertis is the one critic who has made of a felicitous advice (*Saper leggere*, to learn to read sensitively), which states the fundamental condition required for a better understanding of literature. Through his technique he has been instrumental in bringing about a more refined awareness of the harmony and power as well as the beauty and nuance of poetry.

His sustained criticism was for many years confined to a detailed study of the moderns: his book on Leopardi, his essays on Foscolo and Manzoni, represent the limitations as well as the achievements of his approach. His *Saggio sul Leopardi* (originally printed in 1922 but subsequently enlarged and brought up-to-date) seeks to follow the artistic growth of the poet from Recanati by means of a methodical examination of the numerous drafts left by the poet, which are *exempla* of a work in progress to be studied and evaluated in its final form. Throughout his study, De Robertis assiduously makes sparse use of extra-artistic data (history, biography, and so forth) to clear the ground for a concentration on the expression itself. He has also predicated a study of certain works by a writer whenever they appear to be fundamental in the poetic or in the formation of an artistic conscience. The work of art always is examined internally, without direct reference to external events.

Gianfranco Contini (b. 1900), together with Carlo Bo and Oreste Macrí, has long been identified with the school of hermetic criticism (roughly paralleling, if only chronologically, the hermetic poetry of the thirties and forties). This group has been strongly influenced by Gide, Valéry, Du Bos, and other brilliant unorthodox French critics and writers. Their method—and here it is best to speak of Contini in particular—calls for a thorough philological and philosophical preparation. The critic's attention is given to such problems of structure and diction that present themselves during an attentive reading of the work. His particular approach has been best demonstrated in detailed essay-type papers. Because, as Contini writes, "every critical problem is a problem of knowledge," he makes few concessions to psychological or historical interpretations. The only unfortunate side to his, and hermetic criticism in general, is a tendency to make consistent use of a private critical jargon that obfuscates, rather than clarifies, the problems and issues. It presents the temptation to be brilliant for its own sake.

There is, however, no dearth of critics in Italy who consistently communicate with their readers at a high level. Two outstanding examples are Luigi Russo (1892-1961) and Francesco Flora (b. 1891), both disciples of Benedetto Croce. Luigi Russo was until his recent death an indefatigable commentator of his own literature. His most solid work is his book on Giovanni Verga (originally published in 1919 but greatly expanded and revised in five subsequent editions). He has also studied Neapolitan culture and the work of Salvatore di Giacomo, Machiavelli, De Sanctis and critical trends. His three-volume *Storia della critica contemporanea* (History of Contemporary [Italian]

Criticism), published in various installments between 1935 and 1942, covers from Carducci to the contemporaries and is to this date the only work that attempts to give a comprehensive picture of critical theories and trends in modern Italy. Unfortunately, Russo's history lacks the precision and scholarship of Wellek's *History of Criticism* or the incisiveness of Wimsatt's and Brooks' *Literary Criticism*. One of its most disturbing flaws is its highly polemic tone.

Although a follower of Croce, Russo did not miss the opportunity to show his independence from the *maestro* by his refusal to accept the clear-cut concept of poetry and non-poetry. He devoted a large part of his literary criticism to intensive analyses of the relations between poetry and poetics, the latter considered as the element that establishes a real link between one writer and another. Moreover—and this is what probably distinguished Russo's critical personality—the structure of a work of art is identified with the author's poetic. "The ingenuity of art (and ingenuity is certainly its main character) cannot be an ingenuity of nature, but an ingenuity of conquest. Art is not born, but becomes ingenuous . . . through an increasingly more attentive purification and sublimation of culture."

Francesco Flora, brilliant historian of Italian literature, is a critic whose ornate, involved style may prove to be an irritating reading experience to the Anglo-Saxon audience. He has studied the modern and contemporary periods, and his first important work was *Dal Romanticismo al Futurismo* (From Romanticism to Futurism), published in 1921. He has also authored the controversial study of hermetic poetry (1936) to which reference has been made several times in the previous chapters. After completing a solid, five-volume *Storia della Letteratura italiana* (History of Italian Literature), he undertook to examine in detail the work of contemporary novelists and poets (Montale, Pratolini, Moravia, et al.), collecting his essays in the volume *Scrittori italiani còntemporanei* (1952).

Certainly the work that best illustrates the method of Flora is his *Storia*, which clearly shows the range of the author's interests (unlike Croce, Flora makes ample use of his knowledge of music, the visual arts, as well as philosophy in his evaluations of literary artists) and his ability to choose the significant passages that serve to illustrate his discussions.

While Flora and Russo work within a fairly well-defined Croce orbit, there is still another group who, while aware of Croce's presence, recognize as their masters Carducci and Barbi and consequently belong more properly to the philological school of criticism. Under their guidance, criticism has made some solid contributions to knowledge. Neither Giuseppe Billanovich nor Raffaele Spongano nor Vittorio Branca considers pure erudition the ultimate goal of their activity. Although their research stresses the factual, scientific examination of the work of art and its total milieu, they fix their attention on the verbal structure of the work and on its relation with its time. Typical of this approach is Branca's volume on Boccaccio (*Boccaccio medievale*, 1956), in which the author of the *Decameron* is definitely "frozen" in the frame of medieval culture.

Still another group of "university critics" (it should be noted that the overwhelming majority of critics identify themselves with a center of higher learning) includes Mario Praz, certainly the outstanding student of English literature in Italy, Mario Fubini, and others. Some, notably Praz, have refuted Croce's aesthetics and many of his concepts, for instance, the impossibility of writing literary history. Mario Praz (b. 1896), aside from having written extensively on English and European letters and having produced autobiographical works of great merit (*La casa della fama*, 1959), also authored a very original book *La carne, la morte e il diavolo nella letteratura romantica* (translated as *The Romantic Agony*). This volume is a classical study of European decadence examined through the novels and poetry of dozens of writers, whose erotic sensibilities are minutely explored. More recently, Praz has studied the Victorian hero (*The Hero in Eclipse in Victorian Fiction*) and has collected his essays on Anglo-Italian cultural relations in *The Flaming Heart*.

Mario Fubini (b. 1900) is recognized today as one of the most brilliant and penetrating critics and literary theorists. Much of his work has been devoted to clarifying, extending, and re-evaluating some of the concepts of Croce, with the view in mind of refining them but also opening new horizons in recent critical conquests. Thus, for example, Fubini has reopened a debate on the question of stylistic criticism (rejected a priori by the Neapolitan philosopher); and on the relation between certain cultural currents and problems of creative writing, asking whether there should be a conflict between criticism founded on philology and criticism based on interpretation. Fubini has expanded Croce's concept of the "uselessness" of poetry by showing its "disinterested" character. He then proceeds to divide artistic creation into three groups: poetry (corresponding to Croce's lyrical intuition), fragmentary poetry (or poetry disturbed by the unchecked passions of the poet), and literature, a rather large but more amorphous activity the purpose and aim of which are altogether different from those of poetry.

Militant criticism has traditionally been widely and expertly practiced in Italy through the help of what is still an institution *sui generis,* the *terza pagina* (or cultural page) in which practically every newspaper publishes short stories, essays, criticism, reviews, and occasional scholarly notes that may be of interest to the general reader.

Perhaps one of the finest representatives of this particular group was Pietro Pancrazi (1893-1952). He was an urbane, well-read, tolerant, and sympathetic humanist, who for many years kept the public informed of the creative achievements of Italian writers. His writings, collected in six volumes entitled *Scrittori d'Italia* (Italian Writers, published 1946-53) afford one of the most comprehensive panoramas of Italian fiction and poetry "in the making"—since the individual pieces were written originally as book reviews. Pancrazi's prose succeeds in being literate and intelligent without ever being overbearing or pretentious. His insights have resisted the test of time, and even today their acumen is bound to strike the reader. Decisively middlebrow in taste, Pancrazi succeeded in explaining to the layman some of the complex hermetic texts of the thirties. His method is reminiscent of Sainte-Beuve's, and one of his gifts was his ability to show the writer at work, the artist himself illuminating the work he has created and in turn being illuminated by it.

Another well-known "third-page" critic is Emilio Cecchi (b. 1884), who began his literary career as critic of English literature. Extremely cultivated and sophisticated,

Cecchi is an art critic, a historian of literature, a translator, and a scenario writer. He is also remembered (and rightly so) for his brilliant essays and for the part he played in the Roman magazine *La Ronda,* in its efforts to create and cultivate a classical prose through its frequent "calls to order." Possessing a subtler, more complex, and richer mind than Pancrazi, Cecchi emphasizes the autobiographical element in a work of art, the psychology of the artist and the quality of his style.

Enrico Falqui (b. 1902) is the most prolific of the purely journalistic critics, and he has never been associated with any academic institution. (Cecchi was invited to the United States in the thirties, and was a guest lecturer at the University of California at Berkeley.) He is by far the most inveterate believer in the worth of contemporary literature, to which he devotes all his time. He reviews fiction regularly in the Roman newspaper *Il Tempo* and in the cultural biweekly *La Fiera Letteraria.* He is also one of the few students of Italian literature to have attempted to compile a critical bibliography of Italian studies. As for his method, Falqui has been relying more and more on skillful interpolation of comments by other critics and writers to support his theses or to dramatize the lack of agreement on specific literary problems. Often, his books are not original works as such but mosaics of a strange and interesting sort. Not always easy to read, since they are replete with quotations and references, such articles and books are not truly indicative of Falqui's real gifts which are, more properly, those of a well-informed, enthusiastic, and competent popularizer.

# CHAPTER NINE

# The Reviews

In his book *La coltura italiana*, published in 1923, Giuseppe Prezzolini writes a series of letters to an imaginary friend, in which he categorizes Italian magazines as follows: "Italian reviews could be divided into three groups . . . those that thrive, those that are successful and those that count." This statement is appropriate even today, and its chief merit seems to be its applicability to practically any Western nation, irrespective of geographical or cultural differences.

In Italy, the reviews that have "survived" the times are those that, like the *Nuova Antologia* (1866) and *L'illustrazione italiana*, have a vast appeal and address themselves to an educated but essentially conservative middle-class audience. They are the staple reading of doctors, lawyers, and other professional people, in whose waiting rooms they are certain to be found. The reviews that really "count," on the other hand, are read faithfully by a cultural elite that believes passionately in them because they offer a more varied and attractive fare and are, by virtue of their ideas, far more stimulating than the ordinary, run-of-the-mill periodicals. In this country, the publications that correspond to this general description are known as the "little magazines."

An understanding of the currents and cross-currents, the personalities and achievements, of contemporary Italian letters can hardly be achieved without a brief description and analysis of the reviews published in Italy during the first half of this century.

A thorough study completed in 1946 by Messrs. Hoffman, Allen, and Ulrich discusses in detail, in an exemplary scholarly manner, the scope, the nature, and the influence exerted by the little magazines on American literature. The editors of *The Little Magazines* found that these publications "have stood, from 1912 to the present, defiantly in the front ranks of the battle for a mature literature." Many of them "have sought persistently to discover good artists, or to promote the early works of talented innovators. They have frequently published, for the first time, writers and poets of eventual distinction and fame, as Sherwood Anderson, T. S. Eliot, Hemingway, Faulkner. Furthermore, they have introduced and sponsored every noteworthy literary movement or school that has made its appearance in America during the past thirty years." Written by small nuclei of talented, original novelists and critics anxious to inject new blood into the arteries of their culture, the little magazines have usually addressed themselves to an extremely limited audience—hence the reason for the qualification "little." Finally, these reviews "usually came into being for the purpose of attacking conventional modes of expression and of bringing into the open new and unorthodox literary methods and practices."

The importance of the reviews has long been recognized and acknowledged by Italian literary historians. Natalino Sapegno, for example, in his survey of contemporary Italian letters, writes: "In spite of the scarce clarity of the ideological orientations and the intentional avant-gardism that all too frequently hides the absence of a revolutionary content, it may be said that, taken as a whole, these reviews have exercised a useful and progressive function in the history of twentieth-century Italian literature."

Although there is still no comprehensive, up-to-date study of Italian magazines comparable to the one by Hoffman et al., one or two volumes and several essays studying the positive contribution of such periodicals have appeared in recent years. Between 1958 and 1961, several excellent anthologies of writings originally published in the reviews were brought out. In 1960, an intelligent commentator of the Italian scene, writing in the *Italian Quarterly*, remarked: "It is in these literary magazines that the new movements are christened, new problems formulated, new writers introduced to the public. They, more than any other kind of publication, reveal the state of literature at any given moment, give expression to the dissatisfaction and uncertainties of writers and critics, and present their hopes and suggestions for the future. No one interested in the mechanics that guide literary movements in Italy can afford to pass them by."

Even on the surface, there would seem to be more than a casual similarity between the American and the Italian reviews. In both countries, for instance, such publications experienced their richest and most fruitful period during approximately the same years, 1910-40. In both instances there seems to be a similar explanation for the phenomenal rise and success of the little magazines—an explanation connected with a new awareness of contemporary creative writing and an intense desire to participate more actively in the artistic life of the Western world. One of the chief functions of the little magazines has been to re-examine their respective cultures against the background of the needs and values of the new times. Similarly, they have committed themselves to an urbane, civilized, and highly intelligent position with regard to international culture and politics. Through them, the literary and artistic achievement of other nations have become better understood and, as a result, properly evaluated and appreciated.

The parallel between the American little magazines and the Italian reviews, tempting as it may be, must not be carried too far. However similar they may seem and indeed are in many respects, they are the products of different sensibilities and milieux. Qualitatively, the Italian reviews have mantained unusually high standards, and have been almost invariably quite serious in their approach to their topics. Quantitatively, they do not come anywhere near the staggering figure of more than six hundred magazines reportedly published in English since 1912. (Hermet, the official historian of the reviews in Italy, lists roughly two hundred such publications as having come into existence during the same period.) Although the majority of prominent writers were first published in the *riviste* (Silone and Pavese being conspicuous exceptions), the Italian publications have constantly been given more to bringing out criticism and philosophical and political essays, rather than creative writing. Their editors have invariably been men of sophistication and intelligence who have given to their publications the clear sense of direction and purpose often absent in American magazines. Moreover, in addition to their being not quite as kind to creative writing as they might have been, they have never been prone (except in the futuristic or similarly "committed" reviews) to allow their reviews to be a testing ground for experiments. Although even today most of the literary magazines devote some pages to poetry and fiction, it is rare to find a review which, like the now-defunct *Botteghe oscure,* publishes exclusively creative writing. Finally, the Italian reviews have invariably been, however indirectly, the expression of a cultural *and* political point of view. In the best cases (as in *Nuovi Argomenti* and *Tempo presente* of recent years) they are the articulate spokesmen of radical positions; in the worst cases they may be expressions of either the "official" culture, orthodox, sterile, ultraconservative, or, as in the case of the serious *La critica* (edited by the late Benedetto Croce) organs of the aesthetics of a single person or a school and therefore frequently unfriendly toward new ideas or theories of literature.

It is not always clear what it is that attracts the writer to the literary reviews. In the case of the prosperous dailies or the rotogravure magazines (which have become increasingly popular in Italy since the end of the last war), the prime factor that induces writers to publish their work in that format is of course an economic one. Since few writers (and fewer teachers) can live off their royalties or stipends, it is only natural that they should seek in the wealthy periodicals a badly needed source of extra income. It is not surprising, therefore, to find that such prominent university professors as Natalino Sapegno and Gianfranco Contini also play the role of militant critics. The same holds true for several writers of distinction: Moravia, Pratolini, Quasimodo, and Montale, to mention a few names, hold positions either as editors of the literary page, or as cinema and theater critics in one of the newspapers or weeklies. Those who edit or contribute to the little magazines, on the other hand, do so out of a profound belief in their effectiveness and vitality and not for financial remuneration. They value, in short, their importance in the creative life of the nation.

When contrasted with the pieces published in the more commercial publications, the material that appears in the little magazines is bound to strike the reader as far more brilliant and coherent, certainly destined to have more than a passing importance—an assumption supported by the yearly appearance of anthologies of writing previously published in the reviews.

The greater number of the reviews published in Italy from just before the First World War to the thirties appeared in Florence, the cultural capital of the nation. It is interesting to note that, as Rome became the focal point for artists and writers, the reviews, too, followed the trend and moved from Florence to the capital.

In the period between the two wars, several dozen reviews appeared. Many of them survived only a few issues; some lasted a full decade (like *Il Frontespizio,* 1929-38). More commonly, they disbanded after a relatively short period of publication, usually four to six years. As in the case of the American little magazines, financial difficulties, but more often quarrels and misunderstandings among the members of the editorial staff, were the main reasons for their ceasing publication. Frequently the editors became dissatisfied with the program they had originally formulated, or perhaps they believed that the reforms they had set out to bring about had been accomplished, and that the review therefore had no further reason for existing. Typical of such programs, and of the ambitious nature of their aims, is the one published by the review *Il Leonardo,* directed by Giovanni Papini and the true forerunner of the magazines that were to appear later in Florence.

> A group of young men desirous of freedom, eager for universality, anxious for a superior intellectual life, have gathered in Florence under the symbolic and augural name of "Leonardo," in order to intensify their own existence, to elevate their own thought, to exalt their own art.
>
> In life they are pagans and individualistic lovers of beauty and of intelligence, adorers of true nature and of a full life, enemies of any form of antiquated or sheeplike existence or of plebeian servitude.

In thought they are idealists and individualists, superior to any system and to any limits; they are convinced that any philosophy is nothing but a personal mode of living —and deny any other form of existence outside of thought.

In art they love the idealistic transfiguration of life and combat any of its inferior forms—they aspire to beauty— which is a suggestive figuration and revelation of a profound and a serene life.

As an expression of their forces, their enthusiasms, and of their dislikes there will be a review entitled *Leonardo* which they will publish in eight pages, illustrated, with woodcuts and printed with the best of care.

Of the many reviews published between 1908 and 1940, four stand out and are particularly noted for their vitality and daring: *La Voce* (1908-16); *La Ronda* (1919-23); *Solaria* (1926-37); and *Letteratura* (1937-43, when it suspended publication, resumed in 1946). A point that must be emphasized here is that these four were by no means the only influential magazines of this period. There were several others: *Il Convegno, Novecento, Cahiers d'Italie et d'Europe* (1926-9); *Campo di Marte* (1938-9), *Primato, Corrente, Il Meridiano di Roma*—all of which served as rallying points for writers and critics of different tendencies and interests. These magazines also fulfilled a useful function partly by encouraging and publishing those writers who, because of their literary or even political beliefs, or their relative inexperience, were not always warmly received by the more commercial, established periodicals.

The first review to achieve considerable resonance was *La Voce*, founded in 1908 by Giuseppe Prezzolini, who directed it until 1914, at which time the editorship was entrusted to Giuseppe de Robertis, who had been a contributor to the magazine.

An evaluation of *La Voce* depends necessarily on whether we are examining the first or the second phase of its activity, as its tone, content, and direction changed along with its editors. Under Prezzolini it was an eclectic magazine, issued in a format between that of a review and a tabloid, and with a vivacious interest in culture in its broadest manifestations. Moreover, from its first issue, the review reflected the temperament of its editor, Prezzolini, who was anxious to reform, deprovincialize, and inject new blood into the desiccated veins of Italian culture. As such, *La Voce* sought to present, study, and discuss not only the creative writers of its time, but the political and philosophical figures of Western civilization.

> At a certain point in my life, having buried the romantic turmoils and aspirations, I decided to become the "useful man" for others; to clarify certain ideals to Italians, to indicate their inferiorities in order to overcome them, to characterize foreign people and foreign movements, to translate from different languages, to reveal promising young men, to point out hidden greatness; that is, what one calls work of culture is very much like building ditches, plowing the soil, planting trees, pruning, sowing, weeding, trimming, and all the operations of a good agriculturist. Yes, I have always wanted to be useful. I don't say I have always succeeded, but that was my intention. I have always put myself at the service of a man who needed to be known, of an idea that needed conquering, of a propaganda that needed dissemination. This was the principal character of *La Voce,* but it is in a way the character of all my work.

In the first issue of *La Voce,* Giovanni Papini, who had joined the staff at the request of his friend, declared that "the problem is to give Italy not only a contact with Europe but a historical consciousness of her own culture, which is so much part of Europe's." Forty years later, looking back to his experience with *La Voce,* Prezzolini reminisced: "*La Voce* was born with an intense wish on the part of all those who participated most intimately [to search for] truth. We had different faiths; we all came from different parts of Italy; we all had different hopes. But one thing united us: the cult of truth. Italian life, poetry, and philosophy seemed to us to lack truth."

Because the young Italian intellectuals lacked faith in their own culture, they looked to those poets and philosophers who had not been read or sufficiently understood in Italy, in order to find the "truth." Shortly after its inception, *La Voce* achieved a popularity never before achieved by similar periodicals. It exposed its readers to the mature achievement of European art and thought, by translating and commenting on a vast array of living writers. Aside from having introduced the work of Claudel in Italy, it published Tolstoi, Dostoevski, Unamuno, and Chekhov, as well as the philosophers Croce, Gentile, James, and Bergson. Its philosophical allegiance wavered between pragmatism and idealism, and eventually it became the organ of what it termed "militant idealism." The review eventually set up a subsidiary publishing house, destined to bring out some of the significant works of literature, philosophy, and political science of modern Europe. Indeed, as the critic Walter Binni has remarked, "to go through the catalogue of [the publishing house] La Voce means to perceive the fluctuations of French and European culture in Italy."

Throughout its first years of publication, first as a weekly, then as a monthly, La Voce also played the part of the critical voice of national policies. It reminded the government of its obligations and duties toward its citizens; it pointed out many flaws inherent to social and political life in Italy, inconsistent and incompatible with the democratic procedure. It exposed crooked politicians, ridiculed and launched vitriolic attacks against senseless policies, and, in the words of Peter Riccio, lambasted "the charlatans, the pedants, the unscrupulous political officials, the artistic and literary shams of the times."

La Voce did not limit its role to that of a polemical observer of life. One of its positive actions was its persistent demands that the publishing houses bring out inexpensive, accurate editions of the classics, some of whom (like Galileo and Giordano Bruno) were barely known because of the general unavailability of their works. Another important contribution to knowledge were the bibliographies (eleven in all) it published on such disparate topics as "Hegelian Philosophy in Italy," "The Sexual Question," and "Church and State in Tuscany." It devoted several numbers to individual questions of timely concern, such as "The Problem of the South," "Irredentism," "Education and the High-School Reform," and so forth. It also published, along with the work of such serious political thinkers as Amendola, Salvemini, and Einaudi, the creative writing of Jahier, Palazzeschi, Ungaretti, and many another young poet.

The philosopher Eugenio Garin has characterized the role played by the many Florentine magazines at the beginning of the century: "To have pointed out the end of ancient myths and the travail they generated; to have felt the hypocrisy and the immobility of a way of life; to have underscored the urgency of a renewal that might contribute to the renewal of society—such was the positive meaning of the Florentine reviews, from *Leonardo* to *La Voce.*" But, if innovation and cosmopolitanism were two of the central features of such magazines, and particularly of *La Voce,* it became evident that those very elements that contributed to their vitality were also their major source of weakness: youth and inexperience, criticism for its own sake, a tenacious belief in the contemporary world, and far more disastrous, the absence of a real moral code. In spite of Prezzolini's plea *"tener duro"* ("to hold on fast and hard") to principles and convictions, the review soon demonstrated (in the eventual shifts of three of its editors, Prezzolini, Soffici, and Papini) how it could compromise with principles by aligning itself with contrasting philosophies and politics, thus betraying its initial promise. For this reason several of the more honest minds either left *La Voce* to found their own reviews (as in the case of Salvemini) or withdrew altogether from active participation in the magazine.

The disparate temperaments that made up the review could not co-exist very long. Profound differences, especially on the political and philosophical plane, developed between them, and the irreconcilable positions taken by Prezzolini and Salvemini (to mention but two of the *Vociani*) first forced some changes in the editorial management, and eventually provoked a split that was to seriously impair its life.

The second phase of *La Voce* began on December 14, 1914, when the editorship was entrusted to Giuseppe de Robertis. With him the periodical changed both physically and ideologically. The color changed to white, its price was increased, and a new program was soon announced by the editor. If the second phase of the review lacked the fire and vitality given it by Prezzolini, it soon revealed a maturity and a fidelity to certain principles that had not always been discernible in its first years.

*La Voce* intends to be a magazine of modern criticism and art; better still: of modern minds. It wishes to gather together the most alive, mature, or initial work produced by the young literature. . . . Hybrid and ambiguous reviews are plentiful in Italy and elsewhere. But there is not one review as solid and whole as *La Voce*: from it is born the new *Voce* which aspires to nothing else if not to making itself worthy of its creators who for six years have directed it and are now leaving it, in order that the magazine may renew itself and continue publication.

When World War I began, *La Voce* began publishing a political supplement (*La Voce Politica*), edited by Prezzolini, who, in his editorials, insisted that Italy participate in the conflict against Germany. When Italy declared war against the Austro-Hungarian Empire, several *Vociani* left for the service. Many of them (Slataper, Bellini, Serra, Carlo Stuparich) eventually lost their lives at the front line. But right through a better part of the First World War the periodical continued its publication. Under the aegis of De Robertis, its order of the day in literary matters became: "*saper leggere.*" And it was the greatest contribution of the "second" *La Voce* (which was known in later years as "the literary *Voce*") to teach its audience that a literary text deserves a meticulous and sensitive reading. Beyond the simple exhortation, the words of De Robertis further admonished the reader to be suspicious of schools and movements, as well as personalities. Poetry could be found anywhere, for it was not the prerogative of any single nation or cultural entity:

> This suggestion *to read carefully* had, beside everything else, the rare merit of not generating any rhetoric, of not defending any particular style, of going neither toward the classic nor the romantic. It only fixed that absolute, categoric *saper leggere*, which is always valid and which is, in fact, the only weapon of art and poetry against philosophy and against dramatizations, against the foolishnesses of any school. . . . To open a book, and to know *how* to read it, with the pleasure of reading it [such was our teaching].

The editor himself paved the way for a new direction in the literary taste of the readers of *La Voce* by showing the enjoyment any intelligent person could derive from

reading not only contemporary literature of his own country, but French letters, for example, and the classics—
from the Renaissance, back to Jacopone, and forward again
to Tasso, to the poetry of the very latest writers, Mallarmé,
Di Giacomo, Rimbaud. De Robertis analyzed the texts and
commented on them profusely, paying much attention to
the value of the individual word, the syllable, the pauses,
the rhythm. In short, De Robertis did for literature what
Soffici had done, in the previous years, for classical and
contemporary painting. Soffici had written extensively
about the French artists of the latter part of the nineteenth
century and of his day, from Medardo Rosso to the work
of Cézanne and the great French Impressionists, Manet,
Degas, Renoir. Moreover, he had been instrumental in making possible the first exhibitions of those artists in Florence.

The new edition of *La Voce* emphasized art and literature at the expense of politics and philosophy. Indeed, its
philosophical posture was one of clear antagonism toward
Croce and some of its earlier contributors, among whom
was Cecchi. Its new critical leaders were De Robertis and
Renato Serra, until the untimely death of the latter in
1915. The writers and poets it published were Rea, Cardarelli, Ungaretti, Bacchelli, Savinio, Sbarbaro, Baldini,
Apollinaire, who were destined to become the leading
writers of their generation.

With the double issue numbered 11-12, brought out at
the end of 1916, *La Voce* suspended publication without
any warning or explanation of its decision or of the factors that had contributed to it. For several years, it had
fulfilled a useful function, in spite of its confused aims,
the occasional superficiality of its method, and the strange
mixture of its ideological orientation. It had published
creative writers, philosophers, and critics alike, regardless
of their nationality and their unorthodoxy. It had brought
life and vigor to a provincial culture, thus assuring for
itself a permanent place in Italian intellectual history.
Only after the experience of *La Voce* could Italy begin
a truly contemporary period.

*La Voce* had been characterized by such deep dissen-
sions among its collaborators that eventually they caused
the review to fold. It had wasted an excessive amount of

its energy in trying to accomplish too many things at one time and in so doing, it had frequently been guilty of shallowness and of being polemical for its own sake. It had experimented with new ways to bring to the attention of the general public sociopolitical problems seldom explored in depth before; it had attempted to awaken its readers to contemporary art; it had acquainted its audience with a vast number of European novelists, poets, and thinkers, and it had "launched" several new writers. By contrast, *La Ronda*, a Roman periodical founded in Rome in 1919, dedicated itself throughout its existence, with more coherency and single-mindedness than had any previous magazine, to re-establishing some sort of order in a cultural scene that was characterized, after the Futurists and even by the *Vociani*, by turmoil and disorder.

*La Ronda* was written almost exclusively by the seven people who founded it: Vincenzo Cardarelli, Riccardo Bacchelli, Antonio Baldini, Lorenzo Montano; one critic, Emilio Cecchi; one musical composer, Bruno Barilli; and the painter Armando Spadini—with the collaboration of a very carefully selected nucleus of other writers. These seven men soon became known in literary circles as "the Seven Sages." Just as the critic De Robertis had advocated a careful reading of a poetic text as the essential act that would bring about understanding by joining reader and poet, so the *Rondisti* called for a literature that was to be an experience of the highest order, and to which the artist himself was to give the best possible part of his creative talent.

The *Vociani* had been the *enfants terribles* of the first fifteen years of the century. The *Rondisti*, on the other hand, showed themselves in favor of order and respectability, in letters as well as in politics (indeed, one recent critic has analyzed the Fascist tendencies of the review). As the historian Natalino Sapegno succinctly puts it:

> The *Rondisti* are opposed to indiscriminate enthusiasm, the distinction and the sense of measure; [they are opposed] to impotent ambition, humility, and the exigencies of the craft; they concentrate their attention on the literary fact itself, in its formal meaning, as a restoration of technical values—grammatical and stylistic. They deny the myth of sincerity, of immediacy, insisting on the importance of

the reflected and conscious elements of artistic elaboration; they look with diffidence upon the contamination [of art] with morality and philosophy, pointing out precisely the concept of literature as a disinterested exercise and an absolute reflection of any content in terms of style.

The interests of *La Ronda* were not nearly as broad as those of *La Voce*. By no means narrowly provincial, it devoted some attention to the writers of Italy and other European nations, at the expense of philosophers or economists. The content of a literary work, which had been so important for the *Vociani*, received less attention from the *Rondisti*, who believed that ultimately the excellence of a literary work would be determined by the degree of stylistic perfection achieved by its author.

The intellectual posture of *La Ronda* was antimodern to the point of sacrificing, whenever necessary, contemporary writing for the classical authors of Italian letters. In this respect, the review showed itself to be one of the most conservative of the little magazines. It refused either to commit itself to encouraging any experimental writing or to dedicate itself to a dispassionate examination of the young poets and writers emerging on the literary scene. It firmly believed in the worth of the classics—and this, too, may be taken as indicative of the reaction against the neoromanticism of *La Voce*, which had clamorously advocated a rejection of too many "sacred cows" of Italian letters. *La Ronda*'s gods became Manzoni and Leopardi, whose work alone, in the history of modern Italian letters, they deemed worthy of serving as models, not to be blindly worshipped and imitated but understood as representative of that stylistic perfection which the *Rondisti* tried to achieve. Cardarelli's program was quite clear in this respect:

It will not seem a paradox if we say that, from the classics (for whom, as in our case, art had no aim other than pleasure), we have learned to be men before being men of letters. We should like to write the word *umanità* with an *h*, as it used to be written in Machiavelli's time, so that one may understand the precise meaning we give to this word. From the romantics we have inherited a rational contempt for the kind of mythological poetry still being written in our days under the pretext of sensibility and images. . . . We will therefore avoid purposely making a fracas with formulae that smell of mold and of youth at the same time. . . . Our own classicism is metaphorical and with a double bottom. To continue making use of a style now passé will have no other meaning for us than that of achieving new elegance, not to perpetuate insensitively the tradition of our art. We would appreciate being modern in an Italian fashion, without emigrating.

Through its four years of publication, *La Ronda* sought to establish not only a certain continuity with the tradition, which in their ideal meant "the conservation of the historical sense transmitted through the knowledge of form in which such a literary tradition had become realized," but in fostering a new genre roughly equivalent to the prose poem. The most exemplary member of *La Ronda* was, in this respect, Emilio Cecchi (b. 1884), a sophisticated writer whose informative essays on English writers appeared as a regular feature in the review. It was he who became the expert practitioner of the essay, and it was thanks to his volumes, *Pesci rossi* (1920), being the best and most representative, that the genre maintained a wide popularity, until the novel was resurrected from the deep slumber into which it had fallen. Delicate as his prose was, it ultimately lacked the breadth and depth that make literature endure. Today the *prosa d'arte* is remembered as the most representative type of writing of the prewar period. Cool, highly controlled, emptied of whatever romantic and effusive element had typified earlier prose style, the essay was the best possible expression of an essentially conservative and static sensibility. Its seriousness lacked daring; its outer brilliancy was itself symbolic of a sensibility that could neither be shaken nor troubled by the spiritual and political turmoil lived intensely by the more courageous Italian intellectuals of those years—among them, Salvemini, Amendola, and Gobetti.

"Italy is about to become a modern nation: here is the stupendous and countless promise offered to our artistic and spiritual future," had declared Cardarelli in the opening number of *La Ronda*. The *Rondisti*, troubled by the long neglect suffered by their literature, wished it to assert itself in the larger frame of European culture.

Strangely enough their efforts led them to reach such an isolated position in their own country that the magazine was avoided by the young writers. Its sustained concentration on stylistic factors was indicative of its unconcern for life.

"Style," wrote Cardarelli in 1920 in his book *Viaggi nel tempo* (Journeys in Time), "is a complete pleasure, an almost delirious musical amusement of a soul tired and nauseated by its own thoughts." The carefully worded programs of *La Ronda* did not produce a single poet, a fact not too surprising in view of the scanty space the magazine devoted to poetry.

When everything is taken into account, *La Ronda's* influence was of a critical, rather than a creative, kind. It pleaded for a serious literature, pointing out that the work of art is not the result of a spontaneous undisciplined workmanship but the product of long meditation and labor, thus expressing its opposition to Croce's concept of art as intuition. For this reason, the *Rondisti* unheld Leopardi (the author not merely of *I canti* but of the *Operette Morali* and, above all, of the *Zibaldone*) as the kind of writer who worked incessantly through many drafts of a poem before achieving a finished composition of which he could be proud.

*La Ronda,* with its program to foster a urbane, literate, and refined prose style, with its frequent "calls to order" (the cover design of a soldier playing the drums was its standard emblem), and with its harking back to the classics of Italian literature (Ariosto, Leopardi, and Manzoni), sailed along a chartered route, with a tendency to run astray from it once in a while. The end of its publication coincided with a crucial period in Italian history. It was in 1922 that fascism began emerging as an important force in Italian politics. The review could have taken a stand on contemporary events, but it chose not to. Its decision represents the first of a long list of concessions made by Italian intellectuals to the party that was soon to achieve full power. In another sense, *La Ronda,* by its undivided attention to creativity, showed the way to a full retreat from life into the ivory tower of the hermetic poets of the thirties.

Unlike *La Ronda, Solaria,* founded in Florence in 1926,

avoided the usual programs to the point of refusing to set down a clear editorial policy to which it would abide. Its activities were in perfect antithesis to those of *La Ronda*, as the *Solariani* tended to establish a more meaningful relation with, and knowledge of, American as well as European literature. Its intentions were clear from the very opening statement in the first issue of the magazine:

> We are not worshippers of stylistic bravuras and exaggerated purisms; should someone among us sacrifice the beautiful rhythm of a sentence, or even the propriety of language, in his attempt to give breath to an art singularly dramatic and human, we shall forgive him beforehand, with feeling. For us, in sum, Dostoevski is a great writer. But we will not forgive even our fraternal contributors those licenses that are not fully justified, and in this we feel that we are *Rondisti*.

When compared with *La Ronda*, the character of *Solaria*, as revealed by the writings it published, stands out as bolder and less provincial. Its contributors were both more numerous and substantially more international in their view of culture. They were people who, like Moravia, Gadda, Vittorini, Tecchi, and Comisso, soon established themselves as the leading novelists of their generation; critics who, like Debenedetti and Gianfranco Contini, proved to be perceptive commentators of literature; poets who, like Ungaretti, Saba, Montale, and Quasimodo, emerged as the poetic conscience of the period between the two wars.

If the preference of *La Ronda* had been for brilliantly written essays and for skillfully executed impressionistic pieces, *Solaria* tended to prefer the more sustained form of creative writing, the novel. It was in *Solaria* that Elio Vittorini published his first work of fiction, *Il garofono rosso*, just as it was in the pages of that review that the art of Svevo was vindicated, once and for all, by the special issue entirely devoted to the psychological novelist from Trieste. There was perhaps a symbolic meaning in the whole story of the interest of *Solaria* for Svevo (or for Tozzi, Joyce, or T. S. Eliot, for that matter). Svevo's novels, written in a curious asyntactical language, itself a mixture of his native dialect with Austrian and Italian, could hardly have won the admiration of *La Ronda,* deeply preoccupied with *"il bello scrivere,"* or of the Fascists, whose distaste for psychological analyses was an obvious indication of their sense of guilt and parochialism. Introducing and studying the distant Nievo or De Marchi, or rereading the more contemporary Tozzi and Svevo meant for the *Solariani* discovering talents, new sensibilities that had little to do with the so-called official culture. Its literary interests (and *Solaria* clearly avoided any concern that was not cultural) closely tied it to its politics, which were of a special kind. The review, it is worthwhile to remember, was founded during a time when fascism was rapidly consolidating its position and through its restrictive policies censured those who questioned or criticized its methods and decisions. *Solaria* began publication barely two years after the famous murder of Matteotti by the Fascists, that is, at a time when the incident was still the subject of private polemics. Its activity ended shortly after the end of the Ethiopian campaign. Although it never took a firm position on political issues, it was not a truly passive spectator of current events. The founder of the review, Alberto Carocci, recently underscored the fact that, while *Solaria* did not develop a program of political or ideological opposition against the party, it succeeded by its very lack of participation in making its moral and intellectual opposition to fascism.

> [*Solaria*] was anti-Fascist one might almost say because it was not fascist. . . . It was a review whose cultural tendencies found themselves in disagreement with official tendencies. . . . [The magazine] remained a literary review, extraneous to any other interest, even if in its last two years it seemed to change its course and forecast those periodicals that soon replaced it [periodicals to which fell the assignment] of steering the rocky boat of a literature in sympathy with European letters toward the more restless waters of the Second World War. We might almost say that *Solaria* formed the island of cultural resistance, were it not for the precise historical meaning such a term has acquired today.

By accepting the isolated position to which official culture had relegated it, it became the "conscientious objector" of its literary values. Even though it continued to publish the best poets Italy was producing (most of whom were not, incidentally, card-carrying Fascists or had withdrawn from the party), it "humbly acknowledged that the most original expressions of modern literature had flourished elsewhere, regardless of whether their names were Joyce or Kafka, and affirmed that Italian writers were also worthy of consideration, but that they were only part of a larger European dialogue." Vittorini, in a reminiscence about his part in *Solaria,* published in *Diario in pubblico,* went even further:

> *Solariano* was a word which, in the literary circles of that time, meant anti-Fascist, sympathizer of European affairs, universalist, antitraditionalist. . . . Giovanni Papini used to insult us from one end, and Farinacci from the other. They called us dirty Jews because we used to publish Jewish writers and because of all the good things we said about Kafka or Joyce. And they called us jackals. They called us hyenas. They called us ditchdiggers.

The *Solariani* gathered at the famous Giubbe Rosse (Red Waistcoats), a Florentine coffeehouse that since the end of the century had served as a meeting place for literati and artists. There, seated around the small tables inside the café or, weather permitting, in the handsome piazza, the young writers discussed their own work and planned the future issues of the review. Frequently, out-of towners interested in the magazine would show up to make the acquaintance of the *Solariani* and, occasionally, they would be asked to become contributors to the review. For it was one of the principles of the magazine not to deny the chance to be published to anyone who had something interesting to say. *Rondisti,* ex-*Vociani,* young and mature critics and writers—all found *Solaria* open and sympathetic to their ideas and writings, provided they were of high quality. Italian, French, and English writers were equally acceptable: the magazine cut across national boundaries, showing by its example that culture is an international affair.

Its critical position was, as to be expected, anti-Crocean, although many *Solariani* readily acknowledged their debt to Croce or to Gentile. Its interests were not restricted to literature but extended to the cinema, philosophy, the theater. Under the heading of *Zibaldone*, the magazine regularly published reviews and notes written by Debenedetti, Montale, Franchi, Morra, Alberti, and others.

Shortly after *Solaria* had ceased publication, a new quarterly review began appearing. Its title: *Letteratura* (1937). There were several ties between the two reviews. Aside from the fact that once again the collaborators of *Letteratura* had had experience on *Solaria*, the new review accepted and continued many of the policies of the former. Italy had just ended the war against Ethiopia and the Spanish Civil War had reached a temporary impasse; Europe was rapidly and inexorably moving toward the Second World War, which was to solve some problems but to generate others even more formidable.

The title of the new magazine, *Letteratura*, boldly proclaimed that its interests would be strictly literary. Such an orientation would hardly surprise the contemporary reader. But in those days it was an act of sheer courage to proclaim that a periodical would not follow the policy of the overwhelming majority of similar publications and turn to politics and to an eventual exaltation of the ruling regime in order to stay in business. Moreover, *Letteratura* showed in no uncertain terms its identification with contemporary writings, thus contradicting by its example the negative views and position of the dean of literary criticism, Benedetto Croce.

Quite unlike any other review that had preceded it, *Letteratura* began the difficult task of showing historically the role played by those philosophers, artists, and critics who had shaped the course of Italian letters since the beginning of the century. Under the rubrics "From *La Voce* to *La Ronda*" and "Foreign Literature" young scholars and critics, like Walter Binni and Giansiro Ferrata, appraised with an amazing sense of perspective the work of Prezzolini, Croce, Boine. For several years, in fact right up to Italy's entrance into World War II, the magazine devoted many of its substantial numbers (many of which were monographs) to translating and commenting on the work of contemporary writers of a definite reputation. T. S. Eliot, Machado, Cocteau, Yeats, Rilke, Melville, O'Neill, Pound, and Cervantes were some of the writers to be anthologized. Essays on the work of Lorca, Pushkin, Stefan George, Roger Martin du Gard, Eluard, and others appeared regularly.

Unlike *La Ronda,* which had slighted poetry in favor of prose, *Letteratura* immediately showed an admirable generosity toward the poets, old and young alike. Montale's *Occasioni,* Ungaretti's *Il sentimento del tempo,* Quasimodo's subtle renditions of the Greek poets, were published along with the young voices destined to be the important new poets: Sandro Penna, Mario Luzi, Vittorio Sereni, Leonardo Sinisgalli, Attilio Bertolucci. Similarly, the novelists Pratolini, Bilenchi, Gadda, and Delfini found hospitality in the pages of the Florentine magazine. In 1938, Elio Vittorini began publishing in *Letteratura* the first installments of his masterpiece, *Conversazione in Sicilia,* and the "abstract furies" of the novel's hero, Silvestro, were in themselves symptomatic of the restlessness felt by a large segment of the Italian artistic avant-garde.

*Letteratura* became the meeting ground of artists and critics of disparate tendencies and schools: Bo and Vigorelli, the exponents of the Catholic group, were published along with the difficult Macrí, Contini, and Bigongiari, the critical theorists of the hermetic group. The offerings of the review were always not only abundant but diversified as well: there was poetry and fiction, brilliant essays and perceptive shorter pieces, notes on the cinema, the theater, and music. *Letteratura* became famous for its serious tone but also for its daring, standing for many years in the forefront of cultural periodicals. It ultimately achieved a reconciliation of the aesthetic and moral attitudes of all its contributors, and the various tendencies and the manifold interests represented in the magazine made it an exciting publication to read. For all those who contributed to the magazine literature was a highly serious business, to which they gave, with untiring and unselfish energy, the very best of their talent.

The war was barely over when the little magazines, many of which had been forced to suspend publication for a number of practical or political reasons, began reappearing at a prodigiously rapid rate. It would be difficult to list all of them, since several survived only a few issues. A number of such periodicals were particularly distinguished, and one only wishes that such reviews as *Aretusa, Mercurio, La Nuova Europa* (the first two predominantly literary, the last a cultural-political sheet), were still being published. Ideologically they had little in common with each other, since reviews are frequently the organs of the views of a person or of a small nucleus of writers. All periodicals of the years immediately following the war shared the irresistible desire to begin the physical, intellectual, and moral reconstruction of Italy. Moreover, all pleaded for a generous understanding of the literature produced under fascism and offered dispassionate evaluations of those writers who had been deceived by the regime. Finally, the new reviews recognized the need for a fresh and meaningful beginning.

Of the numerous postwar reviews. one stands out in particular. To this very day many Italians recall its noble experiments, its rare achievements, its regrettable naïveté: its name was *Il Politecnico*. Although it appeared for a relatively short period (from September 1945 to April 1947), it has never been forgotten by those intellectuals who, even when not in accord with the sociopolitical and cultural aims of the sheet, admired its courage and were sufficiently stirred by it to take an active part in its publication.

The review had a format similar to that of a tabloid and was edited by Elio Vittorini and others who had experienced life with the partisans. Contrasting personalities of slightly different political allegiances participated in the spirited life of the journal. Its goals were carefully stated in its regular editorials, although soon enough there developed a number of contradictions in tone and ideological content. The coveted goal of *Il Politecnico* was "to bring up-to-date, and turn upside down, the meaning of traditional culture." "We no longer want a culture that consoles us in tomes of suffering, but a culture that protects us from such sufferings and will fight to eliminate them."

At no other time had the atmosphere been so propitious as in the immediate postwar months for a basic and thorough re-evaluation of the meaning of culture and of its place in the context of contemporary society. *Il*

*Politecnico* engaged in a valiant battle to demonstrate how "culture must participate in the regeneration of the Italian society." Its audience was a peculiar mixture of liberal intellectuals, many of whom had actively opposed fascism and had been relegated to political confinement; of enlightened bourgeois, aware that somehow the cultural elite could gain the upper hand in Italian politics and achieve a position of power; and the working classes, starved for information and sympathetic intellectual guidance. All looked to the review as a symbol of what could be done to improve the standards of education and give the masses a definite sense of participation in the affairs of the nation.

As an organ of a liberal group, *Il Politecnico* published many of those works of literature, political and social science, and painting that had been kept from the Italian public by fascism. Along with the important "new" French poets, Aragon and Eluard, it published the Symbolists and Decadents, the Russians Pasternak and Mayakovsky, as well as Whitman, T. S. Eliot, Spender, Auden, MacLeish, and a score of novelists (Hemingway, Sartre, Steinbeck), many of whom had been during the war years symbols of the freedom enjoyed in other lands. Along with the mature writers of Italy, such as Saba, Montale, and Ungaretti, young writers, Calvino, Del Buono, Fortini, Sinisgalli—many of whom had been members of the underground, and were then card-carrying Communists —were published by *Il Politecnico*.

From the personal testimonial of Franco Fortini, who took an active part in the review, it is clear that *Il Politecnico* generated more than the usual amount of enthusiasm and approval. For weeks and months manuscripts from working men, ex-partisans, and soldiers kept arriving at the editorial office—all exemplifying the response stirred by the review and the interest that followed it.

Although it was a leftist review, *Il Politecnico* was never an organ of propaganda of the P.C.I. (Italian Communist Party). Ideologically allied with Marxist doctrines of culture and politics, the review soon discovered that there could hardly be a real dialogue between itself and the party's dogmatic bosses. Eventually, Vittorini himself took a position that was deemed too independent by the party leaders. What had been a tolerant, implicit sympathy for each other, soon developed into an open, vocal polemical friction and eventually caused a break between the editor and Togliatti, the Executive Secretary of the P.C.I. Vittorini's belief in the autonomy of art was never better expressed than in one of the last issues of the periodical: "I have always denied that the duty of literature is to make clear the political reasons of a revolution. I denied that the duty of a writer should be the political education of the readers through a subtle literary game. Nevertheless, there are human reasons for a revolution which only a writer, or a poet, can make clear. Only he can have a knowledge of them and put them in relief."

Because Vittorini lacked a rigid ideological discipline, and since the review was really conceived and directed by artists not politicians, it came to an end after a last laconic plea to its readers. It had tried to be a publication interested in informing and discussing important issues. Having failed, in the words of its editor, to be creative on the informative plane, it lost most of its initial drive. Franco Fortini, one of the young editors of the review, has pointed out how the difficulties encountered by the little magazine are still very much part of contemporary Italian culture. They range from the problems "of a language neither technical nor strictly popular, to that of the rapport between cultural and political leaders, to that of the relations between Marxist thought and other currents of contemporary thought, to that of new possible critical methodologies."

*Il Politecnico*, for all the failures of its approach, the indecisions and disagreements of its editors (which was the factor that ultimately caused its untimely end), must go down in the history of modern Italian culture as one of the noblest and most alive experiments by an unorthodox group of intellectuals. Its end coincides with the beginning of a new, less exciting, and more conservative era in the field of periodical literature. Both existing magazines and those which will no doubt emerge in the future should be far wiser thanks to the lesson imparted by the experiences of *Il Politecnico*.

# CHAPTER TEN

# America and Italy: An Encounter

At the end of the last war, several prominent Italian intellectuals readily confessed that their encounter with American literature had been one of their most significant and rewarding experiences. Strange as it may seem, the violence and deep pessimism of Faulkner, Cain, Caldwell, and Steinbeck, whose works were widely read in Italy in the thirties, had actually given them the measure of hope and courage they needed to continue living and writing. Through the fiction of the Americans, they kept in touch with the free world, and were delivered from the sterile conventionality of Fascist "culture."

The story of Italo-American relations, and more specifically, the impact of American fiction in Italy and the interest of the two countries for their respective cultures, has been told, however fragmentarily, over and over during the past years. It is a complex story, the full meaning of which will not be clear until we achieve a better historical perspective toward events that are still too close to us to be assessed objectively. A definite interpretation of this story cannot be written without first studying what was translated during fascism and evaluating the effect such translations had not only upon the readers, but upon the translators themselves. As the young critic Richard Chase recently remarked, "any discussion of the Italian contemporary scene, while it will inevitably attempt to understand Italian politics and development since the fall of the regime in European terms, cannot escape some analysis of American intervention and the various effects resulting from this." The intervention to which Mr.

Chase refers consists of the technical and emotive borrowing that took place when the two countries met.

Traditionally, Italy and the United States have always been tied by bonds of friendship and sympathy. Yet for decades the two nations remained as far apart culturally as they were geographically. There were always then, as there are now, the steady streams of affluent tourists who went to Italy regularly in search of sunshine and tranquillity, as there was always the flock of intellectuals who resided there for varying periods of time. Those who could not afford the journey made certain that at least Dante and Petrarch would become part of their intellectual baggage.

Numerous Americans and Europeans developed sentimental bonds with Italy or were visibly moved by their experience there. James Fenimore Cooper, Hawthorne, Henry and William James, Robert and Elizabeth Browning, William Dean Howells, Edith Wharton, Mark Twain, spent long and often happy years in Rome, Venice, and Florence. Although in general they were delighted with what they found there, occasionally their exposure to Italy was so fraught with shocks and irritations that they were impelled to make pungent comments about the country and its customs. Many, like Norton, Longfellow, Symonds, and D. H. Lawrence, developed such affection and understanding of the classics that they sought through their translations to make such works as those of Dante and Verga better appreciated in the English-speaking world.

For many decades interest in Italy retained a definite intellectual flavor. Eventually and unfortunately, the opinions and interpretations of James and Twain were instrumental in creating an image of Italy that soon became stereotyped, even though it had little relation to reality itself. Italy was either the nation blessed with what seemed to many an ideal climate and an extraordinary wealth of monuments and intriguing museums, or, more often, it was regarded as "the cradle of culture." Few took pains to dig beneath the surface of well-intentioned generalities which had come to be accepted as pearls of interpretative wisdom. Fewer still explored the genuine character of the Italian people and dealt realistically with the agonizing problems of a country that was blessed with a rich cultural tradition while, at the same time, doomed to remain a third-rate political power. Mark Twain, whose chances of being remembered as a sympathetic critic of Italy are slight at best, came closer than many of his contemporaries to making a valid judgment, when he described Italy as "one vast museum of magnificence and misery . . . the wretchedest, princeliest land on earth." Had he only studied in depth the contrasts and contradictions that have resisted the changes of centuries he might well have become the only writer of his generation to reveal the "real" Italy to a vast audience.

Of the multitude of writers who lived in Italy, many made extensive use of the Italian scene for their books. Howells, who lived in Venice for several years as the American consul, and returned to Italy on several occasions as a private citizen, was perhaps the most inveterate Italophile. The debt he owes to Italy is so large that it has warranted a detailed study by James L. Woodress, *Howells and Italy.* "Among the one hundred novels, poems, plays, travelogues, etc., of which Howells was the sole author, the concentration of Italian material is still heavier; for of this group thirty-five, or more than one third, exploit the Italian experience in varying degrees." When Howells did not set his work in Italy, he made indirect use of the Italian background or made "reference to Italian travel, people, politics, art, literature, etc."

Mario Praz, in an essay devoted to interpreting the American attitude toward Italy in the nineteenth century as expressed by the writers, makes an illuminating observation on the nature of their experience:

> Unfortunately the story of our cultural relations with the United States is often made up of travesties and misunderstandings. Admire as they may our nature and art, be they even well-disposed toward the people, and willing to let themselves be warmed by our sun, and say as they do with George Ticknor, who was in Italy between 1817 and 1818: "If I were condemned to live in Europe, Rome is the place I would choose," and "I have experienced the greatest pleasure in Italy more than in any other European country,"

and "Rome alone is worth all the cities in the world"—in spite of it all there comes the moment when the Americans feel ill at ease.

For all the affection Americans felt for Italy, after a period of permanence there would inevitably come the moment when they would say, with Henry James: "I feel I shouldn't care if I never saw the perverted place again." The one notable exception to what appears to have been a widespread and customary uneasiness and unhappiness with living in Italy for prolonged periods seems to have been Bernard Berenson, who found in the hills near Florence a haven, where he worked in happiness and productivity from the turn of the century until his recent death.

Italian interpretations of the United States, on the other hand, were not only fewer in number, but even more one-sided and biased. The Italians of stature who ventured to this side of the ocean were no more than a handful. Because of their unfamiliarity with the language and their provincial feeling of cultural superiority, those who did come could not grasp those problems that were peculiarly American. Toward the end of the last century, the situation was partially remedied by the visit of the playwright Giuseppe Giacosa and the journalist Ugo Ojetti. Their volumes, entitled respectively *Impressioni d'America* (1898) and *L'America vittoriosa* (1899), were, astonishingly enough, the only candid appraisals of the United States written in a language easily accessible to the general public. Both authors, however sympathetically they viewed the positive sides of American life (its efficiency, its inexhaustible energy, its democracy), were appalled by its greedy materialism, its amorality, and its cultural aridity.

For many years after the appearance of the two volumes by Giacosa and Ojetti the concept of America hardly underwent any change. As in most cases where two nations are separated by vast geographical distance the picture of the character of each country was achieved by a composite method—a hybrid mixture of accounts by qualified witnesses, the projection of moral standards and values in official and quasi-official pronouncements and behavior, and whatever cultural or subcultural products managed to reach the other shores. But more important in the formulation of an attitude or an idea of each nation were the secondhand impressions, the hearsays, the contradictory reports of all sorts of people who had visited or had heard stories or who had relatives living in the other country. Such imprecise data made for considerable vagueness and distortion, the necessary ingredients of a legend about modern America that, like all legends, was only partially rooted in truth.

It is important to remember that most Italians, unable to visit the United States in person, had to be content with an imaginary journey made possible through the accounts and letters of relatives and friends. For them, America was a strange, exotic nation, whose extraordinary wealth and generosity were often the subject of animated conversation. America was also the great land of opportunity (fictionalized in the short story by Corrado Alvaro, *"Il rubino"*—*"The Ruby"*) and thus a welcome haven for the hundreds of thousands of immigrants who, during the latter part of the nineteenth century, began leaving en masse for the United States, in search of work. One of the great puzzles of the nature of Italo-American relations was that all the prolonged sojourns of intelligent Americans in Italy and the long stays of Italians in the United States did so little to dispel strange misconceptions about their respective nations.

World War I did not bring the two countries much closer together, despite their being allied against a common enemy. As a matter of fact, as the historian H. Stuart Hughes appropriately notes, "most Americans, if they thought of Italy's part in the alliance at all, reflected the widespread disappointment over the Italian contribution to the war effort: the Italians, they concluded, might be fine artists and stonemasons, but they made poor soldiers." The end of the war and the Peace Conference at Versailles acerbated the situation when Italy's demands failed to be properly considered by Wilson and the Great Powers.

Literature, usually capable of giving extraordinary insights into the life of different nations, was of little help. Italian interest in American letters remained slight right through the first years of this century. Aside from the sporadic work of scholars like Enrico Nencioni (whose interest was in Anglo-American letters), few important American writers were translated into Italian before the early thirties. Curiously enough, when the work of certain American poets and novelists succeeded in breaking the language barrier (Poe, for instance), they did so thanks to their having been translated first into French—thus reaching Italy by an indirect route.

American culture made an initial but short-lived dent in Italy before the First World War due to the vigorous and enthusiastic interest shown by the writer-poet-philosopher Giovanni Papini and the group of the Florentine magazine *La Voce* for William James's pragmatism. But such interest was rare indeed. With the advent of Mussolini, cultural relations between the two countries deteriorated further. To be sure, the yearly American pilgrimages to Italian cities continued even under fascism. But aside from such diverse personalities as Ezra Pound and George Santayana, both quite sympathetic to Mussolini, not many Americans chose Italy as their spiritual residence. The estranged American writer, the expatriate in search of a "real" home away from a place that for him was not home anymore, stopped in Paris, not Rome or Florence. Gertrude Stein, Ernest Hemingway, and the vast group of the "lost generation" made of France what Italy had been for their forefathers. By then a new era was beginning.

The real confrontation of Italy with American culture begins, strangely enough, toward the end of the first decade of Fascist rule, in 1930. The story of the encounter, and the subsequent "discovery" of an America more real than the real America, is a dramatic one. Like all such stories, it has its own cast of "villains" and "heroes." The chief protagonists of the first group were Emilio Cecchi and Mario Soldati, who were the first to combine their intellectual interest with an actual visit to the United States. The other group was composed of people who had become disillusioned with fascism and eventually had come to resent and reject it. Cesare Pavese, Elio Vittorini, and Giaime Pintor were the leaders of a nucleus that for all its profound affection for American culture, never set foot

on American soil. Through their efforts, American literature was at last made available to the Italian reading
audience. Both groups of *Americanisti* were identified
with a political orientation that was to shift to the right
or to the left according to circumstances. Between the two
nuclei, in a class by himself, stood Giuseppe Prezzolini,
former editor of the literary-political sheet *La Voce* who
had left his native country in self-imposed exile. After
arriving in the United States in the late twenties, he was
appointed to a professorship at Columbia University,
where he eventually became the head of the newly
established (partly with Fascist funds) Casa Italiana. He
wrote about the United States from his privileged sanc-
tuary in the ivory tower of Columbia. A humanist and a
sympathizer with Fascism, he addressed himself to the
general public through his short articles and notes that
even today have lost none of their ambivalence and may be
read either as indictments of American life or as the
compassionate and understanding interpretations of a
foreign observer.

The encounter with America took place in different
stages and with different intensity; although their personal
motivation differed, the reasons that drew the two nations
together were basically the same. As Cesare Pavese stated
in a moving essay published after the war: "[Between 1930
and 1940] Italy was estranged, barbarized, calcified. It
was necessary to shake her, to purge her, to expose her
to the spring winds of Europe and of the world." And so
it was the image of America, already firmly fixed in the
minds of most Italians, that began to change. New,
strikingly different images replaced the incomplete, provisional interpretations that had been formulated in the
past by people whose knowledge of America was at best
partial.

Both Soldati and Cecchi visited the United States,
the former as a fellowship student of Columbia University,
the latter as Visiting Professor at the University of
California at Berkeley (from 1931 to 1932 and again in
1938). Both pilgrimages turned out to be intellectual
adventures of the first order. Although they saw America
through the special lenses of their individual interests,
amazingly enough they arrived at strikingly similar con-

clusions. For both, America was a barbaric country without a culture, a fact they particularly noticed in daily American life. Their observations were recorded in two volumes which made their appearance some time after they returned to Italy.

Mario Soldati's sentimental journey to the American shores represented the author's attempt to abandon, physically and intellectually, his beloved European continent and the traditions of his native country—only to discover how hopelessly European, and how deeply rooted in his land, he was. Appropriately enough, Soldati's work bore the title *America primo amore* (America, First Love), a love which, being perhaps too adolescent, was bound to fail in its attempt to formulate a new synthesis of a strange land. Cecchi's volume, on the other hand, was a more intellectual record, based less on sentimental vagaries and impressions than on literary awareness and merciless observation. Although it is not rare to find in Cecchi's book valuable insights into the culture he studied, one senses an attitude of hostility and sarcasm that hardly contributes to the openness and objectivity expected from an intelligent observer. In both Soldati's and Cecchi's books, as Leslie Fiedler aptly summarized, "there is the same vision of a land ravaged by senseless violence, ruled by women, intellectually presided over by professors who despise ideas and play bridge, and in both [books] there is the view of a desperate materialism brought to the edge of despair."

It was natural that Soldati, being a writer rather than a critic, should present his views about America through a series of vignettes, some amusing, others provocative, others amazingly candid. His volume attempts to recapture the spirit of American life (and of the Italian immigrant) through a number of situations. The disquieting side of *America primo amore* is its inability to comprehend and explain the troubles of a nation in crisis (one must not forget that Soldati wrote of America during the Depression). Beyond this flaw, due no doubt to the author's inexperience, there is a certain unwillingness to forecast how the nation might develop and to predict what the future might bring to a people as diversified as the American.

Cecchi's *America amara* is, by contrast, a more intelligently written book and more calculated in its disparaging synthesis of American life. It is the work of a superb literary craftsman and an expert in Anglo-American letters, who turned his literary knowledge to producing a disturbing and distorted indictment of a whole way of life. What was understandably expected of a writer like Soldati becomes puzzling when one bears in mind Cecchi's background in American culture. His devastating condemnation of America was further documented by the numerous photographs that accompanied the book—illustrations chosen to emphasize the raw aspects of the life he described. Thus, the picture of a gangster shot in his automobile or of the lynchings of the thirties or a portrait of the slums helped to create an image of a nation ruled by hoodlums and riddled with violence and despair. It is unfortunate that the author should resort to such puerile stratagems (it is interesting to note that the pictures do not appear in the postwar editions of the work), particularly since his pages are filled with insights and observations that have a strikingly timely meaning:

> From a civilization whose supreme postulate is material well-being and happiness, it was obvious that only an art without illusions, and of disillusion with solace, could be born. . . . The dilemma of the sexes has become increasingly fierce, both because life itself has become tougher and more demanding and because the freedom of customs seems simultaneously to have increased in the continuous relaxation of the puritan code. Also, in such equivocal freedom, the mortified senses of puritanism have not been relaxed and toned down, but have only become emancipated from feelings and have turned more perverse. Once social decency has tumbled down, without being replaced by a sincere capacity to enjoy life, one is confronted by a kind of cold and wild paganism, which has set its feet upon all internal and external prohibitions: a paganism of mere violence, without any appearance of happiness.

Contemporary with the views promulgated by Cecchi and Soldati, there was still another picture of America vastly richer and more colorful, if substantially more distorted. Such an image became deeply embedded in the Italian mind: but this time Hollywood, and not the

American writers, was responsible for conveying an impression of a nation ravaged by gangsters, wild Indians, and tough cowboys. If such an image is mentioned here, it is because for a long time it was the symbol available to the masses and to the less cultured-oriented groups.

In the period between 1930 and the end of the war another America, less stereotyped and more literary, began to emerge. Both Soldati and Cecchi had been instrumental in giving impetus to an interest in America that was soon to produce an extraordinarily sympathetic appreciation of those aspects of life that had once been deemed the worst faults of the new continent. Thus, the Italian conception of the United States held before the last war was that of a country which, for all its violence and materialism, was fundamentally more sincere and humane than humanistic Italy.

Two intellectuals were chiefly responsible for making the achievement and meaning of American fiction better known in their country: Elio Vittorini and the late Cesare Pavese. Through their translations, the perceptive essays and notes they produced, they made possible an understanding of the worth of American writing and the complexity of American life. Indeed the interest shown by Vittorini, Pavese, and all those who soon turned to American letters was itself a protest against the "official" culture, a manifestation of deep-seated resentment and disapproval of Fascist values. Reading American authors soon became equivalent to being a secret sympathizer of a nation that was determined to resist the aggressive plans of the totalitarian countries.

Beginning in 1930, and continuing through the war years, an incredible amount of translating and explaining the work of the Americans took place right under the eyes of the Fascists. The classics and the contemporary authors—from Melville to Poe, from Sinclair Lewis to Faulkner, Steinbeck, and Caldwell, down to the lesser figures of the "hard-boiled" school of writing—were rendered into Italian. At long last, after having only indirect contact with American literature through the summary judgments of Soldati, Cecchi, and others, the Italian reader was able to confront the works he had heard mentioned so often and come to personal conclusions about their merits.

Those whose interest in American literature was motivated by a rebellion against, and a disgust with, the emptiness and provinciality of their own culture eventually reached a more positive position vis-à-vis the United States. There was nothing in the novels they read to justify such a dramatically unorthodox change in their attitude. Yet, because of what they chose to read in those books, they realized that a nation that could afford the freedom necessary to depict reality with such devastating honesty could only be unafraid to show its real face, anxious to change and evolve, conscious of its flaws, unburdened by its past traditions, and, above all, ready to criticize itself. However pessimistic, such a literature could only be produced by a basically healthy nation and not by one Mussolini had called "a decadent democracy."

In 1941 a rich anthology of American writers appeared, entitled *Americana* and accompanied by a long introduction by Elio Vittorini. It was inevitable that the censor, sensitive to the gravity of the times and not well disposed toward foreign literature, should object to the publication of the work and deny the necessary authorization for its distribution. Another edition was quickly produced, this time without Vittorini's critical essay, which interpreted in a very positive manner the selections included in the book. The new edition carried a note by pro-Fascist Emilio Cecchi who, needless to say, showed himself less friendly toward the American texts. One has but to turn to the final paragraphs of the original piece by Vittorini (now available in the volume *Diario in pubblico*) to understand what had impelled the censor to step in:

> Contemporary America is a kind of fabulous Orient, and man appears from time to time under the sign of an exquisite particularity, Philippine or Chinese or Slave or Kurd, only to be in substance the same lyrical "I" protagonist of the creation. What in the old legend is the son of the West, and is pointed out as the symbol of a new man, is now the son of the earth. And America is no longer America, no longer a new world, but the whole world. But the details come to it from everywhere, and meet there: scents of the earth. Life is stated with the simplest of gestures, and without any hidden ideological thoughts, intrepidly accepted even in despair and in death. . . .

Only in 1945, when the war was over, did a brilliant review of the anthology, by the late Giaime Pintor, a young student of German and American letters, appear in *Aretusa*, a magazine then edited by Carlo Muscetta. The piece is more than a review of *Americana*: it is a *mise en point* of the entire problem of Italo-American cultural relations and a severe criticism of Cecchi's position in it. Pintor lost no time pointing out how certain conflicts had arisen between the two countries after America had been misunderstood and misinterpreted for centuries. After the end of World War I, "this complex of diffidence and curiosity found its natural expression in a rich sociology; . . . America drew closer to European life and imposed [upon the Continent] its own taste and tendencies." Pintor viewed Cecchi's *America amara* as a feeble attempt to understand the United States without having either the necessary sympathetic disposition nor the genuine desire to delve into the life of a nation so different from Italy. The author's "geographical inferiority" prevented the achievement of his goal: Cecchi, Pintor continued, "is one of the men least capable of adapting himself to the discoveries of a journey, one of those [minds] most obstinately bound to the prejudices of his motherland." As for the anthology Cecchi had produced, Pintor remarked that the editor "has scrupulously collected a museum of horrors where he has isolated diseases and decadence and recognized a world that is hardly believable"; and yet it is in this world that "we have recognized a voice profoundly near us, the voice of true friends and our first contemporaries." America, in his words, "has now reached the point of equilibrium in which literature ceases to be a lived experience and is not quite an academic tradition: the writers who live in this period have the right to call themselves classics because in them, for the first time, there is a vision of America that has no need of being recalled. . . . Bureaucratic corruption, the gangsters and the crises, everything has become mature in a growing body. This is the real story of America: a growing people who cover with their own unending enthusiasm the previously made mistakes and ransom with their good will future dangers."

The extended contact with American letters began yielding its own fruits, although they were at times of a negative sort. The effects achieved by such novelists as Cain and Steinbeck, Hemingway and Saroyan, were eventually first imitated then thoroughly assimilated by Pavese, Vittorini, and, through their example, Berto and Calvino. The American notion of "style" brought about a drastic change of position in the Italian literati's long-held insistence on the *"bello scrivere."*

Cesare Pavese published, in the review *Cultura*, a series of articles dealing with the writers he was actively translating during the thirties and early forties: Melville (whose *Moby Dick* he translated *con amore*), Whitman, Edgar Lee Masters, Sinclair Lewis. One can take issue with his interpretations of the work of these and other writers, but one must not discount the particular circumstances that had led him to his own activity as a translator. Quite aside from the merit they undoubtedly had as illuminating pieces on certain American figures, his articles are interesting as examples of a search Pavese himself was to continue for years—a search for the perfect amalgamation of the essential qualities of American style as he saw it, *realtà, mito,* and *ritmo* (reality, myth, and rhythm), rendered in his own prose style. Yet the lesson learned from the Americans was not a narrowly stylistic one. *What* the author saw became as important as *how* he described it, and the frantic obsession with linguistic purity greatly diminished. Pavese's own favorite definition (which, for a while, served him as a concept of the essence of literature) was synthesized in Sherwood Anderson's words "the ultimate grip of reality."

In the light of the new situation it was inevitable that the Italian intellectual should turn to America in his quest for freedom and relief from the stifling conformity of his own culture and politics. No other country in the world was as instinctively loved as America: no other nation in the world had provided the Italian imagination with a myth whose validity was traceable to its indefinitude and suggestiveness. America and freedom were synonymous in the stark years before World War II, and it was to the new continent that Italy looked not merely for understanding and help, but for hope. When Soldati was asked to suggest an English title for his book he answered: "When America Was Called Hope."

In addition to opening new vistas for the Italian reader, American fiction, with its directness and simplicity, induced Italian writers to focus on the moment, to concentrate on reality, and to employ, whenever necessary, a violent style.

"The days are gone when we discovered America!" wrote Pavese, this time in his review of Richard Wright's *Black Boy*. In the years 1930-44 dozens of American books had been translated and avidly read by those who, by their very act of reading, had expressed their outrage toward fascism and the longing for new values. "Now it's all over." Once the threat of fascism had disappeared, America and her culture could no longer represent the oasis of freedom and stand as the symbol of courage, the natural place to escape from the artificiality and mediocrity of Fascist Italy. Pavese's essay, written in a mood of deep and bitter disillusionment, is perhaps the most important statement made by an *Americanista* explaining the "real" meaning of the encounter of Italy with the United States.

> [In the thirties] American culture became for us something very serious and precious, a sort of great laboratory where others were working, under different conditions of liberty and with different means, on the same task of creating a style, a modern world, as the best of our writers were, perhaps with less immediacy but with the same stubborn will. And so this culture seemed to us an ideal place for work and experiment, a strenuous and embattled experiment, rather than a mere Babel of clamorous efficiency, of cruel neon-lit optimism that stunned and blinded the naïve —an image that even our provincial-minded rulers found of some use when they came across it in certain hypocritical novels. After several years of study we comprehended that America was not *another* land, *another* historical beginning, but merely the gigantic theater, where, with more frankness than was possible anywhere else, the universal drama was being re-enacted.

No longer could America influence Italian writing, or at least so stated Pavese. "Without fascism to oppose, without a progressive historical idea to personify, even America —for all its skyscrapers and automobiles and soldiers— will no longer be the vanguard of anybody's culture."

More than a decade has passed since the publication of

Pavese's statement, and if his prophecy has not been totally fulfilled, at least some of his contentions have been realized. Numerous works published in the postwar years show beyond a doubt that American literature has indeed left its deep mark. Ugo Moretti's style has been called "ultra-American," as have Arfelli's novels about the disillusionment of what he calls "the fifth generation." Italo Calvino's first books, notably *The Path to the Nest of Spiders,* echo Hemingway and Saroyan; Vasco Pratolini's book *A Tale of Poor Lovers* seems to have borrowed from the Americans (Dos Passos particularly) its rapid succession of scenes; Mario Tobino and Natalia Ginzburg show how pervasively they have felt the impact of Gertrude Stein's stylistic device of repeating and elaborating the same sentence; while the overwhelming majority of southern writers has been attracted by the violence and wretchedness of their native places in a way which, although stemming from a local tradition that goes back to Verga and the *veristi,* is apt to remind the American reader of his own southern school and of Steinbeck's emphasis on the "underdog."

It is impossible to make specific comments on the question of influence, primarily because the number of American books translated into Italian is so staggering. Moreover, as George Lukács correctly perceived, "although the existence of a literature of international scope is an undisputed fact, it is a very complicated fact replete with contradictions. It is neither the sum nor the mean of all national cultures, literatures, and great writers but the living totality of the mutual interactions of their living totalities." It is better, perhaps, to speak of the impact of American fiction in Italy as discernible in the borrowing of certain stylistic or structural techniques or by themes that have long been part of the tradition of American creative writing. Thus, for example, it is probably due to the American influence that many novels authored by women (Ginzburg, Banti, De Céspedes) have attempted to illuminate by way of a special interest in feminine life another slighted facet of Italian reality.

Does "familiarity breed contempt" as is generally assumed? The question is not as facetious as it may seem. Since the end of the war, indeed since the American invasion in Italy and the ensuing military occupation, Italy has literally been flooded by an overwhelming and disconcerting conglomeration of American products—from cigarettes and Coca-Cola to automobiles and books, many of which fall into the category of what may tolerantly be called "trash." The United States Information Agency—despite the great pressure under which it must work, its occasional naïveté and the errors normally expected from such an active agency—manages to do an extremely useful job in helping clear up several misconceptions about American life. Its library and lecture programs, its various exhibits of books and art, its occasional importation of intellectuals capable of addressing their audience in Italian, may be counted among the most felicitous undertakings that have contributed substantially to a better understanding of the United States and its problems.

Italian views of America have undergone a dramatic and much needed change from the thirties, a change that is still under way. Some of the results of these changes are evidenced by a more thorough, less amateurish approach to American letters. The interest in American and English literature has become broader and more intensive than it was before the war. Wallace Stevens, Marianne Moore, Ezra Pound, E. E. Cummings, have been translated as have the novels of Joyce, Robert Penn Warren, J. D. Salinger, William Styron, James Jones, and a score of other major and minor writers. Penetrating essays and monographs on the classics of American literature have made their appearance of late; Melville, Poe, Hawthorne, James, Howells, Stein, Hemingway, Faulkner, and Pound have been studied from fresh perspectives. The nucleus of translators and critics, a small group in the thirties, has grown considerably, becoming at the same time more professional and, regrettably, also more commercial. But their seriousness and competence make them one of the best groups of translators of contemporary Europe. Although the field of American studies is relatively young, one is impressed by the maturity and enthusiasm of its scholars.

The professional and nonprofessional *Americanisti* are too numerous to be listed here. Their interest has received much encouragement from publishing firms which are, as always, eager to please the public and possibly reap some tangible benefit or profit from Italian interest in America. As a result, too many decisively inferior books have been published. Modern and contemporary poetry has been translated with care and feeling by Alfredo Rizzardi and Carlo Izzo, while fiction can always count on the sensibility of Fernanda Pivano. Among the critics, Gabriele Baldini, Nemi d'Agostino, Salvatore Rosati, Paolo Milano, Claudio Gorlier, Glauco Cambon, and Elémire Zolla have made distinguished contributions to scholarship with their fine essays and books. Agostino Lombardo deserves to be singled out here especially on account of his expert editorship of the yearly *Studi americani,* a book-type journal that publishes the more solid analyses of American writing.

The American theater has also enjoyed unusual acclaim in Italy, especially in the past years. Large and faithful audiences flock regularly to those houses where performances of Tennessee Williams and Arthur Miller are given, while the theaters that offer the classical fare are often deserted, despite the high quality of the casts and the brilliant productions. The common explanation offered is still the best: Italians are attracted not only by the honesty of American theater and fiction but by their contemporary relevance. The violence and starkness of American drama has effectively acted as a much-needed antidote against the shallowness and stupidity—not to mention the ludicrous materialism—that pervades the bulk of Hollywood cinematic productions. It is healthy to be, as many Americans indeed are, skeptical and pessimistic even in a rich and powerful nation.

What of the American attitude toward Italian culture? The facts speak eloquently for themselves. Gone are the days when hardly any Italian fiction, and much less poetry, was translated. The list of the writers who have been translated into English is as impressive as it is diverse: there is something for every taste—from Guareschi to Moravia, from Pavese to Pratolini, from Calvino to Morante. There still are many writers of stature who, for a number of reasons (many of them political), have not been made available to the English-speaking public. At the time of this writing, we have unfortunately failed to see in English any absorbing books by Petroni, Del Buono, Fortini, Testori, Manzini, Banti, Pasolini, Gadda, none of whom (with the exception of the last two) present any special problem of translation. Palazzeschi, Alvaro, Piovene (to mention a few names), have only been partially translated, as has Eduardo de Filippo, possibly the finest living Italian playwright.

Despite the formidable difficulties presented by its texts, poetry has not fared badly on the whole. Of the important poets, two have been generously translated (Ungaretti and Quasimodo), and there is reason to hope that now that the quality of Italian postwar letters has received recognition by the award of the Nobel Prize to Quasimodo in 1959, the work of Umberto Saba and Eugenio Montale will soon be presented in English. A rich anthology of Italian poets of this century, edited by Carlo L. Golino, is now in preparation and should at last acquaint the enthusiast of Italian letters with other worthy names. Quite apart from the labors of individual scholars and translators, the magazine *Italian Quarterly,* published at the University of California at Los Angeles by a group of devoted Italianists, and containing vigorous essays on politics, literature, and the arts, has in the past four years done a great deal to keep the general reader well informed about the current state of Italian life.

Some years ago Leslie Fiedler, writing in the *Kenyon Review,* stated that in responding to Italian fiction, "America is welcoming itself, a deliberate reflection of its own stylistic devices." The insight was a brilliant one, but it failed to explain why a writer like Elio Vittorini, so close to the American sensibility, should fail to receive more than a lukewarm reception from the reading public and the critics.

Perhaps, one might conclude, the time is past when in America and in Italy the reader is ready to accept only those books that reflect an image of man with which he can fully identify. Might not the fact that more and more European fiction is being translated into English (even in the case of such unorthodox Italian writers as La Capria, Morante, Calvino, and Parise) be a valid demonstration that the American audience, often surprisingly alert to literary values, has become more sophisticated and discerning than we ordinarily suspect? To judge from the books that have reached us from Italy and other European countries in recent years the answer would seem to be an affirmative one. The trend is a hopeful one: the future might well be brighter than we think.

# CHAPTER ELEVEN

# Panorama of
# Other Contemporary Novelists

In this chapter the reader will find, listed alphabetically, the names of significant novelists whose work has not been discussed in the previous chapters. The list that follows, far from being a complete one, is merely representative of the various tendencies of contemporary Italian fiction. No writer who died before World War II has been included, nor has any writer with whose works the American audience is sufficiently acquainted. For the convenience of the reader, the titles of works that have been translated into English are given, in parentheses, after the original Italian title.

## CORRADO ALVARO (1895-1956)

Poet, essayist, moralist, and novelist, Alvaro was born in the southernmost region of Calabria. Throughout his life he remained an indefatigable traveler, gifted with a keen sense of observation and an insatiable curiosity about people, traditions, and places. Besides several books of verses and travel, he published numerous short stories, the earliest of which were collected in a masterful book, *Gente in Aspromonte* (1930). His best novels are *L'uomo è forte* (1938) (*Man Is Strong*), whose major theme is intellectual freedom, and *L'età è breve* (1946), the first of a three-volume cycle (entitled *Memorie del mondo sommerso*) describing the involvement of its hero, Rinaldo Diacono, with the important social and political events of Italian life from D'Annunzio's days through fascism.

### GIOVANNI BATTISTA ANGIOLETTI (1896-1961)

Angioletti, born in Milan, may be counted among the most productive writers of this generation. He was known primarily for his essays, literary criticism, and for his books on cultural problems and interpretations. He wrote some fiction, the best of which are short stories, collected in a volume entitled *Narciso* (1949). He was until his recent death Secretary of the Italian Writers' Guild.

### SERGIO ANTONIELLI (1920-    )

Antonielli, Roman by birth and a teacher of Italian literature in a school in Turin, has written a fine war novel, *Campo 29* (1949), as well as a most intriguing tale, *La tigre viziosa* (1954), the heroine of which is a tiger who narrates in retrospect the fascinating adventures that led to her death.

### RICCARDO BACCHELLI (1891-    )

Born in Bologna, Bacchelli is widely known for his active participation in the Roman magazine *La Ronda* (q.v.) and for his historical novels. Aside from his plays and poetry, his most sustained work is *Il Mulino del Po* (1935-40) (*The Mill on the Po; Nothing New Under the Sun*), a three-volume saga of Italian life from the Napoleonic wars to our own time.

### GIORGIO BASSANI (1916-    )

One of the best Italian postwar writers, Bassani has written poetry and several short stories, collected in the volume entitled *Cinque storie ferraresi* (1956) and a *novella* about homosexuality, *Gli occhiali d'oro* (1958) (*The Gold-Rimmed Spectacles*). He has fictionalized his native Ferrara and has created a host of characters who live in periods of stress and tension. He directs the publishing house of Feltrinelli and was the former editor of the review *Botteghe Oscure*.

### MARIA BELLONCI (1902-    )

Born in Rome, wife of the well-known literary critic and journalist Goffredo Bellonci, Signora Bellonci specializes in fictionalized biographies, all of which have been translated and widely read in Europe and abroad. A revised edition of *Lucrezia Borgia* (2nd ed., 1947) (*The Life and Times* of *Lucrezia Borgia*) has appeared under the title of *Lucrezia Borgia, la sua vita e i suoi tempi*. Her recent work includes *I segreti di Gonzaga* (1947) (*A Prince of Mantua*) and *Milano viscontea* (1956).

### GIUSEPPE BERTO (1914-    )

Berto, born in Mogliano in the province of Treviso, was one of the first Italian novelists to be "exported" abroad after the war. His most memorable work is still *Il cielo è rosso* (1947) (*The Sky Is Red*), a novel about war and of a group of youngsters caught in it. His later production includes *Le opere di Dio* (1948) (*The Works of God*) and *Il Brigante* (1951) (*The Brigand*), as well as *Guerra in camicia nera* (1955), a novel about the meaning of fighting on the Fascist side during the last war.

### ROMANO BILENCHI (1909-    )

Born in Colle Val d'Elsa, near Siena, Bilenchi is a psychological writer. Although his fiction is autobiographical, the author is gifted with a restrained style. The events are handled in such a way as to bring out the intellectual, moral, and emotional temper of his characters. He has written several short stories and novelettes, a genre in which he excels. His early books, *Anna e Bruno* (1936), *Mio cugino Andrea* (1936), and *La siccità* (1941) have remained his most typical.

### MASSIMO BONTEMPELLI (1884-1959)

Bontempelli had as varied a literary life as any writer would want to have, experiencing the influence first of Carducci and of the Futurists, then of Croce and fascism, and finally of Communism. He wrote poetry, essays, and literary criticism (some of it first rate, such as his volume *Leopardi, Verga e Pirandello*). He also produced numerous plays and edited the well-known literary magazine *Il '900*. A brilliant, original writer, he was the Italian leader of the metaphysical and surrealistic novel. His most solid book is *Gente nel tempo* (1937). His choice short fiction has been collected in *L'amante fedele* (1935).

### VITALIANO BRANCATI (1907-1954)

Brancati, like many of his contemporary fellow novelists, set his stories in his native Sicily. He is an incisive commentator of certain Italian customs, some of which he has satirized in such amusing novels as *Don Giovanni in Sicilia* (1942) and *Il bell'Antonio* (1949) (*Antonio, the Great Lover*), the latter a tale of sexual impotency. Because of his strong stands against censorship (*I fascisti, Ritorno alla censura,* and *Le due dittature*), his play *La governante,* written shortly before his untimely death, was never granted the censor's approval.

## DINO BUZZATI (1906-    )

By awarding Buzzati the Viareggio Prize for Literature in 1958, the critics acknowledged the high esteem in which they hold one of the most singular writers of suspense stories. Often compared to Kafka (of whom he is, at best, a pale imitator), Buzzati has written mostly about man's fears and insecurity. *Il deserto dei Tartari* (1940) (*The Tartar Steppe*), *Il crollo della Baliverna* (1954), *Un caso clinico* (a play, published as a short story in 1958 in *The Paris Review* with the title "A Clinical Case"), and *Sessanta racconti* (1958) are his most representative works. *L'invasione degli orsi in Sicilia* (1945) is a diverting book to be read as a perfect antidote against the chilling atmosphere generally conjured up by the author.

## CARLO CASSOLA (1917-    )

Although Cassola began his literary career shortly before the last war, it is only in recent years that he has shown original talent. He has found ample inspiration for his novels in the Fascist years, in which he set his *Fausto e Anna* (1952) (*Fausto and Anna*) and, *I vecchi compagni* (1953). Keenly interested in the sociopolitical situation of his country, he has also written such notable *engagé* nonfiction as *I minatori della Maremma* (1956). His recent work includes the novels, *La casa di Via Valadier* (1956), *Un matrimonio del dopoguerra* (1958), *La ragazza di Bube* (1960), and *Un cuore arido* (1961).

## GIOVANNI COMISSO (1895-    )

Born in Treviso, Comisso has written an impressive number of short stories, novels, and books about his travels. He has been the recipient of two major literary prizes, the Bagutta (1929) and the Strega (1955), the latter for his collection of short stories *Il gatto attraversa la strada.* Comisso's style has the rare distinction of being at once simple and poetic, peculiarly endowed with a regional flavor without ever falling into the vernacular. The author succeeds in being both a gentle person who delights in describing his country and his farm and the astute observer who travels to the Orient and throughout Europe to give us an imaginative and realistic interpretation of these countries.

### ALBA de CÉSPEDES (1911-    )

De Céspedes is probably one of the most successful women writers in Italy today. Her novels are sympathetic treatments of the predicament of the modern Italian woman, who is destined to give of herself all her life without necessarily being understood and often, alas, unloved by her mate. Her finest novel is *Quaderno proibito* (1954) (*The Secret*), a moving account written in diary form about the obsession of a woman who, through a deliberately careful reflection of the daily events of her life, discovers the failure and tragedy of a marriage she had once believed happy and serene.

### GIUSEPPE DESSÍ (1909-    )

A Sardinian by birth, Dessí has combined an administrative career (he is the Superintendent of Schools, attached to the Roman Accademia dei Lincei) with that of a creative artist. He has written numerous short stories and a very poetic *novella, L'isola dell'angelo* (1957).

### ENNO FLAIANO (1910-    )

Born in Pascara, Flaiano is an unusually able scenario writer, a penetrating essayist, and a clever, sophisticated journalist. He is the author of the remarkable novel *Tempo di uccidere* (1947) (*The Short Cut*), set in Africa during the Italo-Ethiopian war. The hero has an affair with a woman infected with leprosy, and the ensuing fear and sense of guilt that haunts him constitute the dominating themes of this memorable work.

### CARLO EMILIO GADDA (1893-    )

Gadda, born in industrial Milan, is beyond any doubt the most intellectual and "difficult" of the contemporary Italian novelists. His controversial work, *Quer pasticciaccio bruto de Via Merulana* (1957) is the Italian novel closest to James Joyce's *Ulysses*. The novel has as its central episodes a murder and a burglary, committed in Rome in

1927. The real heroes of the book are the curious and truly human witnesses called before the local police officer conducting the investigation—each of whom speaks in his own dialect, generally Roman, which Gadda alternates with a literate, elegant Italian. It is highly doubtful that Gadda will ever achieve substantial popularity, precisely because of the linguistic difficulties that are both his strength and weakness.

### FRANCESCO JOVINE (1902-1950)

Born in Guardalfiera, a small town in the district of Campobasso, Jovine began writing in the early forties and kept quite close to his native region until death cut short a promising career. His mature novels, published in the postwar years, are: *L'impero in provincia* (1945) and *Le terre del Sacramento* (1950). The latter is set in the Molise region and coincides chronologically with the rise of fascism in Italy. Its theme is the eternal struggle to till the soil and the traditional exploitation of the peasants by rich landowners.

### CARLO LEVI (1902-     )

Though primarily known for his penetrating essays on the South: *Cristo si è fermato a Eboli* (1945) (*Christ Stopped at Eboli*), on freedom: *Paura della Libertà* (1946) (*Fear of Freedom*), on Sicily: *Le parole sono pietre* (1955) (*Words Are Stones*), and more recently on Soviet Russia: *Il futuro ha un cuore antico* (1956), Levi is also the author of an interesting work of fiction, *L'orologio* (1950) (*The Watch*). His novel tries to recapture the atmosphere of the first months after the war and the hectic, promising month of Ferruccio Parri's premiership. As a work of fiction, *The Watch* reveals Levi's best qualities: a refined and extensive culture, a superior intellect, and finally, a deftness in handling words and situations much in the manner of a painter. (He is, incidentally, an established painter.) It is unfortunate that his immense culture should be, in the last analysis, precisely the greatest obstacle to his writing a well-made novel.

### CURZIO (SUCKERT) MALAPARTE (1898-1957)

Right up to his death Malaparte was one of the most controversial and brilliant writers of his generation. A faithful Fascist, he recanted his political position and was subsequently imprisoned. His book *Kapputt* (1944) (*Kapputt*) grew out of his experience as a newspaperman covering the Russian campaign.

He was bold, cultured, and ambitious: his curriculum includes an interesting and fruitful excursion as co-editor of the review *Campo di Marte*, published in Florence. One of his last books was *La pelle* (1949) (*The Skin*), which dealt with the Allied occupation of Naples and with the war in the southern sector of Italy. The work was either exalted or condemned, according to the politics and aesthetics of the critic. His literary output exemplifies in a convincing manner the extent of D'Annunzio's influence upon today's literary figures. His prose is bold, striking, and always quite effective. It arouses, more often than not, either an incredible admiration or downright disgust for the writer.

### GIANNA MANZINI (1896-      )

Born in Pistoia, Gianna Manzini is an acute and highly sophisticated writer. Her work abounds with vividness, complexities, and analogies; her preoccupations are with physical sensations and the discomfort and restlessness they engender. Introspective and morose at times, she is nevertheless always lucid and even clairvoyant. Her literary output consists of over a dozen books, of which *La sparviera* (1956) is the most significant.

### GIUSEPPE MAROTTA (1902-      )

Born in Naples, this humorous and brilliant short-story teller, journalist, and scenario writer is one of the prominent members of the so-called southern school, and a writer who has thoroughly identified himself with the weaknesses, sorrows, and unexplainable joys of life that are Naples'. Among his many books, *L'oro di Napoli* (1947) (*The Gold of Naples*) and *Marotta Ciak* are typical of his art and range.

### ELSA MORANTE (1912-      )

Elsa Morante, the wife of Alberto Moravia, has to her credit an impressive literary record. Although numerically her work is unimpressive (she has written three novels and a small volume of poetry), it is also one of the finest to have appeared lately in Italy. Critics on both sides of the ocean have hailed her recent *L'isola d'Arturo* (1957) (*Arturo's Island*) and its poetic prose style. My personal preference goes to the long, complex, fascinating novel *Menzogna e sortilegio* (1948) (*The House of Liars*), very reminiscent of eighteenth-century tales of intrigues and subterfuges.

## MARINO MORETTI (1885-        )

Born in Cesenatico, a lovely fishermen's town on the Adriatic and today a popular summer resort, Moretti is considered by many readers and critics the dean of the more traditional group of contemporary Italian novelists. He began his literary career in 1905 as a crepuscular poet. Soon afterwards he turned to fiction, a genre he has practiced quite prolifically, as evidenced by the forty-odd volumes of novels and short stories he has authored in the past five decades, most of which have a regional setting. Yet Moretti's world—provincial as it may be—has a measure of humanity unknown to many of his contemporaries. Of all his numerous books, my choices are the early *La voce di Dio* (1920) and the humorous *La vedova Fioravanti* (1941).

## ANNA MARIA ORTESE (1914-        )

Born in Rome, Signorina Ortese is the distinguished author of a remarkable collection of short stories, *Il mare non bagna Napoli* (1953) (*The Bay Is Not Naples*), which describes in a poignant manner poverty and loneliness in Naples' slum areas.

## ALDO PALAZZESCHI (1885-        )

Much like his friend Marino Moretti, Palazzeschi (a pseudonym for Aldo Giurlani) began his career writing first crepuscular then futuristic poetry, the latter especially enjoyable even today. He has written some of the wittiest novels of this century, *Il codice di Perelà* (1911) (*Perelà, the Man of Smoke*) and *Il palio dei buffi* (1944). His other novels, principally *Le sorelle Materassi* (1934) (*The Sisters Materassi*) and *I fratelli Cuccioli* (1948), are true gems of irony and humor. Palazzeschi is one of the best contemporary Italian writers, a raconteur in the finest tradition of his native Tuscany (he was born in Florence). He can tell a tale without complexities or hard-to-decipher symbolism. His stories are now humorous, now pathetic, but always supremely human.

## GOFFREDO PARISE (1929-    )

Born in Vicenza, Parise is one of the *enfants terribles* of the younger generation. A brilliant, outspoken novelist, he has written several novels all of which have received controversial notices. Of these, two have been translated: *Le comete* (1951) (*The Dead Boy and Comets*) and *Il prete bello* (1954) (*Don Gastone and the Ladies*).

## PIER PAOLO PASOLINI (1922-    )

Born in Bologna, Pasolini is a versatile member of the postwar crop of Italian intellectuals. He has written poetry in dialect and learned literary essays, and edited several extremely intelligent anthologies of dialect poetry. He co-edits *Officina,* a bold, leftist review published by Bompiani. He has written two highly significant novels, *I ragazzi di vita* (1955) and *Una vita violenta* (1959), soon to appear in English. In both novels, Pasolini has experimented with the use of dialect in fiction. His favorite focus is the working class, and by obvious preference, the youngsters thriving in the Roman slums.

## CESARE PAVESE (1908-50)

There is a general agreement today that had Pavese not chosen to take his life late in the summer of 1950, he would undoubtedly be the leading novelist of today's Italy. He was born in Cuneo (Piedmont). In his novelettes and novels he tried to fuse the myths of Greek literature with contemporary obsessions and problems. His style is intensely personal, very poetic, and full of allusions. "Life has meaning only if we live it for something or someone," shouts one of his characters. It was part of the tragic failure of our age that Pavese should not have been able to reconcile his extremely rare gift as a creative artist with the demands made upon him by his society. His best novel is *La luna e i falò* (1950) (*The Moon and the Bonfires*), which was published shortly before his suicide.

## GUIDO PIOVENE (1907-    )

Born in Piacenza, Piovene has gained a substantial reputation as a man of letters, as an elegant and extremely cultured essayist, and as a shrewd observer of Italian and

American life. His treatment of the United States (*De America*) (1953) is a prime document in the history of Italo-American cultural relations. His best novel is *Lettere di una novizia* (1941) (*Letters of a Novice*).

### GIOSE RIMANELLI (1926-     )

Rimanelli, like a good many other younger novelists of the postwar period, was born in the South, at Casacalenda (Campobasso). He has written an unusual novel about how it felt to be "on the wrong side" during the last war. His *Tiro a piccione* (1953) (*The Day of the Lion*) deals with the adventures of a young Fascist, and with the anguish born out of his position. His second novel, *Peccato originale* (1954) (*Original Sin*) is a realistic tale that takes place in a primitive southern town.

### FORTUNATO SEMINARA (1903-     )

Born at Maropati, near Reggio Calabria, Seminara began his literary career under the direct influence of two other *Calabresi*, Corrado Alvaro and Grazia Deledda, the Sardinia-born Nobel Prize winner for 1925. In the manner of these two writers, Seminara has focused his attention on the provincial world of his native region, blending and correcting what often is a dangerous provincialism with a more modern sense of inquiry on the impossibility of man to understand his fellow man. Loneliness, isolation, and bitterness are often the themes of Southern writers. In Seminara's fiction they are combined with sympathy and kindness, especially in the novel *Il vento nell'oliveto* (1951) (*The Wind in the Olive-Grove*).

### MARIO SOLDATI (1906-     )

Born in Turin, Soldati has become after his first volume, *America primo amore* (1935), a prolific and versatile writer, producing a creditable body of fiction. His collection of stories, *I racconti* (1958), won the Strega Prize. Among his many books, *A cena col Commendatore* (1952) (*Dinner with the Commendatore*) and the striking novels *Le lettere da Capri* (1954) (*The Capri Letters*) and *La confessione* (1955) (*The Confession*), are typical of his art and of its high quality and interest.

### BONAVENTURA TECCHI (1896-     )

Born in Bagnoregio, a small town between the Latium and Umbria, Tecchi is one of the many contemporary

Italians to combine writing with a teaching career. He lectures on German literature at the University of Rome. He has written travel books, short stories, and novels, of which *Il vento tra le case* (1929) and *Tre storie d'amore* (1934) are particularly successful.

## GIOVANNI TESTORI (1923-    )

Born in Novate, near Milan, Testori has undertaken to write about life in the periphery of Milan, and the solitude, alienation, and exploitation suffered by those who elect or are forced to live in big cities. His cycle *I segreti di Milano* is to consist of several volumes, five of which (two of long short stories, two of plays, and one full-length novel) has already appeared. *Il ponte della Ghisolfa* (1958) is quite impressive for its descriptions and psychology. The fifth volume of the series, *Il fabbricone* (1961), is soon to be translated into English.

## MARIO TOBINO (1910-    )

Born in Viareggio, Tobino has been for many years resident psychiatrist at the Lucca Hospital. The perceptive work *Le libere donne di Magliano* (1953) (*The Women of Magliano*) was inspired by his experience in the hospital wards, and in spite of its structural looseness it makes for intriguing reading. Other commendable books are *Il desert della Libia* (1952) and the more recent *novella La brace dei Biassoli* (1956).

## RENATA VIGANÒ (1900-    )

Born in Bologna, Signorina Viganò has already achieved a permanent place in the history of Italian fiction for her touching novel, *L'Agnese va a morire* (1949). She is also a prolific short-story writer; her collection of stories, *Arriva la cicogna* (1954), is quite rewarding.

## ELÉMIRE ZOLLA (1926-    )

Zolla is one of the few truly intellectual novelists of contemporary Italy. He has written numerous essays, distinguished by unusual lucidity and penetration (collected in the volume *Eclissi dell'intellettuale*, 1959), as well as two novels, *Minuetto all'inferno* (1956) and *Cecilia o la disattenzione* (1961).

# CHAPTER TWELVE

# Roman Postscript

My return to Rome, after an absence of barely two years, has been an instructive reminder of how geographical proximity to a culture is instrumental in producing different critical perspectives. Because of my initial choice to work on contemporary Italian literature from the "outside" (although I have frequently been physically close to its "center") the stature of the writers considered in the foregoing pages has not changed as I have drawn closer to them. I have thus become persuaded that the possibility of becoming directly involved with artistic creation (perhaps out of friendship with the artist, or out of personal opinions that have nothing to do with aesthetics) remains one of the greatest sources of distortion of judgment. An illustrative case is offered by Pier Paolo Pasolini, a talented poet, novelist, philologist, and, of late, film director, whose position in his culture awaits the time when the fog of polemics around his work may disappear. It is with double pleasure, therefore, that I remind the reader that the evaluations and opinions advanced in this book have been unaffected by local "literary politics."

Since the completion of this volume, I have not perceived in recent literary events in Italy any reason to modify or correct the judgments expressed in these pages. Thus, to cite some examples, Vasco Pratolini's *Lo scialo* (The Waste), a massive, two-volume sequel to *Metello* (and the second part of the trilogy *Una storia italiana*) adds very little to his reputation or to his artistic personality. If anything, *Lo scialo* has magnified the gifts and deficiencies of the Florentine writer. His novel is one more demonstration of the marvelous ease with which Pratolini can tell a story full of vivid descriptions, enriched by an intimate knowledge of the socio-political events of contemporary Italy. *Lo scialo* has further persuaded me that few novelists can, as Pratolini, re-create a milieu typical of Florence before and during fascism. The method he has chosen to narrate the great saga of a number of Florentine families evidences what is perhaps his greatest weakness as a storyteller. The author, in fact, has set about his goal of describing the thorough corruption of the Italian middle class, reached in stages as it surrendered its moral principles. The detailed vignettes that constitute the book focus on several Florentine families. Their actions, taken together, is what gives the book its tone. Yet, such highly unsatisfactory technique has produced a fragmentary type of fiction robbed of much of its potential vitality and suspense. (It is significant that Pratolini should have chosen to publish, in the review *Nuovi Argomenti,* a long, self-contained chapter from his novel. Much of his long work lends itself to precisely this kind of reading.)

Alberto Moravia, on the other hand, has continued his relentless investigation of the malaises of our century and of the ills plaguing a complacent, overmechanized, empty society, and has produced a new novel aptly entitled *La noia* (*The Empty Canvas*). His book has made much noise in literary circles, has rapidly become one of the best sellers of the year, but has pleased neither readers nor critics. Perhaps it is true, as someone remarked recently, that the middle class reads Moravia for purely masochistic reasons. In his novels, the bourgeoisie may find an accurate reflection of some of its worst features. Although the author was the recipient of the important Viareggio Prize last summer (awarded, however, not for his last published novel, as customary, but for his *opera omnia*), *La noia* has reinforced the suspicion that Moravia may be suffering from an obsession of wanting to "intellectualize" his fiction at the expense of its human content. The result is that his books have the flavor of genuinely calculated works, produced in the secret, cold study room, well thought out and organized (for Moravia can be a master of the well-told tale), but not blessed by that rare, important *soffio di poesia.* These reservations ought not to minimize the author's achievement; he has fictionalized a negative situation (boredom, in the present case) customarily thought to be the concern of the social scientist and the philosopher. Unattractive as a work of fiction

*La noia* may be, it represents another canvas of a series of paintings of decadence begun in 1929 with *Gli indifferenti*. If anything, his most recent novel has served to clarify a question left vague and unanswered in his previous works: brutality, masochism, cruelty, and all acts that do harm to the physical well-being of a person are presented as valid instruments to establish one's own identity in a meaningless world. It is likely that Moravia means that cruelty enables the individual to define a relationship with another human being and makes him aware of his existence in the suffocating and arid climate of indifference and boredom.

Elio Vittorini, another contemporary of Pratolini and Moravia, is apparently under no compulsion to publish regularly. Although I have been repeatedly assured by his intimate friends that his desk drawers are full of eminently readable fiction, Vittorini has chosen the wise course of letting time help him achieve a certain critical perspective toward his own work. Such caution before consigning one's own private vision to the printed page I find extremely commendable; unless I am very much mistaken, we may still expect some real surprises from Elio Vittorini. Meanwhile, the author divides his time between co-editing, with Italo Calvino, the excellent book-type magazine *Il Menabò* (which has now reached its fourth issue) and directing for Mondadori of Milan the series *"La medusa degli Stranieri."* One of the most notable feats of the collection he directs, with astuteness and critical taste, was the publication last year of the first Italian translation of James Joyce's *Ulysses*, a time-consuming labor that demanded the constant devotion and resourcefulness of an obscure teacher, Giulio de Angelis. The translation has at last made available a work that has been a constant point of reference and comparison in Italian cultural circles for several decades. It is difficult to estimate just what impact it will have in the future creative efforts here, though its critical and commercial success have exceeded all expectations. It is likely that Joyce's work, known heretofore to a limited group of specialists, may stimulate considerable interest in rejuvenating or creating new narrative techniques, which in Italy are, with the usual exceptions, antiquated and naïve by all standards. This, by the way, may well serve to explain the success enjoyed this year by *Ferito a morte*, a bril-

liantly executed novel by Raffaele La Capria (winner of
the 1961 Strega Prize), structurally one of the boldest
novels to have appeared of late in Italy.

Another conclusion, supported by fresh evidence, is the
possibility that Italian fiction may be entering a new period.
The bulk of postwar fiction produced in Italy has been
clearly inspired by the catastrophe brought about by the
war. The relative climate of freedom enjoyed by the Italian
novelist has made possible formidable and shocking descriptions of the unbelievably backward social conditions
of certain depressed or underdeveloped areas in both the
South *and* North. It would be false to assert that such
vein of inspiration has been exhausted. Two recently issued books, Leonardo Sciascia's *Il giorno della civetta* and
Giovanni Arpino's *Delitto d'onore* (both will soon appear
in English), serve to remind us that the concern with exploring certain facets of the Italian temperament and
life—whether those be the powerful Mafia or jealousy—
is still vigorous and productive. But as such works continue
to be published—and they should, since they take into
consideration an important slice of Italian life—other
books being written nowadays point out a new need to
continue the personal quest and analyses of the condition
of twentieth-century man in other directions. Such trend
has, to be sure, given its first fruits, discernible in the fiction of Natalia Ginzburg (whose *Le voci della sera* has
just made its appearance), Lalla Romano (*L'uomo che
parlava solo*), and Laura di Falco (whose novels, *Paura
del giorno* and *Una donna disponibile,* have given us significant insights into the fate of modern women). Should
such a trend continue, we may soon witness a more thorough rejection of what the critic Renato Barilli has elsewhere defined as *"il senso comune."* The philosophy of
common sense is one based on practical considerations that
have little or nothing to do with the real aspirations and
problems of our time. Common sense, as defined by Barilli,
means a totality of psychological, sentimental, ethical, and
logical conceptions that serve to regulate our rapports with
the world of our everyday life. The common acceptance
of such a manner of looking at and describing life has
generated a fiction that is frequently conformist and arid,
bordering more upon chronicles and journalism than upon
art. After the experience of neorealism, the Italian novelist

has learned to look at the world around him with honesty and sincerity.

Italian fiction is enjoying today an enviable reputation. Its diversity, its closeness to reality (or, at least, to a certain kind of reality), its brave attempts to depict some of the manifold problems arising out of the conditions of the new times, have impressed the international audience. The shortcomings of contemporary Italian writing continue to parallel strangely those characterizing the very fabric of Italian life: it is humorless, generally conventional, and lamentably unconcerned with problems other than the basic ones. If there is an abundance of novelists who have managed to give us incisive and convincing pictures of Italian life, there is only a handful of genuine artists who have succeeded in truly transcending their own time—the immediate present—and have given us compelling interpretations less of *how* things are or how times have changed, than of the precise *meaning* of such changes. Surely, since there is general agreement that the world of today is radically different from yesterday's, we may expect the novelist to dedicate himself not just to describing what is happening to us but to discovering in what way the evolutionary or revolutionary changes registered by Western society really matter—in which way they have affected the human condition.

The entire postwar period certainly stands a good chance of being remembered as the era when the Italian novelist gained new confidence in his métier and rid his writing of much of the rhetoric that had frequently plagued his culture. Not much of what he produced was certain to survive the test of time, but at least he could console himself with the fact that a similar fate falls upon all writers in any historical period.

It remains to be seen whether the lesson so painfully learned during the past decade and a half can be put to use in creating a type of fiction that will examine in depth other, more polemical aspects of Italian life and that will seek new ways to achieve that finer knowledge of the self toward which every artist gropes. The novels to be issued during future literary seasons will alone serve as useful instruments to record and gauge the development and achievement of modern Italian fiction.

*Rome, November 1961*

# Selected Bibliography

ALBERTO MORAVIA

(Bompiani editions, unless otherwise stated. The translations of Moravia's work have been published in the United States by Farrar, Straus & Cudahy, Inc.)

*Gli indifferenti,* 1929 *(The Time of Indifference,* 1953)
*La bella vita,* 1935
*Le ambizioni sbagliate,* Mondadori, 1935 (Mistaken Ambitions, 1955)
*L'imbroglio,* 1937
*I sogni del pigro,* 1940
*La mascherata,* 1941 *(The Fancy Dress Party,* 1952)
*L'amante infelice,* 1943
*La speranza,* Documento, 1944
*L'epidemia,* 1944
*Agostino,* 1945 (Published together with *La disubbidienza* as *Two Adolescents: The Stories of Agostino and Luca,* 1950)
*La romana,* 1947 *(The Woman of Rome,* 1949)
*La disubbidienza,* 1948 (cf., *Agostino,* above)
*L'amore coniugale,* 1949 *(Conjugal Love,* 1951)
*Il conformista,* 1951 *(The Conformist,* 1951)
*I racconti,* 1952 (Selections of Moravia's short stories have appeared in two books: *Bitter Honeymoon and Other Stories,* 1956, and *The Wayward Wife,* 1960)
*Racconti romani,* 1954 *(Roman Tales,* 1957, a selection)
*Il disprezzo,* 1954 *(A Ghost at Noon,* 1955)
*La Ciociara,* 1957 *(Two Women,* 1958)
*Un mese in URSS,* 1958
*Teatro,* 1958
*Nuovi racconti romani,* 1959
*La noia,* 1960 *(The Empty Canvas,* 1961)

## VASCO PRATOLINI

*Il tappeto verde,* Vallecchi, 1941
*Via de' Magazzini,* Vallecchi, 1942
*Le amiche,* Vallecchi, 1943
*Il quartiere* (1945), Vallecchi, 1948 (*The Naked Streets,*
    A. A. Wyn, 1952)
*Cronaca familiare* (1947), Mondadori, 1960
*Cronache di poveri amanti* (1947), Mondadori, 1960 (*A
    Tale of Poor Lovers,* Viking Press, 1949)
*Mestiere da vagabondo,* Mondadori, 1947
*Un eroe del nostro tempo,* Bompiani, 1949 (*A Hero of
    Our Time,* Prentice-Hall, 1951)
*Le ragazze di San Frediano,* Mondadori, 1961
*Gli uomini che si voltano,* Atlante, 1953
*Il mio cuore a Ponte Milvio,* Cultura sociale, 1954
*Metello* (1955), Mondadori, 1961
*Diario sentimentale,* Vallecchi, 1957 (A collection of ear-
    lier autobiographical works)
*Lo scialo,* Mondadori, 1960


## ELIO VITTORINI

(Bompiani editions, unless otherwise stated. The
translations of Vittorini's works are published in this
country by New Directions.)

*Piccola borghesia,* Solaria, 1931
*Nei Morlacchi-Viaggio in Sardegna,* Parenti, 1936
*Conversazione in Sicilia,* 1941 (Originally published with
    the title *Nomi e lacrime,* Parenti, 1941) (*In Sicily,*
    1949)
*Uomini e no,* 1945
*Il Sempione stizza l'occhio al Frejus,* 1948 (*The Twilight
    of the Elephant,* 1951)
*Il garofano rosso,* Mondadori, 1948 (Previously published
    in installments in the Florentine review *Solaria,* 1933-4)
    (*The Red Carnation,* 1952)
*Le donne di Messina,* 1949 (Previously published with the
    title *Lo zio Agrippa passa in treno* in *Rassegna d'Italia,*
    1947-8)
*Erica e i suoi fratelli; La Garibaldina,* 1956 (*The Light
    and the Dark,* 1961)
*Diario in pubblico,* 1957

POETRY

(Mondadori editions, unless otherwise stated.)

UNGARETTI

*L'allegria* (1914-19), 3rd ed., 1945
*Sentimento del tempo* (1919-35), 1946
*Poesie disperse*, 1945
*Il dolore* (1937-46), 1947
*La terra promessa* (1950), 2nd ed., 1954
*Un grido e paesaggi* (1939-52), 1954

TRANSLATIONS

*40 Sonetti di Shakespeare*, 1946
*Da Góngora e da Mallarmé*, 1948
*Fedra,* di Jean Racine, 1950

PROSE WORKS

*Il povero nella città,* Ed. della Meridiana, 1949
*Il taccuino del vecchio* (1952-60) (ed. by Leone Piccioni), 1960
*Il deserto e dopo*, 1961

UMBERTO SABA

*Il Canzoniere* (1900-47), 5th ed., Einaudi, 1961

PROSE WORKS

*Scorciatoie e raccontini,* 1946
*Storia e cronistoria del Canzoniere,* 1948
*Ricordi e racconti* (1910-47), 1956

EUGENIO MONTALE

*Ossi di seppia* (1920-7), 1948
*Le occasioni* (1928-39), 1949
*Finisterre* (1943), 1954
*La Bufera e altro,* 1957

TRANSLATIONS

*Quaderno di traduzioni,* Ed. della Meridiana, 1948

PROSE WORKS

*La farfalla di Dinard* (1956), 1960

## Salvatore Quasimodo

*Ed è subito sera* (1930-42), 1954
*Giorno dopo giorno* (1946), 1947
*La vita non è sogno,* 1949
*Il falso e vero verde* (1948-55), 1956
*La terra impareggiabile,* 1958
*Tutte le Poesie,* 1960

### TRANSLATIONS

*Lirici greci* (1940), 1959
*Macbeth,* di W. Shakespeare, 1949
*Tartufo,* di Molière, Bompiani, 1957
*Il fiore dell'Antologia Palatina,* Guanda, 1957
*Poesie scelte,* di E. E. Cummings, Schweiwiller, 1957

### PROSE WORKS

*Il Poeta e il Politico,* Schwarz, 1960

## Anthologies of Contemporary Italian Poetry

Accrocca, Elio Filippo, and Volpini, Valerio, *Antologia
    poetica della Resistenza Italiana,* Landi, 1955
Anceschi, Luciano, and Antonielli, Sergio, *La Lirica del
    Novecento,* Vallecchi, 1961
Falqui, Enrico, *La giovane poesia (Saggio e Repertorio),*
    Colombo, 1956
Quasimodo, Salvatore, *Poesia italiana del dopoguerra,*
    Schwarz, 1958
Spagnoletti, Giacinto, *Poesia italiana contemporanea*
    (1909-59), Guanda, 1959

## Books on Poetry

Apollonio, Mario, *Ermetismo,* Cedam, 1945
Binni, Walter, *La poetica del decadentismo italiano,*
    Sansoni, 1936
Casnati, Francesco, *Cinque poeti: Ungaretti, Montale,
    Quasimodo, Gatto, Cardarelli,* Vita e Pensiero, 1944
Chiapelli, Fredi, *Langage traditionel et langage personel
    dans la poésie italienne contemporaine,* Université de
    Neuchâtel, 1951
Falqui, Enrico, *La giovane poesia. Saggio e Repertorio,*
    Palombo, 1956

Flora, Francesco, *La poesia ermetica*, 3rd ed., Laterza, 1947

Frattini, Alberto, and Camilucci, Marcello, *La giovane poesia italiana e straniera; Aspetti e problemi*, ed. del "Fuoco," 1959

Macrí, Oreste, *Caratteri e figure della poesia italiana contemporanea*, Vallecchi, 1956

Mariani, Gaetano, *Poesia e tecnica del Novecento*, Nistri-Lischi, 1951

Pasolini, Pier Paolo, *Passione e ideologia*, Garzanti, 1960

Petronio, Giuseppe, *I crepuscolari*, Leonardo, 1936

Petrucciani, Mario, *La poetica dell' Ermetismo italiano*, Loescher, 1955

———, *Poesia pura e poesia esistenziale*, Loescher, 1957

Rosa, Titta G., *La poesia italiana del Novecento*, Maia, 1953

BILINGUAL EDITIONS OF POETRY

Kay, George (ed.), *The Penguin Book of Italian Verse*, Penguin Books, 1958

Mandelbaum, Allen (ed. and trans.), *Life of a Man* [Giuseppe Ungaretti, *Vita d'un uomo*], New Directions, 1958

———, *Selected Writings of Salvatore Quasimodo*, Farrar, Straus & Cudahy, 1960

Pacifici, Sergio, *The Promised Land and Other Poems: An Anthology of Four Contemporary Italian Poets* [Saba, Ungaretti, Montale, and Quasimodo], Vanni, 1957

GENERAL WORKS ON ITALIAN LITERATURE

Crémieux, Benjamin, *Panorama de la littérature italienne contemporaine*, Kra, 1928

Galletti, Alfredo, *Il Novecento*, Vallardi, 1957

Gargiulo, Alfredo, *La letteratura italiana del Novecento*, Le Monnier, 1958

Nicastro, Luciano, *Il Novecento*, Mondadori, 1947

Pellizzi, Camillo, *Le lettere italiane del nostro secolo*, Libreria d'Italia, 1929

Sapegno, Natalino, *Compendio di storia della letteratura italiana: dal Foscolo ai moderni*, La Nuova Italia, 1958

Varese, Claudio, *Cultura italiana contemporanea*, Nistri-Lischi, 1951

332     SELECTED BIBLIOGRAPHY

Volpini, Valerio, *Prosa e narrativa dei contemporanei*, Studium, 1957

Whitfield, John H., *A Short History of Italian Literature*, Penguin Books, 1960

Wilkins, Ernest H., *A History of Italian Literature*, Harvard University Press, 1954

## BIBLIOGRAPHIES

Acrocca, Alio Filippo, *Ritratti su misura di scrittori italiani*, Sodalizio del Libro, 1960

Bosco, Umberto, *Repertorio Bibliografico della Letteratura Italiana*. Vol. I (1948-9) and Vol. II (1950-3), Sansoni, 1953, 1959

Frattarolo, Renzo, *Bibliografia speciale della letteratura italiana*, 2nd ed., Marzorati, 1959

Pacifici, Sergio, "A Selected Bibliography of Recent Criticism in English of Contemporary Italian Literature," *Italian Quarterly*, Nos. 13-14 (1960), pp. 50-4

Prezzolini, Giuseppe, *Repertorio Bibliografico della Letteratura Italiana*, Vols. I-II (1902-32), Vanni, 1930-6; Vols. III-IV (1932-42), Ed. Roma, 1936-8

Russo, Luigi, *I Narratori: 1850-1957*, Principato, 1958

Vallone, Aldo, *Gli studi di letteratura italiana contemporanea dal 1937 al 1957*, Vallardi, n.d.

## BOOKS ON THE NOVEL

Astaldi, Maria Luisa, *Nascita e vicende del romanzo italiano*, Treves, 1939

Fernandez, Dominique, *Le roman italien et la crise de la conscience moderne*, Grasset, 1958

Lombardi, Olga, *Scrittori neorealisti*, Nistri-Lischi, 1957

Paoluzi, Angelo, *La letteratura della Resistenza*, Cinque Lune, 1956

Piccioni, Leone, *Lettura leopardiana e altri saggi*, Vallecchi, 1952

——, *La narrativa italiana tra romanzo e racconti*, Mondadori, 1959

——, *Sui contemporanei*, Fabbri, 1953

—— (ed.), *La narrativa meridionale*, ed. di Cultura e di Documentazione, 1956

Pullini, Giorgio, *Il romanzo italiano del dopoguerra: (1940-1960)*, Schwarz, 1961

Scaramucci, Ines, *Romanzi del nostro tempo,* La Scuola, 1956

Sticco, Maria, *Il romanzo italiano contemporaneo,* Vita e Pensiero, 1953

Various Authors, *Le Lettere italiane a metà di questo secolo, Ulisse,* II, No. 2 (1948-50)

————, *Le sorti del romanzo, Ulisse,* X, Nos. 24-5 (1956-7)

## LITERARY CRITICISM

Antonielli, Sergio, *Aspetti e figure del Novecento,* Guanda, 1955

Apollonio, Mario, *I contemporanei,* La Scuola, 1956

Bertacchini, Renato, *Figura e problemi di narrativa contemporanea,* Cappelli, 1961

Bo, Carlo, *Inchiesta sul neorealismo,* RAI, 1951

————, *Riflessioni critiche,* Sansoni, 1953

Cecchi, Emilio, *Di giorno in giorno. Note di letteratura italiana contemporanea* (1945-54), Garzanti, 1954

Contini, Gianfranco, *Esercizi di lettura,* Le Monier, 1946

————, *Un ano di letteratura,* Le Monnier, 1946

Debenedetti, Giacomo, *Saggi critici,* Solaria, 1929

————, *Saggi critici,* 2nd ed., Mondadori, 1955

De Robertis, Giuseppe, *Saggi,* Le Monnier, 1939

————, *Scrittori italiani del Novecento,* 3rd ed., Le Monnier, 1946

Falqui, Enrico, *Letteratura del Ventennio nero,* ed. della Bussola, 1948

————, *Prosatori e Narratori del Novecento italiano,* Einaudi, 1950

————, *Tra racconti e romanzi del Novecento,* D'Anna, 1950

Flora, Francesco, *Scrittori italiani contemporanei,* Nistri-Lischi, 1952

Gadda, Carlo Emilio, *I viaggi—la morte,* Garzanti, 1958

Guarnieri, Silvio, *Cinquant'anni di narrativa in Italia,* Parenti, 1955

Muscetta, Carlo, *Realismo e controrealismo,* Del Duca, 1958

Pancrazi, Pietro, *Scrittori d'oggi,* I-VI, Laterza, 1946-53

Ravegnani, Giuseppe, *Uomini visti,* I-II, Mondadori, 1955

Salinari, Carlo, *La questione del realismo. Poeti e narratori del Novecento,* Parenti, 1960

334     SELECTED BIBLIOGRAPHY

Seroni, Adriano, *Leggere e sperimentare*, Parenti, 1957
————, *Ragioni critiche*, Vallecchi, 1944
Solari, A. G. (pseud. of Giose Rimanelli), *Il mestiere del furbo*, Sugar, 1959

## BOOKS ON THE CINEMA

Bianchi, Pietro, and Berutti, Franco, *Storia del cinema*, Garzanti, 1959
Carpi, Fabio, *Cinema italiano del dopoguerra*, Schwarz, 1958
Ferrara, Giuseppe, *Il nuovo cinema italiano*, Le Monnier, 1957
Gromo, Mario, *Cinema italiano*, Mondadori, 1954
Jarrat, Vernon, *The Italian Cinema*, Falcon Press, 1951
Lizzani, Carlo, *Il cinema italiano*, Parenti, 1954
————, *Storia del cinema italiano: 1895-1961*, Parenti, 1961
Rondi, Brunello, *Il Neorealismo italiano*, Guanda, 1956

# Bibliographical Notes


## ALBERTO MORAVIA

Among contemporary writers, Alberto Moravia has probably received the greatest amount of attention from the critics. The first notices of his work were by Giuseppe Borgese, in *Il corriere della sera* (July 21, 1929), and by Pietro Pancrazi, "Il realismo di Moravia," in *Scrittori d'oggi*, Vol. II (see Bibliog.). Eurialo de Michelis has authored a slim volume that examines Moravia's fiction through the thirties, *Introduzione a Moravia* (La Nuova Italia, 1956). Dominique Fernandez has written a long and exhaustive essay in *Le roman italien* (see Bibliog.). In addition, the reader may find the following essays both useful and stimulating: Francesco Flora, "Alberto Moravia," in *Scrittori italiani contemporanei* (see Bibliog.); Ornella Sobrero, "Il romanzo per Moravia," in *Inventario,* VI, Nos. 1-2 (1954), 155-71, and "Moravia novelliere," ibid., Nos. 3-6, 156-7; Gino Raya, "Alberto Moravia," in *Narrativa*, III (1958), 124-217; Gaetano Trombatore, "Ill punto su Moravia," in *Società*, VII (1951), 610-24; Marcello Camillucci, "Roma e i *Racconti Romani* di Moravia," in *Studi romani*, VI (1958), 564-61; Giorgio Luti, "Alberto Moravia," in *Il ponte*, XVII, No. 1 (1961), 81-92.

In the United States there has been substantial and frequently brilliant criticism of Moravia's work, the most perceptive of which is the essay by R. W. B. Lewis, "Eros and Existence," in *The Picaresque Saint* (Lippincott, 1959), pp. 35-56. Other pertinent essays are those by Thomas Bergin, "The Moravian Muse," in *The Virginia Quarterly Review*, XXIX (1953), 215-25; Frank Baldanza, "The Classicism of Alberto Moravia," in *Modern Fiction Studies*, III (1958), 309-20. See also the exhaustive interview by Ben Johnson and Maria de Dominiciis, published in *The Paris Review*, No. 6 (1955), 17-37.

Among the valuable autobiographical pieces, see "Ricordo de *Gli indifferenti*," in *Nuova Europa*, Feb. 4, 1945; "Perchè ho scritto *La Romana*," in *La fiera letteraria*, July 3, 1947; and "Storia dei miei libri," in *Epoca*, March 8, 1953; "A Fragment of Autobiography: About My Novels," in *Twentieth Century* (1958), pp. 529-32.

## VASCO PRATOLINI

The most complete study of Pratolini is Alberto Asor Rosa's *Vasco Pratolini* (Rome: Ed. Moderne, 1958). The book, for all its many acute insights and thorough analyses, is at times politically slanted, repetitive, and inordinately long. There are also three essays that, however incomplete, are highly readable and intelligent: Francesco Flora, "Vasco Pratolini," in *Scrittori italiani contemporanei* (see Bibliog.), pp. 233-72; Carlo Muscetta's "Metello e la crisi del neorealismo," in *Realismo e controrealismo* (see Bibliog.), pp. 63-113; and Giorgio Pullini, "Vasco Pratolini," in *Belfagor*, VIII (1953), 553-69. The periodical *La fiera letteraria* devoted an entire issue to Pratolini (March 28, 1954) with numerous notes, testimonials, and critical essays. In his *Le roman italien* (see Bibliog.), pp. 258-74, Dominique Fernandez gives a very warm appraisal of the novelist, as does Luigi Russo, in *I narratori* (see Bibliog.), pp. 398-405. The most recent essay on Pratolini is Renato Bertacchini's "Preistoria di Vasco Pratolini," in *Letterature moderne*, X, No. 1 (1960), 28-47.

## ELIO VITTORINI

Although several essays have been written on Elio Vittorini, none of them is satisfactory. The following are the most intelligent appraisals of a difficult novelist: Geno Pampaloni, "I nomi e le lacrime di Elio Vittorini," in *Il Ponte*, XII (1950), 1534-41; Ferdinando Giannessi, "I 'Gettoni' di Elio Vittorini," in *Il Ponte*, XI (1949), 2053-66; Sergio Pannella, "Poetica americana nel romanzo di Elio Vittorini," in *La Parrucca* (1955), pp. 84-6, 105-7; Leone Piccioni, "Coerenza di Vittorini," in *Sui contemporanei* (see Bibliog.), pp. 99-154; Renato Bertacchini, "Preistoria di Vittorini," in *Il Mulino*, V (1956), 661-5, and "Vittorini prima della *Conversazione*," in *Letterature moderne*, VII (1958), 743-58; Fulvio Longobardi, "Vittorini, la vita per la libertà," in *Società*, XIII (1957), 709-29; Pier Francesco Listri, "Il nostro Vittorini," in *Il Ponte*, XIV (1958), 72-83; Dominique Fernandez, *Le roman italien* (see Bibliog.), pp. 228-58.

The translation of the Preface to *Il garofano rosso* has appeared revised by the author and translated by Donald Heiney, with the title "Truth and Censorship: The Story of *The Red Carnation*," in *The Western Humanities Review*, IX (1955), 197-208. In English, the only essays of any import are Diana Trilling's long review of *In Sicily*, in *The New York Times Book Review*, Nov. 27, 1949, and R. W. B. Lewis' article "Elio Vittorini," in *Italian Quarterly*, IV, No. 15 (1961), 55-61.

## POETRY

General articles on Italian poetry are quite numerous and hardly a year goes by without one such survey being printed in a literary periodical. The following essays remain, despite the passing of time, among the most relevant: Antonio Russi, "La poesia italiana dal 1915 e 1945," in *La strada*, I, Nos. 2-3 (1947), 28-51, 39-57; by the same author see also "Il significato della poesia della Resistenza," in *Il Ponte* (1955), pp. 672-83; Giovanni Macchia, "Aspetti della poesia italiana d'oggi," in *La fiera letteraria*, March 25, 1947; Adriano Seroni, "Vent'anni di poesia italiana: 1919-1939," in *Ulisse*, II (1948-50), 501-10; Rodolfo Macchioni Jodi, "Poesia italiana del dopoguerra: 1945-1955" in *Il Ponte* (1955), pp. 2042-53; Eduardo Sanguinetti, "Da Gozzano a Montale," in *Lettere italiane*, I, No. 2 (1955), 188-207; Dante Della Terza, "Postwar Poetics and Poetry," in *Italian Quarterly*, IV, Nos. 13-14 (1960), 39-49; Edward Williamson, "Contemporary Italian Poetry," in *Poetry*, LXXIX, No. 3 (Dec. 1952), 159-81, and No. 4 (Jan. 1952), 233-44.

### UMBERTO SABA

The best critic of Saba is Giacomo Debenedetti, whose essays are to be found in his *Saggi critici*, 1st ed. (see Bibliog.). After the poet's death, he wrote "Ultime cose su Saba," an essay that can be read in *Nuovi Argomenti*,

No. 30 (1958), 1-19. Nora Baldi's slim volume, *Il paradiso di Saba* (Mondadori, 1958), is of some value as a biography. Other good analyses of the poet are: "Umberto Saba," by Fulvio Longobardi, in *Belfagor,* III (1948), 569-74; Claudio Varese, "Attualità di Saba," in *Nuova antologia,* XCII, No. 1882 (1957), 159-72. See also the volumes by Gaetano Marini, Gianfranco Contini, and Claudio Varese in the Bibliography.

### Giuseppe Ungaretti

Gigi Cavalli has recently produced a good volume on the poet (Fabbri, 1958) and the magazine *Letteratura* devoted a long issue to him in 1958 (Nos. 35-6), with testimonials, notes, and essays by the leading critics and writers of Italy. The volume by Mario Petrucciani (see Bibliog.) has a long section devoted to Ungaretti. See also Gaëtan Picon, "Sur la poésie de G. Ungaretti," *Lettres Nouvelles* (Feb. 1956), pp. 738-48; Leone Piccione's essay in *Lettura leopardiana* (See Bibliog.) and G. Nogara, "Pena d'uomo: Ungaretti," in *Lettere italiane,* II (1950), 3-26.

### Montale

Aside from the incomplete study by Raoul Lunardi, *Eugenio Montale e la nuova poesia* (Padova, 1948), there are several essays on Montale's work worth looking into: Sergio Solmi, "La poesia di Montale" (*Nuovi Argomenti,* No. 26, 1-42) is the profoundest and most sensitive; Francesco Flora's article, "Eugenio Montale," in *Scrittori italiani contemporanei* (see Bibliog.), is primarily a stylistic investigation of the poet's complex language; Piero Bigongiari's "I tre tempi della lirica montaliana," *Paragone,* No. 80 (1956), 23-30, is valuable, as are the interpretations of Alfredo Gargiulo, Oreste Macrí, Giuseppe de Robertis, and Gianfranco Contini (see Bibliog.). In English there are two fine essays: Glauco Cambon's "Eugenio Montale's Poetry: the Meeting of Dante and Breughel," in *Sewanee Review,* LXVI (1958), 1-32, and Maria Sampoli Simonelli's recent "The Particular Poetic World of Eugenio Montale," in *Italian Quarterly,* III, No. 10 (1959), 41-53. See also Glauco Cambon, "Ungaretti, Montale and Lady Entropy," in *Italica,* XXXVII (1960), 231-8.

QUASIMODO

There are two monographs on the work of Quasimodo: Mario Stefanile, *Salvatore Quasimodo* (Cedam, 1943), and the recent Natale Tedesco, *Salvatore Quasimodo e la condizione poetica del nostro tempo* (Flaccovio, 1959). Many critics have devoted several pages of their books to the work of Quasimodo, as is the case of Macrí and of Francesco Casnati (see Bibliog.). The following essays are also especially recommended: Vincenzo Valente, "Salvatore Quasimodo," in *Il Ponte*, XIV (1958), 979-87; Glauco Cambon, "A Deep Wind: Quasimodo's 'Tindari,'" in *Italian Quarterly*, III, No. 11 (1959), 16-28; Sergio Pacifici, "Salvatore Quasimodo, Nobel Prize for Literature 1959," in *Saturday Review*, Nov. 7, 1959, pp. 20-1, 42. A complete bibliography and a perceptive essay on Quasimodo's art may be found in an anthology edited by Roberto Sanesi, *Salvatore Quasimodo: Poesie* (Guanda, 1959).

EXISTENTIALISM

In the United States and Europe, there is a rich literature about existentialism. The following titles are particularly interesting in that they explore the relations of this philosophy with literature and the arts in general:

William Barrett, *Irrational Man* (Doubleday, 1958); Everett W. Knight, *Literature Considered as Philosophy*, Macmillan, 1960; Walter Kaufmann (ed.), *Existentialism from Dostoevsky to Sartre* (Meridian Books, 1956); F. H. Heinemann, *Existentialism and the Modern Predicament* (Harper, 1958); Kurt F. Reinhardt, *The Existentialist Revolt: The Main Themes and Phases of Existentialism* (Milwaukee Univ. Press, 1952); Marjorie Greene, *Dreadful Freedom: A Critique of Existentialism* (Univ. of Chicago Press, 1948).

Numerous studies, both of the specialized and popular variety, have appeared in Italy since 1939. The reader can still consult with profit the extensive bibliography prepared by Vito A. Bellezza in the publication of the Archivio di Filosofia, *L'Esistenzialismo* (Rome: 1946); the special number on existentialism, published as a separate volume as part of the *Atti del Congresso Internazionale di Filosofia*, edited by Enrico Castelli (Milan: 1948); and the addenda to the bibliographical essay cited above in *Revue Internationale de Philosophie*, III (1949). The Roman magazine *Nuovi Argomenti* published a short symposium on existentialism in its Jan.-Feb. 1955 issue (pp. 161-91). The Italian magazine *Primato* also published a special number devoted to existentialism, in 1943.

Among the more philosophical treatments of the subject are the numerous volumes by Enzo Paci, especially *Pensiero esistenza e valore* (G. Principato, 1940), *L'esistenzialismo* (Cedam, 1943), and *Esistenzialismo e storicismo* (Mondadori, 1950); Nicola Abbagnano, *Introduzione allesistenzialismo* (Taylor, 1947) and *Esistenzialismo positivo* (Taylor, 1948); Oreste Borello, *L'estetica dell'esistenzialismo* (G. d'Anna, 1956). Carlo Falconi's essay, to which reference has been made in this chapter, is entitled "I vent'anni di Moravia," and may be read in *Humanitas*, V (1950), 189-205. The *Yale French Studies* has published two thought-provoking numbers on existentialism: *Existentialism* (I, 1948) and *Foray Through Existentialism* (No. 16, 1955). While this book was on press, there appeared the English translation of an essay by Nicola Abbagnano, "Existentialism in Italy," in the *Cesare Barbieri Courier*, III, No. 2 (1961), 12-18, which includes a rich bibliography.

## LITERARY CRITICISM

The only systematic account of modern Italian criticism available today is Luigi Russo's three-volume *La critica italiana contemporanea* (Laterza, 1946-7). The following are among the best essays and specific treatments of contemporary critics: Giulio Marzot, "La critica e gli studi di letteratura italiana," in *Cinquant' anni di vita intellettuale italiana, 1896-1946*, edited by C. Antioni and R. Mattioli (Ediz. Scient. Ital., 1950), I, 451-522. Aldo Borlenghi, "La critica letteraria da De Sanctis a Croce," in *Letteratura italiana: Le Correnti* (Marzorati, 1956), pp. 937-1054.

There are several essays in English on the more important critics and trends. René Wellek's essay "Francesco de Sanctis," in *Italian Quarterly*, No. 1 (1957), 5-43, is competent and thorough; Joseph Rossi's "De Sanctis' Criticism: Its Principles and Methods," in *PMLA*, LIV (1939), 526-64 is well-informed. Also useful are Dante

Della Terza's "Literary Criticism in the Universities," in *Italian Quarterly*, No. 6 (1958), 55-63; Claudio Gorlier's "Contemporary Italian Literary Criticism," in *The Literary Review*, III, No. 1 (1959), 163-9; P. M. Pasinetti's "*Coscienza Critica*: Aspects of Contemporary Italian Criticism," in *Romanic Review*, XL, No. 3 (1949), 186-97; Aldo Scaglione's "Croce's Definition of Literary Criticism," in *Journal of Aesthetics and Art Criticism*, XVII (1959), 447-56; René Wellek's "Benedetto Croce: Literary Critic and Historian," in *Comparative Literature*, V (1953), 75-82; and finally, the controversial chapter by William K. Wimsatt and Cleanth Brooks, "Expressionism: Benedetto Croce," in *Literary Criticism* (Knopf, 1957), pp. 499-519. For an extremely long and well-informed essay on Italian criticism see Luce Fabbri de Cressatti, "Los Corrientes de Crítica e Historiografía Literarias en la Italia actual," in *Revista de la Facultad de Humanidades y Ciencias*, No. 14 (1955), 231-88. See also Aldo Scaglione, "Literary Criticism in Postwar Italy," in *Italian Quarterly*, Nos. 13-14 (1960), 27-38.

## THE REVIEWS

The most accurate bibliography of the Florentine reviews, with a detailed list of the critical writings that have appeared in them, is Benvenuto Righini, *I periodici Fiorentini 1597-1950* (2 vols.; Sansoni, 1955).

Among the numerous anthologies of writing originally published in the little magazines discussed in Chapter Nine, the following stand out for their critical remarks and completeness: *La Cultura Italiana del '900 attraverso le riviste*, Vols. I, II, and IV, edited respectively by Delia Frigessi, Angelo Romanò, and Gianni Scalia (Einaudi, 1960-1)—Vol. III has not yet been published; Giansiro Ferrata, *La Voce: 1908-16* (Landi, 1961); Giuseppe Cassieri, *La Ronda: Antologia* (Landi, 1955); Enzo Siciliano, *Antologia critica di Solaria* (Lerici, 1958); S. Pautasso and M. Forti, *Il Politecnico* (Lerici, 1960).

There are several accounts of the reviews in Italy and the role played by them in the culture of their time. The earliest study is Aurelia Bobbio's *Le riviste fiorentine dal principio del secolo: 1903-16* (Sansoni, 1936); Augusto Hermet's more complete book, *La ventura delle riviste*

(Vallecchi, 1941) is unfortunately out-of-date and not easily accessible: it is a well-documented, but not always penetrating, investigation of the reviews through the thirties and of the men connected with them. Carlo Martini has published a fundamental work, *La Voce: Storia e Bibliografia* (Nistri-Lischi, 1956), the principal weakness of which is the treatment of the subject, reduced to a series of quotations and exerpts from the comments and writings of those who participated in or studied *La Voce* and the whole Vocian movement. Vittorio Vettori has produced a very slim survey of the reviews during the first half of this century, *Le rivisti italiane* (Gismondi, 1958). In English, the only published accounts of the reviews are by Peter M. Riccio, *On the Threshold of Fascism* (Casa Italiana, Columbia Univ. Press, 1929), and Maria Serafina Mazza, S. C., *Not for Art's Sake: The Story of "Il Frontespizio"* (Columbia Univ. Press, 1948), the latter a sensitive and critical examination of the major and minor contributors of the Florentine magazine *Il Frontespizio*.

There are several articles on the individual contributions of the various magazines. Among them, notable for their acumen and breadth, are the following: Giuseppe Prezzolini, *L'italiano inutile* (Longanesi, 1954) and *Il tempo della "Voce"* (Longanesi-Vallecchi, 1960); Eugenio Garin, "Cultura universitaria e riviste fiorentine agli inizi del Novecento," in *Paragone*, No. 64 (April 1955), 3-18; Carlo Bo, "Papini e le riviste (dal Leonardo a Lacerba)," in *L'Otto-Novecento* (Libera Cattedra di Storia della Civiltà Fiorentina, Sansoni, 1957), pp. 227-54; Piero Jahier, "Contromemorie vociane," in *Paragone*, No. 56 (Aug. 1954), 25-48; Enrico Falqui, " 'La Voce' did De Robertis," in *L'Otto-Novecento*, pp. 255-80; C. Vasoli, "Note su alcune riviste letterarie del Novecento. Considerazioni su 'La Voce,' " in *Il Ponte*, XIII, No. 3 (March 1957), 390-401; Riccardo Scrivano, " 'La Ronda' e la cultura del $XX^0$ secolo," in *Rassegna Lucchese*, No. 15 (1955), 7-17; Giorgio Luti, "Note su alcune riviste letterarie del Novecento. Considerazioni su 'La Ronda,' " in *Il Ponte*, XIII, No. 1 (Jan. 1957), 54-64; Giansiro Ferrata, " 'Solaria,' 'Letteratura,' e 'Campo di Marte,' " in *L'Otto-Novecento*, pp. 371-400; Franco Fortini, "Che cosa è stato 'Il Politecnico,' " in *Nuovi Argomenti*, I, No. 1 (March-April

1953), 181-200; Renato Bertacchini, "Dalla 'Ronda' a 'Solaria,'" in *Studium*, LV (1959), 834-8; Domenico Tarizzo, "L'esperienza del 'Politecnico' tra mitologia di massa ed 'elites' del sapere," in *Nuova Corrente*, No. 18 (1960) 55-72; Olga Ragusa, "Trends: Literary Periodicals," in *Italian Quarterly*, III, No. 2 (1960), 60-9.

## AMERICA AND ITALY: AN ENCOUNTER

The majority of essays dealing specifically with Italo-American relations are scattered in various journals and reviews. Cesare Pavese's *La letteratura americana e altri saggi* (Einaudi, 1953), with a brilliant Preface by Italo Calvino; and Elio Vittorini's numerous pieces on American culture and literature, collected in his *Diario in pubblico* (Bompiani, 1957), are still the most moving testimonials of the Italian rediscovery of America.

The Italian review *Galleria* (No. 4, 1955) has an entire issue devoted to the impact of American literature on Italy, with notable contributions by Alfredo Rizzardi, Elio Vittorini, Glauco Cambon, and others. Likewise, on this side of the Atlantic, *Italian Quarterly* has recently (Spring 1959) re-examined the situation from a new perspective, bringing fresh insights to a complex problem. Carlo Golino's "On the Italian Myth of America" and Leslie Fiedler's "The Rediscovery of Italian Literature: Chance, Chic and the Task of the Critic" are the best treatments of the cultural "discovery" of the two countries since the end of the war. *Sewanee Review* has devoted an entire number (Vol. LXVIII, Summer 1960) to the topic "Italian Criticism of American Literature." The most original and valuable of the numerous contributions by writers and critics are: Agostino Lombardo's lengthy "Introduction" (pp. 353-74) and Elio Vittorini's "An Outline of American Literature" (pp. 423-37). Lombardo's article may also be read in a much longer version in *Studi americani*, No. 5 (1950), 9-50, with the title "La critica italiana sulla letteratura italiana." Several months after the chapter had been written, there appeared in *Studi americani*, No. 6 (1960), a long essay by Vito Amoruso, "Cecchi, Vittorini, Pavese e la letteratura americana." For information on the history and present status of American studies in Italy, the reader may consult with profit the chapter "Italy,"

by Sigmund Skaard, in his *American Studies in Europe*
(Univ. of Pennsylvania Press, 1958), II, 462-513. The
literary relationships between the two nations have been
the topic of recent studies, among which are: Agostino
Lombardo, "Gli scrittori americani e l'Italia," in *Il Veltro*,
IV, Nos. 1-2 (1960), 20-8; Salvatore Rosati, "Gli scrittori
italiani e gli Stati Uniti," in *Il Veltro*, IV, Nos. 1-2 (1960),
60-9; Glauco Cambon, "The Italian Response to American
Literature, or the Second Discovery of America," *Cesare
Barbieri Courier*, II, No. 2 (1960), 3-8.

Other useful essays are the following: Leslie Fiedler,
"Italian Pilgrimage: The Discovery of America," in *An
End to Innocence* (Beacon Press, 1955); M. Cartasegna,
"Scrittori americani e narrativa italiana," in *Studium*,
XLII, Nos. 7-8 (1952), 429-36; Mario Praz, "Heming-
way in Italy," in *Partisan Review*, XV (1947), 1086-1100;
Elio Vittorini, "American Influences on Contemporary Italian Literature," in *American Quarterly*, I, No. 1 (1949),
3-8; Giaime Pintor, "La lotta contro gli idoli," in *Sangue
d'Europa* (Einaudi, 1950), pp. 208-19; Agostino Lombardo, "Elio Vittorini e la letteratura americana," in
*Criterio*, II, No. 1 (1958), 354-68; Richard H. Chase,
"Cesare Pavese and the American Novel," in *Studi americani*, No. 3 (1957), 347-69. An indispensable bibliography
of English translations of Italian fiction has been compiled
by Vincent Luciani, "The Modern Italian Novel in America,
1929-54," in the *New York Public Library Bulletin*, 1956,
pp. 1-25.

The prime documents in the Italian interpretations of
the United States are the following: Mario Soldati, *America primo amore* (Garzanti, 1945); Emilio Cecchi, *America amara* (Sansoni, 1946); Guido Piovene, *De America*
(Garzanti, 1953); Ezio Bacino, *America bifronte* (Vallecchi, 1957); Giuseppe Prezzolini, *Tutta l'America* (Vallecchi, 1957); E. E. Agnoletti, *Idea e realtà dell'America*
(Assoc. per la Libertà della Cultura, n.d.).

# INDEX